KNITWEAR WORKSHOP DESIGNS

KNITWEAR WORKSHOP DESIGNS

DUETS
& INSPIRATIONS

SHIRLEY PADEN

SHIRLEY PADEN

Knitwear Workshop Designs:
Duets & Inspirations

Published by Shirley Paden Custom Knits
414 E 52nd St, New York, NY 10022

© 2021 Shirley Paden.
All rights reserved. No portion of this book may be reproduced in any form without permission from the publisher, except as permitted by U.S. copyright law.
For permissions contact: shirley@shirleypaden.com

Photography: Yeon J Yue

Stylist: Elisa Koizumi

Hair/Makeup: Michelle Reda

Cover and Interior Design: Anne Shannon

www.ShirleyPaden.com

ISBN: 978-1-7371194-3-2

Acknowledgments

In memory of my beloved husband, Mel, who was called away just before this project was completed. For 35 years he was truly the "wind beneath my wings."

SPECIAL THANKS

Tracey Rivers
whose foresight and diligence in forming the *We Love Shirley Paden Ravelry Group* placed us on the path that led to this incredible journey of discovery.

Styleexpo Studio
To Anibal Escobar and the Styleexpo Studio team for coordinating wonderfully professional photo shoots.

Anne Shannon
whose skilled eye and impeccable book design skills brought this project to life.

Elisa Koizumi
whose vision, guidance, wisdom, and intense planning led us through every detail of each photo shoot.

Jay
whose methodical and diligent work behind the lens of the camera captured all aspects of my vision for this project.

Kareem Chapman and Tiesha Adams
whose mission it was to capture the entire experience of building a design book from scratch, and to accurately tell our story through video.

Rafael De Peña
whose incredible artistic talent created the beautiful fashion illustrations throughout the book.

Eleanor Dixon and Naoko Ogawa
whose talent and devotion helped us to achieve precision and accuracy with completing the technical edits on each pattern, and for their patient journey with each designer through pattern writing and technical drawing accuracy.

Chie Ushio
whose wonderful technical illustrations interfaced with the vision of the designers and technical editors, and who meticulously drew and redrew all charts and schematics.

Joan Forgione, Mari Tobita and Suzanne Wakamoto
whose willingness to lend a hand by helping on any part of the project necessary, and for their professionalism and friendship.

Yvette Walton and Alice Schwartz
whose talent and friendship were always there when a helping hand was needed.

FOREWORD

"A thing of beauty is a joy forever. Its loveliness increases.
It will never pass into nothingness, but still will keep a bower quiet for us,
and a sleep full of sweet dreams, and health, and quiet breathing."
—John Keats (1795-1821)

No matter how far we have evolved since the days of admiring cave painters, today, as in the beginning, something in the human psyche forces us to stop and stand in awe when we observe excellence in craftsmanship. It is a deep respect that we feel when we see something meticulously made by hand. The reality is that the ability to achieve that excellence is present in each of us, and there are few modern-day art forms more readily accessible for us to experience and connect to that side of ourselves than in hand knitting.

After years of teaching hand-knit garment design and watching the magic of the creative process, as well as the joy and excitement of even the newest knitters as their first-time design ideas came to life, I decided to translate that class into a book. The goal was to reach an audience well beyond my classroom. With that in mind, in 2010, Knitwear Design Workshop (KDW) was released as a major comprehensive design reference work. The widespread interest in KDW became the basis for a series of online worldwide design events called Design-A-Longs (DALs). Those events were where most of the pieces shown in this book were created. This is the story of our maiden DAL voyage.

A few months before Knitwear Design Workshop was released, one of my students started an online group for people to come together to knit and discuss my designs. Although I had a large body of published work, I had no prior knowledge of the group being formed. You can imagine both my surprise and joy when I received an invitation to join. Since it was newly forming, the direction that it would take was open, and that founding student, who was also the moderator, welcomed my input. When planning for the book release, I had been busily exploring ways to invite knitters to join me online to experience design. As luck would have it, the newly formed group was the perfect platform for launching a worldwide design event. Therefore, plans got underway for the first DAL.

People had heard of Knit-A-Longs (KALs) where everyone worked on the same project together, perhaps selecting different yarns. However, the question that I was asked over and over during the signup phase was, "Exactly what is a DAL?" I could only describe it as a cross between a design workshop and a design "boot camp," where everyone would be invited to work through the four steps of my Design Process, as introduced in Knitwear Design Workshop, and create their own masterpieces. With everyone signing up responding to that explanation with "great!", I knew it was going to be lots of fun, and unlike anything that any of us had ever before experienced with our knitting!

A few weeks later, we took off with 30 intrepid and eager design students, holding hands and eagerly anticipating this new type of creative experience. I began by posting a chart and a swatch that I had used to design a scarf, then announcing the DAL equivalent of, "Ready, set, go!" which was "Profile, sketch, swatch!" And the design process had begun!

Since the group was composed primarily of American and Japanese knitters, we posted instructions in both languages. People would visit the American group site and wonder if they were at the right place, with large passages of text posted in Japanese. However, between the participants, no one seemed to notice that we spoke different languages. We all spoke knitting, and were eager to design. That kept the atmosphere charged with excitement.

Four months passed quickly with everyone interpreting the DAL stitch pattern to create their individual designs. Some were designing garments and some accessories. As in-progress photos were constantly being posted to the group, there was lots of visual stimulation. This resulted in nonstop virtual chatting and learning as we walked together through each step of the process. Each time we completed a step, there would be a burst of energy that would fill the air for weeks. It was that constant creative energy bubbling over that continued to propel us forward. Finally, the participants began crossing the finish line by posting photos of their completed pieces. At that point the group atmosphere became electric! It was then that I realized that the worldwide design experiment had been a wonderful starting point for bigger and better design events.

In the years that followed, four additional Design-A-Longs were held. They were all truly memorable experiences. As you turn the pages here, you will see some of the different "things of beauty" created in those virtual "Design Workshops". They brought out true excellence in design craftsmanship in all of us.

Table of Contents

Acknowledgments 5

Foreword. 6

Introduction 10

Inspirations: A Starting Point 12

Duets & Inspirations:
    Author Note. 26
    Evening Elegance 28
    Cosmopolitan Consciousness. 48
    Rustic Reveries 74
    Restful Reflections. 92

The Designer's Notebook:
    Ada Wolfstein: Renaissance Woman 106
    The Duets Design Team 110

Instructions:
    Abbreviations 116
    Symbol Keys 118
    Special Techniques. 120
    Duets Project Instructions 126

Technical Contributors. 310

Yarn Sources. 312

Yarn Weight Guide. 313

Index. 314

INTRODUCTION

In our fast-paced, mass-produced world, few things remain more cherished than a personal item that has been made by hand.

Hand Knitting is a cloth-making art form that predates the beginning of the last millenium. Because the fabric is created as the piece is shaped and sized, masterful skill is necessary. However, the possibilities for techniques creation are endless. Therefore, with a craft that has been around and in constant evolution for over one thousand years, we see contributions from regions and/or cultures from most countries on earth with deep historical specialties in different types of knit fabric construction. Some examples include fine lacework from Russia, Germany, Italy and Great Britain; colorwork from the Baltic States and Great Britain; cables from Ireland; twist stitch patterns from the Alpine region of Germany, etc. They also include regional specialties in different types of clothing construction such as shawls, hats, gloves, and socks. Many items also represent specific moments in time with the highest examples on display in museums around the world.

Every knitter enters the creative process in their own way. My fascination has been with hand-knit clothing design. Within that realm, my design journey has always begun with a stitch pattern. For me, there is a particular joy in tapping into visually and structurally balanced stitch patterns created in different cultures and especially in different centuries. The joy of design is in wrapping a modern silhouette around them and bringing them forward into my time and place.

In this book, I have asked a group of students to join me in a series of design Duets as a way to celebrate the rich heritage of our art. The concept for Duets was formed in the Design-A-Longs where participants were asked to begin their design journey by selecting a stitch pattern that spoke to them from a collection that had spoken to me. Their assignment was to use my pieces as inspirations or starting points for their own creations. In that way, we get to see two different design perspectives whose inspirations were gathered from a single stitch pattern as the source. As you examine both the inspiration and the Duets pieces that accompany them, you will see that the end result is a beautiful display of creativity that will inspire a sense of awe and spark your own design imagination.

Our Shared Experience

I have spoken of our inspirations and design journeys through the shared experiences of the Design-a-Longs. Now, I trust that you will go beyond observing the results of our creative adventures to be inspired to add your skills to the mix. Follow your heart and make any piece you place on your needles your own.

— Shirley Paden

INSPIRATIONS
DESIGNS BY SHIRLEY PADEN

Vogue Knitting Winter 2004 / 2005 | 1

INSPIRATION

Vogue Knitting Fall 1999

INSPIRATION

Vogue Knitting Winter 2002

3

INSPIRATION

Interweave Knits Winter 2006

INSPIRATION

Vogue Knitting
Fall 2007

5

Vogue Knitting
Winter 2009 / 2010

6

INSPIRATION

Interweave Knits Winter 2004

INSPIRATION

Vogue Knitting
Fall 2007

8

Vogue Knitting
Men's Special Issue 2002

9

INSPIRATION

Vogue Knitting Holiday 2006

INSPIRATION

Knitwear Design Workshop 2010

11

INSPIRATION

Knitwear Design Workshop 2010

12

INSPIRATION

Vogue Knitting Spring / Summer 1998

13

INSPIRATION

Interweave Knits Winter 2000 / 2001

14

Vogue Knitting Fall 2007

15

INSPIRATION

Interweave Knits Summer 2014

16

INSPIRATION

SWATCH
INSPIRATIONS

AUTHOR NOTE

All the designs featured here are classics. That is a design criterion that I believe in. That means that the pieces can be worn for different occasions and by different generations. To show examples, several projects have been styled in different settings and are shown in more than one story. – *Shirley Paden*

DUETS & INSPIRATIONS

EVENING ELEGANCE | INSTRUCTIONS

Zig Zag Gauntlets (Lisa Hoffman) 30	p. 306 - 309
Sazanami Mini Dress (Midori Yaple) 32	p. 230 - 233
En Pointe Pullover (Olga Jankelovich) 34	p. 178 - 181
Bel Fiore Cape (Olga Jankelovich) 36	p. 148 - 151
Ada Dress (Shirley Paden). 38	p. 126 - 135
Coquilles Pullover (Shirley Paden) 40	p. 172 - 177
Coquilles Caplet (Shirley Paden) 42	p. 170 - 171
Winged Surplice Cardigan (Ellen M. Silva) 44	p. 300 - 305
Coleus Coat (Shirley Paden) 46	p. 160 - 169

COSMOPOLITAN CONSCIOUSNESS | INSTRUCTIONS

Sunset Skirt (Ayano Tanaka) 50	p. 250 - 253
Aleria Pullover (Diane Martini) 52	p. 136 - 143
Skihytte Cardigan (Diane Martini) 54	p. 242 - 249
Open Bud Shawl (Joan Forgione) 56	p. 222 - 223
Floating Triangles Hat & Cowl (Joan Forgione) ... 58	p. 182 - 183
Cabled Yoke Pullover (Laura Zukaite) 60	p. 152 - 155
Linden Hoodie - Burgundy (Mari Tobita) 62	p. 198 - 211
Nikki Reeves Pullover (Nicole Reeves) 64	p. 216 - 221
Primavera Dress (Olga Jankelovich) 66	p. 224 - 229
Cascading Cables Cowl (Sima Brason) 68	p. 156 - 159
Balineen Hat (Joan Forgione) 68	p. 144 - 145
Volare Capelet (Shirley Paden) 70	p. 296 - 299
Twisted Rhythms (Trudie Joseph) 72	p. 282 - 295

RUSTIC REVERIES | INSTRUCTIONS

Linden Hoodie - Blue (Mari Tobita) 76	p. 198 - 211
Linden Hoodie - Burgundy (Mari Tobita) 78	p. 198 - 211
Teardrop Cardigan (Miki Ohara) 80	p. 254 - 263
Mesa Poncho (Noriko Oshige) 82	p. 212 - 215
Coleus Coat (Shirley Paden) 84	p. 160 - 169
Coquilles Capelet (Shirley Paden) 86	p. 170 - 171
Tige Cardigan (Shirley Paden) 88	p. 264 - 275
Volare Capelet (Shirley Paden) 90	p. 296 - 299

RESTFUL REFLECTIONS | INSTRUCTIONS

Seseragi Pullover (Ayano Tanaka) 94	p. 234 - 241
Frost Flowers Pullover (Laura Zukaite) 96	p. 184 - 189
Gothic Tracery Cardigan (Gale Page) 98	p. 190 - 197
Twist & Shout Shawl (Iris Schreier) 100	p. 280 - 281
Trellised Arbor Shawl (Joan Forgione) 102	p. 276 - 279
Primavera Dress (Olga Jankelovich) 104	p. 224 - 229

DUETS & INSPIRATIONS

Evening
ELEGANCE

There is always an aura of elegance when a woman wears a piece that she loves, it makes her statement.

Zig Zag Gauntlets

DESIGNED BY LISA HOFFMAN

INSPIRATION | 15

THOUGH it was a complex swatching and charting process, I had so much fun playing with these intricate twisted stitches and lace patterns and felt extremely proud to have tackled this challenge by Shirley to create "mirrored" zig zag patterns for the left and right mitts.

Instructions on page 306.

EVENING ELEGANCE | 31

Sazanami Mini Dress

DESIGNED BY MIDORI YAPLE

INSPIRATION | 3

SAZANAMI means "wavelet" in Japanese. When I saw this cable & twist stitch pattern, the first thing that came to mind was a chain belt around the low waist of a mini dress. At this point I knew I had to knit it sideways so I tried to figure how the garment could be worked just sideways, but realized that it would be hard to create side shaping for the fitted body that I wanted. I finally decided to work the stitch pattern horizontally and separately to create this simple dress where the focus would be on the pattern stitch. The bottom pleats give movement to the dress.

Instructions on page 230.

EVENING ELEGANCE

En Pointe Pullover

DESIGNED BY **OLGA JANKELOVICH**

INSPIRATION | 1

I HAD been thinking of designing a pullover using a diamond shaped stitch pattern in a unique way for some time. So, when Shirley offered this pattern as a sample, I already knew what I wanted to make. With just enough lace to keep it interesting, this simple pullover features a pointed hemline and pointed sleeve cuffs. It can be worn on a cool evening or as an elegant casual daytime garment.

Instructions on page 178.

EVENING ELEGANCE

Bel Fiore Cape

DESIGNED BY OLGA JANKELOVICH

INSPIRATION 12

I AM NOT usually drawn to knitted accessories. However, after seeing a cape that was knit circularly on the internet, I thought I would try designing one. However, I felt that an open front cape with a collar that would echo the stitch pattern would give the piece a more youthful feeling than one knit circularly. Working flat created the challenge of planning the shoulder line. Happily, it all worked out, and just as I set out to accomplish, this lightweight, cashmere cape showcases the detailed travelling stitch pattern, and will provide a light covering on a cool day or evening.

Instructions on page 148.

EVENING ELEGANCE | 37

Ada Dress

DESIGNED BY **SHIRLEY PADEN**

SWATCH INSPIRATION

THIS dress was influenced by the Eloe dress designed by Ada Wolfstein over 50 years ago in 1964 for her daughter. The freshness of the classic style achieves what I strive for in my designs, which is timelessness. Although the Eloe dress was my design inspiration, I did not use the pattern stitches that Ada had used, but I did use the shaping elements and pattern layout direction that she used. For example, her dress was flared at the bottom with one motif separating the flaring panels. That separating pattern was then worked from that bottom flare through the main pattern separations in the body of the dress, ending at the bust. There are also 3 different types of lace patterns used in the Eloe dress and in my Ada dress.

Instructions on page 126.

EVENING ELEGANCE | 39

Coquilles Pullover

DESIGNED BY **SHIRLEY PADEN**

SWATCH INSPIRATION

I WAS attracted to the different motifs in this lacy stitch pattern. I thought they could be used on different parts of the garment. My vision was for a very elegant pullover with a double taper that would follow the natural curves of the body. For a very feminine feeling I also wanted to add bell cuffs and a large collar that could be worn off the shoulder. I used one motif from the stitch pattern for the edgings including the bottom, sleeve cuffs and collar, then used the total pattern in the main section of the body and sleeves. Because the edging motifs reminded me of a shell, I named this pullover Coquilles.

Instructions on page 172.

EVENING ELEGANCE

Coquilles Capelet

DESIGNED BY **SHIRLEY PADEN**

SWATCH INSPIRATION

AFTER designing the collar for the Coquilles pullover, I thought of adding additional length to that piece to create a feminine shoulder cover.

It can be worn over day or evening clothing to add a hint of elegance, or a bit of warmth.

Instructions on page 170.

EVENING ELEGANCE | 43

Winged Surplice Cardigan

DESIGNED BY **ELLEN M. SILVA**

SWATCH INSPIRATION

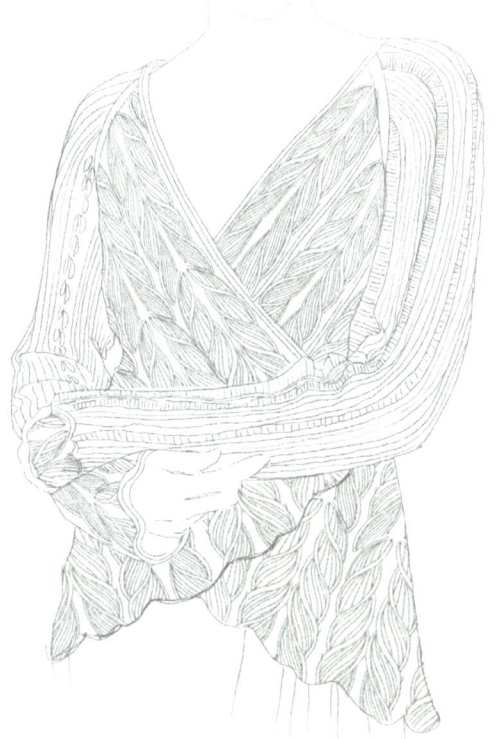

THE STITCH pattern I selected as inspiration for Shirley's fifth design-along looked like lovely wings, wings that I wanted to fly across my garment. It wasn't until I started knitting swatches that I discovered the best way to make that happen was to tip the fabric at an angle. This simple shift added excitement as well as the opportunity to create a wrapped cardigan that flatters most figures. Matching diagonal fronts to vertical sides took some doing and lots of trigonometry, but I'm very pleased with how it has all worked out.

Instructions on page 300.

EVENING ELEGANCE

Coleus Coat

DESIGNED BY **SHIRLEY PADEN**

SWATCH INSPIRATION

I WANTED to create a long beautiful flowing coat that could be worn for multiple occasions where either casual elegance or evening attire was important. I created a very wide round collar made in the same twisted ribbing pattern that runs through the lacy stitch pattern, then trimmed it with a narrow border of the leaf motif from the stitch pattern. This was done to create a subtle body stitch pattern echo in the collar. This collar was added to give the piece a very feminine finish. The name came from the leaves in the stitch pattern, which reminded me of the coleus plant.

Instructions on page 160.

DUETS & INSPIRATIONS

Cosmopolitan
CONSCIOUSNESS

These pieces are worn with a heightened sense of awareness. They combine a touch of class with a hint of self confidence.

Sunset Skirt

DESIGNED BY **AYANO TANAKA**

INSPIRATION | 14

WHEN a friend saw this A-line skirt, she told me it looked like a winter sunset because of the way the colors transitioned from one to the next. It is knit in a gradient yarn with long color changes and is both light and very warm.

Instructions on page 250.

Aleria Pullover

DESIGNED BY DIANE MARTINI

SWATCH INSPIRATION

INSPIRATION | 6

TWO stitch patterns are merged to flow from the hem upward in a flattering asymmetric design that alternately evokes both waterfalls and flames. Versatility is always a key design objective for me – handwork deserves to be worn often and for many years. In this case, what began as a sleeveless shell with a keyhole neckline at the back, became a blouse or tunic in a summery yarn, with the hem pattern reflected in the ¾-sleeves. Worked in the round from the bottom up with optional set-in sleeves and keyhole placement, this pattern works as well in alpaca as in cotton.

Instructions on page 136.

COSMOPOLITAN CONSCIOUSNESS

Skihytte Cardigan

DESIGNED BY DIANE MARTINI

INSPIRATION | 5

THE MEDALLIONS pattern in this cardigan has a timeless quality that I love. It inspired me to use pattern placement to create a border print that would be flattering for all body types. To keep the overall look light, the sleeves have a shorter version of the border pattern. This placement also draws the eye upward to the face, while the pattern itself draws the eye in at the waist without the need for shaping. Worked in one piece from the bottom up with set in sleeves and knitted on front bands, this cardigan is perfect for hanging out at the skihytte (ski lodge) or anywhere else.

Instructions on page 242.

COSMOPOLITAN CONSCIOUSNESS

Open Bud Shawl

DESIGNED BY **JOAN FORGIONE**

INSPIRATION 10

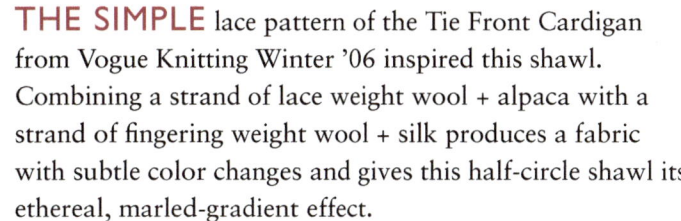

THE SIMPLE lace pattern of the Tie Front Cardigan from Vogue Knitting Winter '06 inspired this shawl. Combining a strand of lace weight wool + alpaca with a strand of fingering weight wool + silk produces a fabric with subtle color changes and gives this half-circle shawl its ethereal, marled-gradient effect.

Instructions on page 222.

COSMOPOLITAN CONSCIOUSNESS

Floating Triangles

HAT & COWL

DESIGNED BY **JOAN FORGIONE**

INSPIRATION | 13

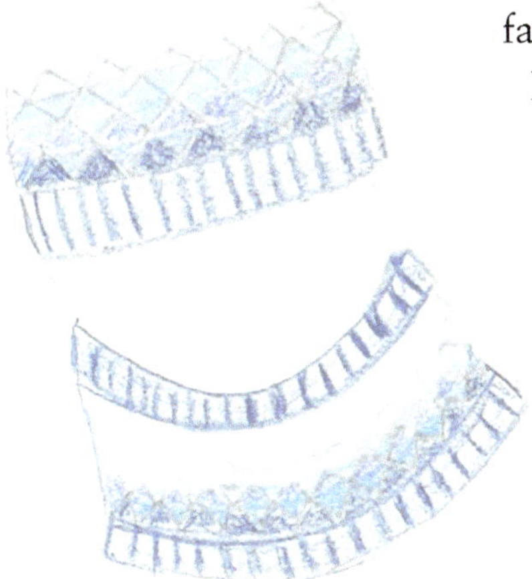

GEOMETRIC colorwork has always been among my favorites. Taking just one of the patterns from Shirley's Lacy Colorwork Tunic and upping the number of colors by using a fantastic gradient set, this hat and cowl were imagined.

Instructions on page 182.

COSMOPOLITAN CONSCIOUSNESS | 59

Cabled Yoke Pullover

DESIGNED BY **LAURA ZUKAITE**

INSPIRATION | 11

THIS pullover is all about calculating the math to perfectly merge the two patterns into a continuous repeat. I immediately loved the density of the Crosses and Twists pattern. It was perfect for a stand-up mock turtleneck collar. The interesting part of the pattern is that besides crossing in a diagonal direction, it also has a vertical, twist-stitch pinstripe that intersects the crosses. I thought it would be great to start with that pinstripe which would seamlessly flow into the Crosses and Twists pattern which gives it a lighter-weight body and denser yoke.

Instructions on page 152.

COSMOPOLITAN CONSCIOUSNESS

Linden Hoodie Burgundy

DESIGNED BY **MARI TOBITA**

SWATCH INSPIRATION

THE TASK of DAL 5 was to combine stitch patterns with different characteristics. I wanted a simple design with a little bit of playfulness for this hooded cardigan with the stitch patterns starting at the hem and flowing up to the hood. I used one pattern repeat as a border that extended from the hem to the top of the hood, but on the back of the cardigan I had enough length to gradually change from one pattern to another. I enjoyed the challenge of this task. The Linden tree provides one of my favorite woods for carving puppets. I named the cardigan after this tree because the stitch pattern reminds me of the shape of its leaves.

Instructions on page 198.

COSMOPOLITAN CONSCIOUSNESS | 63

Nikki Reeves Pullover

DESIGNED BY **NICOLE REEVES**

INSPIRATION | 7

I LOVE CABLES and wanted to express that love with this sweater design. A wide funnel neckline adds interest and serves to complement the classic nature of the cables.

Instructions on page 216.

COSMOPOLITAN CONSCIOUSNESS

Primavera Dress

DESIGNED BY OLGA JANKELOVICH

INSPIRATION | 12

I HAVE always loved knitted dresses. To me they look even more feminine than those made with woven fabric. For this design, I wanted to use three parts of the Double Leaves and Twists stitch pattern, but in a different order than Shirley's inspiration piece. When I swatched this pattern, I noticed the difference in gauges between each of the 3 parts. The stitch count remained the same, but the knitted fabric stretched differently in the different pattern sections. I decided to use this to my advantage to avoid having to do a lot of shaping. I worked the Twisted Ribbing for the central part of the dress, then the Wraps section, which is a denser pattern, beneath the bust, and finally, the Double Leaves pattern for the bust area. In this way, the dress design could flare at the bottom, then very naturally show the curves of the body without having to do many calculations.

Instructions on page 224.

Cascading Cables Cowl
& BALINEEN HAT

COWL DESIGNED BY **SIMA BRASON**

BALINEEN HAT DESIGNED BY **JOAN FORGIONE**

INSPIRATION | 9

COWL: I've been studying with Shirley since 2002 and was excited by the challenge she posed with this design. I selected this cable stitch because of its complexity and designed a tailored, classic cowl. The pattern and finishing of this piece stretched my skills, as I integrated two additional stitch patterns after significant trial and error. The cabled cowl let me reach new levels of precision and intricacy, thanks to charts and written instructions from Joan Forgione. Shirley's steady advice and guidance was unwavering, sharing her in-depth knowledge and expertise with me every step of the way. *Instructions on page 156.*

HAT: When I first saw the Cabled Cardigan in Vogue Knitting's Special Men's issue in 2002, I fell in love. On a smaller scale and by using a crisp, yet soft Targhee wool, the complex cables pop and flow into each other in my dream hat design. *Instructions on page 144.*

COSMOPOLITAN CONSCIOUSNESS

Volare Capelet

DESIGNED BY **SHIRLEY PADEN**

SWATCH INSPIRATION

I WANTED this to be a very pretty lacy poncho that would add elegance to any garment worn beneath. It was designed to be worn with either day or evening apparel. The more open sections of the main stitch pattern were used at the bottom and neck edges for a delicate and feminine feeling. The name for the poncho comes from the Italian word for "fly." The main section resembles an elegant creature that could take flight.

Instructions on page 296.

COSMOPOLITAN CONSCIOUSNESS

Twisted Rhythms

DESIGNED BY **TRUDIE JOSEPH**

INSPIRATION | 4

WITH this design I set out to create a garment design that would flatter my figure. My goal was to craft a cardigan that had sufficient ease in the lower body but was slightly fitted in the upper body. On completion of the design process, the cardigan consisted of a complex lacy bodice with a cabled and twisted rib pattern applied to the lower body. The moss stitch insert that is wrapped in cables is an intricate detail which guides the eye to the lace and cable twists in the bodice. The sleeve patterning consists of a twisted rib pattern borrowed from the lower body stitch pattern. Introducing the second color was a happy accident – I was short on yarn but was determined to complete my garment using yarn from my stash. The garment would also be quite lovely knitted in a single color.

Instructions on page 282.

COSMOPOLITAN CONSCIOUSNESS

DUETS & INSPIRATIONS

Rustic
REVERIES

For a day in the country or an afternoon in the city, these pieces are worn for comfort with an aura of casual elegance.

Linden Hoodie Blue

DESIGNED BY **MARI TOBITA**

SWATCH INSPIRATION

THE TASK of DAL 5 was to combine stitch patterns with different characteristics. I wanted a simple design with a little bit of playfulness for this hooded cardigan with the stitch patterns starting at the hem and flowing up to the hood. I used one pattern repeat as a border that extended from the hem to the top of the hood, but on the back of the cardigan I had enough length to gradually change from one pattern to another. I enjoyed the challenge of this task. The Linden tree provides one of my favorite woods for carving puppets. I named the cardigan after this tree because the stitch pattern reminds me of the shape of its leaves.

Instructions on page 198.

Linden Hoodie Burgundy

DESIGNED BY **MARI TOBITA**

SWATCH INSPIRATION

See design explanation for Linden Hoodie Blue on page 77.

Instructions on page 198.

RUSTIC REVERIES

Teardrop Cardigan

DESIGNED BY **MIKI OHARA**

INSPIRATION | 2

I JOINED Shirley's Cable Design-A-Long for this piece during a time of difficult challenges and change in my life. The first thought before putting pencil to paper for the initial sketch was sadness and teardrops. The teardrops inspired a larger theme of flowing water that led to the choice of shimmering blue yarn and the overall stitch pattern. I also wanted to add the element of hope that keeps us all going amid sadness, resulting in the rising bird in the shape of a teardrop on the back. Since this was going to be a very special keepsake project, I chose to design something a little fancier – elegant, long, and fitted.

Instructions on page 254.

RUSTIC REVERIES

Mesa Poncho

DESIGNED BY **NORIKO OSHIGE**

INSPIRATION 8

THIS comfy and beautiful lace-patterned poncho can be worn two ways: with the lace blocks pointing down at center front or with the straight-edge facing front. The turtleneck collar can be folded over or scrunched down depending on how much warmth you need. My son, Ren named this poncho after a scene from his favorite game.

Instructions on page 212.

RUSTIC REVERIES | 83

Coleus Coat

DESIGNED BY SHIRLEY PADEN

DUET

Pg. 98

I WANTED to create a long beautiful flowing coat that could be worn for multiple occasions where either casual elegance or evening attire was important. I created a very wide round collar made in the same twisted ribbing pattern that runs through the lacy stitch pattern, then trimmed it with a narrow border of the leaf motif from the stitch pattern. This was done to create a subtle body stitch pattern echo in the collar. This collar was added to give the piece a very feminine finish. The name came from the leaves in the stitch pattern, which reminded me of the coleus plant.

Instructions on page 160.

Coquilles Caplet

DESIGNED BY **SHIRLEY PADEN**

SWATCH INSPIRATION

AFTER designing the collar for the Coquilles pullover, I thought of adding additional length to that piece to create a feminine shoulder cover.

It can be worn over day or evening clothing to add a hint of elegance, or a bit of warmth.

Instructions on page 170.

RUSTIC REVERIES

Tige Cardigan

DESIGNED BY SHIRLEY PADEN

SWATCH INSPIRATION

THIS beautiful stitch pattern is composed of mixed panels with different elements including lace, twist stitches and cables. I thought the panel combination could be most elegantly shown on a cropped jacket. I used a double-breasted silhouette and carried the smoother motif that resembles a cornstalk up into the large collar. The more complex but visually stimulating cable and twist stitch panel was placed in the center front and center back. Since the cornstalk type pattern repeats across the garment and is used as an all-over pattern for the collar, I named the jacket Tige. In French, tige de maïs means cornstalk.

Instructions on page 264.

RUSTIC REVERIES

Volare Caplet

DESIGNED BY **SHIRLEY PADEN**

SWATCH INSPIRATION

I WANTED this to be a very pretty lacy poncho that would add elegance to any garment worn beneath. It was designed to be worn with either day or evening apparel. The more open sections of the main stitch pattern were used at the bottom and neck edges for a delicate and feminine feeling. The name for the poncho comes from the Italian word for "fly." The main section resembles an elegant creature that could take flight.

Instructions on page 296.

RUSTIC REVERIES

DUETS & INSPIRATIONS

Restful
REFLECTIONS

These are pieces that provide a sense of comfort no matter where you are, even at home immersed in self reflection.

Seseragi Pullover

DESIGNED BY AYANO TANAKA

INSPIRATION | 16

SESERAGI is a Japanese word which translates as "the relaxing sound of a clear stream." The pullover features an all-over twisted heart stitch pattern with dropped shoulders and triangular insets at each side.

Instructions on page 234.

RESTFUL REFLECTIONS

Frost Flowers Pullover

DESIGNED BY LAURA ZUKAITE

INSPIRATION | 10

WHEN I saw the Frost Flowers pattern I immediately wanted to play with scale. Because the pattern is so versatile, you can adjust the scale, making it larger or smaller by starting the pattern closer or farther apart. So, I kept the sleeves and bottom trim section in small scale, then "exploded" the pattern to fully stretch over the front & back panels. Since the Frost Flowers pattern already had rows of eyelets, I thought it would be nice to repeat them over the upper yoke as well. I love the way the pattern naturally creates a wide scalloped edge and perfectly shapes the bottom opening and sleeves.

Instructions on page 184.

Gothic Tracery Cardigan

DESIGNED BY **GALE PAGE**

SWATCH INSPIRATION

WITH this garment, I set out to design a lace sweater with a slightly fitted silhouette. The shawl collar gently narrows to the center front with a flattering V-neck.

Instructions on page 190.

RESTFUL REFLECTIONS

Twist & Shout Shawl

DESIGNED BY IRIS SCHREIER

INSPIRATION | I

BECAUSE I wanted this to be a really engaging knit, I included an 8-color lineup. The pattern keeps you interested as the next color appears in the sequence. I also wanted to provide an easy to memorize lace pattern with loads of texture, which is why the twist stitches were used.

I've always loved the fabric that knitting on the bias makes, and this shawl is no exception. The orientation of this lace pattern lends itself well to bias knitting and the slanted lines produce a modern, asymmetrical look.

The end result is the perfect generous wrap which can be used in every season; wrap it lightly around the shoulders to avoid air conditioning chill in summer, fasten it with a shawl pin for fall and spring; or wrap it several times around the neck as a scarf to bundle up for winter.

Instructions on page 280.

RESTFUL REFLECTIONS | 101

Trellised Arbor Shawl

DESIGNED BY **JOAN FORGIONE**

INSPIRATION | 12

I ENVISIONED this shawl as a long, asymmetrical triangle finished off in lace. The shape was the perfect canvas to incorporate the way the lines of twisted rib flow into the lace pattern of the Double Leaves & Twists Duster from Knitwear Design Workshop. The "flow" was provided by the lustrous wool and silk blend of the yarn.

Instructions on page 276.

Primavera Dress

DESIGNED BY OLGA JANKELOVICH

INSPIRATION | 12

I HAVE always loved knitted dresses. To me they look even more feminine than those made with woven fabric. For this design, I wanted to use three parts of the Double Leaves and Twists stitch pattern, but in a different order than Shirley's inspiration piece. When I swatched this pattern, I noticed the difference in gauges between each of the 3 parts. The stitch count remained the same, but the knitted fabric stretched differently in the different pattern sections. I decided to use this to my advantage to avoid having to do a lot of shaping. I worked the Twisted Ribbing for the central part of the dress, then the Wraps section, which is a denser pattern, beneath the bust, and finally, the Double Leaves pattern for the bust area. In this way, the dress design could flare at the bottom, then very naturally show the curves of the body without having to do many calculations.

Instructions on page 224.

RESTFUL REFLECTIONS

THE DESIGNER'S NOTEBOOK

Ada Wolfstein: A Renaissance Woman For Our Time

by Shirley Paden

Ada Hüttner Wolfstein possessed that broad range of artistic and intellectual interests and accomplishments that we think of when we use the term "Renaissance Woman." She was the mother of one of my closest friends, Eloe Woolf Laiken.

I first met Ada in 1992 when I was preparing my first design collection. I had heard much about her and her needlecraft talents from her daughter, but since she lived in Sweden, I had never had a chance to meet her. When I learned that she was visiting New York for two weeks, I invited her and Eloe for lunch at my home. After lunch I showed her my work-in-progress knitting on my first custom design collection and asked for any design, knitting, or finishing tips. I still had some pieces that were not put together, and with grace and without hesitation, she helped me with some of the finishing. At that time, Eloe, who is a fine artist, was a very supportive friend. As I knit my collection she would serve as my model. After I showed Ada some of our photos, and she was kind in admiring my first design efforts, we had an impromptu question and answer session where I asked her how she would work different techniques. I remember how patiently and carefully she demonstrated different techniques, explaining every step as she worked. I remember thinking that a seemingly endless array of knitting and finishing techniques appeared to be stored in the forefront of her mind where they could easily and effortlessly be accessed. She was a natural teacher and so polite, secure in her knowledge of an ancient craft. As a relatively new knitter and very new designer, I was both moved and impressed by her unique combination of knowledge, patience, kindness, and humility. As my thoughts of teaching and growing my design business grew, those were the traits that I felt I would aspire toward. The next year after much studying and practicing, I also began to teach, trying to emulate Ada's manner and style into my classes.

When I first met her, Ada was 74. What was most intriguing to me was that she was still actively involved in knitting, crocheting, needlepointing, sewing, and making puppets, and she had a mastery of each needleart that she worked in. We forged a bond of friendship that included a mutual creative respect. It lasted for 26 years, until the end of her life. Each time Eloe would visit her, Ada would send me back a gift of her needlework. As I grew in my design knowledge, and had a book published, she even sent me her hand-cut cardboard pattern pieces. This was the equivalent of a designer's source code, and I was incredibly honored. I felt that watching me grow in my craft from afar she knew that I had finally evolved to the point of truly appreciating what she was sending me. For her, my design book was a type of rite of passage that I had successfully passed through. As I opened the package, I felt much pride in my heart for the trust that she had placed in me by sending me something that would allow me to get a deeper look into her design process at the seed level. I felt like a teenager being given the car keys. She was a "Master" of design and was nodding her head, saying that I could stand in the ranks. I was in constant awe of Ada's amazing, artistic eye, non-stop productivity, endeavor for excellence, and unwavering discipline. All of this continued well into her late 90s. Listening to Eloe tell stories of her mother, I came to find out that Ada's life was rich and varied.

Ada was born in Lwow, Poland (now Lviv, Ukraine) on August 17, 1918. As a Jewish Polish woman coming of age between two World Wars, she spent much of her young adult life maneuvering through a world that was in a state of constant turmoil. Hearing the details from her two biographies (written in her native Polish) is like listening to edge-of-your-seat thrillers or fast-paced spy novels. Yet, even though she and her family suffered numerous hardships, she never stopped learning and creating. It was these two qualities that enabled her to help her family to survive through several critical situations.

During the worldwide depression leading up to WWII, the Hüttner family suffered economically. The young Ada developed her knitting, crochet and needlepoint skills to earn money to help her family. She graduated high school in Jaroslaw, Poland 1936 with excellent grades, but was dissuaded from entering the University of Warsaw due to the intense antisemitism leading up to WWII. Ada was fluent in Russian and German in addition to her native Polish. During WWII, her linguistic abilities would save her life.

In July 1940, Ada and her fiancé Benedykt, a criminal attorney, were forcefully transported by the Red Army from Lwow, Poland to a Soviet labor camp, deep in a forest, approximately 300 miles south of Moscow. It was there that their daughter Eloe was born. Toward the end of 1944, Benedykt and some of the other men decided to follow the newly organized Polish army west in an effort to get back to Poland. He left Ada and his daughter behind with a promise to write as soon as

"I remember how patiently and carefully she demonstrated different techniques, explaining every step as she worked… She was a natural teacher and so polite, secure in her knowledge of an ancient craft."

he could. Although they were able write each other, due to the events of the war, they would not see each other again until Ada and her daughter arrived in Poland in the spring of 1946. Thankfully, because Ada spoke Russian, could knit, and was both resourceful and talented, she was able to earn money knitting pieces for some Russian women, and teaching others how to knit gloves instead of the mittens they were accustomed to. This allowed her and her daughter to survive.

After WW II, when Ada and Eloe were finally reunited with Benedykt in Bytom, Poland, as they began to rebuild their lives, she worked in Benedykt's law practice as secretary and paralegal. However, she never stopped creating handwork and continuously adding different types of designs to her repertoire. Her artistic endeavors expanded as she began creating mixed media collages, dolls and most of her daughter's clothing by hand.

Because her designs were inventive and sophisticated, in the 1960's Ada was encouraged by members of the drama circle at the Bytom Jewish Cultural Agency to create costumes and decorations for the theater. Before the war she had been involved in theater and dance and had even been a student at one of the dance schools influenced by Isadora Duncan. Utilizing these skills, she also began directing and managing the theater. She wrote pieces for performances, taught drama skills and adapted plays and montages for the stage. Her talent was rewarded by requests to take over the management of other cultural circles. She became licensed to do this and won national awards. This is the work that she did until retirement.

In early spring 1982, in a forced relocation, Ada and Benedykt, both retired, left Bytom, Poland to settle in Malmo, Sweden where they quickly learned Swedish and some English and immersed themselves in the cultural life there. After living there a few years they received Swedish citizenship.

Between 2010 and 2012, Ada wrote her two well-received biographies. The first, *To Leave a Trace*, describes life between 1939 at the start of WWII and 1946 when she returned to Poland from the Soviet Union. Her second book, *Life's Screenplay*, describes the struggles that she and Benedykt experienced during the Communist occupation of Poland after WW II, including the loss of friends due to forced emigration.

In her later years, as Ada turned her attention to writing, she was as remarkably disciplined as she had always been with her handwork. Her style was smooth and elegant, and her books are still in demand. Until her late nineties, her knitting and crochet designs remained inventive and sophisticated. I was always amazed at her ability to deconstruct a stitch pattern to flow seamlessly through a design and at her incredible technical skills that included always maintaining perfect tension. Her daughter gave me a collection of her knit and crochet pieces and by studying them I learned to look even deeper at a stitch pattern. Her designs were always classic with stitch patterns that would "dance" across the fabric. This is a design philosophy that I admire and also try to achieve in my pieces.

I am honored to choose one of Ada's meticulously planned designs as my personal inspiration piece. I have entitled my dress "Ada" as a tribute to her. It is inspired by the "Eloe" dress that she designed for her daughter in 1964. I feel that the design is timeless, as fresh today as it was 57 years ago. That is representative of her design stamp.

Ada died on October 28, 2017 at the age of 99 in Malmo, Sweden. She lived with a desire to learn, teach and create that lasted until the very end. Through her handwork and her creative work in cultural institutions throughout Poland, her legacy is secure and will continue to influence generations to come.

> "I am honored to choose one of Ada's meticulously planned designs as my personal inspiration piece. I have entitled my dress 'Ada' as a tribute to her. It is inspired by the 'Eloe' dress that she designed for her daughter in 1964. I feel that the design is timeless, as fresh today as it was 57 years ago. That is representative of her design stamp."

THE DESIGNER'S NOTEBOOK

Sima Brason

As a published knitwear designer, active teacher and former owner of a knitting studio, Sima Brason focuses on creative designs that let the personality of the yarn and the wearer come through. Whether funky, elegant or fun, Sima mixes practical with eclectic to create unique designs. Sima's work has been published in the book Vogue on the Go Bags Two and Knit Simple magazine. As a teacher, she shares her love for knitting and techniques with novice and experienced knitters, hoping to inspire young and old as her mother and grandmother inspired her. Sima is a licensed real estate agent in NY and NJ. Her career spans 25+ years.

RAVELRY: simabrason
INSTAGRAM: @sima_brason

Joan Forgione

Joan Forgione is a knitwear designer and reading teacher. Her design work has been published in leading magazines, nationally and internationally, featured in books, and commissioned by yarn companies. When she's not designing for others, she self-publishes her patterns as Paper Moon Knits on Ravelry. A teacher at heart, she believes every pattern is an opportunity for a knitter to learn, and she loves helping knitters do just that while they create finished pieces of which they can be proud.

RAVELRY: joanforgione
INSTAGRAM: @papermoonknits
WEBSITE: Paper Moon Knits

Lisa Hoffman

Lisa Hoffman is a knitwear designer and knitting teacher. Lisa's designs have been published in Vogue Knitting, Interweave Knits and knit.wear magazines. A collaboration with her cousin, Alice Hoffman, in Faerie Magazine led to a book, Faerie Knitting, a collection of stories and knitting patterns. Lisa is the manager of String Yarns (stringyarns.com). She lives in Manhattan with her husband. When she is not working or knitting, you will find her with her grandchildren.

RAVELRY: LisaHoffmanKnits
INSTAGRAM: @lisahoffmanknits
WEBSITE: Lisa Hoffman Knits

THE DESIGNER'S NOTEBOOK

Olga Jankelovich

Olga was born and raised in Latvia, a country famous for its handknitted folk mittens and socks. From a very early age she was surrounded by pretty hand-made things. Her mother, older sister and aunts enjoyed knitting, crocheting and needlepointing. However, Olga only became interested in knitting at the age of 15. Because her mother couldn't afford to buy her a ready-made woolen dress, she offered to buy yarn so Olga could knit one for herself. Although it was her first knitted garment, it was enough to capture her long-lasting passion for knitting.

While working to achieve the rank of Latvian National Master of Knitting, Olga studied how to design and make all kinds of knitwear from mittens and socks to dresses and coats, all with fine garment details and finishing while being judged on all levels of perfection. It is interesting that many years later, after immigrating to the United States, she found the essence of that course in Shirley Paden's book Knitwear Design Workshop. She has won awards at Stitches West and other knitting competitions and continues to follow a practical principle of keeping her designs simple while showcasing the stitch patterns and elegance of her finished pieces.

RAVELRY: **Olgajanka**

INSTAGRAM: **@olgajankelovich**

Trudie Joseph

Trudie Joseph is an avid knitter who enjoys knitting designs with intricate detail and classic garment construction. Her interest in complex knitwear designs is a natural extension of her love of building software for large corporations. Her experience as a software developer and now director of IT Operations allows Trudie to apply general design principles to knitwear, while being a sewist helps her understanding of translating woven fabric to knitted fabric.

Trudie's interest in garment design is driven by her desire to tailor patterns to fit her body and style. Her first introduction to Shirley Paden was through Shirley's Lace and Design master classes at her local yarn shop. Trudie sat on the sidelines in DAL 2, and then became an active participant in DAL 3 and DAL 4. Her enthusiasm for the DALs led her to become one of the moderators for DAL 5 and for The Knitting Boutique's KAL for Shirley's Recolte Jacket.

A published knitwear designer, Trudie's Corolla Cropped Cardigan was featured in Vogue Knitting, Winter 19/20 with upcoming designs in major publications slated for the coming year.

RAVELRY: **tdevknits**

INSTAGRAM: **@tdevknits**

THE DESIGNER'S NOTEBOOK

Diane Martini

By day, Diane works for an engineering company, but in her free time she "engineers" knitwear, creating unique and stylish garments with classic lines that defy trends for women of all sizes. Diane began as a child, designing and making clothes for her dolls. Now she enjoys the challenges of creating garments with interesting stitch patterns using hand-dyed yarns. She has designed for Brooks Farm Yarn since 2007 and opened her Ravelry Store in 2011. Her designs have won awards at both design and garment competitions. Diane lives and works in Chicago, Illinois.

RAVELRY: rantini

Miki Ohara

Miki Ohara has been drawing and painting since she could hold a crayon. She picked up knitting when she decided she needed a hat and scarf to go to a chilly New Year's Bowl game 11 years ago, and has not put down the needles since. Adding intarsia elements to her designs was a natural combination of her creative passions and extensive professional skills in Excel which turned out to be a great tool for turning her drawings into knitting charts. When in need of more immediate creative gratification, she spends her time in the kitchen. Most recently she has been expanding her spice cabinet and exploring the joy of curries from around the world. In order to support her knitting habit, she works with financial data and reporting during the day. Her two dogs have a home in the San Fernando Valley, and they are kind enough to let her live there and pay all the bills.

RAVELRY: pugmutt

Noriko Oshige

Noriko's love for and interest in knitting, sewing and embroidery began in childhood. She learned to knit from her mother by knitting a scarf. By the age of ten, she was knitting garments for her family. All four seasons in Japan are beautiful, but she likes winter the most because knitting can be done all day. When she's not knitting, Noriko teaches personal computer classes. Noriko lives with her husband, son, and two lovely dogs in Fukuoka, Japan.

RAVELRY: punico
INSTAGRAM: @chihuaet

THE DESIGNER'S NOTEBOOK

Shirley Paden

As an internationally recognized hand knitwear designer, Shirley Paden's designs and articles have appeared in the leading magazines in the hand knitting industry such as *Vogue Knitting, Interweave Knits, Interweave Crochet, Knitters, Family Circle,* and *Knit It* as well as in the collections of leading yarn companies. She has taught and lectured on various aspects of hand knitting and crochet locally, nationally and internationally. She also has a popular online class *Handknit Garment Design* featured on the popular Craftsy website (formerly Blueprint). Her book, **Knitwear Design Workshop**, was the best selling knitting book on Amazon.com in 2010 and remains a key industry reference. Shirley has been featured on HGTV and Knitting Daily TV as well as in designer interviews in the leading knitting magazines and in the well-known *Designer's Studio* series.

The British magazine *The Knitter* has listed her in their "Who's Who in North American Knitting."
She is also the owner of *Shirley Paden Custom Knits* located in New York City.

Gale Page

Gale learned to knit as a child and made a ripple afghan and her first pair of snowflake mittens in college. Since then, she has knitted many garments including sweaters, gloves, hats, and shawls. She enjoys trying out ideas on baby garments and knitting fair isle designs. This is her first published pattern.

RAVELRY: **gale2025**

Nicole Reeves

Nicole Reeves decided that she wanted to learn to knit sweaters, so she taught herself the basics. Since then, she has created many designs featured on her knitting blog, Nik's Knits, where she writes about knitting and the random thoughts in her head. She has also designed for both Interweave Knits and Twist Collective. In addition, one of her designs was published in knit.wear magazine's Wool Studio Vol. VIII. She lives in Raleigh, North Carolina, where she is a knitter/crafter who happens to be a molecular biologist.

RAVELRY: **niksknits**
INSTAGRAM: **@niksknits1**
WEBSITE: **Nik's Knits**

THE DESIGNER'S NOTEBOOK

RAVELRY: **irissch**
INSTAGRAM: **@artyarns**
WEBSITE: **Artyarns**

Iris Schrieier

Iris couldn't find the yarn she wanted for her designs, and with the mission of elevating the art of knitting, decided to create it herself. She is the founder of Artyarns, a company which has built its reputation on producing luxurious, sophisticated, hand-dyed yarns of the highest quality. Since 2004, Artyarns has offered a variety of special yarns, including Merino wool, silk, cashmere and mohair, and has featured fiber blends as well as embellished yarns enhanced with beads, sequins and gold or silver metallic strands.

Iris is the author of 7 knitting books including Modular Knits (Lark, 2007), Lacy Little Knits, and the popular One + One Series. Her original, innovative techniques are used in knitting shops around the world and her patterns and books have been translated into multiple languages. Iris has appeared on the television programs "Knitty Gritty" and "Needle Arts Studio," and she has written articles and published patterns in leading magazines. You can find her on Facebook and Instagram to learn more about her designs and patterns.

Ellen M. Silva

After decades as a serious knitter, years that included blogging and podcasting with her twin sister about the craft and other fiber topics, Ellen got serious about designing. Several of her popular self-published patterns were born out of the desire to personalize her knitting. She credits her participation in Shirley Paden Design-A-Longs for taking her design skills to the next level. Ellen has had her designs featured in Modeknit Yarns Sock Club and 1000 Fabulous Knit Hats, has been published in Cast-On magazine, and has taught classes on her designs at local yarn stores and knitting retreats. She supports several other designers with technical editing services, enjoying the opportunity to knit dozens of original designs in her head. Ellen became a Certified Master Knitter through The Knitting Guild of America in 2018.

RAVELRY: **twinsetellen**

Ayano Tanaka

Ayano Tanaka lives in Japan with her husband. After many years of exploring different creative areas, including attending art school and working at a cloisonné studio, she found her creative passion in hand knitting. She spends her spare time either creating or knitting new designs. Her dream is to travel the world exploring textiles from different countries. Her current interests include Estonian knitting and hand knit glove design. She has participated in Shirley Paden's Design-A-Longs four times. Her knitwear designs have been featured in a number of different magazines, including Interweave Knits.

RAVELRY: **ashika**
INSTAGRAM: **@ichiboku**

THE DESIGNER'S NOTEBOOK

Mari Tobita

Mari moved to New York City from Japan in 1996 to continue her work as a puppet designer/builder. In 2002, she began taking Shirley Paden's classes and started designing in 2005. Her designs have appeared in magazines such as Vogue Knitting, Interweave Knits, Noro Magazine, Brooklyn Tweed Wool People, as well as in several knitting books. She also self publishes her designs at Mari Tobita Designs on Ravelry. Mari also teaches handknitting in her home cities of Sapporo and Tokyo, Japan. She loves knitting gloves using fine gauge needles and collecting knitted gloves that she never wears. She also enjoys participating in knitting events, learning new techniques and meeting new people!

RAVELRY: ChaNY
INSTAGRAM: @mari.tobita

Midori Yaple

Midori is a Maui-based Japanese knitter who loves knitting and photography. She credits her creative family with developing these passions – her grandmother, a wonderful knitter and her father, a renowned photographer in Japan. Her favorite subjects for both are inspired by living in a tropical setting: sunsets, the ocean, waves, swaying palm trees and flowers. She has participated in the Design-A-Longs since 2010 and credits Shirley Paden with motivating her to focus on creating natural movement and freshness in her knitting designs.

RAVELRY: amgreen
INSTAGRAM: @mauigreen7

Laura Zukaite

Laura Zukaite was born and raised in Lithuania, but has lived in New York City for nearly two decades. She studied fashion design at Parsons School of Design and has been designing in the fashion industry for such companies as Ralph Lauren and Gap. Laura has been published in various knitting magazines and is the author of Luxe Knits, Luxe Knits: The Accessories and Inspired Shawls: 15 Creative Patterns for Year-Round Knitting, a book of knitted shawl designs all inspired by recent travels. Laura is also the co-founder of Artisan-Made home décor design brand Ama Connection which specializes in sustainable, hand-made products.

RAVELRY: LauraZukaite
INSTAGRAM: @laurazukaite
WEBSITE: Laura Zukaite Designs

Abbreviations

approx	approximately
beg	beginning; begin; begins
bet	between
BO	bind off
Ch	chain
CC	contrasting color
cm	centimeter(s)
cn	cable needle
CO	cast on
cont	continue(s); continuing
dbl	double
dc	double crochet
dec(s)	decrease(s)
dec'd	decreased
dec'ng	decreasing
dpn(s)	double-pointed needle(s)
estab	established; as established
foll	following; follows
g	gram(s)
inc(s)	increase(s)
inc'd	increased
inc'ng	increasing
k	knit
k1f&b	knit into front and back of same stitch
kfbf	knit into front, then back, then front of same stitch
k1tbl	knit 1 stitch through the back loop
k2tog	knit two stitches together
k'wise	knitwise
LH	left-hand
LHN	left-hand needle

LHS	left-hand side	SKP	slip 1 stitch, knit 1 stitch, pass slipped stitch over the knit stitch (single decrease)
mar(s)	marker(s)		
m	meter(s)	SK2P	slip 1 stitch, knit 2 stitches together, pass slipped stitch over the stitch resulting from the 2 stitches knit together (double decrease)
MC	main color		
mm	millimeter(s)		
M1	make one	S2KP	slip 2 stitches together, knit 1 stitch, pass 2 slipped stitches over the knit 1 stitch
M1 (P)	make one (purl)		
M1R (L)	make one right (left)	sl	slip
oz	ounce(s)	sl m	slip marker
p	purl	sl st	slip 1 stitch (slip 1 stitch purlwise unless told otherwise)
patt(s)	pattern(s)	ssk	slip 2 stitches knitwise, on a right side row, one at a time, from the left needle to the right needle. Insert the left needle tip through both front loops and knit the 2 slipped stitches together from this position (single decrease)
p1f&b	purl into the front and back of same stitch		
p1tbl	purl 1 stitch through the back loop		
p2tog	purl 2 stitches together		
pl mar	place marker		
psso	pass slipped stitch over	ssp	slip 2 stitches knitwise, on a wrong side row, one at a time, from the left needle to the right needle. They are twisted. Slip the 2 stitches back to the left needle in this twisted position. Purl the 2 stitches together through the back loops (single decrease)
p2sso	pass 2 slipped stitches over		
p'wise	purlwise		
rem	remain(s); remaining		
re mar	remove marker		
rep	repeat; repeating	st(s)	stitch(es)
rev sc	reverse single crochet	St st	stockinette stitch
rev St st	reverse stockinette stitch	symm	symmetry
RH	right-hand	tbl	through the back loop
RHN	right-hand needle	thru	through
RHS	right-hand side	tog	together
rib	ribbing	W&T	wrap & turn
rnd(s)	round(s)	WS	wrong side
RS	right side	WSR(s)	wrong side row(s)
RSR(s)	right side row(s)	wyib	with yarn in back
Rt	right	wyif	with yarn in front
sc	single crochet	yd(s)	yard(s)
selv	selvedge stitch	yo	yarn over
sk	skip	*	starting point for repeat instructions (e.g., repeat from *)
		**	repeat all instructions between asterisks
		( )	alternate measurements and/or instructions
		[ ]	repeat instructions inside bracket a specific number of times

Symbol Keys

CABLES, CROSSES, AND TWISTS SYMBOL KEY:

Crosses

#	Symbol	Abbr	Description
1		Cr2L	K 2nd st tbl crossing behind the 1st st, then k the 1st st, sl both tog to RHN
2		Cr2R	K 2nd st crossing in front of 1st st, then k 1st st, sl both tog to RHN

Cables

#	Symbol	Abbr	Description
3		C3F	Sl2 to cn, hold front, k1, then k2 from cn
4		C3B	Sl1 to cn, hold back, k2, then k1 from cn
5		C4F	Sl2 to cn, hold front, k2, then k2 from cn
6		C4B	Sl2 to cn, hold back, k2, then k2 from cn
7		C5F	Sl2 to cn, hold front, k3, then k2 from cn
8		C5B	Sl3 to cn, hold back, k2, then k3 from cn
9		C6F	Sl3 to cn, hold front, k3, then k3 from cn
10		C6B	Sl3 to cn, hold back, k3, then k3 from cn
11		C8F	Sl4 to cn, hold front, k4, then k4 from cn
12		C8B	Sl4 to cn, hold back, k4, then k4 from cn

Special Cable Techniques

#	Symbol	Abbr	Description
13		C7F-P	C7F-P Sl3 to cn, hold front, k3, p1, then k3 from cn
14		C7B-P	C7B-P Sl4 to cn, hold back, k3, then p1, k3 from cn

Twists A - Exchanging Positions of Untwisted Knit and Purl Stitches

#	Symbol	Abbr	Description
15		T3F	Sl2 to cn, hold front, p1, then k2 from cn
16		T3B	Sl1 to cn, hold back, k2, then p1 from cn
17		T3F-2	Sl1 to cn, hold front, p2, then k1 from cn
18		T3B-2	Sl2 to cn, hold back, k1, then p2 from cn
19		T4F	Sl2 to cn, hold front, p2, then k2 from cn
20		T4B	Sl2 to cn, hold back, k2, then p2 from cn
21		T4F-2	Sl3 to cn, hold front, p1, then k3 from cn
22		T4B-2	Sl1 to cn, hold back, k3, then p1 from cn
23		T4F-3	Sl2 to cn, hold front, p2, then k2 from cn
24		T4B-3	Sl2 to cn, hold back, k2, then p2 from cn
25		T5F	Sl3 to cn, hold front, p2, then k3 from cn
26		T5B	Sl2 to cn, hold back, k3, then p2 from cn
27		T5F-2	Sl2 to cn, hold front, p3, then k2 from cn
28		T5B-2	Sl3 to cn, hold front, k2, then p3 from cn
29		T5L	Sl2 to cn, hold front, k1, p1, k1, then k2 from cn
30		T5R	Sl3 to cn, hold back, k2, then k1, p1, k1 from cn

Twists B - Exchanging Positions of Knit and Purl Stitches while twisting the Knit Stitches (K1tbl)

#	Symbol	Abbr	Description
31		TT2F	Sl1 to cn, hold front, p1, then k1tbl on st from cn
32		TT2B	Sl1 to cn, hold back, k1tbl, then p1 from cn
33		TT3F	Sl2 to cn, hold front, p1, then k1tbl on each of the 2 sts from cn
34		TT3B	Sl1 to cn, hold back, k next 2 sts, each tbl, then p1 from cn
35		DBLT3F	Sl2 to cn, hold front, k1tbl, then k1tbl on each of the 2 sts from cn
36		DBLT3B	Sl1 to cn, hold back, k next 2 sts, each tbl, then k1tbl on st from cn

Special 2-Stitch Twisted Crossings

37	Tw2-F	K 2nd st crossing behind 1st, k 1st st tbl, drop both tog from LHN
38	Tw2-B	K 2nd st tbl crossing in front of 1st, k 1st st, drop both tog from LHN
39	Tw2-F-P	Sl1 to cn, hold front, p1, then k1tbl from cn
40	Tw2-B-P	Sl1 to cn, hold back, k1tbl, then p1 from cn
41	Tw2-CrF	K 2nd st tbl crossing behind the 1st, k 1st st tbl, drop both tog from LHN
42	Tw2-CrB	K 2nd st tbl crossing in front of 1st, k 1st st tbl, drop both tog from LHN

Special 3-Stitch Twisted Crossings

| 43 | Cr4L W/YO | 1)Sl1 st p'wise to RHN, 2)sl2 sts to cn, hold front, 3)slip st from RHN back to LHN and k2tog with the next st on the LHN, 4)yo, then, k2 from cn |
| 44 | Cr4R W/YO | 1)Sl1 st to cn, hold back, 2)k2, yo, 3)sl st from cn onto RHN, 4)k1 from LHN, 5) pass slipped st from cn (now returned to RHN) over knit st from LHN |

Special 2-Stitch Twisted Decreases

45	Tw2-L	Sl1tbl-k1-psso
46	Tw2-R	1)Sl2 p'wise one at a time to RHN, 2)Sl 1st st back to LHN tbl by reaching across the st with the LHN and entering through the RHS (Rt-to-left) to twist the st, 3)Sl 2nd st back to LHN without twisting it, 4)knit the 2 sts tog. The twisted st will be on top.
47	Tw3-L	Sl1tbl-k2tog-psso
48	Tw3-R	1)Sl3 sts p'wise one at a time to RHN, 2)Sl 1st st back to LHN tbl by reaching across the st with the LHN and entering through the RHS (Rt-to-left) to twist the st before slipping it to the LHN, 3)Sl the next 2 sts back to the LHN without twisting them (one at a time), 4)k3tog. The twisted st will be on top.

Special Single Decreases Techniques

49	TD4F	Sl2 to cn, hold front, p2tog, then k2 from cn
50	TD4B	Sl2 to cn, hold back, k2, then p2tog on sts from cn
51	CD4F	Sl2 to cn, hold front, k2tog, then k2 on sts from cn

LACE SYMBOL KEY:

1. K on RS, P on WS
2. P on RS, K on WS
3. K2tog on RS, P2tog on WS
4. Ssk on Rs, Ssp on WS
5. Sl2-k1-p2sso
6. K1tbl on RS, P1tbl on WS
7. Slip stitch wyib
8. K1f&b
9. No stitch
10. Patt rep
11. Yarn Over
12. K3tog on RS, P3tog on WS
13. Sl1-k2tog-psso
14. Kfbf
15. P2tog
16. K2togtbl
17. P1tbl on RS, K1tbl on WS
18. K first and last st on each row
19. M1 pwise on RS, M1 on WS
20. M1 on RS, M1 pwise on WS
21. (_____) Wrap = # of sts + # of times sts wrapped
22. 1)Lift 3rd st on LHN backward over the first 2 sts, 2)K1, yo, k1 on 2 rem sts
23. 1)Lift 3rd st on LHN backward over the first 2 sts, 2)K1, yo, 3)Sl 2nd st from LHN knitwise, 4)Knit next st on LHN, 5)Pass the slipped st over the knit st
24. 1)Slip the st before these 3 sts, 2)Lift 3rd st backward over the 2nd st on LHN, 3)Return slipped st to LHN, 4)K2tog, yo, k1

Special Techniques

4-STITCH DOUBLE WRAP (worked over 4 sts)

With RS facing, k1tbl, p2, k1tbl, then sl the 4 sts just worked onto cable needle (Fig 1.1). With RS still facing, bring yarn to front between the cn and left-hand needle, then holding cn at front, wrap the sts twice (Fig 1.2 and Fig 1.3)—4 sts on cn have been double-wrapped. Return the 4 sts on cn to right-hand needle (Fig 1.4) and cont in patt.

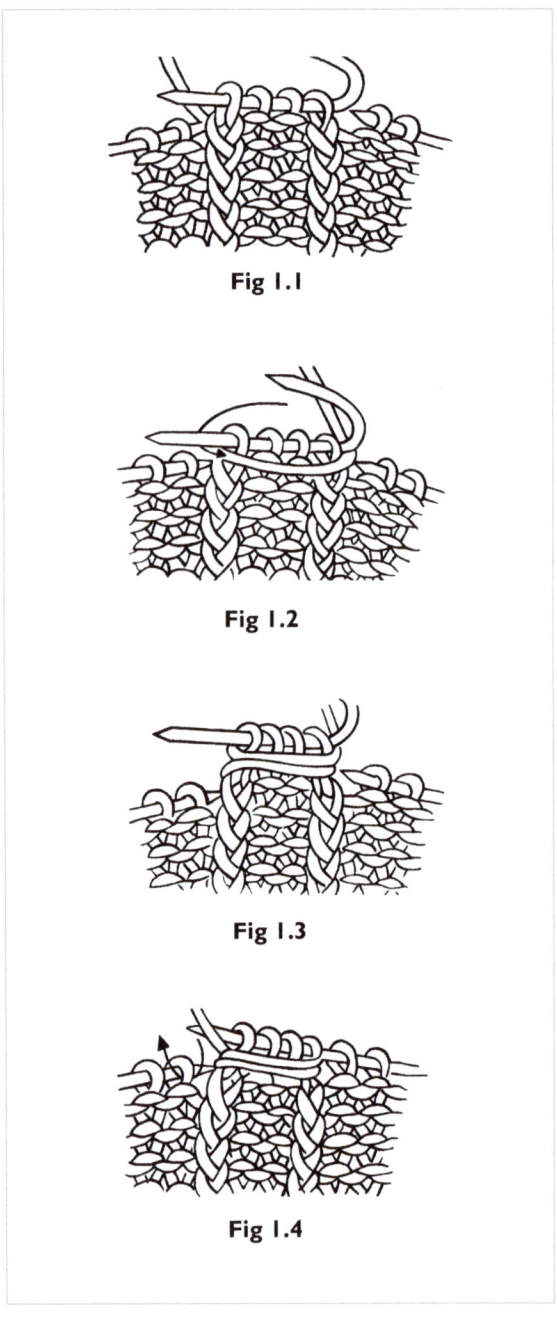

Fig 1.1

Fig 1.2

Fig 1.3

Fig 1.4

ALTERNATING LONGTAIL CAST ON

The Alternating Cast On technique produces a lovely, rolled edge. It is used for K1/P1 ribbing. The stitches are placed on the needle in the exact structure that they will be worked in as the fabric is constructed above the cast on edge. The recommendation is to use a needle a few sizes smaller than the needle being used for the body of the project.

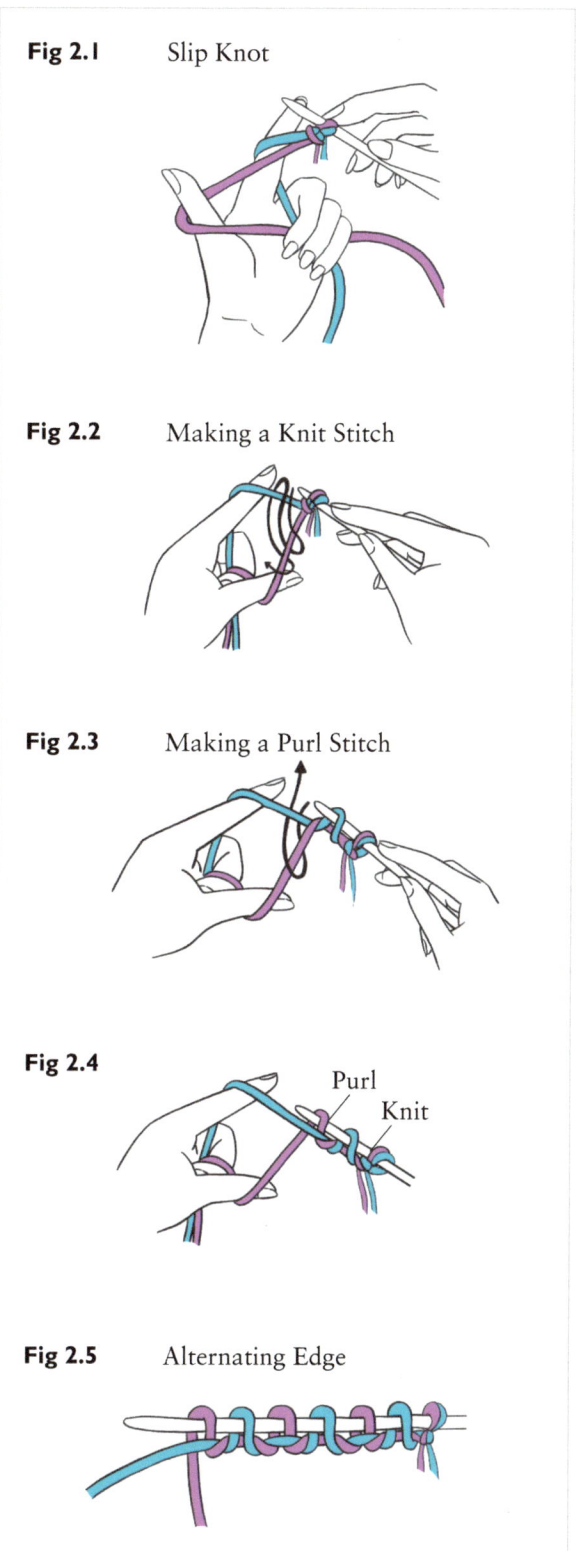

Fig 2.1 — Slip Knot

Fig 2.2 — Making a Knit Stitch

Fig 2.3 — Making a Purl Stitch

Fig 2.4 — Purl / Knit

Fig 2.5 — Alternating Edge

Forming a Knit Stitch

(Fig 2.1) Begin with a slip knot. (Fig 2.2) Bring the needle above the two strands of yarn. One strand will be crossing the thumb and the other strand will be crossing the forefinger. Bring the needle forward and go beneath the thumb strand. Next, bring the needle up over the forefinger strand. Press down against the forefinger strand and bring the needle forward beneath the thumb strand until the forefinger strand becomes the next stitch on the needle. The thumb strand will twist around the forefinger strand at the bottom, just below the needle. Both strands will be back in their starting positions. Lift the needle to begin forming the purl stitch

Forming a Purl Stitch

(Fig 2.3) Take the needle back behind the forefinger strand. Next, bring the needle all the way forward going beneath both strands until it is in front of the thumb strand. When the needle is at the front, push it back against the thumb strand until that strand has been moved back beneath the forefinger strand and the thumb strand has formed a stitch on the needle. The two strands will be twisted with the forefinger strand crossing in front of the thumb strand at the bottom. That forefinger strand is now in position to make a purl bump as you begin the movements for the knit stitch. (Fig 2.4) Here we see both types of stitches completely formed.

(Fig 2.5) Here we see alternating knit and purl sts as they cross the bottom edge.

TUBULAR CAST ON

The Tubular Cast On technique produces a lovely, rolled edge. It is used on projects with a K1/P1 or K2/P2 edging. The edging can also be planned to begin and end with one or two knit stitches. In our example, we are planning an edging that is worked in K1/P1 and that begins and ends with one knit stitch. To begin this type of edging, a temporary cast on or crochet chain is worked with waste yarn in a contrasting color. In our example we are using a crochet chain. Approximately half the number of stitches planned for the edging are either cast on or picked up in a crochet chain. The exact number will be based on the type of edging and the planned edge stitch symmetry. Increasing to the full stitch count is done on a planned tubular construction row. Because the rolled bottom (tube) is always planned with the smooth face of stockinette, there is always a set number of rows that will be worked in that patt and planned to turn under during the tubular construction row. The tubular row is the single row that pulls the bottom edge up to have the appearance of a hemmed edge. In our example, we are working three rows in the St. st. patt before the tubular row. They include the knit pick-up row, one purl row and one knit row. See example below:

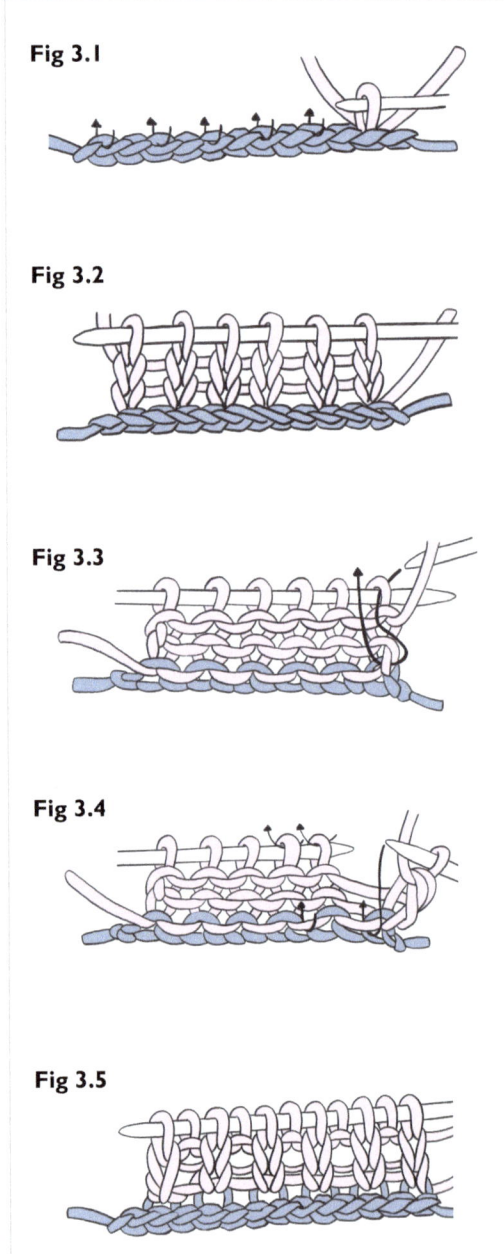

Fig 3.1

Fig 3.2

Fig 3.3

Fig 3.4

Fig 3.5

(Fig 3.1) Begin by making a crochet chain with waste yarn in a contrasting color. We are planning a K1/P1 rib. We also want our edge to begin and end with a knit st for symmetry. This means that we will need an odd stitch count. At the conclusion of the tubular row we want 11 stitches in our edging. We will plan to make an 11 st chain. We can add extra chains. However, we cannot have fewer than the number of stitches planned in the full edging width. We will begin picking up in the first chain, then skip every other chain picking up the remaining 5 stitches in chains 3, 5, 7, 9, and 11. This means that we have picked up 6 stitches and have 5 unworked chains between the pick ups.

(Fig 3.2) After working the pick up row, turn and work a WSR, then turn again and work a RSR, then turn work. **(Fig 3.3)** Next, work the tubular construction row. This is the row that will turn the St. sts under to create the hemmed look at the bottom. On this row, while the bottom edge is being formed into a tube, the sts on the needle at the top edge will be transformed into the K1/P1 ribbing structure. When we are looking at the RS of our work we see 6 knit sts facing. On this row the yarn crossing each chain that was skipped during the pick up will become a purl stitch. The sts seen at the bottom of the chain will intersperse with the St. St. knit stitches on the needle. This is how the planned stitch count and ribbing structure will be achieved. For this example, we have planned 11 stitches. Begin by purling the first stitch on the needle together with the yarn below the first stitch that was made when the work was turned to the WS after completing the stitch pick ups in the crochet chain. This first P2tog will begin the tubular process.

(Fig 3.4) Next, we begin to work in the K1/P1 format across the row by alternating between purling one of 5 remaining stitches on the LHN needle then knitting one of the stitches showing in the project yarn at the bottom of the contrasting crochet chain. When the work is turned to the RS, the stitches that were knit on the WSR from the spaces between the crochet chains will be purl stitches and the stitches that were on the needle that were purled will be knit sts.

(Fig 3.5) At the end of this process the full stitch count will be on the needles, the K1/P1 pattern structure will be established, and the beautiful, rolled bottom edge will be visible. In our example there are now 11 stitches on the needles. Remove the waste yarn at the bottom and continue working in the K1/P1 rib patt on the full stitch count for the planned length of your edging.

THREE NEEDLE BIND OFF

This technique is a seaming technique that is worked on "live" stitches. That means the stitches have not been bound off. You will be binding off the stitches and seaming two sections together simultaneously. It can be worked from the Wrong Side (two Right Sides facing) or from the Right Side (two Wrong Sides facing).

The techniques can be used for many seaming purposes when you want a perfect line up of stitch patterns in your seam, and/ or when you want a barely visible finished seam. Here in Duets this technique has been used primarily for seaming the shoulders of garments where it has been worked with the Right Sides Facing. It is a strong seam because the stitches are knit together before they are bound off. Because the stitches are live, the normal bulk that is caused by the bind off procedure is eliminated. It produces a very smooth, thin seam.

Getting Started

Work in the same way as a standard Pullover Bind Off with one additional step. For a classic bind off two single stitches are knit from the left needle onto the right needle before the first stitch placed on the right needle is lifted over the second and off. With this 3-needle method you are seaming two sections together, so two stitches being held on two different needles are knit together (one from each needle) and placed on the RHN as a single stitch. Then, the same method of lifting the first stitch over the second and off the RHN needle (as is used in the standard bind off) is worked.

Shoulder Stitches

For shoulder stitches, when you are working in a stitch pattern, it is important to check to make sure not only that the stitch count is the same on both sections, but that the stitch patten lines up perfectly. This final check should be made before you knit the last row of your project. Make any adjustments on that final row. If while working this technique you find that you have an extra stitch, or that the pattern alignment is one stitch off, you can place two stitches on the 3rd needle from the needle where the extra stitch is located (back or front), then place only the single stitch from the opposite needle on that 3rd needle and knit all 3 stitches together.

1. Hold both needles side by side so the wrong sides are facing outward, then insert a 3rd needle through the front of the first stitch on the front needle, then through the front of the first stitch on the back needle and knit those two stitches together. In the 1st illustration, (Fig 4.1) you see that the first stitches have been knit together and made into one, and that stitch has been placed on the RHN. You can see that the process is being repeated.

2. When Step 1 (Fig 4.1) has been repeated twice and 2 stitches are on the RHN, lift the 1st stitch placed on that needle over the second to bind off. In the 2nd illustration (Fig 4.2) you see the bind off in progress.

Fig 4.1

3. Continue working in this manner of knitting 2 stitches together to convert them to a single stitch on the RHN, then binding off the previous stitch placed on that needle over the latest stitch added.

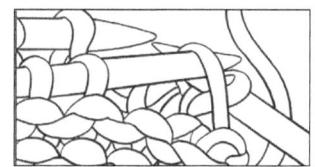

Fig 4.2

Remember, as you move across the double row of live stitches knitting them together, there should only be one stitch remaining on the RHN after each new stitch is added and the bind off technique is worked on the previous stitch.

WHIPSTITCH SEAM

Collars (as well as hem facings and buttonbands) are typically attached using a whipstitch, which forms a tidy join without bulk. A whipstitch can be worked either vertically or horizontally. Begin by pinning or basting the pieces together, matching the widths and lengths as necessary. With the right side facing, and working close to the edges, bring the threaded needle down into the edge of one piece and up through the other piece directly opposite, then pull the working yarn to close the seam. Space the stitches fairly close to one another and maintain an even tension as you work.

Fig 5.1

Horizontal Whipstitch Seam

PULLOVER CIRCLES MOTIF

(Fig 6.1) Work a Reverse Pullover BO by lifting the 3rd st on the LHN backwards over the first 2 sts and off the needle. (Fig 6.2) This BO stitch will circle the first 2 sts. Work a k1 on the first of the 2 circled sts. (Fig 6.3) Make a yo to replace the bound off st. (Fig 6.4) Work another k1 on the 2nd circled st. There are now 3 circled sts.

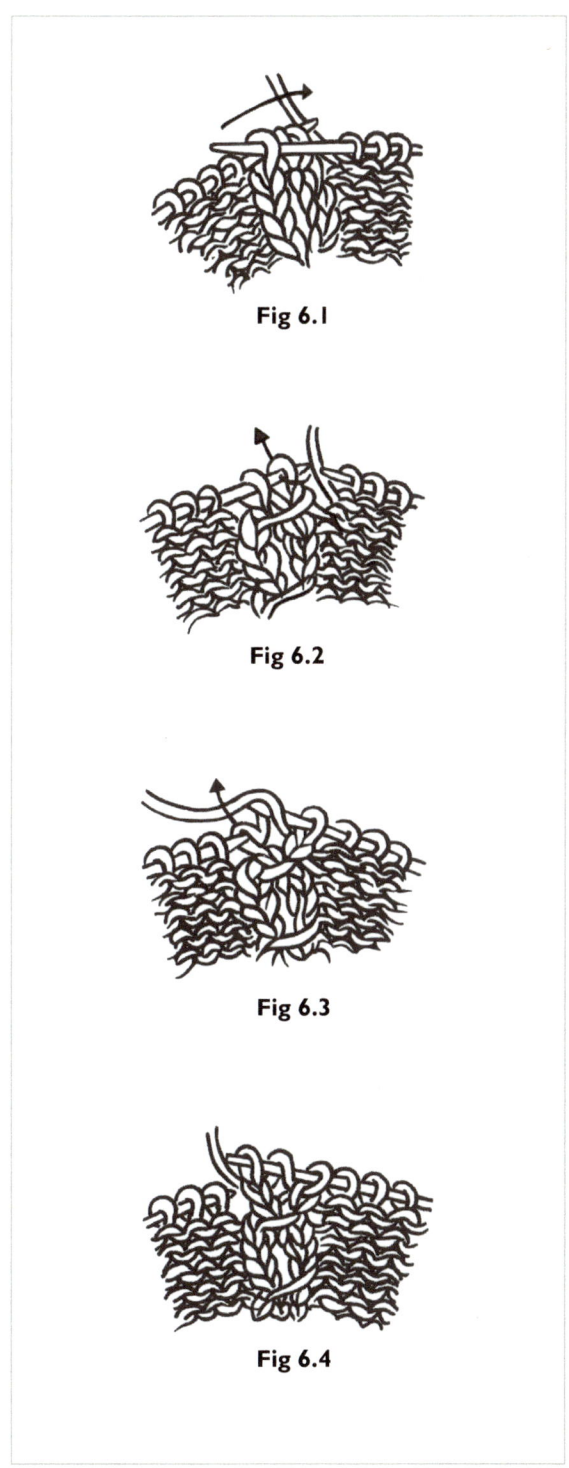

Fig 6.1

Fig 6.2

Fig 6.3

Fig 6.4

SPECIAL TECHNIQUES | 125

Ada Dress

FINISHED SIZES

To Fit Bust Sizes: S (M, L, XL) 33-35 (36-38, 39-41, 42-44)" 84-89 (91.5-96.5, 99-104, 106.5-112) cm
Finished Bust Sizes: 36 (39, 42, 45)" 91.5 (99, 106.5, 114.5) cm
To Fit Hip Sizes: S (M, L, XL) 35-37 (38-40, 41-43, 44-47)" 89-94 (96.5-101.5, 104-109, 112-119.5) cm
Finished Hips: 39 (42½, 45½, 49)" 99 (108, 115.5, 124.5) cm

Sample Size: S

YARN

6 (7, 8, 9) 4.5 oz /115 g skiens (each approx 480 yds / 439 m) of Knitting Boutique's "Susquehanna" 85% Polwarth, 15% Silk, in color Fawn.

NEEDLES & HOOKS

Size US 3 (3.25 mm) – 40" (100 cm) circular needle
Size US 4 (3.5 mm) - 40" (100 cm) circular needle
Size US 5 (3.75 mm) – 40" (100 cm) circular needle
Size US 6 (4 mm) – 32" (80 cm) and 40" (100 cm) circular needles, and spare for 3-needle bind off
*If preferred, use a 24" (60 cm) circular needle in each size for swatching.

Size E (3.5 mm) crochet hook

NOTIONS

Stitch markers; stitch holders; tapestry needle; 8 (9, 10, 11) buttons, size ⅜" / 9.5 mm

GAUGES

Needle Sizes and Gauges

Circles & Butterflies Patt (Total Circular Circumference given) Note: F/B = Across Front & Back
6 (4 mm) Needle – 88 sts = 13" (33 cm) = 6½" (16.5 cm) F/B, 46 rnds = 6" (15 cm)
5 (3.75 mm) Needle – 88 sts = 12" (30.5 cm) = 6" (15 cm) F/B, 66 rnds = 8" (20.5 cm)
4 (3.5 mm) Needle – 88 sts = 11" (28 cm) = 5½" (14 cm) F/B, 62 rnds = 7" (18 cm)
3 (3.25 mm) Needle – 88 sts = 10½" (27 cm) = 5¼" (13.5 cm) F/B, 74 rnds = 8" (20.5 cm)

Gauges per inch

6 (4 mm) 6.75 sts and 7.65 rnds = 1"
5 (3.75 mm) 7.33 sts and 8.25 rnds = 1"
4 (3.5 mm) 8 sts and 8.9 rnds = 1"
3 (3.25 mm) 8.38 sts and 9.25 rnds = 1"

Lacy Zigzag Patt (Worked Flat for Sleeves and Bodice)
6 (4 mm) Needles – 70 sts = 10" (25.5 cm), 64 rows / rnds = 8" (20.5 cm)

Reverse St st Patt
Size 6 (4 mm) Needles – 80 sts = 15" (38 cm), 51 rnds = 6" (15 cm)

Ladder Patt (Used bet Dress and Bodice)
Size 6 (4 mm) Needles – 156 rnds = 20" (51 cm)

STITCH GUIDE

Circles & Butterflies Patt (Circular Dress) – See Chart.

Lacy Zigzag Patt: Multiple of 3 sts and 8 rnds / rows (Worked flat on sleeves and upper body).

Circular Patt
Rnd 1: K3tog, YO.
Rnd 2: K1, YO, K1.
Rnd 3: K3.
Rnd 4: K3.
Rnd 5: YO, Sl1-k2tog-psso.
Rnd 6: K1, YO, K1.
Rnd 7: K3.
Rnd 8: K3.

Lacy Zigzag-2 (Flat Patt)
See Chart.

Ladder Patt (Seamed between Dress and Bodice): Multiple of 3 sts and 2 rows (Rep sts 20 - 22 on rows 17 & 18 of the Circles & Butterflies Patt)
Patt is Worked Horizontally
Row 1: Selv, Sl1 tbl-k1-psso, YO, K1tbl, Selv.
Row 2: Selv, P1tbl, K1, P1tbl.

Reverse St st Patt
Row 1: Purl on RS rows.
Row 2: Knit on WS rows.

Single Crochet (sc)
Insert the hook into the work. Wrap the yarn over the hook and draw the yarn through the work. Wrap the yarn around the hook again and draw it through both loops on the hook.

Double Crochet (dc)
Wrap the yarn over the hook and insert the hook into the work. Wrap the yarn over the hook again and draw it through the work. Wrap the yarn over the hook again and draw it through the first 2 loops. Wrap the yarn around the hook again and draw it through the last 2 loops.

Crochet Neck Edging: Multiple of 4 + 4
1ch, sk 1ch, 1dc into next ch; Rep * to *, to end.

NOTES

Stitch Pattern Notes
The Ada dress is composed of 2 different stitch patterns. Each pattern has a different stitch multiple and a different row count. Patt A: Lacy Zigzag: Multiple of 3 sts and 8 rows. This Patt changes the number of sts in the multiple to 2 sts on rows 1 and 5. This will change the stitch count on those pattern rows.

For final calculations, the 3-st version is used throughout in the patt. Example: Rnds 1 & 5 of Ruffle: P6 version P6 + 2 Patt A sts = 8 sts 48 (52, 56, 60) x = 384 (416, 448, 480) sts on needles. Rnds 2, 3, 4, 7 & 8 = P6 + 3 Patt A sts = 9 sts 48 (52, 56, 60) x = 432 (468, 504, 540) sts on needles

Patt B: Circles & Butterflies: Multiple of 22 sts and 30 rnds.

Pattern Notes

1. This dress is made using the re-gauging technique which means the widths and lengths of the fabric are altered by changing needle sizes instead of using increases and decreases.

2. Above the bottom ruffle, the dress is worked with the hip, waist and bust shaping planned by needle size changes. There are 4 needle size changes used for the body.

3. All measurements were taken on blocked swatches.

4. Garter Stitch Selvedge: Used at each edge of all pieces worked flat. Worked by knitting the first and last stitch on each row.

6. Sloped Bind Off – This technique is used to shape armholes, neckline and sleeve caps for smooth edges (no stair-steps). Work as foll: do not work the last stitch on the row before the BO row. On the BO row, slip the first stitch from the LHN purlwise, then BO the rem st from the previous row over the slipped st. This technique is used only on the first bind off stitch. If there are more BO sts, the others will be worked, then bound off as usual.

6. Circles and Butterflies Patt swatched in-the-round. Lacy Zigzag Patt when used alone for top and sleeves swatched flat.

INSTRUCTIONS

Ruffle Working Notes: The ruffle is composed of a combination of the Reverse St st Patt and the 3-st Lacy Zigzag Patt. It begins with 6 purl sts separating each Lacy Zigzag stripe and decreases to 2 purl sts separating each Lacy Zigzag stripe over 53 rnds. Then, the ruffle is worked even for 10 rnds = 64 total rnds in the ruffle.

With the 40" (100 cm) Size 6 (4 mm) needle cast on 432 (468, 504, 540) sts. Making certain that the sts are not twisted, join in a circle. Knit one rnd. On the knit rnd, set up a beg rnd mar and mars for 48 (52, 56, 60) sections of 6 purl sts and 3 Lacy Zigzag sections = 9 sts bet each mar. Foll the Lacy Zigzag chart, on rnds 1 and 5 the st count will be dec'd by 1 st in each of the 3-st sections. There will be 8 sts bet each mar on those rnds. On rnds 2, 3, 4, 6, 7, 8 there will be 9 sts in each of the Purl and Lacy Zigzag sections. When working with 8 sts there are 2 Lacy Zigzag sts + P6. When working with 9 sts there are 3 Lacy Zigzag sts + P6. Work even foll the 8 rnd Lacy Zigzag Patt for 15 rnds. **Work Purl Dec's as foll: Rnd 16:** P2, P2tog, P2 in every P6 section = P5 rem in every purl section. **Rnd 29:** Work P1, P2tog, P2 in every P5 section = P4 rem, **Rnd 42:** Work P2, P2tog in every P4 section = P3 rem in every purl section. **Rnd 53:** Work P1, P2tog in each P3 section = P2 rem in every purl section. There are 240 (260, 280, 300) total sts on the needles. Work 10 rnds even through Rnd 63. On Rnd 64 sl sts around the needle repositioning the markers as foll: Beg Rnd mar, * P2 + 3-st Lacy Zigzag Patt + P2 = 7 sts, pl mar, 13 sts, pl mar * Cont to sl and pl mar from * to * around. Each section will have a 2 patt set.

Ruffle to Dress Transition Notes

As you transition from the bottom ruffle into the dress pattern there are several things to be aware of: **Please read the following 7 notes carefully while examining the Circles and Butterflies Chart #1)** The 22-st main dress patt consists of 2 sections: Patt A) 3-st Lacy Zigzag Patt and Patt B)15-st Circles & Butterflies Patt. **#2)** There are 2 purl sts before each patt = 4 purl sts in each rep. On the transition rnd

(Rnd 65), 2 inc's will be worked in each rep. **#3)** When the patt layout is complete and the inc's have been worked, the 22-st patt layout will be as foll: P2, 3-st Patt A, P2, 15-st Patt B. **#4)** As the ruffle was being constructed, the dec's were planned to have it end with the 5-st structure of Patt A = P2, 3-st Lacy Zigzag Patt sts. The 3-st lacy vertical lines of Patt A will run unbroken vertically from the beg of the ruffle to the top of the dress section. **#5)** For Patt B, as the ruffle transitions into the dress patt, only 13 sts of the final 5-st ruffle patt will line up beneath each Patt B section as foll: [3-sts of Patt A, P2] 2x, 3 sts of Patt A. Because 15 sts are needed for Patt B, on the transition rnd (Rnd 64) bet the final rnd of the ruffle and the first rnd of the dress, after placing mar(s) to separate the 20 sts of each rep, also place a mar in a different color after the 7th in each rep to isolate the 13 sts of Patt B. **#6)** Patt B has two 7-st panels separated by a single purl stitch. For that patt, inc's will be worked in the 2 separate panels after the 5th and 9th sts. **#7)** On Rnd 65, both Patts A & B are planned to beg with a patt rnd 1. For Patt A it will be rnd 1 of the 9th 8-rnd rep.

Rnd 64: after slipping and placing mars, knit the rnd inc'ing 2 sts in each of the 13-st Patt B sections as foll: 1 st after the 1st st in the 6-st beg panel = 7 sts in that panel. Next, work across 12 sts, then work another inc, = 2 sts added in that 13-st section. 15 sts are now established in Patt B as foll: 7-st panel, P1, 7-st panel.

Rnd 65: Beg working the rnds as established, foll the chart for Patts A and B.

Work 12 (13, 14, 15) 22-st reps. There are now 264 (286, 308, 330) sts on the needle. Work even for approx. 90 rnds, until piece measures 19¼" (49 cm) from the beg, 11¾" (30 cm) from top of ruffle.

Shape Hips

Change to size 5 (3.75 mm) needles and work 1" = 8 rnds even. Next, change to the size 4 (3.5 mm) needle and work 9 rnds. Piece should measure 21¼" (54 cm) from beg, 13¾" (35 cm) from top of ruffle. Crosswise width should measure 16½ (17⅞, 19¼, 20⅝)" 42 (45.5, 49, 52.5) cm.

Waist

Change to size 3 (3.25 mm) needles and work 10 rnds even. Crosswise width should measure 15¾ (17, 18⅜, 19¾)" 40 (43, 46.5, 50) cm

Waist-to-Bust

Change to the size 4 needles, (3.5 mm) and work 18 rnds, then change to size 5 (3.75 mm) needles and work 28 rnds. Piece should measure 28½" (72.5 cm) from beg. Crosswise measurement should be 18 (19½, 21, 22½)" 45.5 (49.5, 53.5, 57) cm.

Total Circumference: 36 (39, 42, 45)" 91 (99, 106.5, 114) cm. Bind off all sts.

Ladder Patt Border Strip

This strip attaches the body and top of the dress. With size 6 (4 mm) needles work the Ladder Patt until the strip measures 36 (39¼, 42, 45)" 91.5 (99.5, 106.5, 114.5) cm = approx 282 (306, 328, 352) rows. Steam block.

Note: Dress top section is made in one piece using the Lacy Zigzag Patt + 2 Purl sts = 5-st Patt

Top of Dress

With the size 6 (4 mm) needle pick up 249 (284, 304, 324) sts in the Ladder Strip as foll: **Left Back:** (RS) selv + 2 Plus sts, pl mar, + 60 (70, 75, 80) sts = 12 (14, 15, 16) reps of the 5-st Lacy Zigzag-2 Patt = 63 (73, 78, 83) sts, pl mar. **Front:** Pick up 125 (140, 150, 160) sts = 25 (28, 30, 32) reps of the 5-st patt, pl mar. **Right Back:** 61 (71, 76, 81) sts = 12 (14, 15, 16) reps of the 5-st Lacy Zigzag and Purl Patt +1 selv. After row layout, purl across the foll row = WS row.

Shape Armholes (Use Sloped Bind Off Technique)

Note: Armholes shaped over 12 (16, 16, 18) rows = 1½ (2, 2, 2¼)" 4 (5, 5, 5.5) cm.

After purling across the WS row, on the foll RS row work across the 63 (73, 78, 83) Left Back sts, then place them on a holder. Bind off 4 sts for the RHS front armhole shaping. The 5th st is on the needle from the bind off. Work across the rem 120 (135, 145, 155) Front sts to marker, then Slip 61 (71, 76, 81) sts of the Right Back onto a holder. Continue working only on the front stitches, shaping both sides of the armhole as foll: BO 4 sts for the LHS front = 8 sts BO. Beg on the next RS row and working only on the rem 117 (132, 142, 152) sts, cont binding off as foll: 3 sts at the beg of the next 4 (6, 6, 6) rows, 2 sts at the beg of the foll 4 (6, 6, 6) rows, 1 st at the beg of the foll 2 (2, 2, 4) rows = 30 (40, 40, 42) sts BO, 15 (20, 20, 21) sts on each side. There are 95 (100, 110, 118) sts rem in the front cross-back (including 2 selv sts).

Shape Neck: (Use Sloped Bind Off Technique)

Sizes S (M): Beg neck shaping on the foll RS row after completing the armhole shaping. **Sizes L (XL):** Work even for ½ (1)" 1.5 (2.5) cm = 4 (8) rows then beg neck shaping.

All Sizes: On the first neck shaping row work across 39 (41, 46, 50) sts, BO the center 17 (18, 18, 18) center neck sts, then work across the rem 38 (40, 45, 49) sts. Working only on the LHS, BO on RS rows at neck edge as foll: 5 sts once, 4 sts once, 3 sts once, 2 sts 1 (1, 2, 2) time(s), 1 st 2 (2, 1, 1) time(s) = 16 (16, 17, 17) sts BO, 23 (25, 29, 33) shoulder sts rem. Convert the first and last sts at each edge to Garter st selvedge sts and work on these sts until piece measures 6¾ (7½, 8, 8¾)" 17 (19, 20.5, 22) cm from the pick-up row. 6½ (7¼, 7¾, 8½)" 16.5 (18.5, 19.5, 21.5) cm = 52 (58, 62, 68) total armhole rows. Re-attach the yarn at the RHS neck edge and working on WS rows, BO as for the LHS, reversing all shaping, then place the 23 (25, 29, 33) shoulder sts on a holder in prep for working the 3-needle bind off technique for shoulder seaming.

Armhole Shaping Cont

Left Back: Slip sts from holder back onto needle and attach yarn to armhole. Working on a WS row work as foll: Bind off 4 sts at the beg of the next 1 (2, 2, 2) WS row(s), 3 sts at the beg of the foll 2 (3, 3, 3) WS rows, 2 sts at the beg of the foll 2 (3, 3, 3) WS rows, 1 st at the beg of the foll 1 (0, 0, 1) WS row = 15 (23, 23, 24) sts BO, 48 (50, 55, 59) sts rem. Work even on these sts until piece measures 6¾ (7½, 8, 8¾)" 17 (19, 20.5, 22) cm from pick-up row. BO 25 (25, 26, 26) neck sts. Place rem 23 (25, 29, 33) shoulder sts on a holder in prep for working the 3-needle bind off seaming technique.

Right Back: On RS row, Sl sts from holder back onto needle and attach yarn to armhole edge. Work as foll: Bind off 4 sts at the beg of the next 1 (2, 2, 2) RS row(s), 3 sts at the beg of the foll 1 (2, 2, 2) RS row(s), 2 sts at the beg of the foll 2 (3, 3, 3) RS rows, 1 st at the beg of the foll 2 (1, 1, 2) RS row(s) = 13 (21, 21, 22) sts BO, 48 (50, 55, 59) sts rem. Work even on these sts until piece measures 6¾ (7½, 8, 8¾)" 17 (19, 20.5, 22) cm from pick-up row. Bind off 25 (25, 26, 26) neck sts. Place 23 (25, 29, 33) shoulder sts on a holder in prep for working 3-needle bind off seaming technique.

Sleeves

Bell Bottom

With size 6 (4 mm) needles, cast on 178 (187, 196, 205) sts. Patt layout is as foll: Selv, P1, [3-st Lacy Zigzag Patt, P6] 19 (20, 21, 22) times, 3-st Lacy Zigzag Patt, P1, Selv. Work 6 rows even. On Row 7 dec 19 (21, 21, 22) sts = dec 1 st in each P6 section by working as foll: P2, P2tog, P2 = 5 purl sts rem in each purl section = 159 (167, 175, 183) sts on needles. Work 9 rows even. On Row 17 dec 19 (20, 21, 22) sts by working P1, P2tog, P2 in each P5 section = P4 in each purl section, 140 (147, 154, 161) sts on needle. Work 9 rows even, on Row 27 dec 19 (20, 21, 22) sts by working P2, P2tog in each P4 = P3 in each purl section, 121 (127, 133, 139) sts on needles. Work 7 rows even. On Row 35 dec 19 (20, 21, 22) sts by working P1, P2tog in each P3 section = P2 in every purl section = 102 (107, 112, 117) sts on the needles. Work even on these sts until piece measures 7 (7½, 7¾, 8¼)" 18 (19.5, 20, 21) cm. Widthwise measurements 14¼ (15, 15¾, 16⅜)" 36 (38, 40, 41.5) cm.

Shape Cap

Size S: Bind off 4 sts at the beg of the next 2 rows, [3 sts at the beg of the next 4 rows, 2 sts at the beg of the foll 2 rows] 3 times, 3 sts at the beg of the next 2 rows, 4 sts at the beg of the final 4 rows = 78 sts BO, 24 sts rem. BO all rem sts. **Size M:** Bind off 4 sts at the beg of the next 2 rows [3 sts at the beg of the next 6 rows, 2 sts at the beg of the foll 4 rows] 2 times, 3 sts at the beg of the next 2 rows, 4 sts at the beg of the final 4 rows = 82 sts BO, 25 sts rem. BO all rem sts. **Size L:** Bind off 4 sts at the beg of the next 2 rows, [3 sts at the beg of the next 2 rows, 2 sts at the beg of the foll 4 rows] 4 times, 3 sts at the beg of the next 2 rows, 4 sts at the beg of the final 4 rows = 86 sts BO, 26 sts rem. BO all rem sts. **Size XL:** Bind off 4 sts at the beg of the next 2 rows, [3 sts at the beg of the next 2 rows, 2 sts at the beg of the foll 8 rows] 3 times, 4 sts at the beg of the final 4 rows = 90 sts BO, 27 sts rem. BO all rem sts.

Finishing

Block Pieces to measurements. Working on one side at a time, slip the 23 (25, 29, 33) shoulder sts from holders onto needles and seam the shoulders using the 3-needle bind off technique making certain that the st patt lines up properly. Work one row of the Crochet Neck Edging Patt around the neckline. Center the dress patt on the front and sew the dress to the bottom edge of the Ladder Patt, using the whip stitch sewing technique with very closely spaced stitches.

Back Placket Border

With Size E (3.5 mm) crochet hook work as foll: Beg at the neck on the RHS with the RS of the work facing. Work 1 row of sc around the center back opening as foll: sc 36 (40, 44, 48) sts to bottom, pl mar in center of opening, then work 36 (40, 44, 48) sc to top of LHS, ch1 and turn. Work a 2nd row of sc. On the 3rd row work one row of Picot Crochet as foll: Beg with 1 sl st, then work *3ch, sk 1sc, 1sl st in each of the next 3sc*, Rep from * to * 8 (9, 10, 11) times, then sk the next sc and work 1 sl st in the next 6sc leading to the center opening. Work 1 sl st in the marked center st, then in the first 6sc on the LHS. *3ch, then sk 1sc, then sl 1 st in each of the next 3sc *; Rep * to* 8 (9, 10, 11) times. End with 3ch, sk 1sc, 1 sl st in the last sc at the top of the neck edge. There should be 8 (9, 10, 11) picots on each side. Next, sew 8 (9, 10, 11) buttons opposite the 8 (9, 10, 11) picots on the RHS bet the first 2 sc rows. For back closure, use the picot chains as button loops.

Note: On the back of women's clothing, buttons are placed on the opposite side from the side they are placed on the front.

Sew sleeve seams. Set in sleeves.

Ada Dress

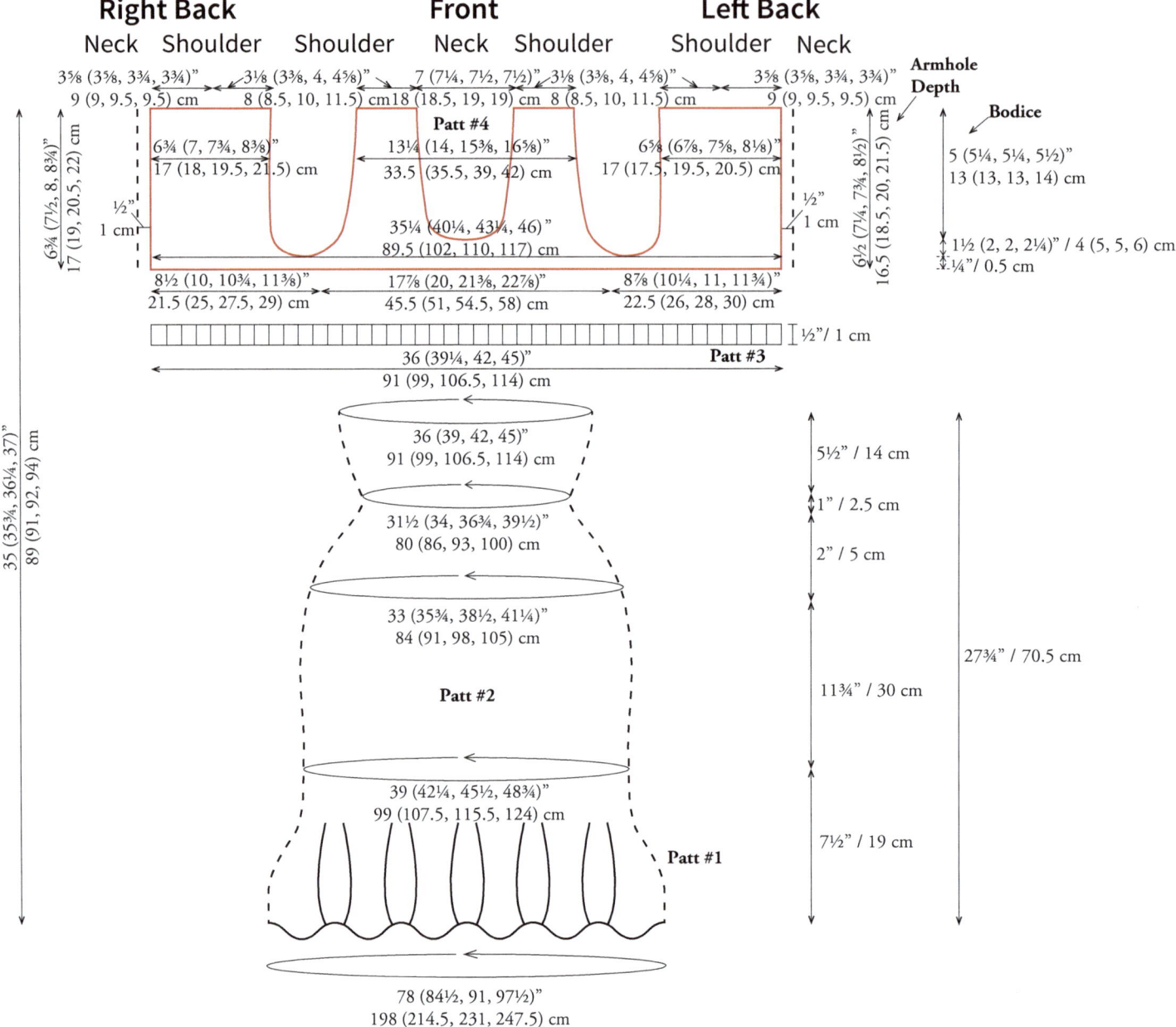

Ada Dress Sleeve

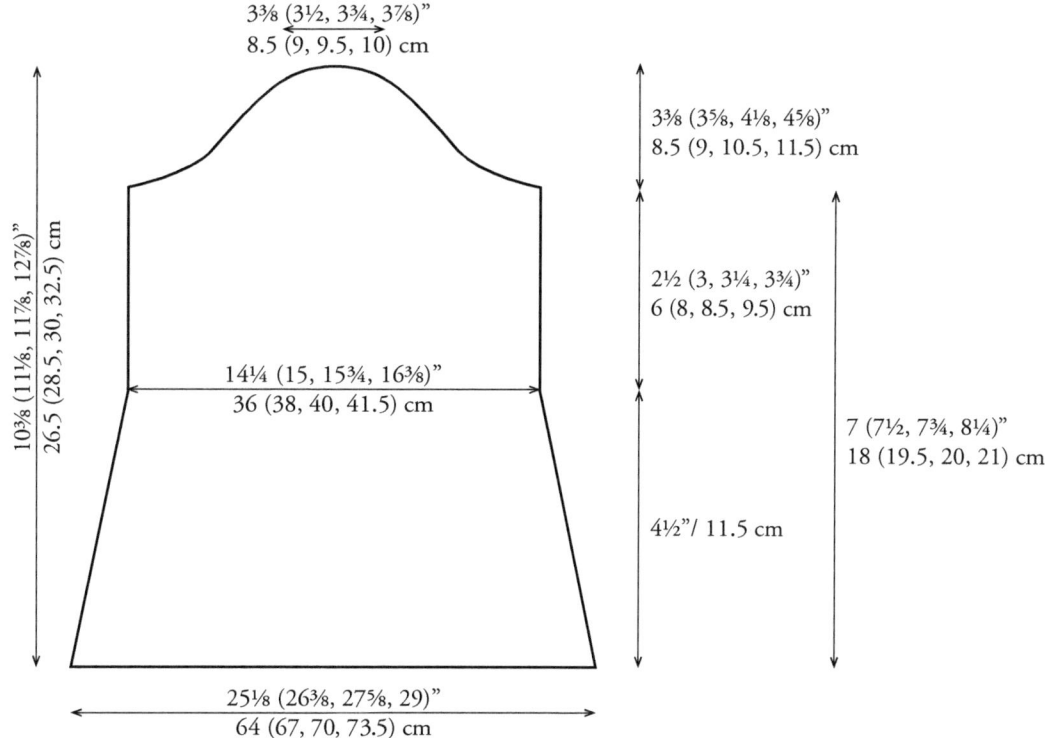

Circles & Butterflies
(Multiple of 22 / 30 rnds)

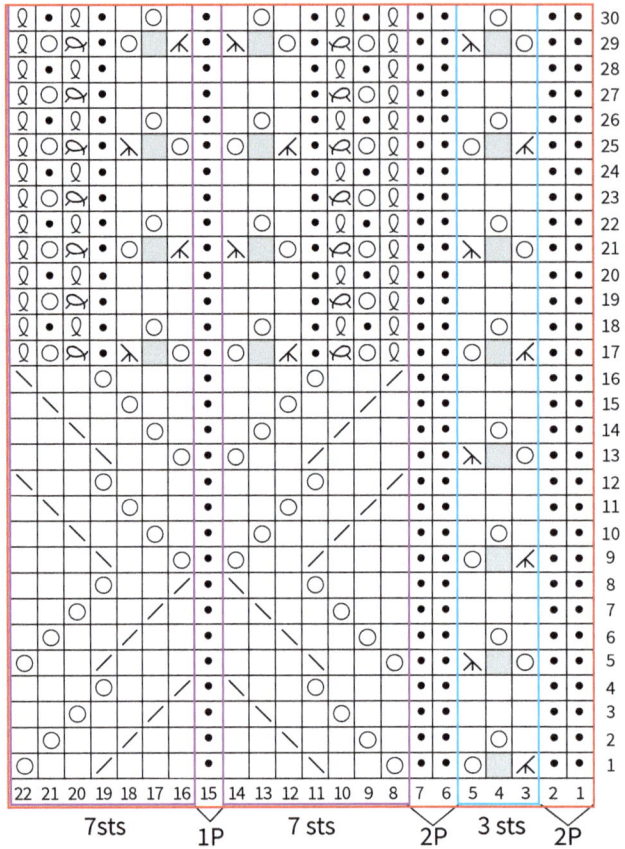

Lacy Zigzag-2
(multiple of 5+2/ 8 rows)

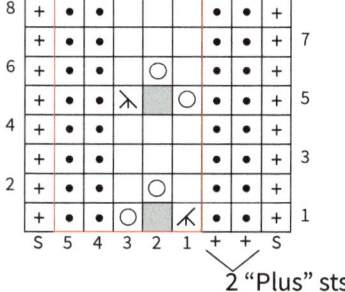

2 "Plus" sts

- ☐ K1 on RSRs, P1 on WSRs
- • P1 on RSRs, K1 on WSRs
- ○ Yarn Over
- ⅄ Sl1-k2tog-psso
- ⼊ K3tog
- ▓ No stitch
- ✛ Selvedge st = K first and last st on each row
- ☐ Patt rep

DIANE MARTINI

Aleria Pullover

FINISHED SIZES

S (M, L, XL)
To Fit Bust Sizes: 34 (38, 42, 46)" / 86.5 (96.5, 106.5, 117) cm
Finished Bust Sizes: 36 (38¾, 44¼, 47)" / 91.5 (98.5, 112.5, 119.5) cm
Finished Hip Sizes: 38¼ (41¼, 47, 50)" / 97 (105, 119.5, 127) cm

Sample Size: M

YARN

As shown, 8 (9, 10, 11) 1.75 oz/50 g skeins (approx. 150 yds / 137 m each) of Berroco Corsica 90% cotton, 10% cashmere in Color 3624 Venus. Or 1200 (1300, 1500, 1600) yds / 1100 (1190, 1370, 1465) m of sport weight yarn.
For sleeveless version, 7 (8, 8, 9) skeins – 1000 (1100, 1200, 1300) yds / 915 (1005, 1100, 1190) m
For tunic length, add 200 - 300 yds (185-275 m)

NEEDLES & HOOKS

Size 4 (3.5 mm) - 32" (80 cm) circular needle or size to obtain gauge
Size G (4 mm) crochet hook

NOTIONS

stitch markers
stitch holders
cable needle
tapestry needle
1 button – 3/8" (10 mm) diameter

GAUGES after blocking

Border Lace Pattern: 24.5 sts and 26.5 rows = 4" / 10 cm with size 4 (3.5 mm) needles.
Cable Pattern: 29 sts and 31 rows = 4" / 10 cm with size 4 (3.5 mm) needles.
Stockinette stitch: 23 sts and 31 rows = 4" / 10 cm with size 4 (3.5 mm) needles.

STITCH GUIDE

1. Aleria Sleeve Chart: Twisted rib and lace
2. Aleria Front Cable Chart: Cable and lace
2. Alternating cast on
3. C4F – Sl2 to cn, hold front, k2, then k2 from cn
4. C4B – Sl2 to cn, hold back, k2, then k2 from cn

DESCRIPTION

A-line pullover with standard ease at hip and bust. Styled with ¾ sleeves, keyhole neckline and stand-up collar. Sleeves are optional. The armhole edge will naturally roll under and require no finishing if sleeves are not added.

PATTERN NOTES

Get Gauge – Check all of the stitch patterns.

Row Gauge: The measurements provided are rounded to the nearest 0.25 inch and 0.5 cm, and nearest even row, your results may be slightly different.

Make The Sleeves First – and block them, being careful not to stretch the ribbing. This will help you to get familiar with the cast on and the lace patterns, confirm your gauge, and let you practice maintaining the patterns while shaping.

Alternating cast on: The Alternating cast on is an "invisible cast on" that sets up the cast-on row for k1, p1 ribbing. As the stitch pattern begins in k1, p1 rib with an extra purl stitch every 9th stitch, we found it easier to CO in k1, p1 ribbing and then add the extra sts in the first row, than to try to CO these sts in the Alternating CO. The Tubular cast on may also be used to create a rolled edge in ribbing. See pages 121 and 122 in Special Techniques.

Pattern repeats: Sizes S and XL have an odd number of repeats for the border pattern. As the pullover is worked in the round, the side seam marker is placed in the middle of a pattern repeat for these sizes.

Intrinsic Decreases and stitch counts: Pattern Row 35 decreases the stitch count by 2 sts for every pattern repeat that is outside the front motif. Pattern Rows 45, 61, 77, 93, and 157 also decrease the number of sts for the front and are on the right front. For the sleeves, these decreases are centered and are covered in the increase rows.

To break up pooling for hand-dyed yarn: Use 2 skeins at once, alternating every 1 or 2 rows, carrying on WS. This also helps to blend any variation between skeins. Hand-dyed yarns will tend to make horizontal stripes in the round, and diamonds or argyles in the flat portions.

Binding off at neck edge: We recommend binding off the back neck sts, then adding the neck band. The BO edge helps to prevent the neck from stretching and keeps the fit at the armhole. If the sts of the back neck are left live the neck will stretch and the sleeve will hang low on the arm.

Options for this Pattern:

- Sleeves are optional, the sleeves require 200 - 300 yds / 185 - 275 m of yarn. The armhole edge will roll under and needs no other finishing
- Tunic length – To increase to Tunic length, insert 32 rnds beginning at Rnd 106. Armhole shaping will start 32 rows (about 4" / 10 cm) later than as-written instructions.
- Back keyhole closure – Divide for neck on back, rather than Front. The second half of the front neck shaping will remain in the front, but will be joined, rather than separate.

INSTRUCTIONS

Sleeves

Use the Alternating cast on to CO 64 (64, 64, 80) sts on size 4 (3.5 mm) needles.

Begin Row 1 of Sleeve Chart at Border Pattern, making 1 st every 9th st as follows: *p1, (k1tbl, p1) 4 times, M1P; rep from * across row 7 (7, 7, 9) more times to total 72 (72, 72, 90) sts. Join into round, being careful not to twist.

Alternate: Use the Tubular cast on or another technique to: CO 72 (72, 72, 90) sts and work Row 1 of chart.

Starting with stitch 19 (19, 19, 10) in the border chart, work through Rnd 52 (50, 48, 52). On next rnd, inc 1 st at each end. Then inc every 8 (6, 4, 8) rnds 3 (3, 8, 3) times, then every - (4, -, 4) rows - (2, -, 1) times to total 72 (76, 82, 90) sts.

Work even for 2" (5 cm), about 15 rnds, until sleeve measures 12¾ (12¾, 13¼, 13¼)" / 32.5 (32.5, 33.5, 33.5) cm including the border [about 92 (92, 96, 96) rnds].

Shape Cap: Work back and forth.

BO 5 (5, 5, 7) sts at beg of next 2 rows. 62 (66, 72, 76) sts rem.

Keeping 1 knit st at each edge for seaming, dec 1 st each end of every 2 rows 9 (8, 9, 9) times, then every 3 rows - (2, 2, 4) times, then every 2 rows 8 (8, 9, 8) times.

BO 3 sts at beg of next 4 rows, then BO rem 16 (18, 20, 22) sts.

Block to measurements and check gauge before proceeding.

Make a second sleeve.

Body and Back

Use the Alternating cast on to CO 208 (224, 256, 272) sts on size 4 (3.5 mm) circular needle. Begin Row 1 of Sleeve Chart at Border Pattern, making 1 st every 9th st as follows: *p1, (k1tbl, p1) 4 times, M1P; rep from * across row 25 (27, 31, 33) times to total 234 (252, 288, 306) sts. Join into round, being careful not to twist.

Sizes S, L: Beg at st 1 in the border pattern and work 18-st full rep 13 (-, 16, -) ending with a 9 st half rep.

Sizes M, XL: Beg at st 10 in the border pattern, work 9-st half rep once, then 18-st full rep - (13, -, 16) times, then the other half rep once. (Note for wrapped sts in Rnd 23: These sizes start at mid-repeat. Slip the first 3 sts, work around to last 3 sts, work wrapped sts using last 3 and first 3 sts of the rnd)

Work even through Rnd 33 maintaining chart patt.

On Rnd 34, mark the location for the front motif and side seams as foll: Work 45 (54, 63, 72) sts, pl mar, work 54 (54, 54, 54) sts, pl mar, work 18 (18, 27, 27) sts, pl mar (side seam), work 117 (126, 144, 153) sts. All stitch markers should be between 2 purl sts. The front cable panel is worked over 54 sts.

After Rnd 35, there will be 6 more sts on the front than on the back. These sts will be removed as the front motif is worked. Total 214 (230, 262, 278) sts rem, 110 (118, 134, 142) for front and 104 (112, 128, 136) for the back.

Cont working. After Rnd 45, the back will be in Stockinette st.

Cont working until piece measures 16½ (16¼, 16, 15¾)" / 42 (41.5, 40.5, 40) cm. Total 120 (118, 116, 114) rnds. **The front will have one more st than back at this point, on the left front.**

Alternate: For tunic length, work even in Front Cable Chart to rnd 139, then rep rnds 107 - 138 once more. When piece measures 20½ (20¼, 20, 19¾)" / 52 (51.5, 50.5, 50) cm, total of 152 (150, 148, 146) rnds, beg armhole shaping.

Begin Armhole

Divide for armhole (RS). BO 5 (5, 7, 7) sts for left front armhole. Work to side seam marker. Place front sts just worked on holder. BO 5 (5, 5, 7) sts for back underarm, work to end of row. The garment will be worked flat from here forward.

Turn work (beg WS row) and BO 5 (5, 7, 7) sts, work to end of row. 94 (102, 114, 122) sts rem for back.

Dec 1 st at each edge every 2 rows 4 (3, 8, 11) times as foll: K1, ssk work to last 3 sts, k2tog, k1.

Work even on rem 86 (96, 98, 100) sts until armhole measures 7¼ (7¾, 8¼, 8¾)" / 18.5 (19.5, 21, 22) cm, ending after a WS row [about 56 (60, 64, 68) rows total].

Alternate: If placing keyhole neckline in Back, beg keyhole shaping below when armhole measures 2 (2¼, 2½, 3)" / 5 (6, 6.5, 7.5) cm and do not do keyhole shaping on Front.

BO 8 (9, 9, 9) sts at beg of next 4 rows, BO 6 (7, 7, 7) sts at beg of next 2 rows.

BO rem 42 (46, 48, 50) sts. Total about 190 (192, 194, 196) rows and 24½ (24¾, 25, 25¼)" / 62 (63, 63.5, 64) cm, including hem.

Front

Transfer front sts from holder to needle. Join yarn with WS facing. Begin armhole shaping at armhole edge as for back, maintaining motif on right front following Front Cable chart.

At the same time, when armhole measures 2 (2¼, 2½, 3)" / 5 (6, 6.5, 7.5) cm [about 16 (18, 20, 24) rows from beg of armhole, and at about Row 136 (136, 136, 138) of body] Divide for KEYHOLE shaping as foll:

With RS facing, work 43 (48, 49, 50) sts, CO 1 st (neck edge), join new yarn for right front, CO 1 st (neck edge), work rem 44 (49, 50, 51) sts. Total 44 (49, 50, 51) sts for left front, and 45 (50, 52, 53) sts for right front. The extra st on the right front is taken out at Row 157. The two extra sts at the neck edge create a clean rolled edge for the front neck. Pl mar at 22 (25, 25, 25) sts from each armhole edge to mark shoulder BO sts for future.

Work fronts simultaneously until armhole measures 6 (6¼, 6½, 7)" / 15 (16, 16.5, 17.5) cm, about 46 (48, 50, 54) rows.

Begin front neck shaping –

With RS facing, work 31 (36, 37, 36) sts. Slip 13 (13, 13, 15) sts at neck edge to holder for left front. Work 13 (13, 13, 15) sts at right neck edge, then slip them to holder and work rem 31 (36, 37, 36) sts. Dec 1 st at neck edge every row 8 (9, 9, 8) times, then every 2 rows 1 (2, 3, 3) time(s), working even until shoulder BO is completed.

At the same time, when armhole measures 7¼ (7¾, 8¼, 8¾)" / 18 (20, 21, 22) cm, [about 56 (60, 64, 68) rows], begin shoulder BO as for back as foll: BO 8 (9, 9, 9) sts at beg of next 4 rows, BO 6 (7, 7, 7) sts at beg of next 2 rows.

Blocking

Gently block pieces to measurements as shown in the schematic before proceeding being careful not to stretch ribbing.

Shoulder Seams

After blocking, sew shoulder seams.

Neck Band

With RS facing, pick up one st for each st and row along neck edge as follows: work 13 (13, 13, 15) sts from right front holder, pick up 16 (18, 20, 20) sts from right neck edge, 42 (46, 48, 50) sts from back neck, 16 (18, 20, 20) sts from left front neck edge and 13 (13, 13, 15) sts from holder. Total 100 (108, 116, 122) sts picked up.

Turn work, p 1 row, dec - (-, 2, 4) sts evenly to total 100 (108, 114, 118) sts.

Work 1½" / 4 cm (about 12 rows) in St st.

Row 13: K2, *yo, k2tog; rep from * to last st, k1.

Row 14: P

Rows 15 - 25: Work in St st.

Row 26: BO p'wise.

Fold collar in half, RS facing. Sew front edges of collar together. Turn RS out and use tapestry needle to sew down inside edge of collar. Block or press collar to flatten.

Button Loop

At point of join between collar and neck on right front, using a size G (4 mm) crochet hook, chain about 1" / 2.5 cm. Fasten chain in a loop. Sew one ⅜" (10 mm) button onto left front.

Finishing

Pin sleeves into armholes, with right sides facing.

Sew armhole seams easing to fit.

Weave in all ends.

Aleria Pullover Sleeve

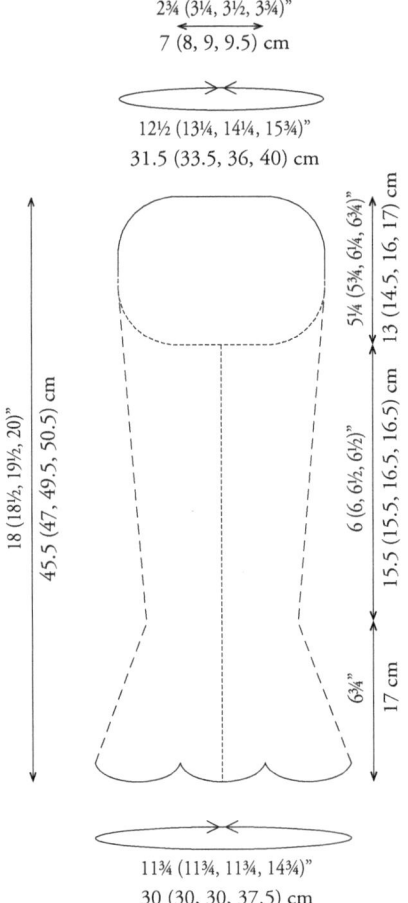

Aleria Pullover Body

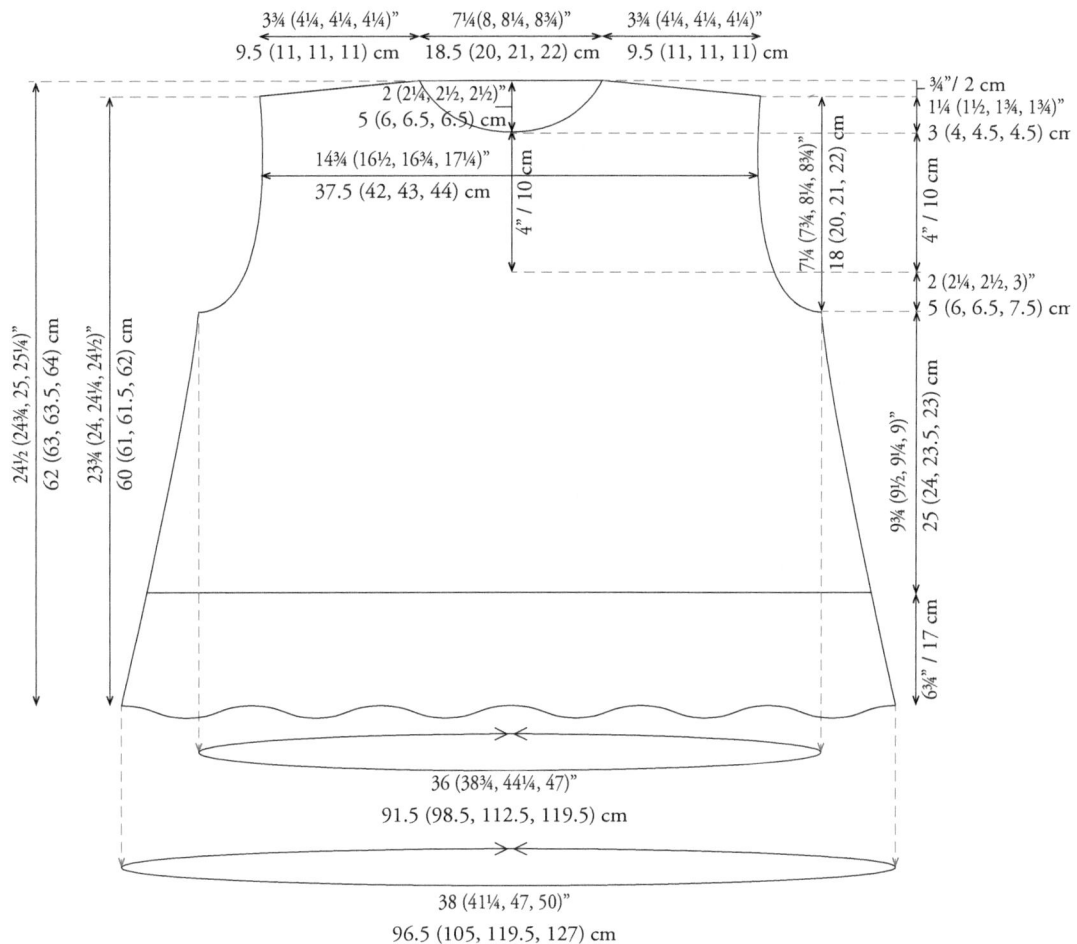

Aleria Sleeve and Body Chart

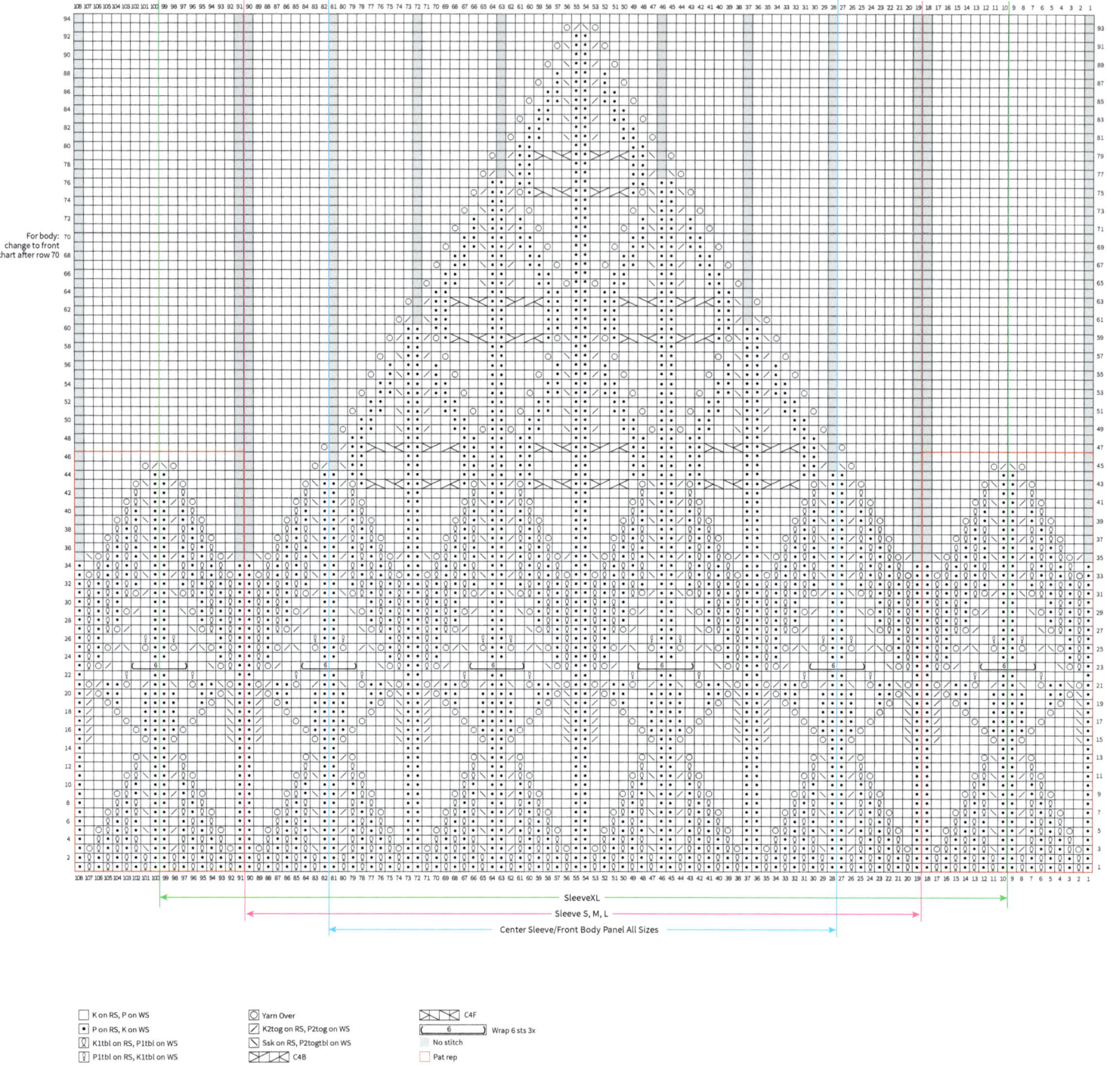

	K on RS, P on WS		Yarn Over		C4F
	P on RS, K on WS		K2tog on RS, P2tog on WS		Wrap 6 sts 3x
	K1tbl on RS, P1tbl on WS		Ssk on RS, P2togtbl on WS		No stitch
	P1tbl on RS, K1tbl on WS		C4B		Pat rep

Aleria Front Cable

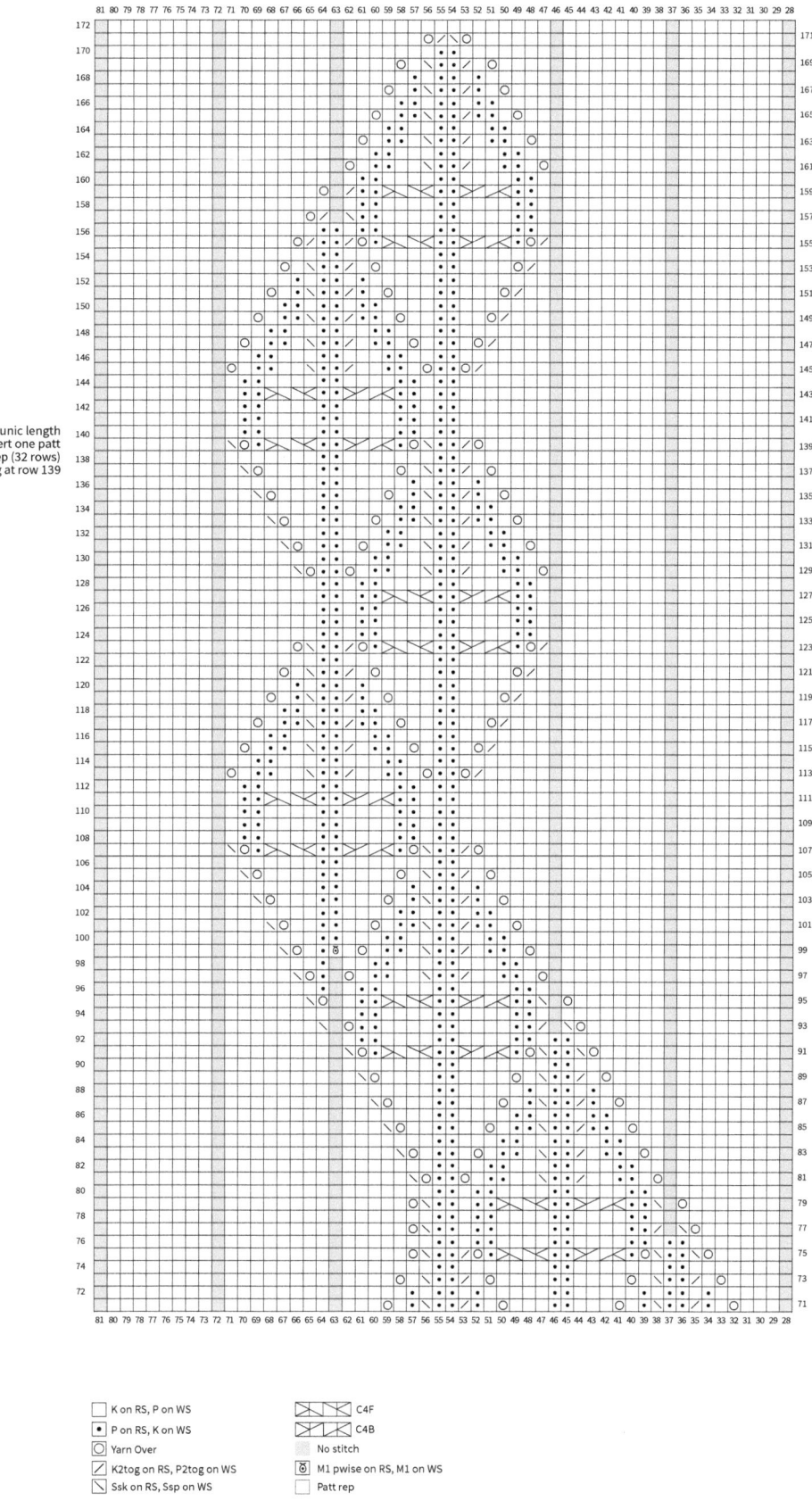

JOAN FORGIONE

Balineen Hat

FINISHED SIZE

Circumference: 17" / 43 cm
Height: Cap – 8" / 20.5 cm   Slouch – 9" / 23 cm
Stretches to fit head sizes 18-21" / 45.5 – 53.5 cm

YARN

Brooklyn Tweed Arbor (100% Targhee wool; 145 yds [133 m] / 1.75 oz / 50 g): Alizarin (red), 2 skeins or Klimt (gold), 2 skeins

NEEDLES

Size US 4 (3.5 mm) - 16" (40 cm) circular or dpn's
Size US 7 (4.5 mm) – 16" (40 cm) circular and/or dpn's

NOTIONS

stitch marker
pom pom (optional)
tapestry needle

GAUGES

30 sts and 40 rnds = 4" / 10 cm in 2x2 ribbing with smaller needles, blocked and slightly stretched
33 sts and 33 rnds = 4" / 10 cm in cable patt with larger needles before blocking
30 sts and 34 rnds = 4" / 10 cm in cable patt with larger needles, blocked and slightly stretched.

STITCH GUIDE

C4B – Sl2 to cn, hold back, K2, then K2 from cn.
C4F – Sl2 to cn, hold front, K2, then K2 from cn.
T4B – Sl2 to cn, hold back, K2, then P2 from cn.
T4F – Sl2 to cn, hold front, P2, then K2 from cn.
T3B – Sl1 to cn, hold back, K2, then P1 from cn.
T3F – Sl2 to cn hold front, P1, then K2 from cn.
TD4B – Sl2 to cn, hold back, K2, then P2tog on sts from cn. (1 st dec)
TD4F – Sl2 to cn, hold front, P2tog, then K2 from cn. (1 st dec)
CD4F – Sl2 to cn, hold front, K2tog, then K2 from cn. (1 st dec)

NOTES

- The hat is worked in the round from the bottom up.
- The height of the hat can be adjusted by adding more rounds of ribbing. Instructions show measurements for cap (slouch).

INSTRUCTIONS

Ribbing

With smaller needles, CO 128 sts, pl mar and join to work in the rnd, being careful not to twist. Set up rib as follows: K1, p2, [k2, p2] to last st, k1. Rep this rnd until ribbing measures 1¼ (2½)"/3 (6.5) cm.

Begin Main Chart

Set-up rnd 1: K1, p2, [T3F, T3B, p2] to last 5 sts, T3F, sl2 to RHN, re mar, sl2 back to LHN, T3B, replace beg of rnd marker.

Set-up rnd 2: P2, [p1, k4, p3] to last 6 sts, p1, k4, sl1 to RHN, re mar, sl1 back to LHN, replace beg of rnd marker. Change to larger needles.

Body

Rnd 1: [P4, C4B] to end.
Rnd 2: [P4, k4] to end.
Rnd 3: P2, [T4B, T4F] to last 6 sts, T4B, sl2 to RHN, re mar, sl2 back to LHN, T4F, replace beg of rnd marker.
Rnd 4: K2, [p4, k4] to last 6 sts, p4, sl2 to RHN, re mar, sl2 back to LHN, replace beg of rnd marker.
Rnd 5: [C4F, p4] to end.
Rnd 6: [K4, p4] to end.
Rnd 7: K2, [T4F, T4B] to last 6 sts, T4F, sl2 to RHN, re mar, sl2 back to LHN, T4B, replace beg of rnd marker.
Rnd 8: P2, [k4, p4] to last 6 sts, k4, sl2 to RHN, re mar, sl2 back to LHN, replace beg of rnd marker.
Rnd 9: Rep Rnd 1.
Rnd 10: Rep Rnd 2.
Rnd 11: [P2, T4B, T4F, p2, k4] to end.
Rnd 12: [P2, k2, p4, k2, p2, k4] to end.
Rnd 13: [P2, k2, p4, k2, p2, C4B] to end.
Rnd 14: Rep Rnd 12.
Rnd 15: [P2, T4F, T4B, p2, k4] to end.
Rnd 16: Rep Rnd 2.
Rep Rnds 1 – 16 twice more.]

Crown shaping

Rnd 1: [P2tog, p2, C4B] to end - 112 sts rem.
Rnd 2: [P3, k4] to end.
Rnd 3: P1, [TD4B, TD4F, T3B, T3F] 7x, TD4B, TD4F, T3B, sl2 to RHN, rem m, sl2 back to LHN, T3F, replace beg of rnd marker – 96 sts rem.
Rnd 4: K2, [p2, k4] to last 4 sts, p2, sl2 to RHN, re mar, sl2 back to LHN, replace beg of rnd marker.
Rnd 5: [CD4F, p2] to end – 80 sts rem.
Rnd 6: [K1, k2tog, p2tog] to end – 48 sts rem.
Rnd 7: [k2tog, p1] to end– 32 sts rem.
Rnd 8: [Ssk] to end – 16 sts rem.
Rnd 9: [Ssk] to end – 8 sts rem.

Finishing

Cut 6" [15cm] tail, thread tapestry needle and weave yarn through rem sts. Cinch to close. Pull tail through to inside of hat and weave in all ends. Block to finished measurements. Sew on optional pom pom.

Ballineen Main Chart

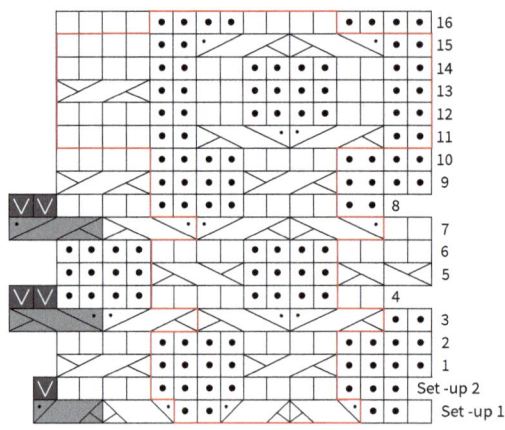

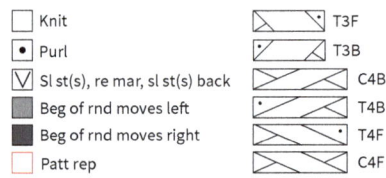

- ☐ Knit
- • Purl
- V Sl st(s), re mar, sl st(s) back
- ▨ Beg of rnd moves left
- ▧ Beg of rnd moves right
- ☐ Patt rep
- T3F
- T3B
- C4B
- T4B
- T4F
- C4F

Crown Shaping Chart

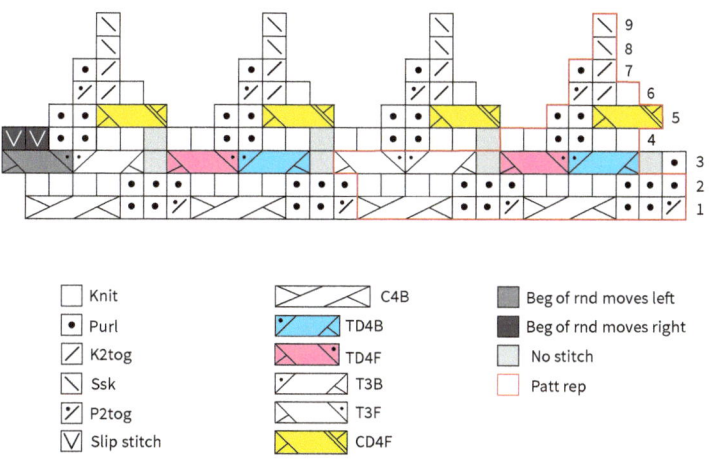

- ☐ Knit
- • Purl
- ╱ K2tog
- ╲ Ssk
- ╱ P2tog
- V Slip stitch
- ╲╱ C4B
- ╲╱ TD4B
- ╲╱ TD4F
- ╲╱ T3B
- ╲╱ T3F
- ╲╱ CD4F
- ▓ Beg of rnd moves left
- ▓ Beg of rnd moves right
- ☐ No stitch
- ▢ Patt rep

OLGA JANKELOVICH

Bel Fiore Cape

FINISHED SIZE
One size – to fit adult woman.
Circumference: 52" (128 cm)
Length (not including collar): 22½" (58 cm)

YARN
Jade Sapphire Mongolian Cashmere 4-Ply (100% Cashmere; 200 yds [183 m] / 2 oz / 55 g): #35 Sterling, 7 skeins

NEEDLES
Size US 4 (3.5 mm) 48" (120 cm) circular needle
Size US 3 (3.25 mm) needles, for collar
Adjust needle size if necessary to obtain the correct gauge.

NOTIONS
locking stitch markers (2); closure for collar
tapestry needle

GAUGES
Double Leaves and Twists pattern:
24 sts and 36 rows = 3¼" x 5" (8 cm x 13 cm) (one patt rep) on larger needles

STITCH GUIDE
Twisted Ribbing #1 with I-cord edging
(worked flat over multiple of 3 sts + 2, plus 4 edge sts at each end)
Row 1 (RS): [Sl1, k1] twice, [p2, k1tbl] to last 6 sts, p2, [sl1, k1] twice.
Row 2 (WS): [Sl1, k1] twice, [k2, p1tbl] to last 6 sts, k2, [sl1, k1] twice.
Rep Rows 1- 2 for pattern.

Twisted Ribbing #2 with I-cord edging
(worked flat over multiple of 2 sts + 3, plus 4 edge sts at each end)
Row 1 (RS): [Sl1, k1] twice, p2, [k1tbl, p1] to last 5 sts, p1, [sl1, k1] twice.
Row 2 (WS): [Sl1, k1] twice, k2, [p1tbl, k1] to last 5 sts, k1, [sl1, k1] twice.
Rep Rows 1- 2 for pattern.

4-stitch double wrap (W4) - Sl4 to cn and hold to front. With working yarn, wrap these 4 sts by taking the yarn behind the cable needle and then to the front and around twice. *Yarn should be wrapped loosely enough so that when blocked, the 4 sts do not appear distorted.* Then work 4 sts from cn: k1tbl, p2, k1tbl. See Page 120.

Double Decrease
Sl2-k1-p2sso – Slip 2 sts together k'wise, k1, pass 2 slipped sts over. 2 sts dec

SPECIAL DECREASE TECHNIQUES
RSR 4-st Vertical Dec
1) Sl2 sts p'wise to the RHN, 2) Sl the 3rd st to a cn and hold it at front, 3) Sl 2 additional sts p'wise to RHN, 4) Place the st from the cn onto the LHN, 5) Sl the rem 4 sts from the RHN to the LHN and K5tog = 4 sts dec'd.

The st slipped to the CN will be positioned as the center st running vertically.

WSW 4-st Vertical dec

1) Sl2 sts p'wise to the RHN, 2) Sl the 3rd st to a cn and hold at back. 3) Sl the 2 sts back to the LHN without twisting them, then Sl the 3rd st from the cn back onto the LHN. 4) place the RHN into these 3 sts, then into the next 2 sts = 5 sts in dec, 5) P5 sts tog. The st slipped to the cn will be positioned as the center st running vertically.

NOTES

- Cape is worked flat in one piece from the bottom up.
- To avoid having to estimate length of "long tail" for cast on, use second ball of yarn.
- The slipped stitches in the I-cord edging produce a different row gauge from the pattern stitches. To correct this, after every 12 rows work edge as follows: [Sl1, k1] twice, bring yarn to front, sl1, move yarn to back, sl1 back to LHN, turn work to other side, [sl1, k1] twice. Work next row to end, then repeat same at other end before working next row.
- The I-cord edging is not shown on the charts.

INSTRUCTIONS

Hem and Body

With larger needles CO 394 sts and work in Twisted Ribbing # 1 for 32 rows or until piece measures 4"/10 cm.

Estab Double Leaves and Twists patt from Row 1 of chart as foll: [Sl1, k1] twice (I-cord edge), work 3 "plus" sts, work 24-st patt rep 15 times, work 23 "plus" sts, [sl1, k1] twice (I-cord edge). Cont as estab, working entire chart three times – 108 rows total. Piece measures about 19"/49 cm.

Shoulders

Cont in patt as estab and work 18 rows of Twist Decrease chart – 267 sts rem.

Place stitch markers on last (16th) st of 4th and 12th patt reps to mark the shoulder stitches at each side. The marked stitches will be the middle stitches of the centered double and quadruple decreases.

Work Row 1 of Twisted Ribbing #2, working sl2-k1-p2sso at each marked stitch – 263 sts rem. Cont in patt for 18 more rows, working RSR 4-st vertical dec and WSW 4-st vertical dec (see stitch guide) – 119 sts rem. Work one WS row in patt with no decs.

Collar

Change to smaller needles. Knit 1 RS row, with 4-st I-cord at each end and decreasing 1 st in middle of row – 118 sts rem. Estab Small Double Leaves patt, beg with Row 2, as foll: [Sl1, k1] twice (I-cord edge), work 22-st chart 5 times total, [sl1, k1] twice (I-cord edge). Work in patt rows 3 - 16.

Next row (RS): BO 4-st I-cord, p to last 4 sts, [sl1, k1] twice.

Next row (WS): BO 4-st I-cord, estab Twisted Ribbing #1 pattern without I-cord as foll: [k2, p1tbl] to last 2 sts, k2.

Work 15 rows in pattern. BO all sts loosely on WS.

Carefully block garment. Fold collar in half to inside and stitch in place. Add desired closure at collar.

Bel Fiore Cape

8"/20 cm
2"/5 cm
22 ¾"/58 cm
19"/49 cm
26"/64 cm

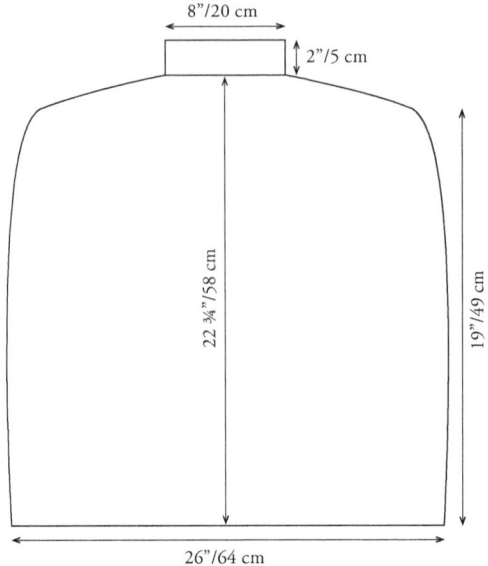

Double Leaves & Twists Chart

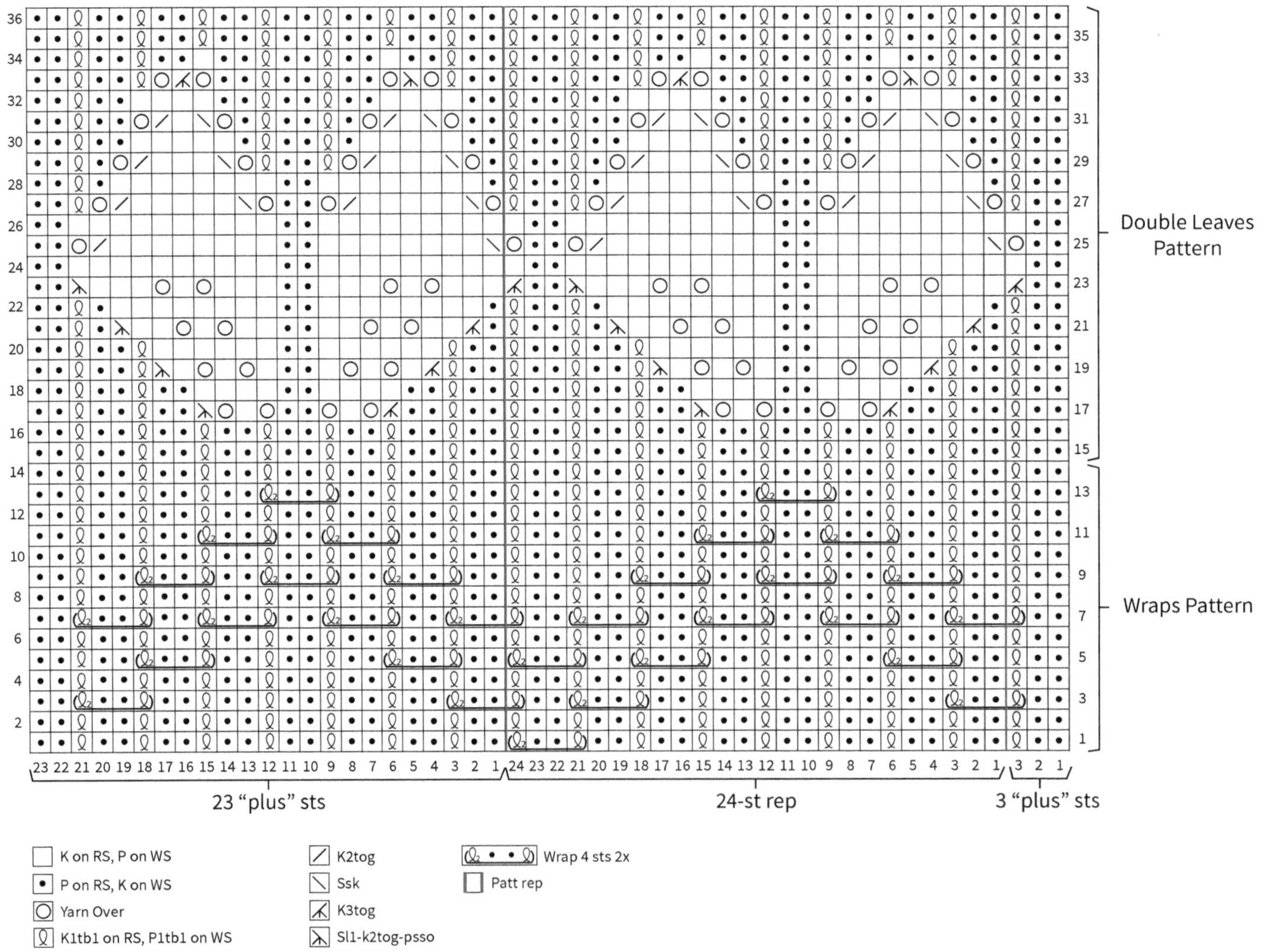

Double Leaves Pattern
Wraps Pattern
23 "plus" sts
24-st rep
3 "plus" sts
K on RS, P on WS
P on RS, K on WS
Yarn Over
K1tbl on RS, P1tbl on WS
K2tog
Ssk
K3tog
Sl1-k2tog-psso
Wrap 4 sts 2x
Patt rep

Small Double Leaves Chart

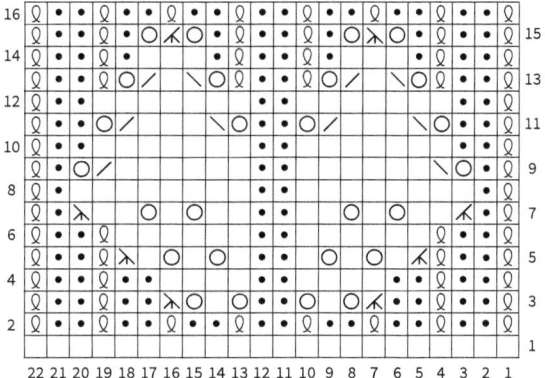

Q	K1tbl on RS, P1tbl on WS
☐	K on RS, P on WS
•	P on RS, K on WS
╱	K2tog
╲	Ssk
○	Yarn Over
⋏	K3tog
⋏	Sl1-k2tog-psso

Twists Decrease Chart

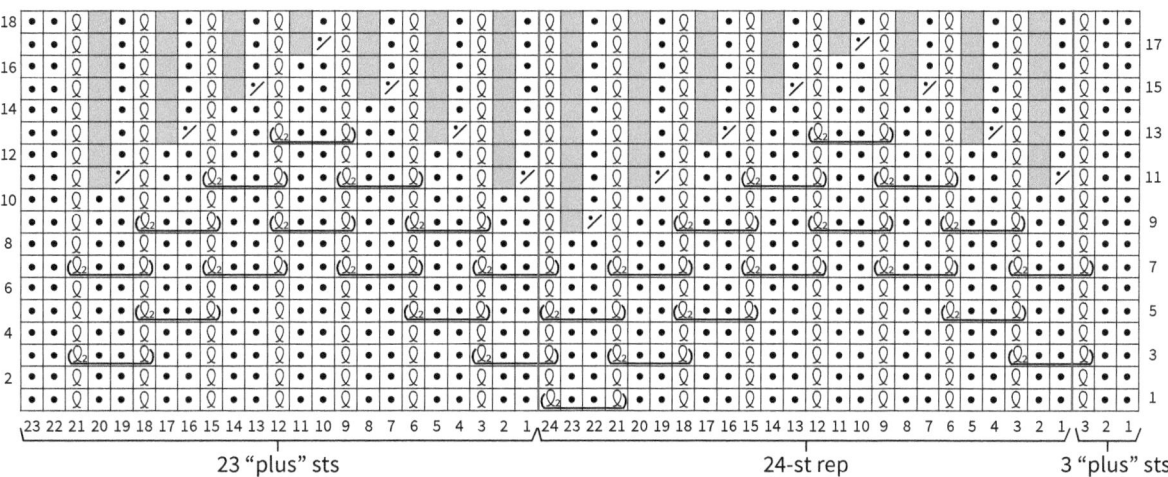

23 "plus" sts | 24-st rep | 3 "plus" sts

☐	K on RS, P on WS
•	P on RS, K on WS
Q	K1tb1 on RS, P1tb1 on WS
╱	P2tog
Q₂ • Q	Wrap 4 sts twice
▓	No stitch
☐	Patt rep for body

BEL FIORE CAPE

Cabled Yoke Pullover

FINISHED SIZES

Women's S (M, L, XL)

Finished bust: 37 (40, 46, 49)" / 92.5 (100, 115, 122.5) cm

To fit bust sizes: 33-35 (36-38, 39-44, 45-47)" / 83.5-89 (91.5 -96.5, 99-111.5, 114-119.5) cm

Sample Size: S

YARN

Madelinetosh Silk/Merino (50% silk / 50% merino; 205 yds [187 m] / 3.5 oz / 100 g): colorway Aura, 7 (8, 8, 9) skeins

NEEDLES

Size US 6 (4 mm) & Size US 5 (3.75 mm)
Adjust needle size if necessary to obtain the correct gauge.

NOTIONS

stitch markers

tapestry needle

GAUGES

Pin Stripe Pattern:
24 sts and 26 rows = 4" / 10 cm in patt with larger needles

Crosses & Twists Pattern:
33 sts and 16 rows = 5 x 2½" / 13 x 6.5 cm in patt with larger needles

STITCH GUIDE

C5B – Sl3 sts onto cn and hold in back, k2, k3 from cn.
C5F – Sl2 sts onto cn and hold in front, k3, k2 from cn.
T4B-3 – Sl2 to cn, hold back, k2, then p2 from cn.
T4F-3 – Sl2 to cn, hold front, p2, then k2 from cn.

NOTES

- A Garter stitch selvedge is worked at both edges of all pieces: Knit the first and last sts of every row. These sts are not shown on the charts but are included in the pattern instructions.
- Marker placement is not specified. Use them as desired to mark pattern repeats.

INSTRUCTIONS

Back/Front (make 2)

With larger needles CO 100 (109, 127, 136) sts.
Knit 1 row.

Shape hem and set up Pinstripe pattern
Row 1 (RS): K1, p8, [k1tbl, p8] to last st, k1.
Row 2 (WS): K1, k8, [p1tbl, k8] to last st, k1.
Row 3: K1, m1L, work in patt to last st, m1R, k1 – 2 sts inc.
Row 4: K1, p1tbl, work in patt to last 2 sts, p1tbl, k1.
Row 5: K1, m1Lp, work in patt to last st, m1Rp, k1 – 2 sts inc.
Row 6: K1, work in patt to last st, k1.
Rep last 2 rows 4 more times – 112 (121, 139, 148) sts.

Establish patt from Row 1 of Pinstripe Pattern chart as foll: K1 (selvedge st), work 5 "plus" sts, work 9-st patt rep 11 (12, 14, 15) times, work 6 "plus" sts, k1 (selvedge st). Cont in estab patt until piece measures 15 (15¼, 15½, 15¾)"/38 (38.5, 39.5, 40) cm or desired length to underarm, ending with a WS row.

Shape Armholes

Shaping is worked by binding off sts at beg of rows and working k2tog's at end of rows.
In rows with no bind offs, slip the first st and end k1.

Row 1 (RS): BO3, work to end – 3 sts dec.
Row 2: BO3, work to last 2 sts, k2tog – 4 sts dec.
Rows 3 & 4: BO2, work to last 2 sts, k2tog – 6 sts dec.
Rows 5 & 6: BO1, work to last 2 sts, k2tog – 4 sts dec.
Row 7: Work to last 2 sts, k2tog – 1 st dec.
94 (103, 121, 130) sts rem.

Next row, re-estab selvedge and work WS set-up row as foll: K1, k5, [p1tbl, k4, m1Lp, k4] to last 7 sts, p1tbl, k5, k1 – 103 (113, 133, 143) sts.

Establish patt from Row 1 of Crosses & Twists chart as foll: K1 (selvedge st), work 5 "plus" sts, work 10-st patt rep 9 (10, 12, 13) times, work 6 "plus" sts, k1 (selvedge st). Cont in establ patt until armhole measures 8½ (8¾, 9, 9¼)"/21.5 (22, 23, 23.5) cm from initial BO, ending with a WS row.

Shape Shoulders

Using Sloped Bind-Off method, cont in patt and BO5 at beg of next 8 (10, 12, 14) rows – 63 (63, 73, 73) sts.
Work even in patt with selvedge for 20 (20, 22, 22) rows.
Change to smaller needles and knit 2 rows tightly.
BO all sts knitwise.

Sleeves (make 2)

With smaller needles CO 63 (67, 73, 77) sts.
Knit 2 rows.

Change to larger needles and set up Crosses & Twists Pattern as foll (WS): K1 (selv), k0 (2, 0, 2) sts (rev St st), work chart Row 8 (6 "plus" sts, then 5 (5, 6, 6) 10-st patt reps, then 5 "plus" sts) to last 1 (3, 1, 3) st(s), k0 (2, 0, 2) sts (rev St st), k1 (selv).

Work even in patt for 2"/5 cm, ending with a WS row.

Next row – inc (RS): K1, m1Rp, p0 (2, 0, 2), work chart to last 1 (3, 1, 3) st(s), p0 (2, 0, 2), m1Lp, k1 – 2 sts inc.

Cont in patt and rep inc row every 4th RS row 9 times more - 83 (87, 93, 97) sts. Work new sts into pattern, working any extra sts in rev St st.

Work even in patt until sleeve measures 17 (17½, 18, 18½)"/43 (44.5, 45.5, 47) cm or desired length to underarm, ending with a WS row.

Work 7-row armhole shaping as for body – 65 (69, 75, 79) sts rem.

Work even in patt for 1 row.

Next row, dec as follows (RS): K1, p2tog, work in patt to last 3 sts, p2tog, k1 – 2 sts dec.

Note: As the decs break the pattern repeat, work any extra sts in rev St st.

Cont in patt and rep dec row every other RS row 5 (6, 7, 8) more times – 53 (55, 59, 61) sts.

At beg of next RS row, BO3 then work to end – 50 (52, 56, 58) sts.

Work next 7 rows as follows: BO3, work to last 2 sts, k2tog – 22 (24, 28, 30) sts.

Next row (RS): Work to last 2 sts, k2tog - 21 (23, 27, 29) sts.

BO all sts in patt on WS.

Finishing

Block pieces to measurements. Sew Front to Back along side seams. Sew sleeve seams then set in sleeves.

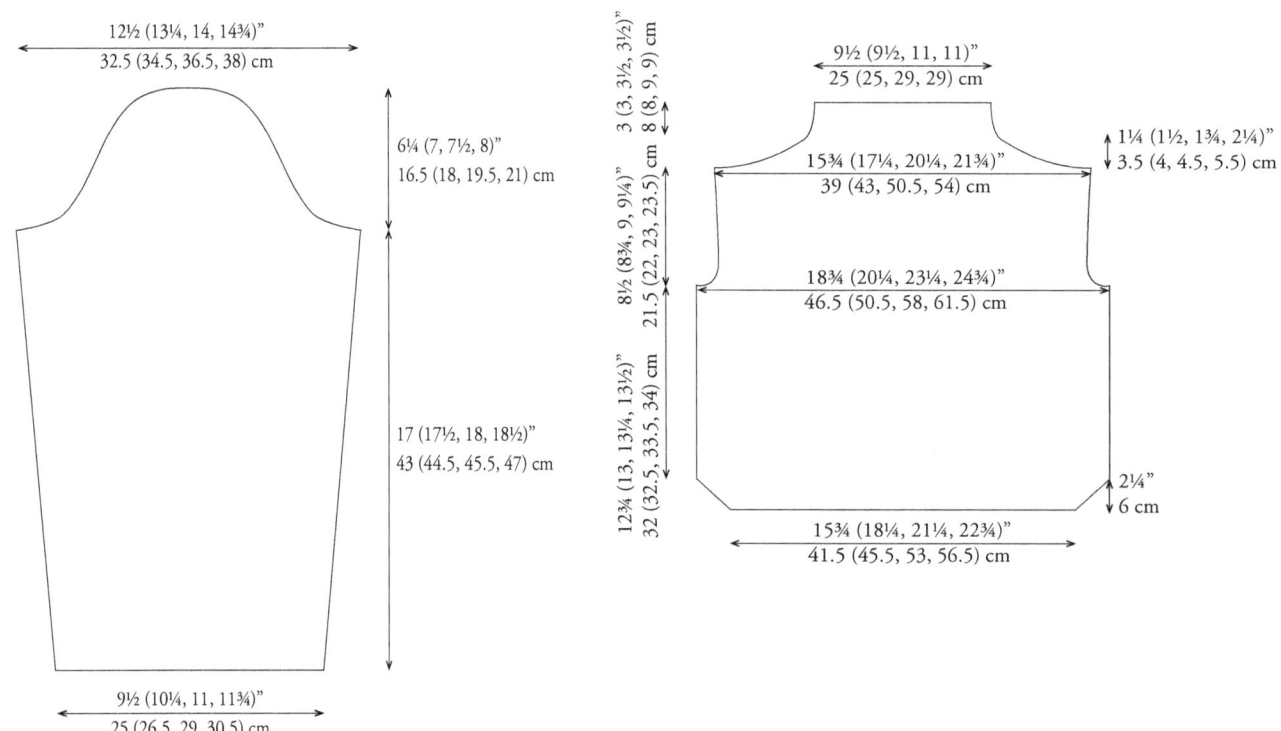

Crosses & Twists Chart
(multiple of 10 +11 + 2 selv)
8 row repeat

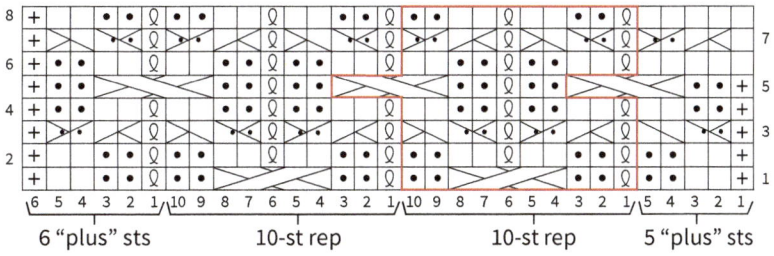

- ☐ K on RS, P on WS
- • P on RS, K on WS
- Q K1tbl on RS, P1tbl on WS
- + K first and last st on each row
- ☐ Patt rep
- T4F-3
- T4B-3
- C5B
- C5F

Pinstripe Pattern

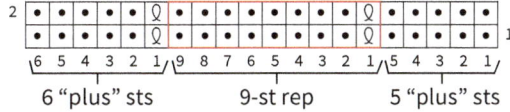

- • P on RS, K on WS
- Q K1 tbl on RS, P1 tbl on WS
- ☐ 9-st patt rep

CABLED YOKE PULLOVER

SIMA BRASON

Cascading Cables Cowl

FINISHED MEASUREMENTS

Circumference: approximately 31 (34)" / 78.5 (86.5) cm
Length: 13½"/34.5 cm

YARN

Brooklyn Tweed Arbor (100% American Targhee Wool; 145 yds [133 m] / 1.75 oz / 50 g): colorway Alizarin (red), 6 skeins or Klimt (gold), 7 skeins

NEEDLES

Size US 5 (3.75 mm) 29" (74 cm) circular needles and 2 dpn's
Size US 4 (3.5 mm) 29" (74 cm) circular needles

NOTIONS

cable needle; stitch marker; crochet hook; waste yarn; tapestry needle

GAUGES

Interlocking Cables Pattern:
16 sts and 16 rnds = 1⅝" / 4.25 cm in patt with larger needles

Cabled Rib Pattern:
49 sts and 45 rnds = 5" / 12.75 cm in patt with larger needles

Gauge is not critical to this project's construction; however, a change in gauge will affect the finished measurements and the yarn requirements.

STITCH GUIDE

C4B – Sl2 to cn, hold back, K2, then K2 from cn.
C4F – Sl2 to cn, hold front, K2, then K2 from cn.
T4B – Sl2 to cn, hold back, K2, then P2 from cn.
T4F – Sl2 to cn, hold front, P2, then K2 from cn.
T3B – Sl1 to cn, hold back, K2, then P1 from cn.
T3F – Sl2 to cn hold front, P1, then K2 from cn.

Cabled Rib Edging

(multiple of 8 sts, worked in the rnd)

Rnd 1: [P1, k2, p1, C4B] to end.

Rnds 2-4: [P1, k2, p1, k4] to end.
Rep Rnds 1-4 for patt.

Interlocking Cable Stitch

(multiple of 16 sts, worked in the rnd)

Rnd 1: [P4, C4B] to end.
Rnd 2: [P4, k4] to end.
Rnd 3: P2, [T4B, T4F] to last 6 sts, T4B, sl2 to RHN, re mar, sl2 back to LHN, T4F, replace beg of rnd marker.
Rnd 4: K2, [p4, k4] to last 6 sts, p4, sl2 to RHN, re mar, sl2 back to LHN, replace beg of rnd marker.
Rnd 5: [C4F, p4] to end.
Rnd 6: [K4, p4] to end.
Rnd 7: K2, [T4F, T4B] to last 6 sts, T4F, sl2 to RHN, re mar, sl2 back to LHN, T4B, replace beg of rnd marker.
Rnd 8: P2, [k4, p4] to last 6 sts, k4, sl2 to RHN, re mar, sl2 back to LHN, replace beg of rnd marker.
Rnd 9: Rep Rnd 1.
Rnd 10: Rep Rnd 2.
Rnd 11: [P2, T4B, T4F, p2, k4] to end.
Rnd 12: [P2, k2, p4, k2, p2, k4] to end.
Rnd 13: [P2, k2, p4, k2, p2, C4B] to end.
Rnd 14: Rep Rnd 12.
Rnd 15: [P2, T4F, T4B, p2, k4] to end.
Rnd 16: Rep Rnd 2.
Rep Rnds 1-16 for patt.

Cabled Trim

(6 sts, worked flat)

Row 1 (RS): K1 (selv), k4, k1 (selv).
Row 2 (WS): K1 (selv), p4, k1 (selv).
Row 3: K1 (selv), C4B, k1 (selv).
Row 4: Rep Row 2.

Rep Rows 1-4 for patt.

NOTES

- The samples shown are identical except for color and number of pattern repeats. To adjust the circumference, alter the cast on by a multiple of 16 sts.

INSTRUCTIONS

Section 1 - Cabled Ribbing

With larger needles and using the long-tail method, CO 304 (336) sts, pl mar, and join in the rnd being careful not to twist your sts. Work 16 rnds in Cabled Rib Edge patt, ending with patt Rnd 4.

Section 2 – Interlocking Cables

Work Rnds 1-16 of the Interlocking Cable Stitch patt 5 times, then rep Rnds 1-9 once more (89 rnds total).

Section 3 - Cabled Ribbing

Beg with Rnd 2, work 16 rnds in Cabled Rib Edge patt, ending with patt Rnd 1. BO all sts in patt, working every 3rd purl st as a k2tog with the following knit st – 4 sts dec for every 4 patt reps.

Section 4 – Trim (make 2 – lengths will differ)

Using the crochet hook and waste yarn, make a 10-st crochet chain. With working yarn and dpn skip the first 2 chains, then pick up 6 sts and work as follows:

Set-up row (WS): P6.

Work back and forth on dpn's in Cabled Trim patt until trim measures approximately 6"/15 cm less than the edge of the cowl. Keeping the trim sts on the dpn, baste the trim to the cowl to see how much more length is needed. Continue working back and forth to appropriate length, ending with patt Row 4.

Finishing

Remove the waste yarn chain from the bottom of the cabled trim and place the 6 CO sts on a dpn, then seam the two ends together using the 3-needle bind off technique. Weave in ends. Next, with RS of both pieces facing, attach the edge of the cabled trim to the appropriate edge of the cowl using mattress stitch.

With the smaller circular needle pick up stitches along the remaining edge of the cabled trim, placing the needle just below the garter st bumps formed by the K1 selvedge sts along the edge. Join the pickup sts in a circle and work 4 rnds in St st. Do not bind off. Instead, place the live stitches on waste yarn. To create a neat covering that will encase the seam where the cabled trim was attached to the cowl edge work as foll: Fold the trim to the inside of the cowl and, using the tapestry needle, carefully sew down the live St sts to the sts beneath the mattress st seam one at a time. When the seamed edge is completely covered, remove the waste yarn and weave the ends in.

Repeat with second cabled trim to finish remaining cowl edge.

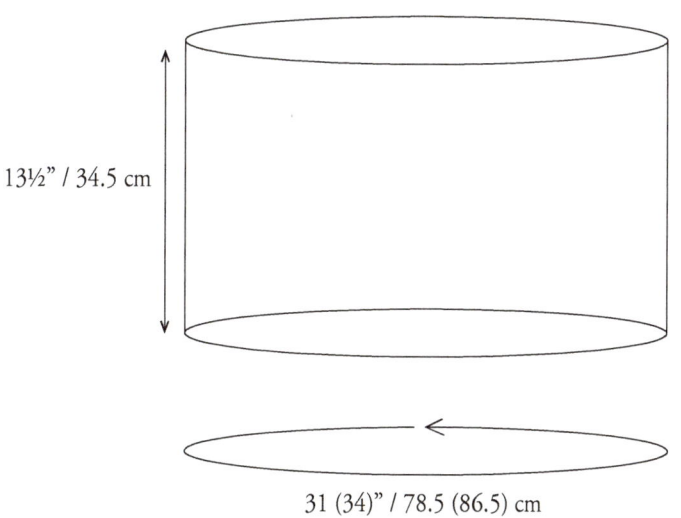

13½" / 34.5 cm

31 (34)" / 78.5 (86.5) cm

Cabled Rib Edge

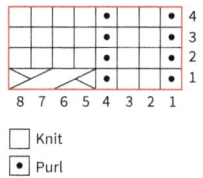

- ☐ Knit
- • Purl
- ⧖ C4B
- ☐ Patt rep

Cabled Trim

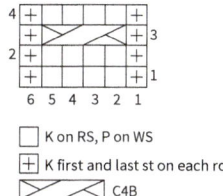

- ☐ K on RS, P on WS
- + K first and last st on each row
- ⧖ C4B

Interlocking Cable Stitch

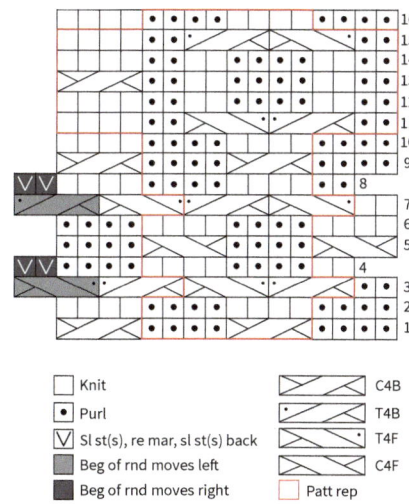

- ☐ Knit
- • Purl
- V Sl st(s), re mar, sl st(s) back
- ▨ Beg of rnd moves left
- ▨ Beg of rnd moves right
- ⧖ C4B
- ⧗ T4B
- ⧗ T4F
- ⧖ C4F
- ☐ Patt rep

CASCADING CABLES COWL | 159

SHIRLEY PADEN

Coleus Coat

FINISHED SIZES

Women's S (M, L)

Finished bust: 38 (42½, 47)" / 96 (108, 120) cm
To fit bust sizes: 34-36 (38-40, 41-45)" / 86-91.5 (96.5 -101.5, 104-114) cm
Finished hip: 46½ (51, 56)" / 118 (130, 142) cm
To fit hip sizes: 36-42 (44-48, 50-54)"/ 91.5-106.5 (111.5-122, 127-137) cm

Sample Size: S

YARN

Trendsetter Yarn Group GGH Merino Soft (100% Virgin Wool; 185 yds [170 m] / 1.75 oz / 50 g): #140 Pearl Grey, 15 (16, 17) balls

NEEDLES & HOOKS

Size US 4 (3.5 mm) - 40" (100 cm) circular
Adjust needle sizes if necessary to obtain the correct gauge.

Size E (3.5 mm) crochet hook for provisional cast on, crochet edging, and button backs

Spare needle for 3-needle bind off

NOTIONS

Stitch markers; tapestry needle; 1" / 25.5 mm buttons (2)

GAUGES

Swatches #2 Pattern (body): 48 sts x 60 rows = 7" x 8" / 18 cm x 20.5 cm on larger needles
Swatches #2 Pattern (collar edging): 32 sts = 4" / 10 cm on smaller needles
Twisted Rib Pattern: 32 sts x 30 rows = 4" / 10 cm

STITCH GUIDE

Swatches #2 Pattern - see chart

Twisted Rib Pattern
(odd number of sts)
Row 1 (RS): P1, [k1tbl, p1] to end.
Row 2 (WS): [K1, p1tbl], to last st, k1.
Rep Rows 1-2 for patt.

Single Crochet (sc):
Working from right to left, *insert hook into st, yarn round hook (yrh), draw loop through, yrh, draw yarn through 2 loops on hook; rep from *.

TECHNIQUES

Tubular Cast On

Cable Cast On

Whipstitch Seaming

Five-Stitch One-Row Buttonhole:

1. Work to buttonhole, pull yarn to the front.
2. Slip 1 stitch purlwise from left needle to right.
3. Pull yarn to the back (circling the slipped stitch). Leave yarn in back.
4. Slip 1 stitch purlwise, then pass the circled slipped stitch over the new slipped stitch. This is the first cast off for your buttonhole.
5. Continue to slip purlwise from left needle to right and pass the previously slipped stitch over the new one 4 more times until you have cast off 5 stitches total.
6. Slip the last cast-off stitch back to the left needle. Turn your work.
7. With yarn at back, cable CO 5 stitches, bring yarn forward, then CO 1 more. Turn your work.
8. Slip 1 stitch knitwise from left needle and pass the extra cast-on stitch over it. Continue to work across the row.

Sloped Bind Off (Used to smoothly shape the armholes, neckline, sleeve caps and collar edges)
The technique begins with the 2nd bind-off row. Work the first bind-off row as instructed, but do not work the last stitch. When you turn the work, this will be the first stitch on the RHN. Slip the next stitch purlwise from the LHN to the RHN, then pass the first stitch (leftover from the previous row) over the slipped stitch to bind off. If there are additional bind-off sts on this row work them as usual, then work to the last st and turn, repeating the process for all rem bind-off rows.

Collar Edging Swatch: Use smaller needles and the Tubular Cast On, beg with a 45-loop crochet chain and picking up 41 sts to CO a total of 81 sts. Work Rows 1-9 of the Swatches #2 Patt, with a selvage st at beg and end (4 patt reps + 15 sts + 2 selv). Skip Rows 10-11 and work Row 12, then work a k2tog dec on all sts across the row. Next, take a width measurement. For gauge specified (8 sts per 1"/2.5 cm), this decreased measurement should be 10"/25 cm measured along the 79 sts inside the selv sts.

Picot Crochet Edging (to finish center front edges): Working from right to left, *work 1 sl st in sc, chain 4, skip 1 sc *; rep from * to last st, work 1 sl st in final sc. Cut yarn and pull through to fasten off.

Crocheted Button Backs: Using crochet hook, make a slip knot, then ch2. **Rnd 1:** work 8 sc in the 2nd ch from the hook (this is the slip knot). **Rnd 2:** *Work 2 sc in the first sc, then 1 sc in the foll sc; rep from * three more times = 12 sts. **Rnd 3:** Work 1 sc in each of the 12 sc. Slip the last st to the first sc. Fasten off. At center, thread the starting tail onto a tapestry needle. Pull the starting yarn through the first round of sts and pull to close the center hole.

NOTES

- A Garter stitch selvedge is worked at both edges of all pieces: Knit the first and last sts of every row. All shaping is to be worked inside these selvedge stitches.
- The smaller needles are used only for the collar edging; use the larger needles if not otherwise specified.

INSTRUCTIONS

Back

Tubular Cast On (see illustrated instructions on page 122 in Special Techniques)

1. Using the crochet hook and waste yarn, make a chain of 85 (93, 101) loops. Using the working needle and beginning with the 3rd chain from the end, pick up 1 st from the back of each loop until you have 81 (89, 97) sts on your needle. Cut the waste yarn. (Fig 3.1)

2. Join working yarn and purl 1 row, then knit 1 row (= 2 rows St st, ending with RS row). (Fig 3.2)

3. Turn to WS. (Tubular Construction Prep)

4. Insert the RHN into the first st in the bottom row (just above the waste yarn) and purl it together with the first st on the LHN. (Tubular First Stitch) (Fig 3.3)

5. Work across the row, adding knit sts between the purl sts as follows: *K1 from st picked up in the crochet chain (strand of working yarn between waste yarn loops), p1 from LHN; rep from * to end. (Fig 3.4) 161 (177, 193) sts (Fig 3.5) Full stitch count.

6. Gently unravel the crochet chain to remove the waste yarn.

Establish Swatches #2 patt as foll, beg with chart Row 1 (RS): K1 (selv), work 16-st patt rep 9 (10, 11) times, work 15 "plus" sts, k1 (selv).

Work chart rows 1-30 three times (90 rows total). Piece should measure 12"/30.5 cm.

Transition Row

Next row (RS), establish Twisted Rib patt at either side of Swatches #2 patt as foll: K1 (selv), M1P, [k1tbl, p1] 16 times (Twisted Rib), pl mar, work chart Row 1 patt rep 5 (6, 7) times, work 15 "plus" sts (Swatches #2), pl mar, [p1, k1tbl] 16 times, M1P (Twisted Rib), k1 (selv). 33 Twisted Rib sts at each side; 95 (111, 127) Swatches #2 sts; 163 (179, 195) sts total.

Work 1 WS row in patt as estab.

Hip-to-Waist

Cont in patt and dec 1 st at beg and end of next 2 RS rows, then dec 1 st at beg and end of every other RS row 22 times, ending with WS row. 92 shaping rows total; 9 Twisted Rib sts at each side; 115 (131, 147) sts total.

Waist

Work even in patt for 14 rows.

Waist-to-Bust

Next row (RS), work in patt inc 1 st at beg and end of row. 2 sts inc'd.

Cont in patt and *inc 1 st at beg and end of every RS row 3 times, then inc 1 st at beg and end of every other RS row twice; rep from * once more then end with WS row. 30 shaping rows total; 20 Twisted Rib sts at each side; 137 (153, 169) sts total.

Work even in patt for 18 rows or until piece measures 33"/83 cm or desired length to underarm.

Shape Armhole (Use the Sloped Bind-Off Technique)

BO 4 sts at beg of next 2 rows, 3 sts at beg of foll 4 (4, 6) rows, 2 sts at beg of foll 6 rows, 1 st at beg of foll 6 rows. 1 (1, 0) Twisted Rib st(s) rem at each side; 95 (111, 123) Swatches #2 sts rem; 99 (115, 125) sts total.

Work even in patt for 36 (40, 42) rows or until armhole measures 7¼ (7¾, 8¼)"/19 (20, 21) cm, ending with a WS row.

Next row (RS): Work 25 (33, 38) right shoulder sts, BO 49 sts for Back Neck, work rem 24 (32, 37) shoulder sts. Place shoulder sts on holders.

Right Front

Foll the Tubular Cast On Instructions, beg with crochet chain of 58 (62, 66) loops, then picking up 54 (58, 62) sts. After Step 5 you will have 107 (115, 123) sts, including 2 selv sts.

Establish Swatches #2 patt as foll, working from center front edge to side edge, beg with chart Row 1 (RS).

Sizes S (L): K1 (selv), work sts 8-16 of patt rep once, work 16-st patt rep 6 (7) times, k1 (selv).
Size M: K1 (selv), p1, work 16-st patt rep 7 times, k1 (selv).
All sizes: Work chart rows 1-30 three times (90 rows total). Piece should measure 12"/30.5 cm.

Transition Row
Next row (RS), establish Twisted Rib patt at side edge as foll: Work in patt to last 33 sts (final 2 patt reps + selv), pl mar, [k1tbl, p1] to last st (Twisted Rib), k1 (selv). 32 Twisted Rib sts at side edge (as worn); 73 (81, 89) Swatches #2 sts; 107 (115, 123) sts total.

Work 1 WS row in patt as estab.

Hip-to Waist
Cont in patt and dec 1 st at end of next 2 RS rows, then dec 1 st at end of every other RS row 22 times, ending with WS row. 92 shaping rows total; 8 Twisted Rib sts at side edge; 83 (91, 99) sts total.

Waist & Buttonhole
Work even in patt for 6 rows, ending with chart row 10.

Next row (RS): K1 (selv), work in patt for 38 (38, 46) sts, work a 5-st one-row buttonhole, cont in patt to end of row. This places the buttonhole in the center of a leaf motif, with 2 sts on either side of the center purl st. Work even in patt for 3 more rows.

Begin V-Neck Shaping (Use Sloped Bind Off Technique)
Note: Read ahead before continuing; waist-to-bust shaping and armhole shaping is worked at same time as V-neck shaping.

Size S: BO 1 st at beg of next 50 RS rows.
Size M: *BO 1 st at beg of next 23 RS rows, then 0 sts at beg of foll RS row; rep from * once more, then BO 1 st at beg of foll 4 RS rows.
Size L: *BO 1 st at beg of next 11 RS rows, then 0 sts at beg of foll RS row; rep from * 3 times more, then BO 1 st at beg of the foll 6 RS rows.

Waist-to-Bust
AT THE SAME TIME, on 5th row of V-neck shaping (RS), work in patt inc 1 st at end of row. 1 st inc'd at side edge.

Cont in patt and *inc 1 st at end of every RS row 3 times, then inc 1 st at end of every other RS row twice; rep from * once more then end with WS row. 30 shaping rows total; 19 Twisted Rib sts at side edge.

Work even in patt, cont V-neck shaping, for 18 rows or until piece measures 33"/83 cm or same length as Back to underarm.

Shape Armhole (Use Sloped Bind Off Technique)
Cont V-neck shaping and BO 4 sts at beg of next WS row, 3 sts at beg of foll 2 (2, 3) WS rows, 2 sts at beg of foll 3 WS rows, 1 st at beg of foll 3 WS rows.

Once all shaping is complete, you should have 25 (33, 38) shoulder sts rem.

Work even until armhole measures 7¼ (7¾, 8¼)"/19 (20, 21) cm, ending with a RS row.

Place shoulder sts on holder.

Left Front

CO as for Right Front.

Establish Swatches #2 patt as foll, working from side edge to center front edge, beg with chart Row 1 (RS).

Sizes S (L): K1 (selv), p1, work 16-st patt rep to last st, ending with half rep on st#8, k1 (selv).

Size M: K1 (selv), p1, work 16-st patt rep 7 times, k1 (selv).

All sizes: Work chart rows 1-30 three times (90 rows total). Piece should measure 12"/30.5 cm.

Transition Row

Next row (RS), establish Twisted Rib patt at side edge as foll: K1 (selv), [p1, k1tbl] 16 times (Twisted Rib), pl mar, work in patt to end. 32 Twisted Rib sts at side edge (as worn); 73 (81, 89) Swatches #2 sts; 107 (115, 123) sts total.

Work 1 WS row in patt as estab.

Hip-to Waist

Cont in patt and dec 1 st at beg of next 2 RS rows, then dec 1 st at beg of every other RS row 22 times, ending with WS row. 92 shaping rows total; 8 Twisted Rib sts at side edge; 83 (91, 99) sts total.

Waist

Work even in patt for 11 rows, ending with chart row 15.

Begin V-Neck Shaping (Use Sloped Bind Off Technique)

Note: Read ahead before continuing; waist-to-bust shaping and armhole shaping is worked at same time as V-neck shaping.

Size S: BO 1 st at beg of next 50 WS rows.

Size M: *BO 1 st at beg of next 23 WS rows, then 0 sts at beg of foll WS row; rep from * once more, then BO 1 st at beg of foll 4 WS rows.

Size L: *BO 1 st at beg of next 11 WS rows, then 0 sts at beg of foll WS row; rep from * 3 times more, then BO 1 st at beg of the foll 6 WS rows.

Waist-to-Bust

AT THE SAME TIME, on 4th row of V-neck shaping (RS), work in patt inc 1 st at beg of row. 1 st inc'd at side edge.

Cont in patt and *inc 1 st at beg of every RS row 3 times, then inc 1 st at beg of every other RS row twice; rep from * once more then end with WS row. 30 shaping rows total; 19 Twisted Rib sts at each side.

Work even in patt, cont V-neck shaping, for 18 rows or until piece measures 33"/83 cm or same length as Back to underarm.

Shape Armhole (Use Sloped Bind Off Technique)

Cont V-neck shaping and BO 4 sts at beg of next RS row, 3 sts at beg of foll 2 (2, 3) RS rows, 2 sts at beg of foll 3 RS rows, 1 st at beg of foll 3 RS rows.

Once all shaping is complete, you should have 25 (33, 38) shoulder sts rem.

Work even until armhole measures 7¼ (7¾, 8¼)"/19 (20, 21) cm, ending with a RS row.

Place shoulder sts on holder.

Sleeves

Foll the Tubular Cast On Instructions, beg with crochet chain of 46 loops, then picking up 42 sts. After Step 5 you will have 83 sts, including 2 selv sts.

Establish Swatches #2 patt as foll, beg with chart Row 1 (RS): K1 (selv), p1, work 16-st patt rep 4 times, work 15 "plus" sts, p1, k1 (selv).

Work even in patt until piece measures 3"/7.5 cm, ending with a RS row.

Next row (WS): K1 (selv), [p9, M1P] twice, pl mar, work in patt for 47 sts (15 "plus" sts, then 2 patt reps), pl mar, [M1P, p9] twice, k1 (selv). 87 sts.

Next row (RS), establish Twisted Rib at each side as foll: K1 (selv), p1, [k1tbl, p1] to mar (Twisted Rib), sl mar, work Swatches #2 patt as estab (2 patt reps, then 15 "plus" sts), sl mar, p1, [k1tbl, p1] to last st (Twisted Rib), k1 (selv).

Shape Sleeve

Cont in patt and inc at beg and end of RS rows as foll, working incs into Twisted Rib patt:

Size S: Work incs every 10th row 9 times. 28 Twisted Rib sts each side; 105 sts total.

Size M: *Work incs in 6th row, then in foll 8th row; rep from * five times more, then work incs in foll 6th row once more. 32 Twisted Rib sts each side; 113 sts total.

Size L: Work incs every 4th row 6 times, then every 6th row 11 times. 36 Twisted Rib sts each side; 121 sts total.

All sizes: Work even until sleeve measures 17½"/ 44.5 cm from CO edge.

Shape Cap

All Sizes: BO 4 sts at beg of next 2 rows. 97 (105, 113) sts rem.

Size S: [BO 2 sts at beg of next 4 rows, then 3 sts at beg of foll 2 rows] 3 times, then [BO 2 sts at beg of next 2 rows, then 3 sts at beg of foll 4 rows] twice. 23 sts rem. BO all rem sts.

Size M: BO 1 st at beg of next 2 rows, 2 sts at beg of foll 2 rows, 3 sts at beg of foll 2 rows, then [BO 2 sts at beg of next 4 rows, then 3 sts at beg of foll 2 rows] 4 times, then BO 3 sts at beg of the next 4 rows. 25 sts rem. BO all rem sts.

Size L: [BO 2 sts at beg of next 4 rows, then 3 sts at beg of foll 2 rows] 5 times, then BO 2 sts at beg of foll 2 rows, then 3 sts at beg of foll 4 rows. 27 sts rem. BO all rem sts

Collar

Using a regular long-tail method, CO 355 (367, 379) sts.

Establish Twisted Rib patt as foll:

Row 1 (RS): K1 (selv), p1, [k1tbl, p1] to last st (Twisted Rib), k1 (selv).

Row 2 (WS): K1 (selv), [k1, p1tbl] to last 2 sts, k1 (Twisted Rib), k1 (selv).

Cont in patt and shape collar edges as foll, using the Sloped Bind Off Technique:

Rows 3 – 14: BO [2 sts at beg of next 2 rows, then 1 st at beg of foll 2 rows] 3 times. 18 sts BO; 337 (349, 361) sts rem.

Rows 15 – 22: BO 2 sts at beg of next 4 rows, then 1 st at beg of foll 4 rows. 12 sts BO; 325 (337, 349) sts rem.

Rows 23 – 40: BO [2 sts at beg of next 4 rows, then 1 st at beg of foll 2 rows] 3 times. 30 sts BO; 295 (307, 319) sts rem.

Rows 41 – 52: BO [3 sts at beg of next 2 rows, then 2 sts at beg of foll 4 rows] twice. 28 sts BO; 267 (279, 291) sts rem.

Rows 53 – 68: BO 3 sts at beg of next 2 rows, then 4 sts at beg of foll 2 rows, then [3 sts at beg of foll 4 rows, then 4 sts at beg of foll 2 rows] twice. 54 sts BO; 213 (225, 237) sts rem.

Rows 69 – 72: BO 3 sts at beg of next 2 rows, then 4 sts at beg of foll 2 rows. 14 sts BO; 199 (211, 223) sts rem.

Rows 73 – 98: BO 3 sts at beg of next 2 (2, 0) rows, then 4 sts at beg of foll 6 (2, 2) rows, then 5 sts at beg of foll 4 (8, 10) rows, then 6 sts at beg of foll 6 (6, 6) rows, then 7 sts at beg of foll 8 (8, 8) rows. 142 (146, 150) sts BO; 57 (65, 73) sts rem.

Next row (RS): BO all rem sts.

Collar Edging

With smaller needles and foll the Tubular Cast On Instructions, beg with crochet chain of 205 (213, 221) loops, then picking up 201 (209, 217) sts. After Step 5 you will have 401 (417, 433) sts, including 2 selv sts.

Establish Swatches #2 patt as foll, beg with chart Row 1 (RS): K1 (selv), work 16-st patt rep 24 (25, 26) times, work 15 "plus" sts, k1 (selv).

Work chart rows 1-9 once, then skip chart rows 10 & 11 and work chart row 12, dec'ng 1 st. 400 (416. 432) sts.

Next row (RS): K2tog across. 200 (208, 216) sts.

BO all sts.

Edging should measure 50½ (52½, 54½)"/128 (133.5, 138.5) cm.

Finishing

Block pieces to measurements. Attach fronts to back at shoulders using the 3-needle bind off, making sure that the stitch pattern is aligned at each shoulder. Sew side seams.

Crochet Edging

Left Front: With RS facing and crochet hook join yarn at the base of the V neck. Work in sc along left front edge to bottom, making sure that the number of sc is odd. Turn and work a second row of sc. Turn and work the Picot Crochet edging along the front from the V neck to the bottom.

Right Front: With RS facing join yarn at bottom edge. Work in sc along right front edge to the base of the V neck. Turn and work 2 sc then make button loop as foll: sl1 st in sc of previous row, ch5, skip 2 sc, slip 1 st in the next sc. Cont working sc to the row end. Turn and work the Picot Crochet edging to 1 st before the 5 ch button loop, work 1 sl st in the next sl st, then work 10 sc in the 5-chain loop, then 1 sl st in the foll sl st. Work a sl st in each of the 2 rem sc.

Buttons: Make 2 crocheted button backs and sew them to the leaf motifs on the Left Front, corresponding with the Right Front buttonhole and button loop, respectively. Sew the 2 buttons onto the button backs.

Collar: Baste, then sew edging to the outer collar, gathering it into a ruffle if necessary. Baste, then sew collar to the neckline. For an invisible join, use the Whipstitch technique with very close stitches. The RS of the collar should be facing inward during seaming as collar will turn outward when worn.

Sleeves: Sew sleeve seams. Baste, then set sleeves into the armholes.

Horizontal Whipstitch Seam

Coleus Coat

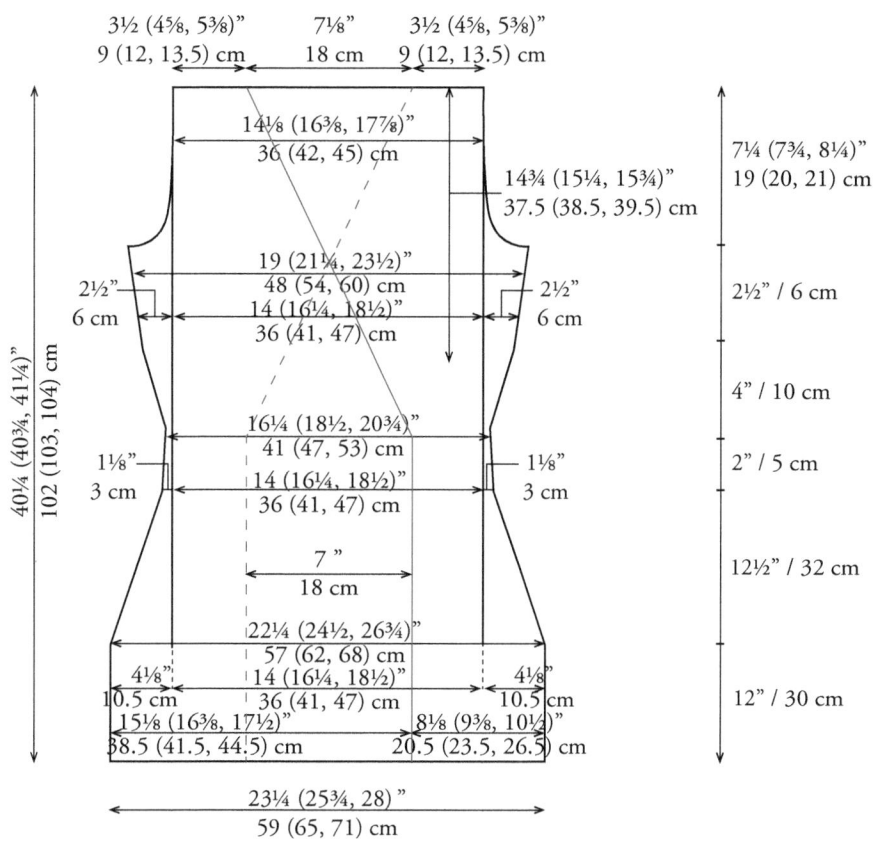

Sleeve

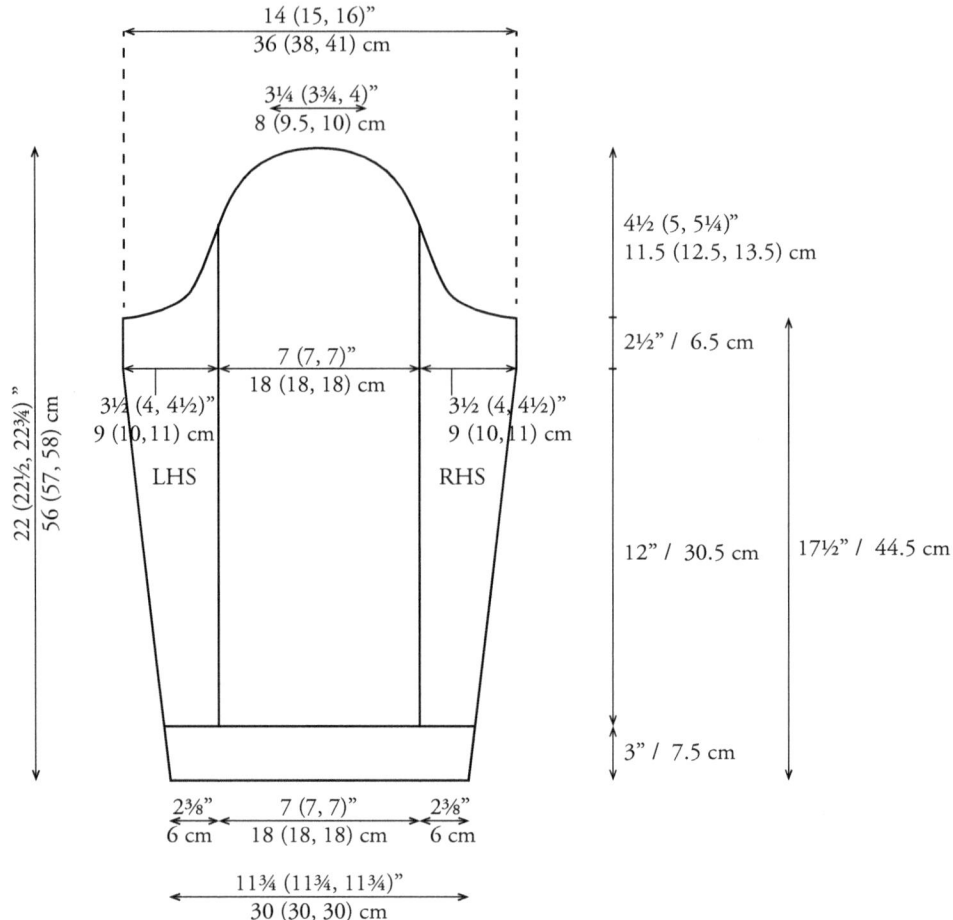

Collar

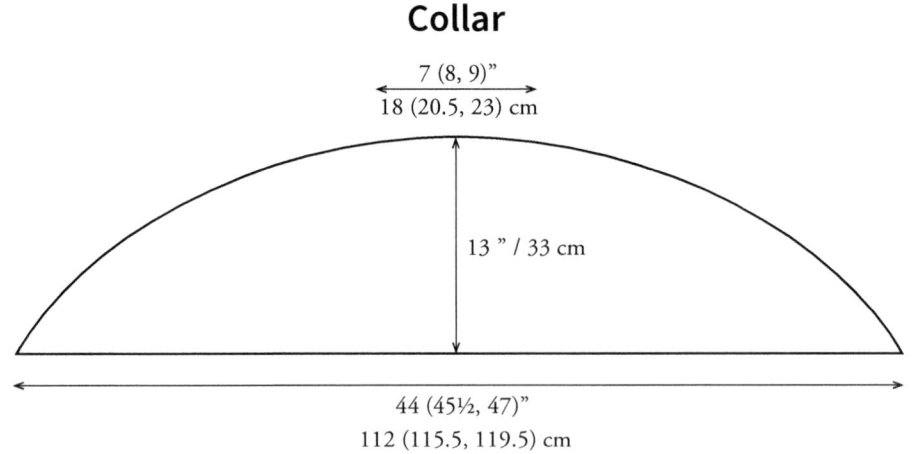

Swatches #2
(mult of 16 + 15/30 rows)

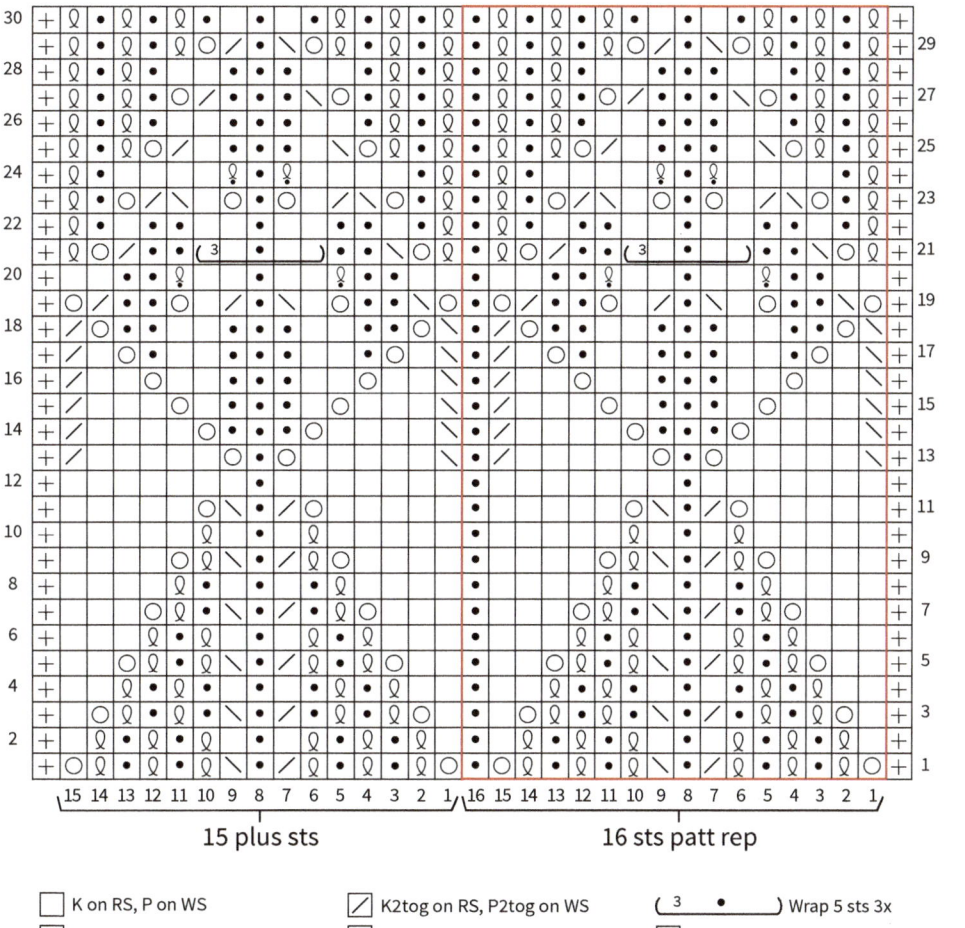

Twisted Rib Pattern
(Mult of 2 + 1 / 2 Rows)

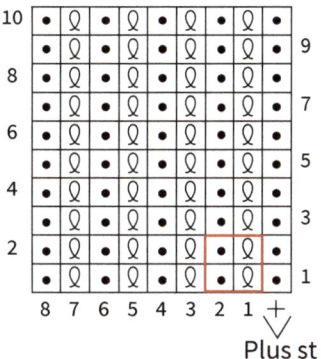

Coquilles Capelet

SHIRLEY PADEN

FINISHED SIZES

Women's S (M, L, XL)

Total Circumference:
Capelet Bottom (Shoulders): 35 (41, 41 46¾)" / 89 (104, 104, 119) cm
Capelet Top (Neck): 29 (33¾, 33¾, 38¾)" / 73 (85, 85, 98) cm

Front and Back Widths:
Capelet Bottom (Shoulders): 17½ (20½, 20½, 23⅜)" / 44.5 (52, 52, 59.5) cm
Capelet Top (Neck): 14½ (16⅞, 16⅞, 19⅜)" / 36.5 (42.5, 42.5, 49) cm

Sample Size: M

YARN

Mariposa Yarn Atelier Monarch (100% Silk; 410 yds [375 m] / 3.5 oz / 100 g): #3001 Sage, 1 (1, 2, 2) skein(s)

NEEDLES

Size US 3 (3.25mm) – 32" (80 cm) circular needle
Size US 2 (2.75mm) – 32" (80 cm) and 24" (60 cm) circular needles
Size US 1 (2.25mm) – 32" (80 cm) circular needle

NOTIONS

Stitch markers, tapestry needle

GAUGES

Shells Pattern
57 sts x 32 rnds = 8¾" x 4" / 22.25 cm x 10 cm on largest needles
57 sts x 32 rnds = 8" x 4" / 20 cm x 10 cm on medium needles
57 sts x 36 rnds = 7¼" x 4" / 18.5 cm x 10 cm on smallest needles

Garter Stitch (Edging)
26.5 sts and 80 rnds = 4" / 10 cm on largest needle

STITCH GUIDE

Shells Pattern – See Chart

Garter Stitch
(worked in the rnd)
Rnd 1: Knit.
Rnd 2: Purl.
Rep Rnds 1-2 for patt.

INSTRUCTIONS

With largest needle, CO 228 (266, 266, 304) sts, pl mar and join to work in the rnd, being careful not to twist the sts. Work 5 rnds in Garter st, beg and ending with a knit rnd.

Next rnd: Establish Shells patt from Rnd 1 of chart as foll: work 19-st patt rep 12 (14, 14, 16) times, placing markers between reps.

Work 8-rnd chart 3 (3, 4, 4) times. 24 (24, 32, 32) rnds.

Change to medium needles and work 8-rnd chart 3 (3, 4, 4) more times. 24 (24, 32, 32) rnds.

Change to smallest needles and work 8-rnd chart 4 (4, 3, 3) more times. 32 (32, 24, 24) rnds.

Piece should measure about 9¾ (9¾, 10⅞, ⅞)"/25 (25, 27.5, 27.5) cm from bottom edge.

80 (80, 88, 88) chart rnds total.

Work 5 rnds in Garter st, beg and ending with a knit rnd.

BO all sts.

Finishing

Weave in ends and block to measurements.

Coquilles Capelet

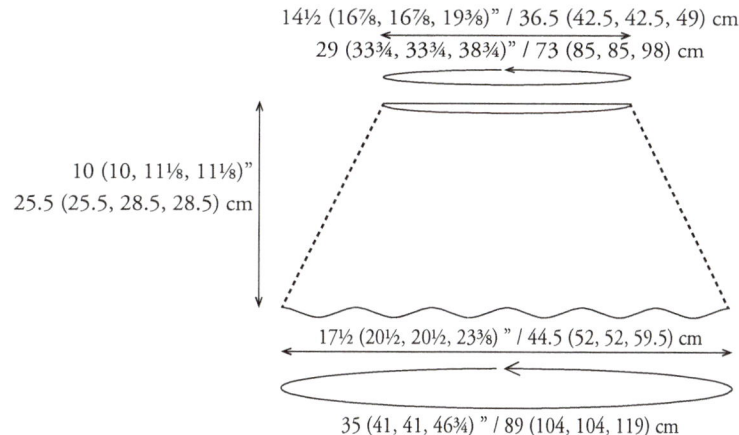

Shells
(multiple of 19 sts / 8 rnds)

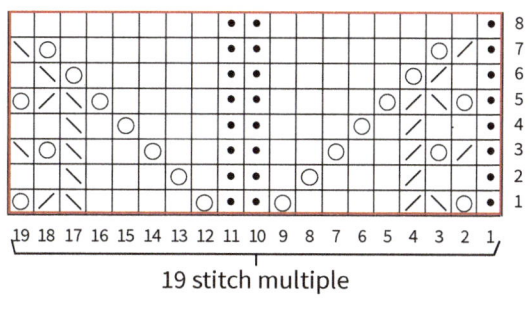

19 stitch multiple

- ☐ Knit
- • Purl
- ╱ K2tog
- ╲ Ssk
- ○ Yarn Over
- ▭ Patt rep

SHIRLEY PADEN

Coquilles Pullover

FINISHED SIZES

Women's S (M, L, XL)

Finished bust: 34 (39¾, 45½, 51)" / 86 (101, 116, 130) cm
To fit bust sizes: 32-33 (34-38, 39-44, 45-49)" / 81-84 (86-97, 99-112, 114-124) cm

Sample Size: M

YARN

Mariposa Yarn Atelier Monarch (100% Silk; 410 yds [375 m] / 3.5 oz / 100 g): #3001 Sage, 5 (6, 7, 8) skeins

NEEDLES

Size US 3 (3.25mm) – 32" (80 cm) circular needle
Size US 2 (2.75mm) – 32" (80 cm) and 24" (60 cm) circular needles plus spare for 3-needle bind off
Size US 1 (2.25mm) – 32" (80 cm) circular needle

NOTIONS

Stitch markers; stitch holders (or scrap yarn); tapestry needle; elastic thread (optional)

GAUGES

Shells Pattern (chart rows 1-8):
57 sts x 32 rows = 8¾" x 4" / 22.25 cm x 10 cm on largest needles
57 sts x 32 rows = 8" x 4" / 20 cm x 10 cm on medium needles
57 sts x 32 rows = 7¼" x 4" / 18.5 cm x 10 cm on smallest needles

Ovals & Arrows Pattern (chart rows 1-30):
57 sts x 30 rows = 8½" x 3½" / 21.5 cm x 9 cm on largest needles
57 sts x 30 rows = 7½" x 3½" / 19 cm x 9 cm on medium needles
57 sts x 30 rows = 7" x 3¼" / 18 cm x 8.5 cm on smallest needles

Garter Stitch:
26.5 sts and 80 rows = 4" / 10 cm on largest needles

Ribbing:
37 sts and 40 rows = 4" / 10 cm on medium needles

STITCH GUIDE

Shell Pattern
See Swatches #1 Chart Rows 1-8

Ovals & Arrows Pattern
See Swatches #1 Chart Rows 9-30

1x1 Rib
All rnds: [K1, p1] to end.

Garter Stitch
(worked flat)
Knit every row.

(worked in the rnd)
Rnd 1: Knit.
Rnd 2: Purl.
Rep Rnds 1-2 for patt.

Reverse Stockinette Stitch
RS rows: Purl.
WS rows: Knit.

TECHNIQUES

Full Fashion Raglan Decreases
Note: Right-slanting decs are worked at the beg of row; left-slanting decs are worked at end of row.

Single Decrease at each side (RS):
1. K1 (selv), k1, slip st back to LHN, insert RHN into 2nd st on LHN and lift it backward over the slipped stitch and off the needle, slip st p'wise back to the RHN.
2. Work in patt as estab to last 3 sts.
3. Sl1, k1, psso, k1 (selv). 2 sts dec total.

Double Decrease at each side (RS):
1. K1 (selv), ssk, slip st back to LHN, insert RHN into 2nd st on LHN and lift it backward over the slipped stitch and off the needle, slip st p'wise back to the RHN.
2. Work in patt as estab to last 4 sts.
3. Sl1, k2tog, psso, k1 (selv). 4 sts dec total.

NOTES
- A Garter stitch selvedge is worked at both edges of all pieces: Knit the first and last sts of every row.

INSTRUCTIONS

Back/ Front (make 2)
With largest needles CO 116 (135, 154, 173) sts.

Border
Work 5 rows in Garter st.

Next row (RS): Estab Shells patt from Row 1 of Swatches Chart as foll: K1 (selv), work 9 "plus" sts, pl mar, work 19-st patt rep 5 (6, 7, 8) times placing markers between reps, pl mar, work 10 "plus" sts, k1 (selv).

Cont in patt as estab, work Chart Rows 1-8 six times. (48 rows total)

Piece should measure about 6¼"/16 cm.

Shape Top of Hip
Change to medium needles and work Rows 1-8 twice more. (64 rows total)

Piece should measure about 8¼"/21 cm.

Waist

Change to smallest needles and beg Ovals & Arrows patt, working chart Rows 9-26 as estab. (82 rows total)

Piece should measure about 10¼"/26 cm.

Note: From this point you will work full chart reps, repeating Rows 1-30 of the Swatches Chart.

Waist-to-Bust Increase

Change to medium needles and work even for 18 rows, ending with chart row 14. (100 rows total)

Piece should measure about 12¼"/31 cm.

Bust

Change to largest needles and work even for 34 rows, ending with chart row 18 and dec 0 (1, 0, 1) st(s) at end of final row. (134 rows total) 116 (134, 154, 172) sts. Piece should measure about 16¼"/41 cm.

Shape Raglan Yoke

Note: Use Full Fashion Raglan Decreases – see Techniques Section.

Cont in patt and BO 7 sts at beg of next 2 rows, then dec 2 sts at beg and end of every RS row 0 (4, 10, 15) times, then dec 1 st at beg and end of every RS row 19 (19, 15, 12) times, then dec 1 st at beg and end of every other RS row 1 (0, 0, 0) time(s). 14 sts bound off; 40 (54, 70, 84) sts dec'd; 62 (66, 70, 74) sts rem. Place all sts on stitch holder.

Sleeves (make 2)

Sizes S, M, & L, use largest needles; size XL, use medium needles.

CO 78 (97, 97, 116) sts.

Border

Work 5 rows in Garter st.

Bell Cuff

Next row (RS): Estab Shells patt from Row 1 of Swatches Chart as foll: K1 (selv), work 9 "plus" sts, pl mar, work 19-st patt rep 3 (4, 4, 5) times placing markers between reps, pl mar, work 10 "plus" sts, k1 (selv).

Cont in patt as estab, work chart rows 1-8 six times. (48 rows total)

Sleeve should measure about 6¼"/16 cm.

Sizes S, M & L: change to medium needles; **Size XL:** cont with same needles.
Rep chart rows 1-8 twice more. (64 rows total)
Sleeve should measure about 8¼"/21 cm.

Top of Bell Cuff

All sizes, change to smallest needles and beg Ovals & Arrows patt, working chart Rows 9-26 as estab. (82 rows total)

Sleeve should measure about 10¼"/26 cm.

Note: From this point you will work full chart reps, repeating Rows 1-30 of the Swatches Chart.

Upper Arm Shaping

Sizes S & L only: Change to medium needles and cont in patt inc 1 st at beg and end of every 8th row 4 times, working new sts in Rev St st. 8 sts inc'd; 86 (-, 105, -) sts.

AT THE SAME TIME, change to largest needles after 18 rows (starting with chart row 15). After incs are complete (chart row 30), work 20 rows even, ending with chart row 18.

Sizes M & XL only: Change to medium needles and work even for 18 rows, ending with chart row 14.
Change to largest needles and work even for 34 rows, ending with chart row 18.
Sleeve should measure about 16¼"/41 cm.

Shape Raglan

Note: Use Full Fashion Raglan Decreases (described under Techniques section on page 173).

All Sizes: Bind off 7 sts at the beg of the next 2 rows. 72 (83, 91, 102) sts rem.

Sizes S, M & L: *Dec 1 st at beg and end of every RS row 4 (10, 12, -) times, then dec 0 sts on the foll RS row; rep from * 3 (1, 0, -) time(s) more, then dec 1 st at beg and end of every RS row 1 (1, 12, -) time(s). 34 (42, 48, -) sts dec'd; 38 (41, 43, -) sts rem. Place all sts on stitch holder.

Size XL: Dec 2 sts at beg and end of next RS row, then dec 1 st at beg and end of every RS row 26 times. 56 sts dec'd; 46 sts rem. Place all sts on stitch holder.

Finishing

Block pieces to measurements. Sew Sleeves to Back and Front along raglan edges. Sew side and sleeve seams.

Yoke

With smallest needle and RS facing, place held sts on needles as foll: 38 (41, 43, 46) sts for Left Sleeve; 62 (66, 70, 74) sts for Front; 38 (41, 43, 46) sts for Right Sleeve; 62 (66, 70, 74) sts for Back. 200 (214, 226, 240) sts total. Pl mar and join to work in the rnd.

Knit 1 rnd, inc 24 (26, 26, 32) sts as foll: *[K9 (9, 9, 7), M1] 4 (3, 9, 8) times, [k8, M1] 8 (10, 4, 8) times; rep from * once more to end. 224 (240, 252, 272) sts.

Change to medium needles and work in 1x1 rib for 16 rnds or 1½" (4cm).

Knit 1 rnd.

Changing to 24" (60 cm) circular needle, dec 40 (44, 46, 52) sts as foll: *[K4, k2tog] 12 (10, 11, 6) times, [k3, k2tog] 8 (12, 12, 20) times; rep from * once more to end. 184 (196, 206, 220) sts rem.

Knit 1 rnd.

Leave sts on needle and set aside.

Collar

With largest needle, CO 228 (266, 266, 304) sts, pl mar and join to work in the rnd, being careful not to twist the sts. Work 5 rnds in Garter st, beg and ending with a knit rnd.

Next rnd: Establish Shells patt from Row 1 of Swatches Chart as foll: work 19-st patt rep 12 (14, 14, 16) times, placing markers between reps.

Work Rows 1-8 three times, working all chart rows from right to left.

Change to medium needles and work Rows 1-8 three more times.

Change to smallest needles and work Rows 1-8 three more times.

Piece should measure about 8½"/21.5cm.

Change to medium needles and knit 1 rnd.

Next rnd, dec 44 (70, 60, 84) sts as foll: *[K4 (2, 2, 2), k2tog] 4 (28, 17, 26) times, [k3 (1, 3, 1), k2tog] 18 (7, 13, 16) times; rep from * once more to end. 184 (196, 206, 220) sts rem.

Knit 1 rnd even.

Assembly

With RS of both pieces facing and collar needle behind body needle (RS of collar to WS of body), hold needles together so sts are aligned, and use spare needle to work the 3-needle bind off seaming technique, joining the pieces.

Note: Collar is to be worn folded to the outside along the ribbing at the shoulders. Because silk is a non-resilient fiber, if the ribbing does not pull the piece in sufficiently at the shoulders, run three lines of elastic thread through the ribbing at the top, bottom and middle, threading the elastic thread through a tapestry needle and weaving it under the each knit stitch.

Weave in all ends.

Coquilles Pullover

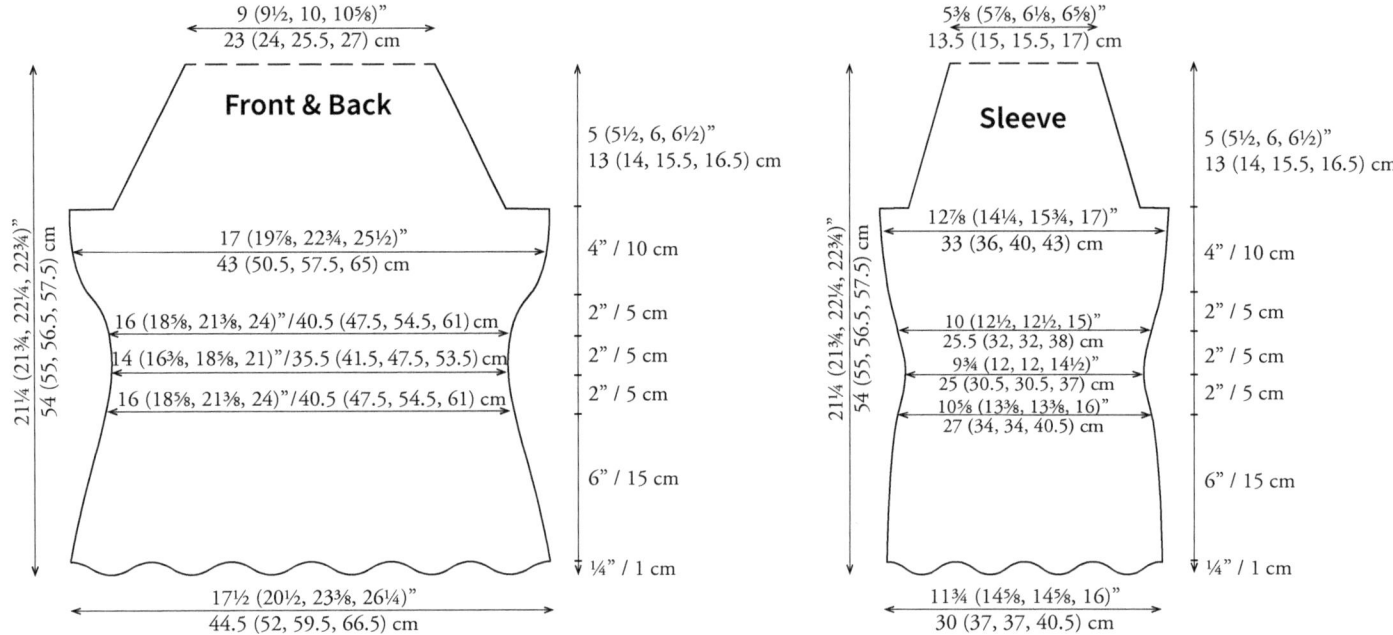

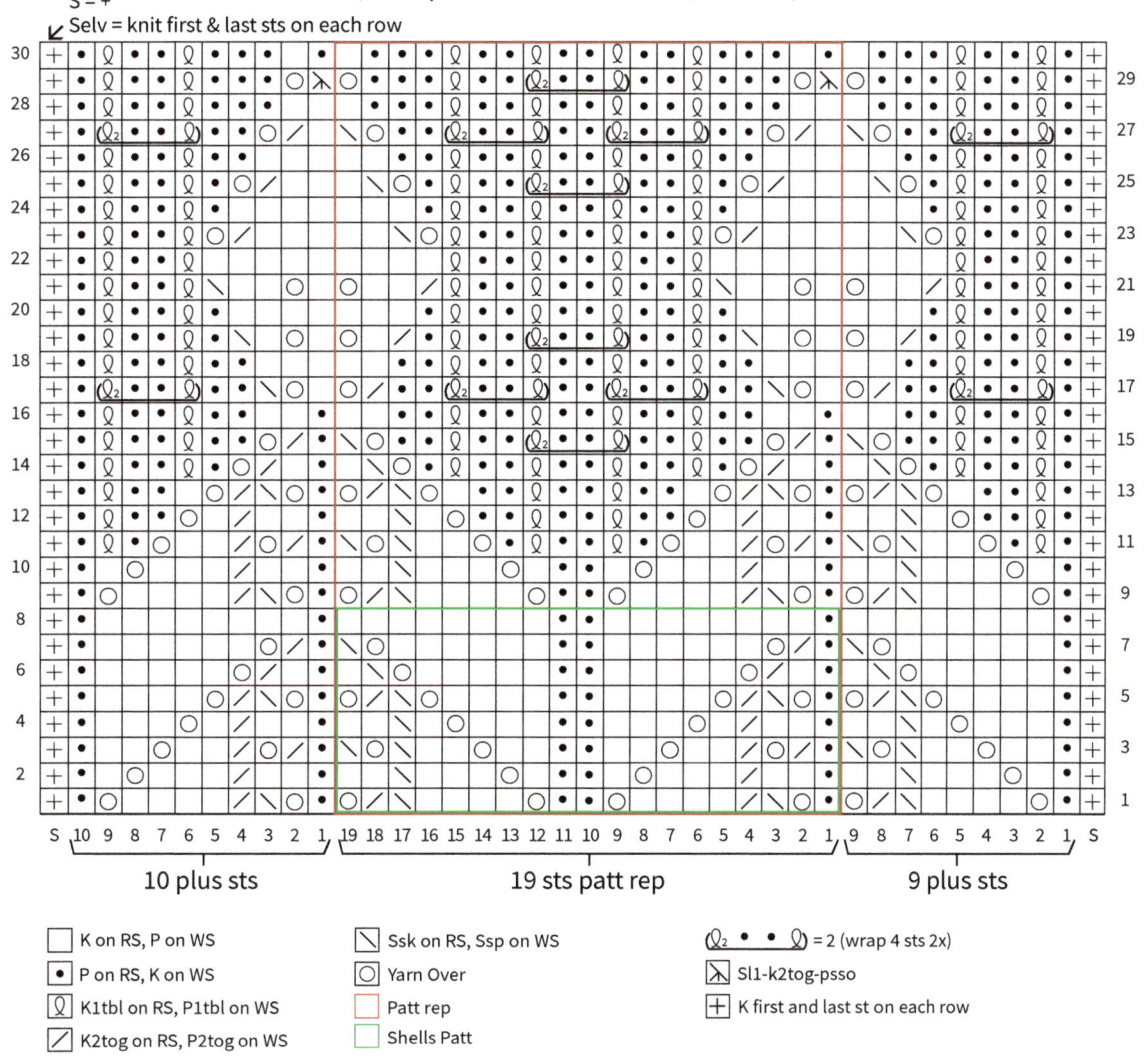

En Pointe Pullover

OLGA JANKELOVICH

FINISHED SIZES

Women's S (M, L)
Finished bust: 35½ (40½, 47¾)" / 87.5 (104.5, 121.5) cm
To fit bust sizes 28-30 (32-38, 40-44)" / 71-76 (81-96.5, 101.5-112) cm
Sample Size: M

YARN

Blue Sky Fibers Alpaca Silk (50% Alpaca / 50% Silk; 146 yds [133 m] / 1.75 oz / 50 g): #113 Ice, 7 (8, 9) skeins

NEEDLES

Size US 2 (2.75 mm)
Adjust needle size if necessary to obtain the correct gauge.

NOTIONS

stitch holders (4) or waste yarn; tapestry needle; Size D (3.25 mm) crochet hook; locking marker (optional)

GAUGES

Smiling Diamonds pattern:
22 sts and 20 rows = 3⅓" x 2½" / 8.5 x 6.5 cm (one patt rep)

STITCH GUIDE

Crab stitch (crochet edging)

Rnd 1: Single crochet – Insert hook into next st, yo hook and pull up a loop (2 loops on hook), yo hook and draw through both loops.

Rnd 2: Reverse single crochet – Work from left to right. Insert hook into next st to the right, yo hook and pull up a loop (2 loops on hook), yo hook and draw both loops.

NOTES

- Pullover is worked flat in pieces.
- Selvedge sts (k1 at beg and end of every row) are included in the charts.
- If desired, mark center stitch with locking marker and move the marker up periodically. Keeping track of the precise center is especially helpful when beginning the V-neck.

INSTRUCTIONS

Back

CO 5 sts. Work Smiling Diamonds Triangle chart for 51 (61, 71) rows, beg with WS Row 0 and repeating from Row 11 – 113 (135, 157) sts.

Estab Smiling Diamonds patt from Row 1 of chart as foll: K1 (selvedge st), work 1 "plus" st, work 22-st patt rep 5 (6, 7) times, k1 (selvedge st). Work entire chart 3 times – 60 rows total. Note single decrease at beg of chart row 20.

Shape armholes

Row 1 (RS): BO 1 st, omit first yo, k2togtbl, work in patt to last 4 sts, k2tog, omit yo, k2tog – 4 sts dec.
Row 2 (WS): K1, omit yo, p2tog, work in patt to last 3 sts, p2togtbl, omit yo, k1 – 2 sts dec.
Row 3: K1, omit yo, k2togtbl, work in patt to last 3 sts, k2tog, omit yo, k1 – 2 sts dec.
Rep last 2 rows 3 times more then rep Row 2 once more – 91 (113, 135) sts.

Size L only: Rep last 10 rows once more – 113 sts.

All sizes: Work even in patt for 40 rows.

Neck shaping

Next row (RS): Work 24 (35, 35) sts in patt, join a second ball of yarn, BO next 43 sts, work in patt to end – 24 (35, 35) sts each shoulder. Work each side separately for 9 more rows, then place sts on separate holders or waste yarn.

Front

Work as for Back to end of armhole decs – 91 (113, 113) sts.

Sizes M & L only: Work even in patt for 10 rows.

All sizes, beg V-neck shaping in next row (RS) as follows: Work in patt for 43 (54, 54) sts ending 2 sts before ctr, k3tog; join a second ball of yarn, k2togtbl, work in patt to end – 44 (55, 55) sts each side. Working each side separately, cont to dec 1 st at each neck edge for 8 more rows, working 2 edge sts as p2togtbl/k2togtbl at RF and p2tog/k2tog at LF – 36 (47, 47) sts.

Next row (WS): Work RF to last 3 sts, p3togtbl; beg LF p3togtbl, work to end – 34 (45, 45) sts.

Dec 1 st at each neck edge for 9 more rows, then in next row (WS) work p3togtbl at each neck edge (do not omit adjacent yo) – 24 (35, 35) sts.

Work even in patt for 30 (20, 20) rows, then place sts on separate holders or waste yarn.

Sleeves

CO 5 sts. Work Smiling Diamonds Triangle chart for 20 rows – 47 sts.

Estab Smiling diamonds patt for sleeves as foll: CO 22 sts at beg of next row, work Row 1 of Smiling Diamonds chart to end, working patt rep 3 times. CO 22 sts at end of row – 91 sts.

Sizes S/M only: Cont working even in patt for 119 more rows (6 chart reps total). Then work 10-row armhole shaping as for back three times (30 rows total) – 25 sts rem. BO all sts.

Size L only: Cont in patt for 89 more rows. At the same time, inc 1 st at beg and end of every 8th row 11 times, working new sts into pattern - 113 sts. Work even in patt for 20 rows, then work 10-row armhole shaping as for back four times (40 rows total) – 25 sts rem. BO all sts.

Finishing

Block pieces to measurements. Hold Front and Back with right sides together; join shoulders with 3-needle bind off. Set in sleeves, then sew underarm and side seams.

With crochet hook work Crab Stitch around neckline, cuffs and hem.

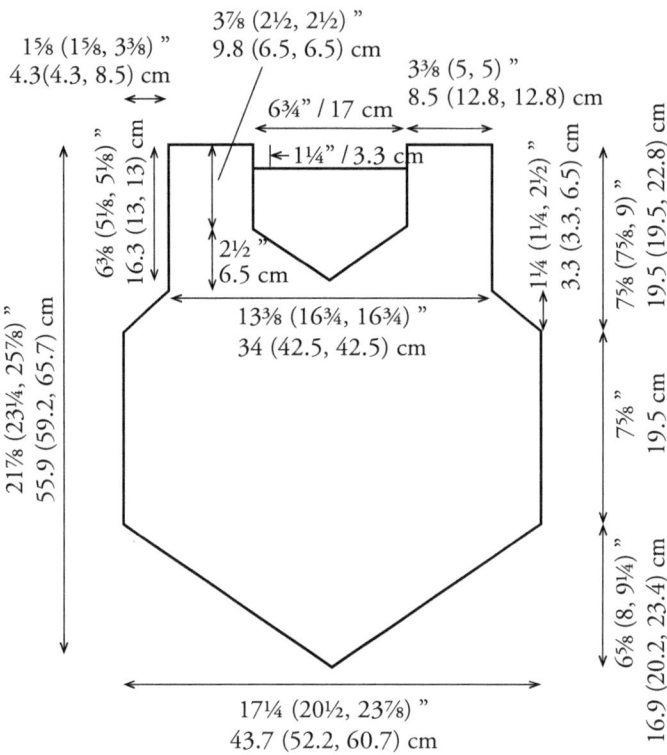

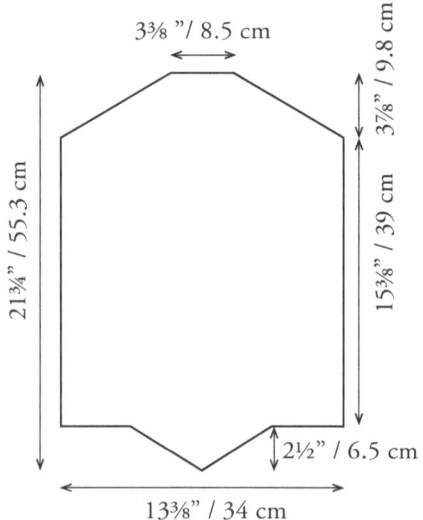

Smiling Diamonds Triangle Chart

- K on RS, P on WS
- P on RS, K on WS
- K1tb1 on RS, P1tb1 on WS
- Yarn Over
- P3tog
- K2tog
- Ssk
- Patt rep
- Selvedge stitch

Smiling Diamonds Chart

- K on RS, P on WS
- P on RS, K on WS
- K1tb1 on RS, P1tb1 on WS
- Yarn Over
- P3tog
- K2tog
- Ssk
- K first and last st on each row
- Patt rep

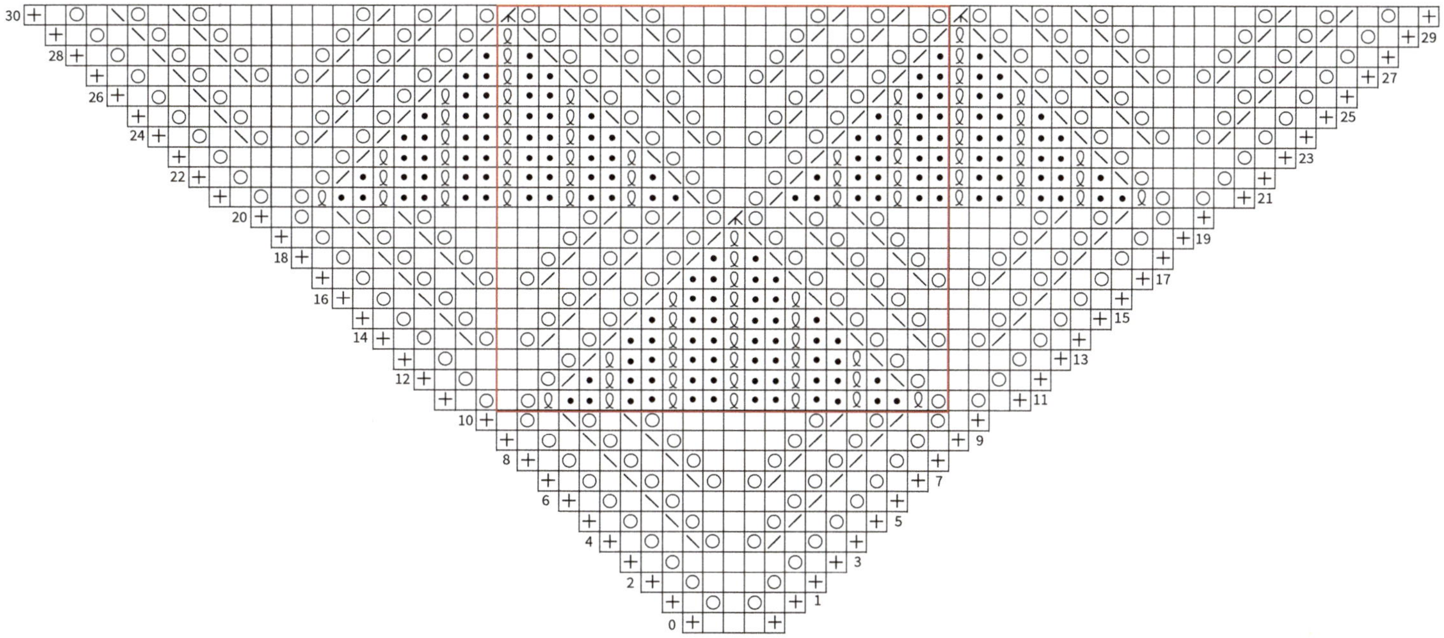

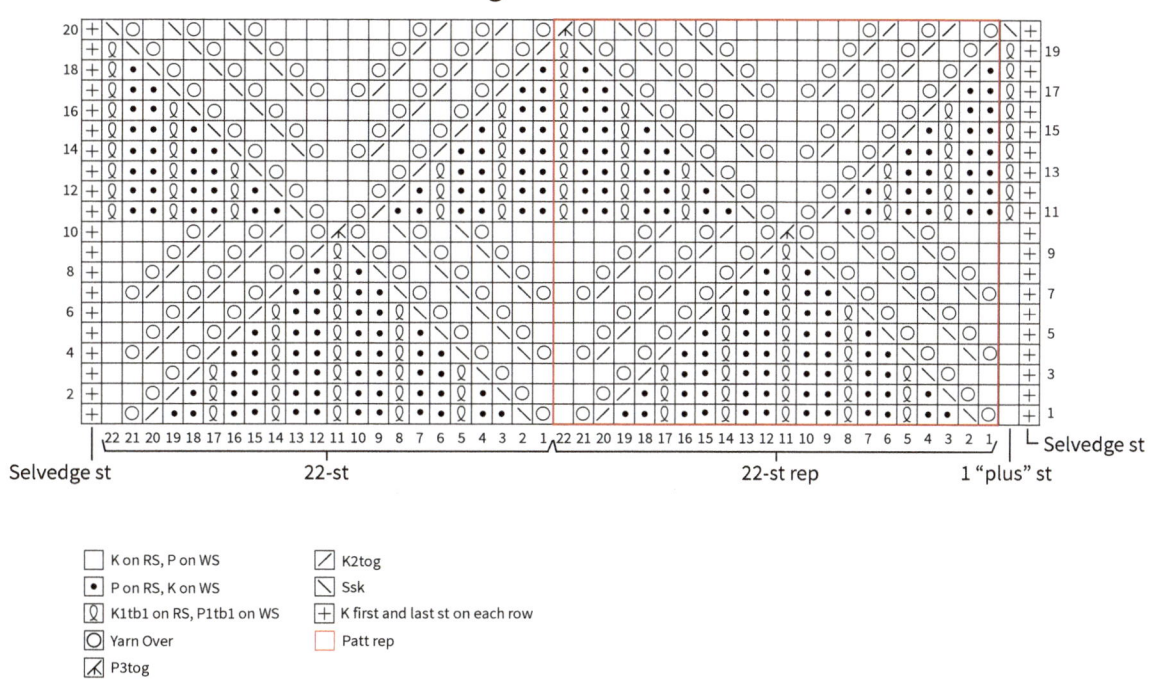

JOAN FORGIONE

Floating Triangles Hat & Cowl

FINISHED SIZE

Hat
Circumference: 18" / 45.5 cm
Height: 8½" / 21cm

Cowl
Circumference: 45¾" / 114.5 cm
Height: 9" / 22 cm

YARN

Neighborhood Fibers Studio DK Gradients (100% Merino wool / 720yds [658 m] / 10.5 oz / 300 g): Shades of Lilac, 1 set of 5 mini skeins (each 144 yd [132 m] / 2.25 oz / 60 g)

NEEDLES

Size US 4 (3.5 mm) - 16" (40 cm) circular or dpn's (for ribbing)
Size US 6 (4 mm) - 16" (40 cm) circular and/or dpn's (colorwork)
Adjust needle size if necessary to obtain the correct gauge.

NOTIONS

stitch marker; tapestry needle; pom pom (optional)

GAUGE

Ribbing:
24 sts and 38 rounds = 4" / 10 cm in 3x1 ribbing with smaller needles, blocked and slightly stretched'
Colorwork chart:
21 sts and 31 rounds = 4" / 10 cm in color pattern with larger needles, blocked and slightly stretched.

STITCH GUIDE

3x1 Ribbing
(worked in the round over a multiple of 4 sts)
Every rnd: [K3, p1] to end.

NOTES

- The hat and cowl are both worked in the round from the bottom up.
- The height of the hat or cowl can be adjusted by adding more rounds of ribbing, however, additional yarn will be necessary.
- The circumference of the cowl can be adjusted by casting on any multiple of 8 sts. Yardage will vary based on circumference.
- Colors are labeled A to E, dark to light.
- The subtle change in color pattern after Rnd 35 in the cowl chart is intended to avoid running short of any one color. If you have ample yardage available, you may replace Rnds 36-49 of the cowl chart with Rnds 16-29 of the hat chart, then finish with a rnd of color A.

INSTRUCTIONS

HAT

Ribbing

With smaller needles and color A, CO 96 sts, pl mar and join to work in the rnd, being careful not to twist. Work in 3x1 Ribbing for 1¼"/3 cm.

Body

Change to larger needles and work all rnds of Hat Chart, 12 times per rnd.

Crown

Remainder of hat is worked with color E only.

Rnd 1: [K2, sl2-k1-p2sso, k2, p1] to end - 72 sts rem.

Rnd 2: [K5, p1] to end.

Rnd 3: [K1, sl2-k1-p2sso, k1, p1] to end - 48 sts rem.

Rnd 4: [K3, p1] to end.

Rnd 5: [Sl2-k1-p2sso, p1] to end - 24 sts rem.

Rnd 6: [Ssk] to end– 12 sts rem.

Finishing

Cut 6"/15 cm tail, thread tapestry needle and weave yarn through rem sts. Cinch to close. Pull tail through to inside of hat and weave in all ends. Block to finished measurements. Sew on optional pom pom.

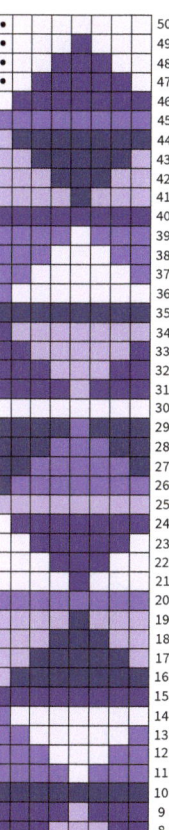
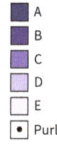

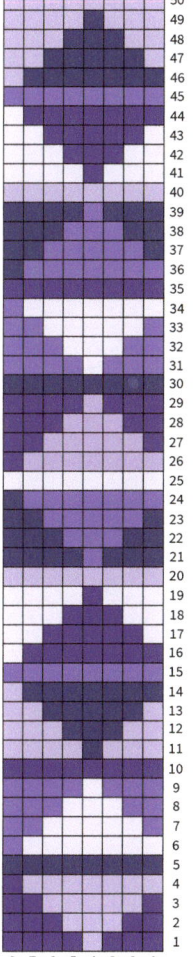

COWL

With smaller needles and color C, CO 240 sts, pl mar and join to work in the rnd, being careful not to twist. Work in 3x1 Ribbing for 1¼"/3 cm.

Change to larger needles and work all rnds of Cowl Chart, 30 times per rnd.

Change to smaller needles and cont with color D only. Work in 3x1 Ribbing for 1¼"/3 cm. BO all sts.

Finishing

Weave in all ends. Block to finished measurements.

FLOATING TRIANGLE HAT & COWL

LAURA ZUKAITE

Frost Flowers Pullover

FINISHED SIZES

Women's S (M, L)
Finished bust: 35½ (38¾, 44)" /88.5 (97, 110) cm
To fit bust sizes: 33-35 (36-38, 39-42)"/ 84-89 (91.5 -96.5, 99-106.5) cm

Sample Size: S

YARN

Artyarns Ensemble Light (50% silk / 50% cashmere; 400 yds [366 m] / 2.75 oz / 80 g): #307 Pale Sky, 3 (4, 4) skeins

NEEDLES

Size US 5 (3.75mm) – 24" (60 cm) circular needle
Adjust needle size if necessary to obtain the correct gauge.

NOTIONS

stitch markers; stitch holders (or scrap yarn); tapestry needle

GAUGES

Frost Flowers Pattern:
28 sts and 28 rows = 4" / 10 cm

Ribbing:
36 sts and 28 rows = 4" / 10 cm in 1x1 Rib

STITCH GUIDE

1x1 Rib
RS: [K1, p1] to end.
WS: Knit the knits and purl the purls.

YOKE PATTERN

(worked in the rnd over an even number of sts)
Rnd 1: Knit.
Rnd 2: Purl.
Rnd 3: [Yo, k2tog] to end.
Rnd 4: Purl.
Rnd 5: Knit.
Rep Rnds 1-5 for patt.

NOTES

- A Garter stitch selvedge is worked at both edges of all pieces until the armhole: Knit the first and last sts of every row. These sts are not shown on the charts but are included in the pattern instructions.
- When working the body, each size has its own Panel 1 chart. Panel 2 uses the same chart for all sizes. When working the sleeves, all sizes use the Size L Panel 1 chart, working 50 sts as indicated.
- Each row of Panel 2, whether RS or WS, is worked from right to left to center marker, then is worked in reverse with mirrored decreases. In odd rows, work chart as shown with ssk decreases, then work same row from right to left with k2tog decreases. In even rows, you will use p2tog decreases before the center marker, then work the second half of the row with p2togtbl decreases.
- Waist shaping is worked with ribbing rather than decreases, maintaining the pattern stitch in the center front and back.

INSTRUCTIONS

Back/Front (make 2)

CO 126 (138, 156) sts.
Work 1 WS row as follows: K1, p to last st, k1.

Lower Body

Estab patt from Panel 1 (Size S, M or L) Row 1 as foll: K1 (selvedge st), p1 (1 "plus" st), work 41- (45-, 51-) st patt rep 3 times, placing markers at beg and end of middle patt rep, k1 (selvedge st).

Size S: Work Rows 1-12, rep Rows 3-12 twice more, work Rows 13-15.
Size M: Work Rows 1-39.
Size L: Work Rows 1-43.

Waist Shaping

All sizes: Work rem 11 rows of Panel 1 as foll:

Next row (WS): K1 (selvedge st), k1 (extra rib st), [k1, p1] to m (1x1 Rib), sm, work chart patt rep one time only, sm, [p1, k1] to last 2 sts (1x1 Rib), k1 (extra rib st), k1 (selvedge st).

Next row (RS): K1, p1, work 1x1 Rib to m, work chart patt rep once, work 1x1 Rib to last 2 sts, p1, k1.

Remove markers on final WS row.

Upper Body

Estab upper body patt from Panel 2 (same chart for all sizes) Row 1 as foll:

K1 (selvedge st), p1 (rev St st edge), k5 (11, 20) (St st), pm, work 56 chart sts, pm, work same chart row in reverse with mirrored decreases (see Pattern Notes), pm, k5 (11, 20) (St st), p1 (rev St st), k1 (selvedge st).

Next row (WS): K1 (selvedge st), k1 (rev St st), work St st to m, work next chart row right to left, work same chart row in reverse with mirrored decreases, work St st to last 2 sts, k1 (rev St st), k1 (selvedge st).

Work even in patt, working Rows 1-28 twice, then rep Rows 1-4.

Shape Armholes

Shaping is worked by binding off sts at beg of each row and working equivalent number of k2tog's at end of row.

In rows with no bind offs, slip the first st and end k1.

Sizes S/M only: Remove first and last markers when necessary. Maintain patt as estab, eliminating sts from beg and end of chart rows as they are bound off/decreased.

Row 5 (RS): BO3, work in patt as estab to last 6 sts, [k2tog] 3 times – 120 (132, 150) sts rem.

Row 6: BO1, work in patt to last 2 sts, k2tog – 118 (130, 148) sts rem.

Row 7: BO2, work in patt to last 4 sts, [k2tog] 2 times – 114 (126, 144) sts rem.

Work all rem chart rows and at the same time BO/dec 1 st at beg/end of next 4 rows, then every RS row 4 (6, 8) times – 98 (106, 120) sts rem.

Place all sts on stitch holder.

Sleeves (make 2)

CO 62 (66, 70) sts.

Work 1 WS row as follows: K1, p to last st, k1.

Row 1 (RS): K1 (selvedge st), p1 (rev St st), k4 (6, 8) (St st), pm, work first 25 sts of Panel 1 Size L sleeve sts, pm for center sleeve, work rem 25 chart sts, pm, k4 (6, 8) (St st), p1 (rev St st), k1 (selvedge st).

Row 2 (WS): K1 (selvedge st), k1 (rev St st), work St st to m, work next chart row to last m, work St st to last 2 sts, k1 (rev St st), k1 (selvedge st).

Work Rows 3-43 in patt as estab, working sleeve incs and shaping armholes as instructed below.

Note: In Rows 44-46 the first and last 2 sts are worked as estab, but the St st sections are omitted so that the patt st extends across. (You may have to remove the first and last markers, and replace them before/after the center 50 sts when repeating Row 1.)

Row 44 (WS): K all sts.

Row 45 – 1st time (even number of sts to ctr marker): K1, p1, k1, work chart to last 3 sts, k1, p1, k1.

Row 45 – 2nd time (odd number of sts to ctr marker): K1, p1, work chart to last 2 sts, p1, k1.

Row 46: K all sts.

Rep Rows 1-46.

At the same time on Row 15 (first time) begin incs as foll: K1, p1, m1R, work in patt to last 2 sts, m1L, p1, k1 – 2 sts increased. Cont in patt and rep inc row every 10 rows 7 (8, 9) more times – 78 (84, 90) sts, then work even for 29 (23, 15) more rows. End Row 22 (26, 28). Sleeve measures approx. 16½ (17, 17¼)"/41 (42.5, 43) cm.

Shape Armholes

In rows with no bind offs, slip the first st and end k1. Remove markers as necessary.

Next row (RS): BO3, work in patt to last 6 sts, [k2tog] 3 times – 72 (78, 84) sts rem.

Next row (WS): BO1, work in patt to last 2 sts, k2tog – 70 (76, 82) sts rem.

Next row (RS): BO2, work in patt to last 4 sts, [k2tog] 2 times – 66 (72, 78) sts rem.

BO/dec 1 st at beg/end of next 4 rows – 58 (64, 70) sts rem.

BO/dec 1 st at beg/end of every RS row 4 (5, 4) times - 50 (54, 62) sts rem. End chart row 37 (43, 43).

Size S only: Work rem 9 rows of Panel 2, beg each row with sl1.

Size M only: Knit 1 row then work Row 45 as follows: BO1, work chart over next 50 sts, k2tog – 52 sts rem. Knit 1 row, then work 4 rows in St st.

Size L only: Knit 1 row then work Row 45 as follows: BO1, [yo, ssk] to ctr marker, [k2tog, yo] to last 2 sts, k2tog – 60 sts rem. Knit 1 row. Work in St st for 6 rows and at the same time BO/dec 1 st at beg/end of RS rows – 54 sts rem.

Place rem sts on stitch holder.

Finishing

Block pieces to measurements. Sew Front to Back along side seams. Sew sleeve seams then set in sleeves.

Yoke

Place 98 (106, 120) Back sts on needle, pm, then place 50 (52, 54) Left Sleeve sts on needle, pm, place Front sts on needle, pm, place rem slv sts on needle - 296 (316, 348) sts. Join to work in the rnd.

Work 1 dec rnd as follows: *[Ssk, k8] 4 (5, 5) times, ssk, k14 (2,16), [k2tog, k8] 4 (5, 5) times, k2tog, sm, [ssk, k5] 3 (3, 3) times, ssk, k4 (6, 8), [k2tog, k5] 3 (3, 3) times, k2tog; rep from * once more – 88 (94, 108) sts each Back /Front; 42 (44, 46) sts each sleeve; 260 (276, 308) sts total.

Work 5-rnd yoke patt then work dec rnd as follows: *[Ssk, k7] 4 (5, 5) times, ssk, k12 (0, 14), [k2tog, k7] 4 (5, 5) times, k2tog, sm, [ssk, k4] 3 (3, 3) times, ssk, k2 (4, 6), [k2tog, k4] 3 (3, 3) times, k2tog; rep from * once more – 78 (82, 96) sts each Back/Front; 34 (36, 38) sts each sleeve; 224 (236, 268) sts total.

Work 5-rnd yoke patt then work dec rnd as follows: *[Ssk, k6] 4 (4, 5) times, ssk, k10 (14, 12), [k2tog, k6] 4 (4, 5) times, k2tog, sm, [ssk, k3] 3 (3, 3) times, ssk, k0 (2, 4), [k2tog, k3] 3(3, 3) times, k2tog; rep from * once more – 68 (72, 84) sts each Back/Front; 26 (28, 30) sts each sleeve; 188 (200, 228) sts total.

Work 5-rnd yoke patt then work dec rnd as follows: *[Ssk, k4] 5 (5, 6) times, ssk, k4 (8, 8), [k2tog, k4] 5 (5, 6) times, k2tog, sm, [ssk, k2] 2 (3, 3) times, ssk, k6 (0, 2), [k2tog, k2] 2 (3, 3) times, k2tog; rep from * once more – 56 (60, 70) sts each Back/Front; 20 (20, 22) sts each sleeve; 152 (160, 186) sts total.

Work 5-rnd yoke patt then work dec rnd as follows: *[Ssk, k3] 5 (5, 6) times, ssk, k2 (6, 6), [k2tog, k3] 5 (5, 6) times, k2tog, sm, [ssk, k1] 2 (2, 3) times, ssk, k4 (4, 0), [k2tog, k1] 2 (2, 3) times, k2tog; rep from * once more – 44 (48, 56) sts each Back/Front; 14 (14, 14) sts each sleeve; 116 (124, 140) sts total.

Size S only: Work Rnds 1-4 of yoke patt, then BO all sts knitwise in next rnd.

Size M only: Work 5-rnd yoke patt, then knit 1 rnd, purl 1 rnd, then BO all sts knitwise in next rnd.

Size L only: Work 9 rnds in yoke patt, then BO all sts knitwise in next rnd.

Block the yoke. Weave in all ends.

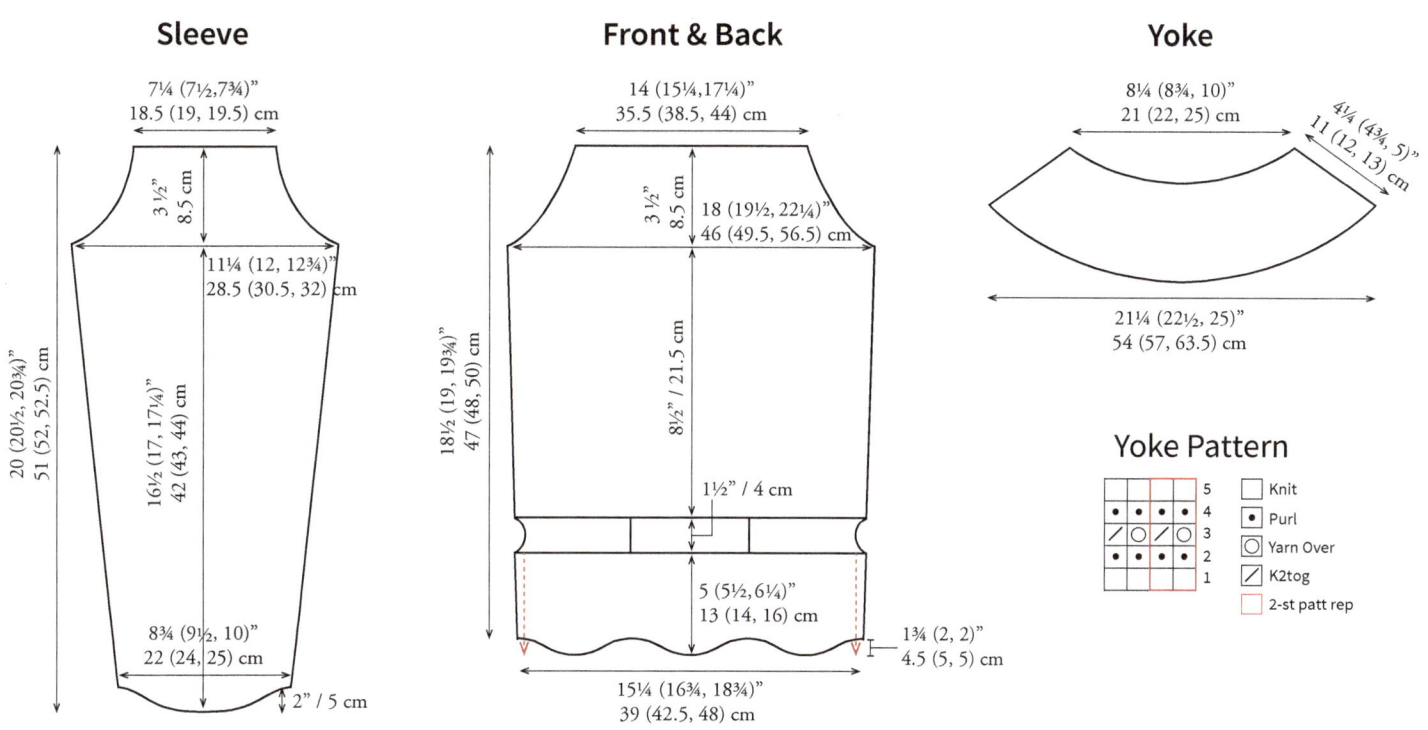

Panel 1 Size S

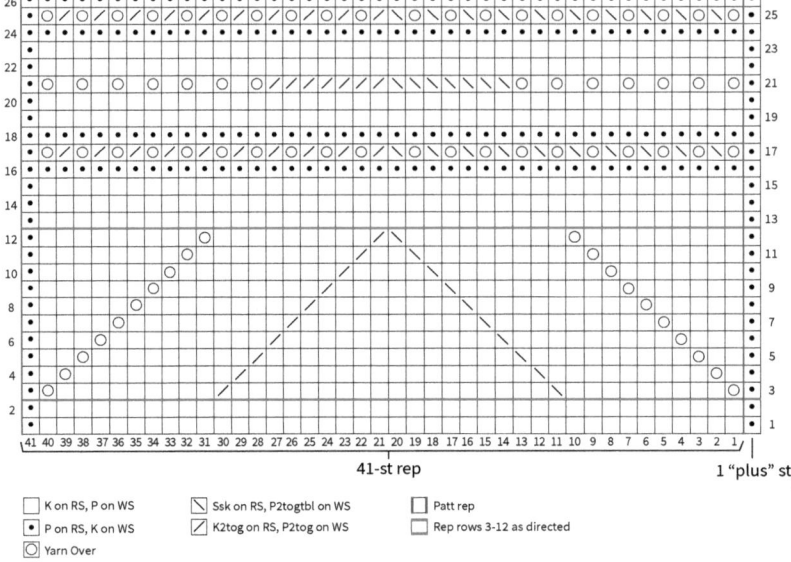

Panel 1 Size M

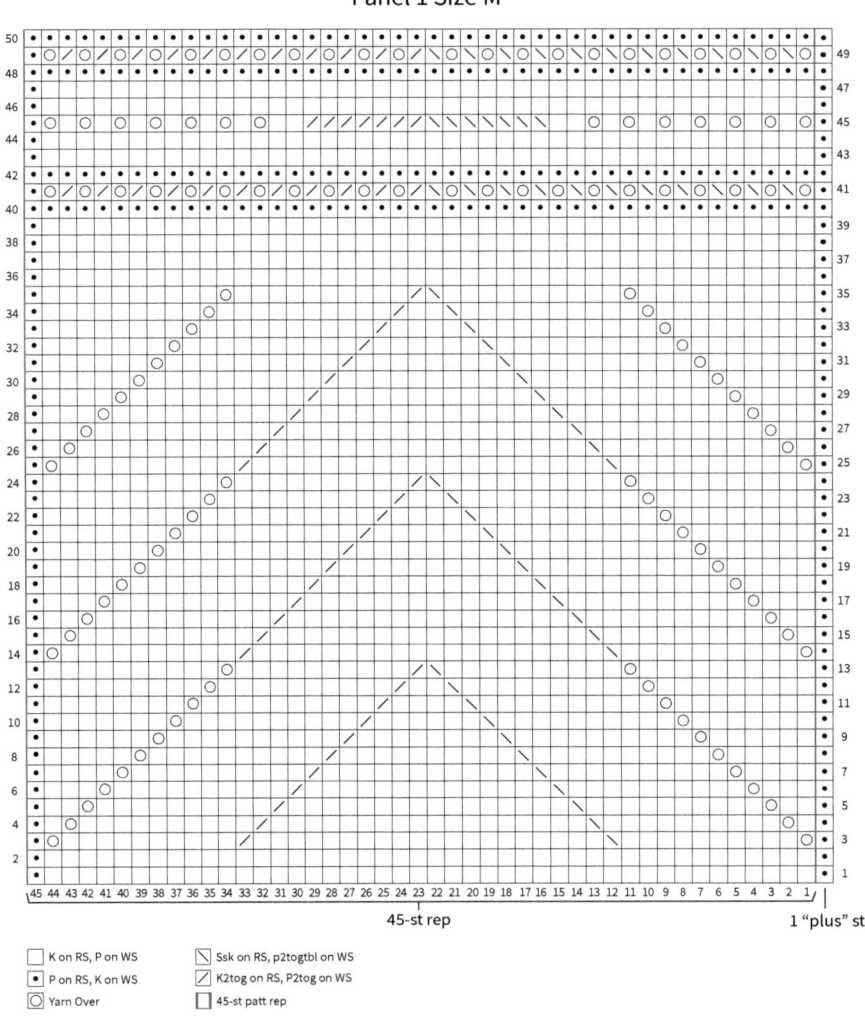

Panel 1 Size L & Sleeves (all sizes)

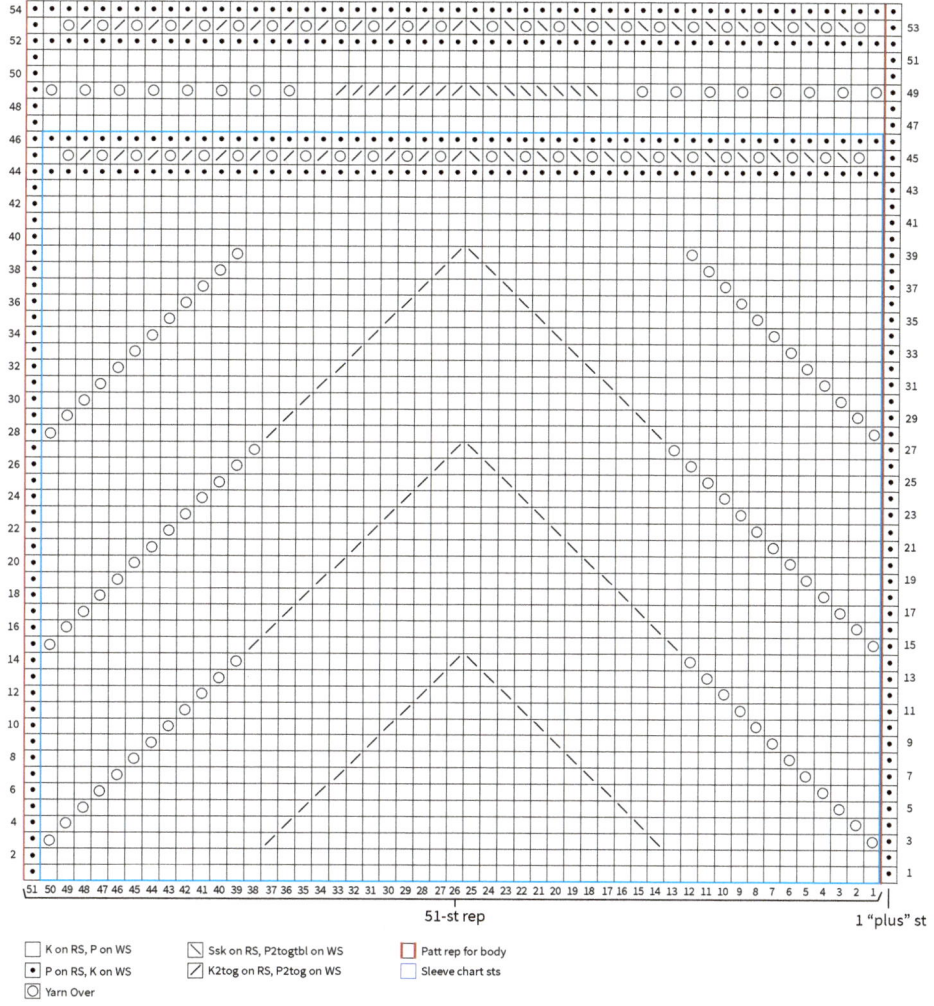

- ☐ K on RS, P on WS
- • P on RS, K on WS
- ○ Yarn Over
- ◺ Ssk on RS, P2togtbl on WS
- ◸ K2tog on RS, P2tog on WS
- ▭ Patt rep for body
- ▭ Sleeve chart sts

Panel 2 All Sizes

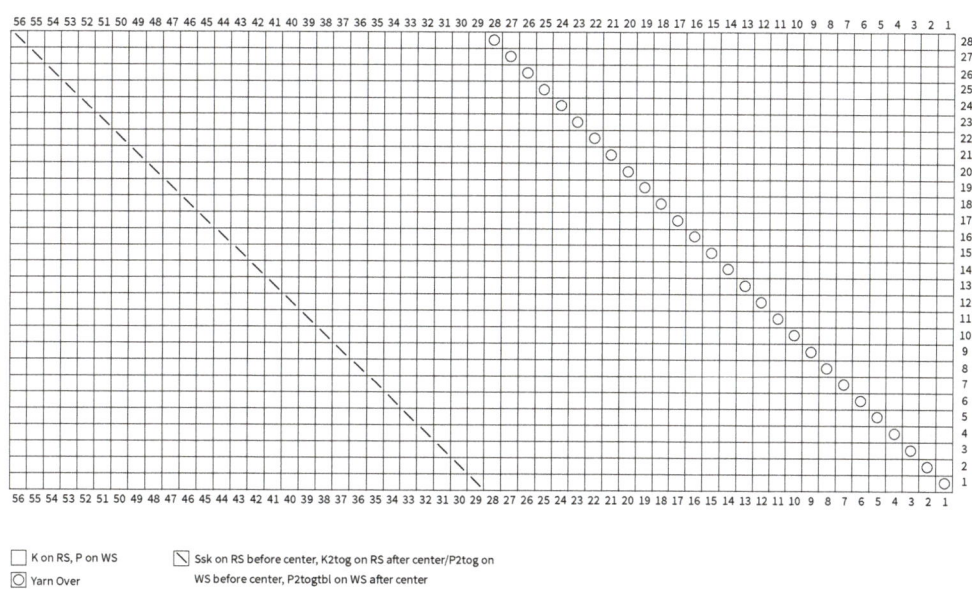

- ☐ K on RS, P on WS
- ○ Yarn Over
- ◺ Ssk on RS before center, K2tog on RS after center/P2tog on WS before center, P2togtbl on WS after center

FROST FLOWERS PULLOVER | 189

GALE PAGE

Gothic Tracery Cardigan

FINISHED SIZES

Sizes: S (M, L, XL)
Finished bust: 36¼ (38¼, 42¾, 46½)" / 92.5 (97, 108.5, 118.5) cm
To fit bust 32-33 (34-36, 37-39, 40-44)" / 80-85 (86-92, 94-99, 102-112) cm

Sample Size: M

YARN

Valley Yarns Northfield 70% Merino / 20% Baby Alpaca / 10% Silk: 124 yds [13 m] / 1.75 oz / 50 g): color Natural, 12 (12, 14, 16) balls

NEEDLES

US 4 (3.5 mm) or size to obtain gauge.

NOTIONS

cable needle
stitch markers
tapestry needle
buttons: 3 - 3¾" / 19 mm buttons

GAUGES

25 sts and 32 rows in Lace pattern = 4" / 10 cm, blocked

STITCH GUIDE

1) Stockinette Selvedge: K on RS, p on WS
2) Yarn-over Selvedge

NOTES

- It is highly recommended that you knit a practice swatch of at least 10" (25 cm), and preferably 12" (30 cm), to establish gauge and get familiar with the stitch pattern before beginning sweater. The wraps should be made with a very firm tension.

- One leaf pattern has 16-st rep with 8-st halves, and each half has a yo-dec pair. When you have partial repeats (fewer than 8 sts) at the ends of work and can't work this yo-dec pair, omit the yo or replace the dec with a k or p st to keep the st count constant.

- As a rule, all inc and dec should be worked just inside the selvedge, however, when you become familiar with the stitch pattern, you may find ways to inc or dec that take advantage of the design. The important thing is to make the pattern look continuous right up to the selvedge edge, and to shape invisibly when you can. For example, if you need to dec 1 st, and the stitch pattern calls for a yo at the end of the row, simply skip working the yo and you will have dec'd 1 st. Avoid working yo's on the first and last sts of the row. If the pattern calls for a yo, and you need a stitch to maintain the proper st count, make a st; this will avoid the hole that the yo would create.

- On both front sections, the front center border consists of a 2-st yo selvedge and a 3 sts button band, 5 sts in total. This band is worked as you go, thus there is no attached button band to work at the end.
- There are 3 buttonholes in this design. Make whatever method of buttonhole you prefer, but it should be unobtrusive and blend into the lace design. Instructions for a 2-row eyelet buttonhole are given here. This makes a very small, almost invisible, buttonhole located between the two twisted stitches in the front band.

INSTRUCTIONS

Back

CO 119 (127, 139, 151) sts and p 1 row. Do not count these preliminary rows in row count.

On next row (RS), establish patt using Body and Sleeve Chart as foll: K1 (selv), starting at stitch 6 (2, 12, 6) through st 16, then work 6 (6, 8, 8) full rep of 16-st patt placing mars at the end of each rep, work 10 (14, 4, 10) more st(s), k1 (selv)

Work even for 6 more rows, ending with a WS row (7 rows worked in total).

Shape Waist

On next row (WS), dec 1 st at each side. Then dec every 5th row 1 (1, 3, 5) more time(s), then dec every 4th row 7 (7, 5, 3) times, 101 (109, 121, 133) sts rem. 41 (41, 43, 45) rows worked.

Work patt as set for 13 rows (about 1½" / 4 cm), ending with a WS row.

On next row (RS), inc 1 st each side. Then inc 1 st each side every 8th row 4 (2, 2, 0) times, then inc every 9th row 1 (3, 3, 5) time(s). 113 (121, 133, 145) sts on needle. 96 (98, 100, 104) total rows worked.

Work even for 16 rows (2"/ 5 cm), ending with a WS row. Back should measure 14 (14¼, 14½, 15)" / 35.5 (36, 37, 38) cm, 112 (114, 116, 120) rows worked.

Shape Armholes

BO 5 (5, 5, 6) sts at the beg of the next 2 rows, then BO 3 (3, 3, 4) sts at the beg of the next 2 rows, then BO 2 (2, 2, 3) sts at the beg of the next 2 rows, then BO 2 sts at the beg of the next 0 (0, 2, 2) rows, then BO 1 st at the beg of the next 2 (4, 4, 6) rows. 8 (10, 12, 14) rows worked in total for armhole.

Then re-establish selvedge sts, and work even for 60 (60, 64, 66) rows on rem 91 (97, 105, 109) sts. On next RS row, work 21 (24, 27, 29) sts, BO next 49 (49, 51, 51) sts for back neck, and work rem 21 (24, 27, 29) sts. Place right and left shoulder sts on holder. 180 (184, 192, 200) rows worked in total. Back should measure 22½ (23, 24, 25)" / 57 (58.5, 61, 63.5) cm.

Left Front

CO 65 (69, 75, 81) sts and p 1 row. Do not include these preliminary rows in row count.

Front Band: 5 sts in total, including a 2-st yo selvedge and 3-st button band

RS: p1, k1tbl twice, k2.

WS: hold yarn in back as if to k, then yarn forward over the top of the needle making a yo, p2tog (1 yo and 1 dec'd st on needle), p1tbl twice, k1.

Row 1 (RS): Set up row as foll: K1 (selv), start Body and Sleeve Chart at stitch 6 (2, 12, 6) through st 16, then work 3 (3, 4, 4) full rep, work front band, placing mars at the end of each patt rep and at front band.

Work 6 rows in patt (7 rows worked in total).

Shape Waist

On next row (WS), dec 1 st at side seam. Then dec every 5th row 1 (1, 3, 5) time(s), then dec every 4th row 7 (7, 5, 3) times, 56 (60, 66, 72) sts rem, 41 (41, 43, 45) rows worked in total.

Work patt as set for 13 rows (about 1½" / 4 cm), ending with a WS row.

On next row (RS), inc 1 st at side seam, then inc 1 st every 8th row 4 (2, 2, 0) more times, then inc 1 st every 9th row 1 (3, 3, 5) time(s). 62 (66, 72, 78) sts on needle, 96 (98, 100, 104) total rows worked.

Work even for 16 rows (2" / 5 cm), ending with a WS row. Front should measure 14 (14¼, 14½, 15)" / 35.5 (36, 37, 38) cm, 112 (114, 116, 120) rows worked.

Shape armholes

Match armhole shaping as described for back over the next 8 (10, 12, 14) rows. 51 (54, 58, 60) sts rem. Work next 5 (5, 9, 11) rows in patt as set ending with a RS row. Front should measure 15¾ (16¼, 17¼, 18¼)" / 40 (41, 44, 46.5) cm, 125 (129, 137, 145) rows worked.

V-neck shaping

On next row (WS), BO 6 sts including the 5 front band sts and work in patt to end. Work V-neck using a Sloped BO to create a tight, firm edge. This will make attaching the collar easier. Dec 1 st at neck edge every other row 22 (22, 25, 25) times, then every 3rd row 2 (2, 0, 0) times, ending with a WS row. 21 (24, 27, 29) sts remain. 176 (180, 188, 196) rows worked in total. Work next 4 rows in patt without shaping. Garment should measure 22 ½ (23, 24, 25)" / 57 (58.5, 61, 63.5) cm. 180 (184, 192, 200) rows worked in total. Place rem shoulder sts on separate holder.

Right Front

CO 65 (69, 75, 81) sts and p 1 row. Do not include these preliminary rows in row count.
Front Band: 5 sts in total, including a 2-st yo selvedge and 3-st button band
RS – hold yarn in front as if to purl, then yarn back, ssk (1 yo and 1 dec'd st on needle), ktbl twice, p1.
WS – p2, p1tbl twice, k1.

Row 1 (RS): Set up row as foll: work the 5-st front band, p1, work 3 (3, 4, 4) full patt rep of Body and Sleeve Chart, placing mars between patt reps work 10 (14, 4, 10) sts, k1 (selv), placing mars between patt rep.

Work as for left front, reversing shaping until piece measures 12¼ (12¾, 13¾, 14¾)" / 31.5 (32.5, 35, 38) cm and you have worked 99 (103, 111, 119) rows.

Buttonholes

*Work next WS row until 3 sts rem on LHN. Work a yo and complete the row. Next row, work 2 sts and with yarn in back, slip the next st as if to k. P into the yo but do not drop it from the LHN. Pass the slipped st over the st just worked. Transfer the st from RHN to LHN. K2tog. Buttonhole complete. Work the rest of the row in patt as set, while shaping armhole**.

Work 10 more rows and rep between * and ** for second buttonhole.

Work 10 more rows and rep between * and ** for third buttonhole. Work next row in patt. 126 (130, 138, 146) rows worked.

At the same time, beg armhole shaping when you have worked 112 (114, 116, 120) rows and garment measures 14 (14¼, 14½, 15)" / 35.5 (36, 37, 38) cm.

Begin V-neck shaping following instructions and reverse shaping as for left front. Work last 3 rows in patt without shaping. Place rem 21 (24, 27, 29) sts on holder.

Sleeves

CO 47 (49, 55, 59) sts and p 1 row. Don't count these preliminary rows in row count.
Row 1 (RS): K1 (selv), beg Body and Sleeve Chart with st 10 (9, 14, 12), pl mar, then, work 2 (2, 3, 3) full rep

placing marker(s) between rep, work 6 (7, 2, 4) sts, k1 (selv).
Cont patt as set for 11 rows, ending with a WS row.

On next row (RS), inc 1 st at each side, then every 6th (6th, 6th, 5th) row 19 (19, 19, 6) more times, then for XL only, every 6th row 0 (0, 0, 14) times. 87 (89, 95, 101) sts on needle.

Work even for 13 (17, 17, 17) rows. 140 (144, 144, 144) rows worked in total. Sleeve should measure 17½ (18, 18, 18)" / 44.5 (45.5, 45.5, 45.5) cm from Row 1.

Shape cap

BO 5 (5, 5, 6) sts at the beg of the next 2 rows, 3 sts at the beg of the next 2 rows, 2 sts at the beg of the next 4 (2, 2, 2) rows. 63 (69, 75, 79) sts rem, 8 (6, 6, 6) rows worked.

Then, dec 1 st at each edge every RS row 16 (18, 21, 22) times (XL only: work a RS row without dec once). 31 (33, 33, 35) sts rem, 40 (42, 48, 52) cap rows worked in total. BO 3 sts at the beg of the next 4 rows, then BO rem 19 (21, 21, 23) sts.

Collar

Collar is worked in two sections and joined at center back with a 3-needle BO. Collar is shaped using short rows to make attaching to the sweater body easier.

Left Collar

Make a slip knot on the left hand needle, and work patt as shown on chart through Row 44.

Next row (RS): work Row 45 of leaf patt, then p9, k1.

Next row (WS): p1, k9, work Row 46.

Next row (RS-WS): work Row 47 of patt rep, p6 to last 4 sts of row, with yarn in front, sl next st to RHN, yarn back, return slipped st to LHN, turn work (W&T complete), k6, work Row 48 of leaf patt.

Work Rows 49-50 as set.

Next row (RS-WS): work Row 51 of patt rep, p6 to the last 4 sts of row, W&T, k6, and work Row 52.

Work Rows 53-54 as set.

Cont in this manner through Row 74, working short rows every 4th row. Then return to Row 45 and cont short row shaping every 4th row. At the end of Row 51, pl mar for shoulder seam. Rep short rows at Rows 53-54 (=last short row). 10 short rows worked in total.

Work Rows 55-74, then Rows 45 to 52 (52, 54, 54) in patt as set. 112 (112, 114, 114) rows worked in total. Place sts on a holder.

Right Collar

Make a slip knot on the left hand needle, and work patt as shown on chart through Row 44.

Next row (RS): k1, p9, work Row 45.

Next row (WS): work Row 46, k9, p1.

Next row (RS): k1, p9, work Row 47.

Next row (WS-RS): work Row 48 of chart, k6 to the last 4 sts of row, W&T, p6, work Row 49.

Work rows 50-51 as set.

Cont in this manner through Row 74, working short rows every 4th row. Return to Row 45 and cont short row shaping every 4th row. At the end of Row 50, pl mar for shoulder seam. Rep short row at Rows 54-55 (=last short row). 10 short rows worked in total.

Work Rows 56-74, then Rows 45 to 61 (61, 63, 63) in patt as set. 111 (111, 113, 113) rows worked in total. Place sts on a holder.

Finish Collar

Place right sides of collar pieces together, and using 3-needle BO, attach left collar to right collar beg at the outside edge.

Finishing

Block all pieces to measurements in schematic. Sew shoulder seams using 3-needle BO, placing right sides together, and starting at the neck edge. Sew side seams and sleeve seams. Attach sleeves to body. Pin center back of collar to center back of sweater. Pin collar around neck evenly and sew in place. Sew buttons in place.

Gothic Tracery Cardigan Back

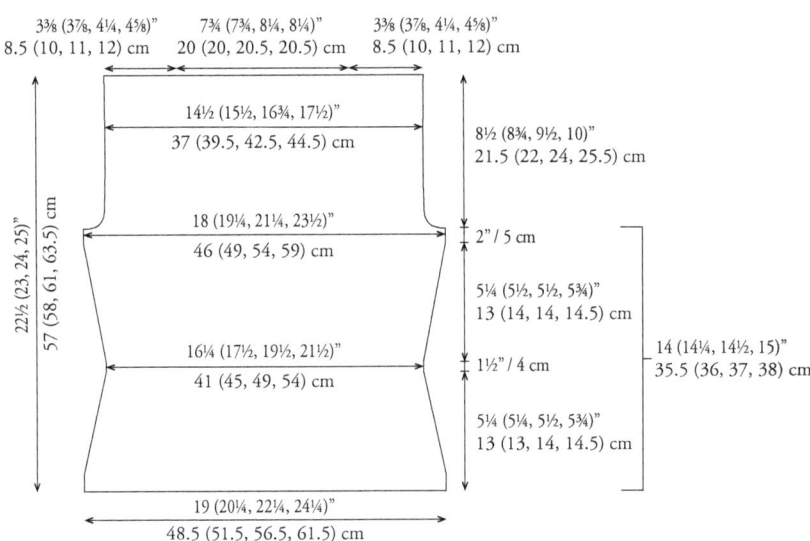

Gothic Tracery Cardigan Left Front

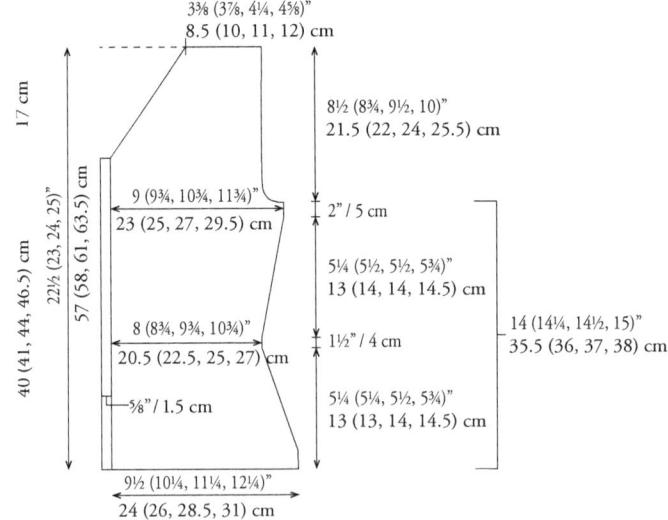

Gothic Tracery Body and Sleeve Chart
(mult of 16+15 / 30 rows)

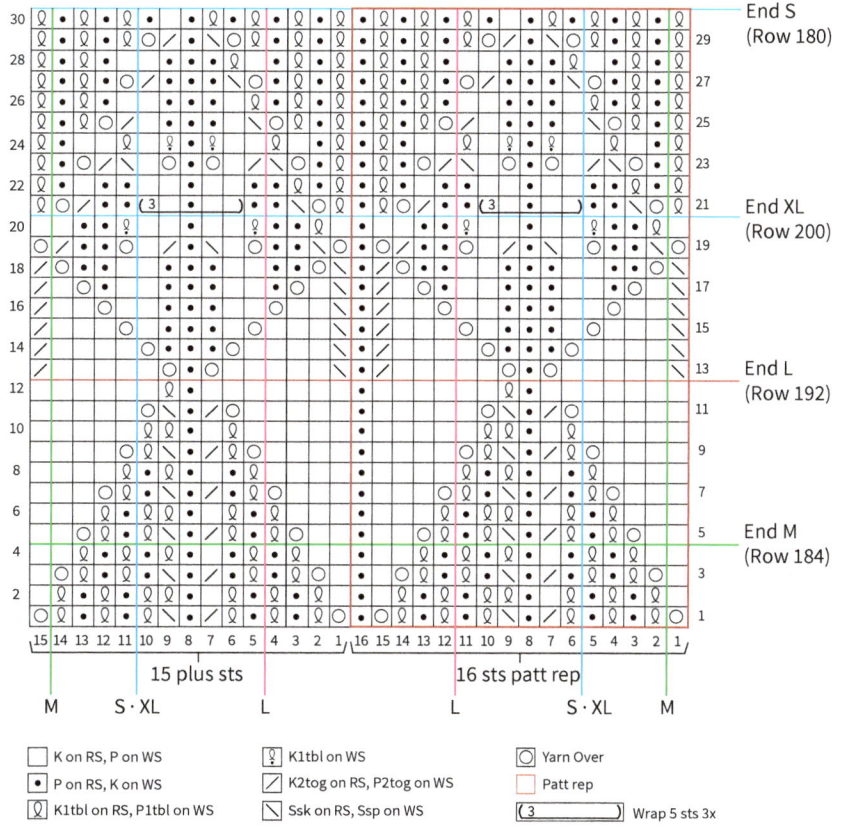

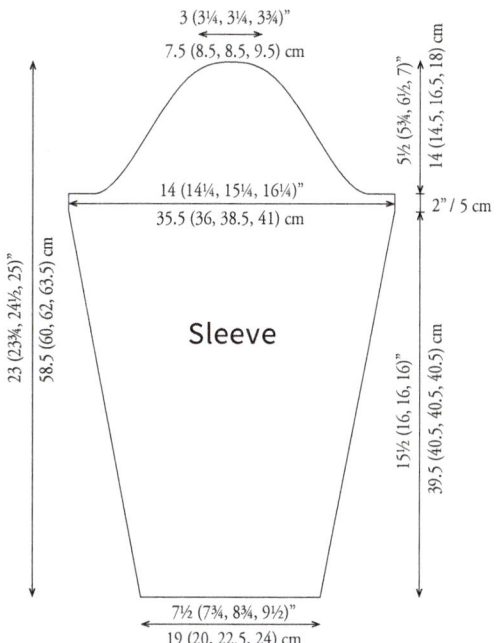

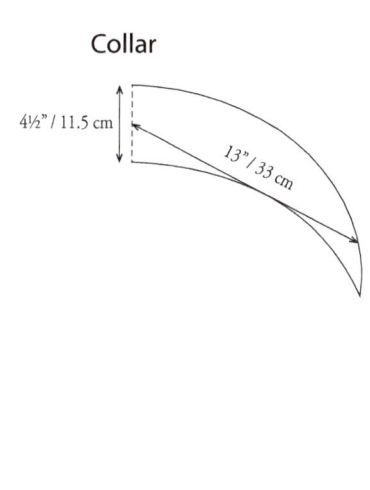

Gothic Tracery Cardigan
Left Collar

Left Collar Short Rows

Legend:
- ☐ K on RS, P on WS
- • P on RS, K on WS
- ○ Yarn Over
- ╲ Ssk on RS, Ssp on WS
- ╱ K2tog on RS, P2tog on WS
- ℚ K1tbl on RS, P1tbl on WS
- V K1f&b
- M1 on RS, M1 pwise on WS
- M1 pwise on RS, M1 on WS
- Wrap and turn
- ▨ No stitch
- ▢ Patt rep

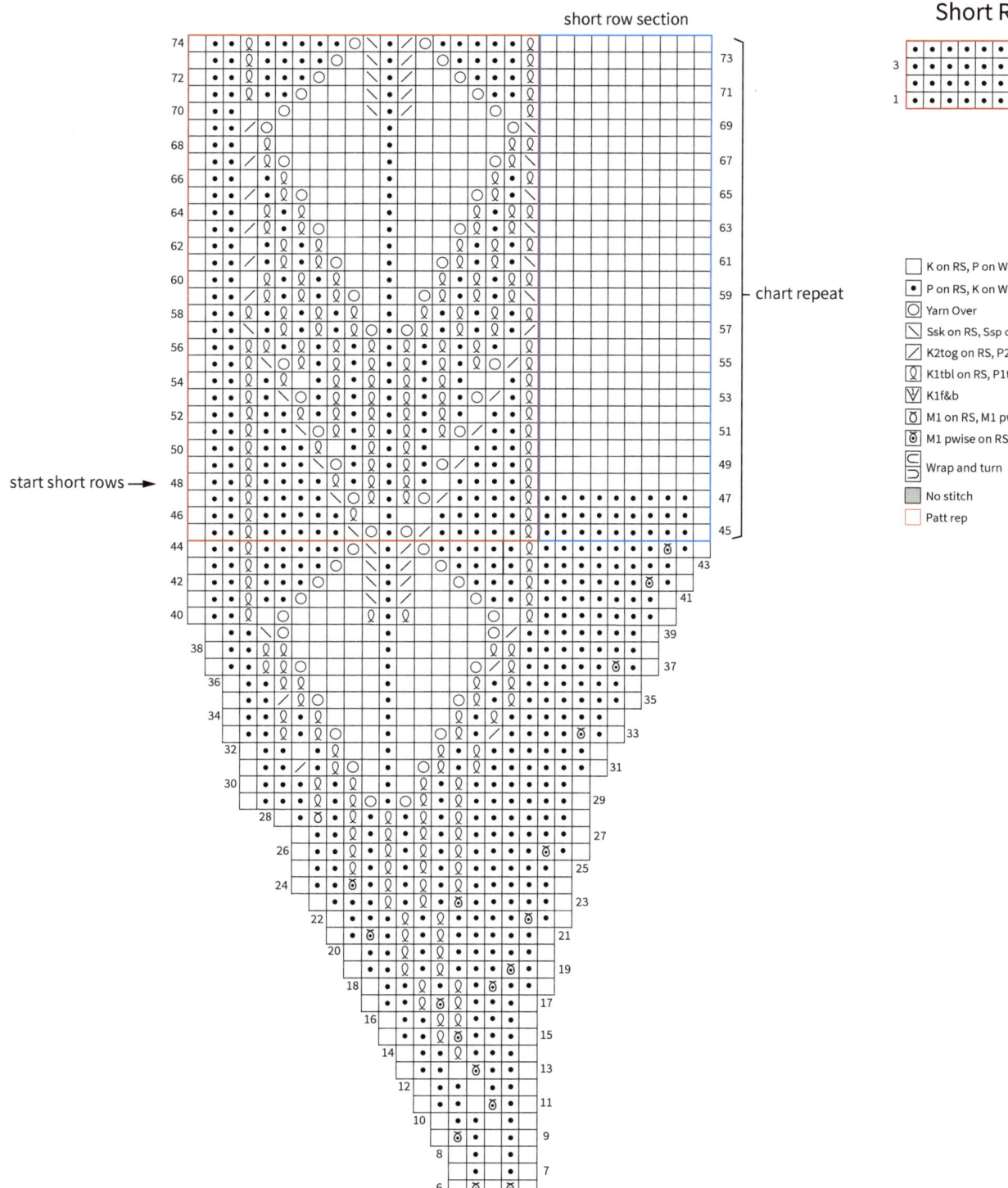

MARI TOBITA

Linden Hoodie (Burgundy or Blue)

SIZES

S (M, L, XL)
To fit Bust Sizes: 32-34 (36-38, 40-42, 44-46)" / 81.5-86.5 (91.5-96.5, 101.5-106.5, 112-117) cm

Sample Size: S

FINISHED MEASUREMENTS

Bust: 35½ (39½, 43, 47½)" / 90 (100, 109, 121) cm
Length: 21½ (22, 22¼, 23)" / 54.5 (56, 56.5, 58.5) cm

YARN

Blue:
Elsebeth Lavold's Silk Wool (45% Wool / 35% Silk / 20% Nylon; 192 yds [176 m] / 1.75 oz / 50 g): color 110 Spring Sky 7 (7, 8, 8) skeins

Burgundy:
Elsebeth Lavold's Silk Wool (45% Wool / 35% Silk / 20% Nylon; 192 yds [176 m] / 1.75 oz / 50 g): color 106 Black Currant 7 (7, 8, 8) skeins

NEEDLES

US size 6 and 7 (4.0 and 4.5 mm) 24" / 60 cm and 32" / 80 cm circular needles

NOTIONS

Stitch markers, stitch holders, tapestry needle

GAUGES

22.5 sts and 24 rows = 4" / 10 cm in lace pattern using size 7 (4.5 mm) needles.
22.5 sts and 28 rows = 4" / 10 cm in Stockinette stitch using size 6 (4.0 mm) needles.
24.5 sts and 28 rows = 4" / 10 cm in lace pattern using size 6 (4.0 mm) needles.

STITCH GUIDE

1. **Chain selvedge for Front edges**
   RS rows: Sl 1 k'wise, work to last st, k1.
   WS rows: Sl 1 p'wise, work to last st, p1.

2. **Garter st selvedge for seaming edges**
   Knit the first st and last st on every row.

3. **Lifted increases**
   RLI: K into the st one row below the first st on LHN.
   LLI: K into the st two rows below the st just worked.

NOTES

- The body of this cardigan is worked back and forth in one piece from the bottom to the underarm, then divided for working the fronts and back separately.
- The body and sleeves begin with lace border, then are worked in Stockinette stich. The lace pattern flows into the front borders, at the center back, and on the sleeves.

INSTRUCTIONS

Note: Work Chain selvedge for Front edges. These selvedge sts are included in charts A and C.

Body

With size 7 (6, 6, 7) longer circular needle, CO 243 (275, 307, 307) sts. Do not join.

Next row (RS): K1, *p1, k1tbl; rep from * to last 2 sts, p1, k1.

Next row (WS): Sl 1 p'wise, *k1, p1tbl; rep from * to last 2 sts, k1, p1.

Beg charts A, B, C and D

Row 1 (RS): Work chart A, pl mar, work chart D 4 (5, 6, 6) times, p1, pl mar, work chart B, pl mar, work chart D 4 (5, 6, 6) times, p1, pl mar, work chart C.

Cont in this manner thru Row 12.

Size S and XL only

Change to size 6 (4.0 mm) needle.

Row 13 (RS): Work chart A, sl mar, *work chart D 4 (6) times, k1*, sl mar, work chart B, sl mar, rep * to *, sl mar, work chart C.

Work 3 more rows in patt.

Row 17: Work chart A, sl mar, *work chart D 2 (3) times, pl mar, work chart D 2 (3) times, k1*, sl mar, work chart B, sl mar, rep * to *, sl mar, work chart C.

Work 1 more row.

Size M only

Row 13 (RS): Work chart A, sl mar, *[omit 2 yos of chart D] 5 times, k1*, sl mar, work chart B, sl mar, rep * to *, sl mar, work chart C. 20 sts dec'd – 255 sts.

Row 14: Work chart C, sl mar, *p1, [yo, p4, ssp, k1, p2tog, p4, yo, p1] 5 times*, sl mar, work chart B, sl mar, rep * to *, sl mar, work chart A.

Row 15: Work chart A, sl mar, *[k2, yo, k3, k2tog, p1, ssk, k3, yo, k1] 5 times, k1*, sl mar, work chart B, sl mar, rep * to *, work chart C.

Row 16: Work chart C, sl mar, *p1, [p2, yo, p2, ssp, k1, p2tog, p2, yo, p3] 5 times*, sl mar, work chart B, sl mar, rep * to *, sl mar, work chart A.

Row 17: Work chart A, sl mar, *[k4, yo, k1, k2tog, p1, ssk, k1, yo, k3] 2 times, k4, yo, k1, k2tog, pl mar, p1, ssk, k1, yo, k3, [k4, yo, k1, k2tog, p1, ssk, k1, yo, k3] 2 times, k1*, sl mar, work chart B, sl mar, rep * to *, sl mar, work chart C.

Row 18: Work chart C, sl mar, *p to mar, sl mar, p to mar*, sl mar, work chart B, sl mar, rep * to *, sl mar, work chart A.

Size L only

Row 13 (RS): Work chart A, sl mar, *omit last yo of chart D, [omit 2 yos of chart D] 4 times, omit first yo of chart D, k1*, sl mar, work chart B, sl mar, rep * to *, sl mar, work chart C. 20 sts dec'd – 287 sts.

Row 14: Work chart C, sl mar, *p2, yo, p4, ssp, k1, p2tog, p4, yo, p1, [yo, p4, ssp, k1, p2tog, p4, yo, p1] 4 times, yo, p4, ssp, k1, p2tog, p4, yo, p2*, sl mar, work chart B, sl mar, rep * to *, sl mar, work chart A.

Row 15: Work chart A, sl mar, *k3, yo, k3, k2tog, p1, ssk, k3, yo, k1, [k2, yo, k3, k2tog, p1, ssk, k3, yo, k1] 4 times, k2, yo, k3, k2tog, p1, ssk, k3, yo, k3*, sl mar, work chart B, sl mar, rep * to *, sl mar, work chart C.

Row 16: Work chart C, sl mar, *p4, yo, p2, ssp, k1, p2tog, p2, yo, p3, [p2, yo, p2, ssp, k1, p2tog, p2, yo, p3] 4 times, p2, yo, p2, ssp, k1, p2tog, p2, yo, p4*, sl mar, work chart B, sl mar, rep * to *, sl mar, work chart A.

Row 17: Work chart A, sl mar, *k5, yo, k1, k2tog, p1, ssk, k1, yo, k3, [k4, yo, k1, k2tog, p1, ssk, k1, yo, k3] 2 times, pl mar, [k4, yo, k1, k2tog, p1, ssk, k1, yo, k3] 2 times, k4, yo, k1, k2tog, p1, ssk, k1, yo, k5*, sl mar, work chart B, sl mar, rep * to *, sl mar, work chart C.

Row 18: Work chart C, sl mar, *p to mar, sl mar, p to mar*, sl mar, work chart B, sl mar, rep * to *, sl mar, work chart A.

All sizes: Begin to work in St st bet front lace panels (charts A and C) and the center back panel (chart B, then E).

Row 19: Work chart A, sl mar, k to mar, re mar, k1, pl mar, k to mar, sl mar, work chart B, sl mar, k to mar, sl mar, k to mar, sl mar, work chart C. 66 (69, 77, 82) sts for each front, 111 (117, 133, 143) sts for back.

Row 20: Work chart C, sl mar, *p to mar, sl mar, p to mar*, sl mar, work chart B, sl mar, rep * to *, sl mar, work chart A.
Cont in patt through Row 22 (40, 24, 26).

Note: For M size, dec begin at Row 41, after switching to chart E at Row 31.
Read ahead under Dec row.

Dec row (RS): Work chart A, sl mar, *k to 3 sts before mar, k2tog, k1, sl mar, k1, ssk, k to mar*, sl mar, work chart B or E, sl mar, rep * to *, sl mar, work chart C.
Work Dec row every 10 (30, 12, 14)th row 1 (1, 4, 1) more time(s), 12 (-, -, 16)th row 3 (-, -, 2) times. 20 (8, 20, 16) sts dec'd – 223 (247, 267, 291) sts, 61 (67, 72, 78) sts for each front and 101 (113, 123, 135) sts for back.

At the same time, at Row 31 (RS), switch to 19-st rep of charts A and C, and chart E for center back panel as foll: Work Row 31 of chart A over 19 sts (selv + 18 sts), pl mar, k to mar, re mar, k to mar, sl mar, k to mar, re mar, k14, pl mar, work chart E, pl mar, k to mar, re mar, k to mar, sl mar, k to mar, re mar, k14, pl mar, work Row 31 of chart C over 19 rem sts.

Work even in patt for 17 more rows, ending with a WS row – 88 (90, 92, 92) rows have been worked for Body. Piece measures 13 (13, 13¼, 13½)" / 33 (33, 33.5, 34.5) cm from CO edge.

You have finished 26 (28, 30, 30)th row of chart E and 56 (58, 60, 60)th row of charts A and C.

Divide for fronts and back

Next row (RS): Work chart A, sl mar, k to 4 (4, 5, 6) sts before mar, place right front sts onto holder, BO next 7 (7, 9, 11) sts, k to mar, sl mar, work chart E, sl mar, k to 3 (3, 4, 5) sts before mar, place back sts onto holder, BO next 7 (7, 9, 11) sts, k to mar, sl mar, work chart C – 57 (63, 67, 72) sts for each front and 95 (107, 115, 125) sts for back.

Left Front

Shape Armholes (Use the Sloped BO Technique)

Work back 1 WS row in patt, then BO 3 (4, 4, 4) sts at beg of next RS row, 2 (3, 3, 3) sts at beg of next RS row 1 (1, 1, 2) time(s), - (2, 2, 2) sts at beg of next RS row - (2, 3, 3) times. 5 (11, 13, 16) sts dec'd – 52 (52, 54, 56) sts.

Dec row (RS): K1, ssk, work to end.

Rep Dec row every other row 3 (2, 2, 2) more times. 4 (3, 3, 3) sts dec'd – 48 (49, 51, 53) sts.

Work even in patt for 41 (43, 41, 43) more rows, ending with a WS row and re mar. Armhole measures 7¾ (8¼, 8¼, 8¾)" / 19.5 (21, 21, 22) cm.

Shape neck and shoulder (Use the Sloped BO Technique and short rows)

Row 1 (RS): BO 7 (7, 8, 8) sts, k20 (21, 22, 24), W&T.

Row 2 (WS): P to last st, turn.

Row 3: BO 6 (7, 7, 8) sts, k9 (9, 10, 11), W&T.

Row 4: P to last st, turn.

Row 5: BO 6 (6, 7, 7) sts, break yarn.

Place rem 29 (29, 29, 30) sts onto holder.

Right Front

Return 57 (63, 67, 72) right front sts onto needle and with WS facing, rejoin yarn.

Work 2 rows in patt.

Shape Armholes (Use the Sloped BO Technique)

BO 3 (4, 4, 4) sts at beg of next WS row, 2 (3, 3, 3) sts at beg of next WS row 1 (1, 1, 2) time(s), - (2, 2, 2) sts at beg of next WS row - (2, 3, 3) times. 5 (11, 13, 16) sts dec'd – 52 (52, 54, 56) sts.

Dec row (RS): K to last 3 sts, k2tog, k1.

Rep Dec row every other row 3 (2, 2, 2) more times. 4 (3, 3, 3) sts dec'd – 48 (49, 51, 53) sts.

Work even for 41 (43, 41, 43) more rows, ending with a WS row and re mar. Armhole measures 7¾ (8¼, 8¼, 8¾)" / 19.5 (21, 21, 22) cm. Break yarn.

Shape neck and shoulder (Use the Sloped BO Technique and short rows)

Row 1 (RS): Sl 20 sts, join new yarn, k to end.

Row 2 (WS): BO 7 (7, 8, 8) sts, p20 (21, 22, 24), W&T.

Row 3: K to last st, turn.

Row 4: BO 6 (7, 7, 8) sts, p9 (9, 10, 11), W&T.

Row 5: K to last st, turn.

Row 6: BO 6 (6, 7, 7) sts, break yarn.

Place rem 29 (29, 29, 30) sts onto holder.

Back

Return 95 (107, 115, 125) Back sts onto needle and with WS facing, rejoin yarn.

Shape Armholes (Use the Sloped BO Technique)

Next row (WS): Work to last st, turn.

BO 3 (4, 4, 4) sts at beg of next 2 rows, 2 (3, 3, 3) sts at beg of next 2 (2, 2, 4) rows, - (2, 2, 2) sts at beg of next - (4, 6, 6) rows. 10 (22, 26, 32) sts dec'd – 85 (85, 89, 93) sts.

Dec row (RS): K1, ssk, work to last 3 sts, k2tog, k1.

Rep Dec row every other row 3 (2, 2, 2) more times. 8 (6, 6, 6) sts dec'd –77 (79, 83, 87) sts.

Work even for 21 (17, 13, 11) more rows until the 3rd chart E rep is completed, ending with a WS row.

Beg chart F for center panel as foll: K to mar, re mar, k1, pl mar, work Row 1 of chart F, pl mar, k1, re mar, k to end.

Work chart F thru Row 12 one (1, 1, 2) time(s).

Next row (RS): K to 3 sts before mar, pl mar, k1, k2tog, re mar, p1, k1, yo, [p1, k1tbl] 6 times, p1, yo, k1, p1, re mar, ssk, k1, pl mar, k to end.

Next row (WS): K1, p to mar, sl mar, p2, k1, p2, [k1, p1tbl] 6 times, [k1, p2] twice, sl mar, p to last st, k1.

Next row (RS): K to mar, sl mar, k2tog, p1, k1, yo, [k1tbl, p1] 7 times, k1tbl, yo, k1, p1, ssk, sl mar, k to end.

Next row (WS): K1, p to mar, sl mar, p1, k1, p1, [k1, p1tbl] 8 times, [k1, p1] twice, sl mar, p to last st, k1.

Beg chart G for center panel as foll: K to mar, re mar, k1, pl mar, work Row 1 of chart G, pl mar, k1, re mar, k to end.

Work even for 3 (9, 11, 3) more rows with chart G, ending with a WS row. Armholes measure 7¾ (8¼, 8¼, 8¾)" / 19.5 (21, 21, 22) cm.

Shape Shoulder

Cont with chart G and beg shaping on next RS row as foll: BO 7 (7, 8, 8) sts at beg of next 2 rows, 6 (7, 7, 8) sts at beg of next 2 rows, 6 (6, 7, 7) sts at beg of next 2 rows. 38 (40, 44, 46) sts dec'd – 39 (39, 39, 41) sts. End with Row 10 (16, 2, 10) of chart G. Piece measures 8½ (9, 9, 9½)" / 21.5 (23, 23, 24) cm from beg of armhole.

Place rem 39 (39, 39, 41) sts onto holder.

Sleeves

Note: Knit the first st and last st on every row for seaming edges. These selvedge sts are included in the written instructions.

With size 7 (7, 6, 6) shorter circular needle, CO 49 (49, 65, 65) sts.

Next row (RS): K1, *k1tbl, p1; rep from * to last 2 sts, k1tbl, k1.

Next row (WS): K1, *p1tbl, k1; rep from * to last 2 sts, p1tbl, k1.

Size S and M only

Beg charts B

Row 1 (RS): K1, work Row 1 of chart B, k1.

Row 2 (WS): K1, work Row 2 of chart B, k1.

Cont with chart B thru Row 12 (WS).

Change to size 6 (4.0 mm) needle. Beg to inc 1 st each side and work these inc sts in St st.

Row 13: K1, pl mar, RLI, work from 2nd to 46th sts of chart B, LLI, pl mar, k1 – 49 (49) sts.

Work even thru Row 20 (18).

Next row (RS/inc): K1, RLI, sl mar, chart B, sl mar, LLI, k1 – 51 (51) sts.

Work even for 5 more rows.

Inc row (RS): K1, RLI, k to mar, sl mar, chart B, sl mar, k to last st, LLI, k1.

Rep Inc row every 6 (6)th row 13 (10) times then every - (4)th row - (5) times.

30 (34) sts total inc'd – 79 (83) sts.

Work even for 13 more rows, ending with Row 28 of 3rd rep of chart E.

120 rows have been worked for Sleeve.

At the same time, at Row 31, beg chart E for center panel as foll: K1, k1 (RLI), k1 (2), re mar, k14 (14), pl mar, work Row 1 of chart E, pl mar, k14 (14), re mar, k1 (2), k1 (LLI), k1.

Piece measures 17½"/ 44.5 cm from CO edge.

Size L and XL only

Beg charts B and half of D.

Row 1 (RS): K1, RLI, work from 11th to 16th sts of chart D, p1, pl mar, work chart B, pl mar, work 1st to 7th sts of chart D, LLI, k1 – 65 (65) sts.

Row 2 (WS): K1, work 8th to 1st sts of chart D, sl mar, work chart B, sl mar, k1, work 16th to 10th sts on chart D, k1.

RS row: K1, work 10th to 16th sts of chart D, p1, sl mar, work chart B, sl mar, work 1st to 8th sts of chart D, k1.

WS row: K1, work 8th to 1st sts of chart D, sl mar, work chart B, sl mar, k1, work 16th to 10th sts of chart D, k1.

Rep last 2 rows 4 more times.

Row 13 (RS / dec row): K1, ssk, k5, p1, re mar, omit first and last yos of chart B, re mar, p1, k5, k2tog, k1. 4 sts dec'd – 61 (61) sts.

Row 14: K1, p2tog, p4, yo, pl mar, work chart B, pl mar, yo, p4, ssp, k1.

Row 15: K1, ssk, k3, yo, k1, sl mar, work chart B, sl mar, k1, yo, k3, k2tog, k1.

Row 16: K1, p2tog, p2, yo, p2, sl mar, work chart B, sl mar, p2, yo, p2, ssp, k1.

Row 17: K1, ssk, k1, yo, k3, sl mar, work chart B, sl mar, k3, yo, k1, k2tog, k1.

Row 18: K1, p2tog, yo, p4, sl mar, work chart B, sl mar, p4, yo, ssp, k1.

Work even for 2 (-) more rows, with St st for each side of chart B.

Beg to inc 1 st each side and work these inc sts in St st.

Inc row: K1, RLI, k to mar, sl mar, chart B, sl mar, k to last st, RLI, k1.

Rep Inc row every 8 (6)th row 3 (11) times then every 6 (4)th row 10 (5) times.

28 (34) sts inc'd – 89 (95) sts.

Work even for 15 more rows. 122 rows have been worked for Sleeve, ending with Row 30 of 3rd rep of chart E.

At the same time, at Row 31, beg chart E for center panel as foll: K1, k1 (RLI), k7 (8), re mar, k14, pl mar, work Row 1 of chart E, pl mar, k14, re mar, k7 (8), k1 (LLI), k1.

Piece measures 17½"/ 44.5 cm from cast-on edge.

All sizes

Shape Cap (Use Sloped BO Technique)

Cont working with chart E.

BO 4 (4, 5, 6) sts at beg of next 2 rows, 2 sts at beg of 2 rows - (-, 1, -) time, [1 st at beg of 2 rows, 2 sts at beg of 2 rows] 6 (7, 7, 8) times, 1 st at beg of 4 (2, -, -) rows, 3 sts at beg of 4 rows. There are 19 (19, 21, 23) sts rem. BO all rem sts on next RS row.

At the same time, when the 4th chart E rep is completed on Row 32 (32, 30, 30) of sleeve cap, work [k1tbl, p1] rib for center panel to final BO.

Piece measures 22¼ (22¾, 23, 23¼)"/ 56.5 (58, 58.5, 59) cm from CO edge.

Hood

Block body piece to measurements. Join shoulders.

With size 6 (4.0 mm) shorter circular needle and RS facing, place 29 (29, 29, 30) sts from Right Front, 39 (39, 39, 41) sts from Back, 29 (29, 29, 30) from Left Front – 97 (97, 97, 101) sts.

Size S, M and L only

Row 1 (RS): Work 19 sts of chart A, pl mar, k2, M1, [k3, M1] twice, ssk, k2tog, k1, M1, [k3, M1] twice, pl mar, work chart G, pl mar, [M1, k3] twice, M1, k1, ssk, k2tog, M1, [k3, M1] twice, k2, pl mar, work 19 sts of chart C. 8 sts inc'd – 105 sts.

Size XL only

Row 1 (RS): Work 19 sts of chart A, pl mar, [k4, M1] twice, ssk, k2tog, k2, M1, k4, M1, k3, pl mar, work chart G, pl mar, k3, M1, k4, M1, k2, ssk, k2tog, [M1, k4] twice, pl mar, work 19 sts of chart C.

4 sts inc'd – 105 sts.

Shape lower hood

All sizes

Work even for 5 more rows, ending with a WS row.

Inc Row (RS): Work chart A, sl mar, k to 1 st before mar, LLI, k1, sl mar, work chart G, sl mar, k1, RLI, k to mar, sl mar, work chart C – 107 sts.

Rep Inc row every 6th row once and every 8th row 4 times. 12 sts inc'd – 117 sts.

Work even 9 rows, ending with a WS row.

Shape upper hood

Dec Row (RS): Work chart A, sl mar, k to 2 sts before mar, k2tog, sl mar, work chart G, sl mar, ssk, k to mar, sl mar, work chart C.

Rep Dec row every 6th row once, every 4th row once, and every other row 4 times. 14 sts dec'd – 103 sts

Work 1 WS row in patt.

Next row (RS /dec): Work chart A, sl mar, k to 2 sts before mar, k2tog, sl mar, work chart G, sl mar, ssk, k to mar, sl mar, work chart C.

Next row (WS /dec): Work chart C, sl mar, p to 2 sts before mar, ssp, sl mar, work chart G, sl mar, p2tog, p to mar, sl mar, work chart A.

Rep last 2 rows 3 more times. 16 sts dec'd – 87 sts

Short row 1 (RS): Work chart A, re mar, k12, k2tog, sl mar, work chart G, sl mar, ssk, turn.

Short row 2 (WS): Sl 1 from RHN to LHN, ssp, sl mar, work chart G, sl mar, p2tog, turn.

Short row 3: Sl 1 from RHN to LHN, k2tog, sl mar, work chart G, sl mar, ssk, turn.

Short row 4: Sl 1, sl mar, work chart G, sl mar, sl 1, turn.

Short row 5: Sl 1 from RHN to LHN, k2tog, sl mar, work chart G, sl mar, ssk, turn.

Short row 6: Sl 1 from RHN to LHN, ssp, sl mar, work chart G, sl mar, p2tog, turn.
Short rows 7 - 8: As Short rows 5 - 6.
Short row 9: As Short rows 5.
Short rows 10 - 15: As Short rows 4 - 9.
BO in pattern only center 23 sts on WS – 38 sts rem.

Cont with 2 Front Lace panels.

With RS facing, join new yarn at Left corner of BO row, work as foll: K1f&b, work chart C – 20 sts.
Next row (WS): Work chart C, k1. Using working yarn for Right Front, p1f&b, work chart A.

Work even for 12 more rows, using Chain selvedge for outside of Front panels and Garter selvedge for inside. End with a WS row. Join Front panels with 3-needle BO. Sew Center panel to the side of Front panels.

Finishing

Block pieces to measurements. Seam sleeves and set them into armhole

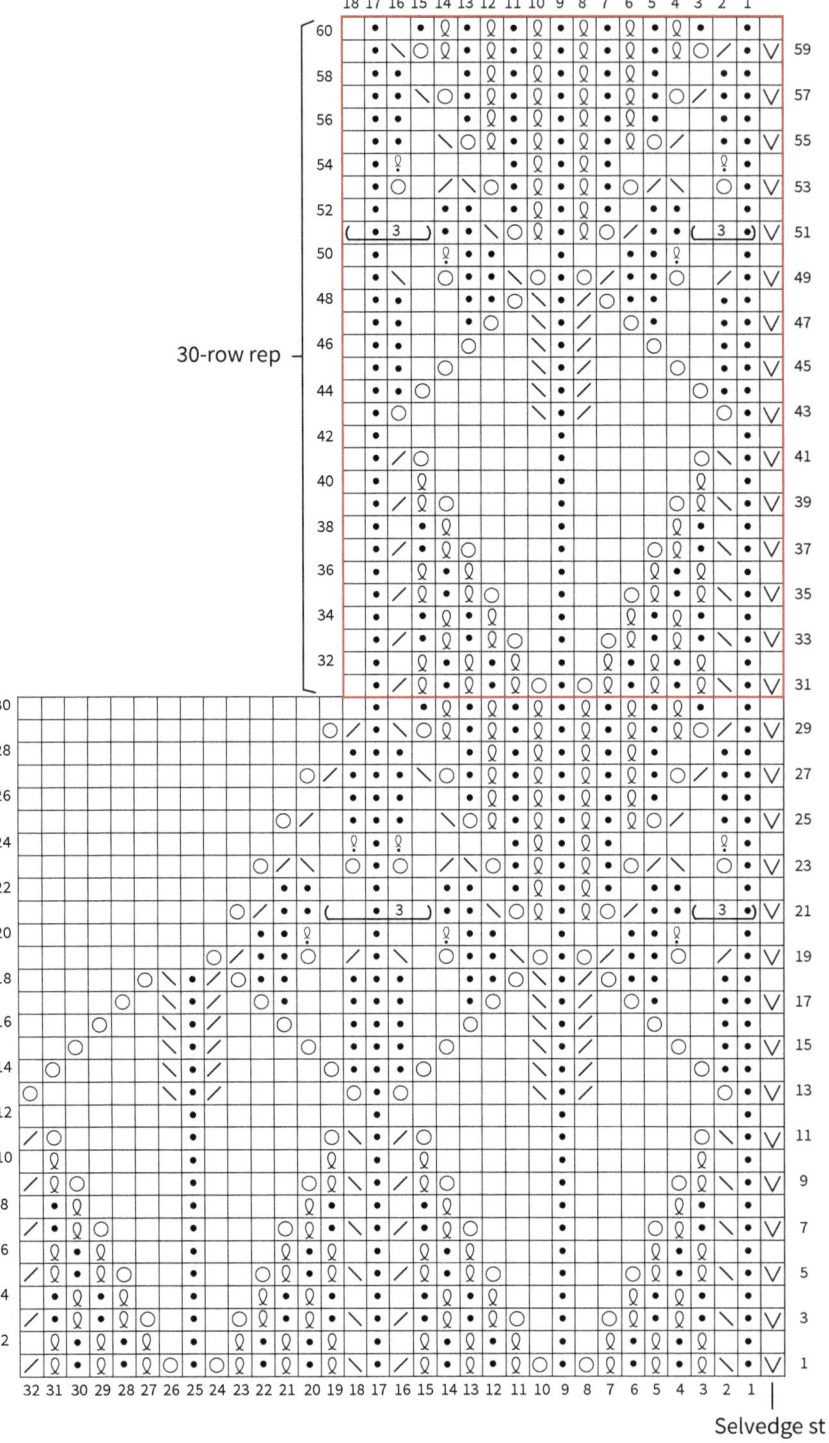

Chart B

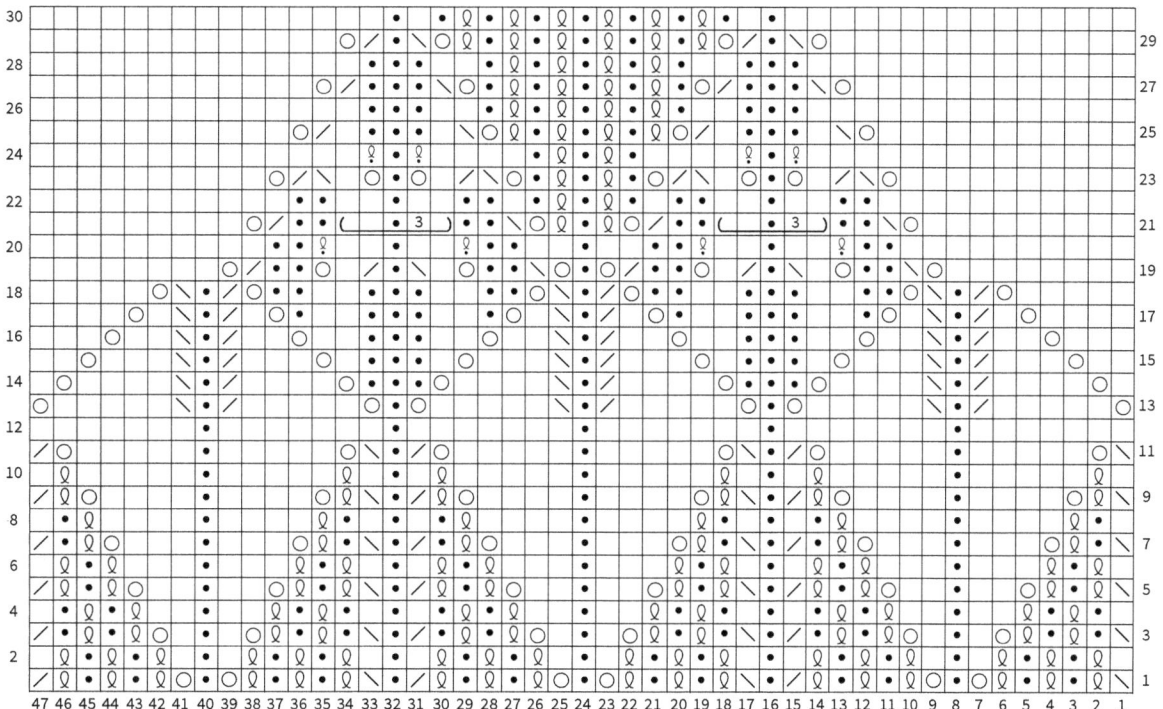

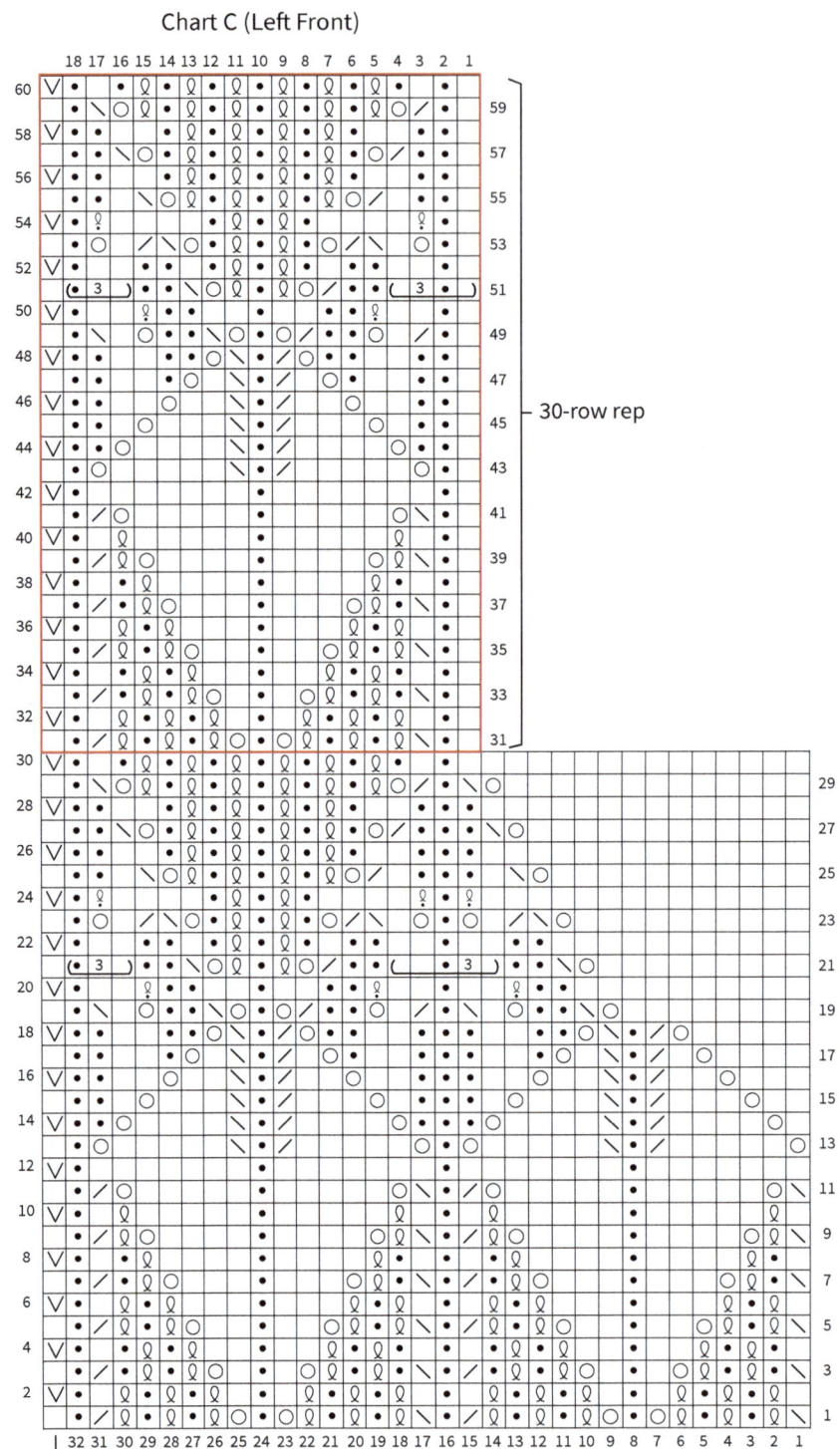

Chart C (Left Front)

30-row rep

Selvedge st

208

Chart D (Hem repeat)

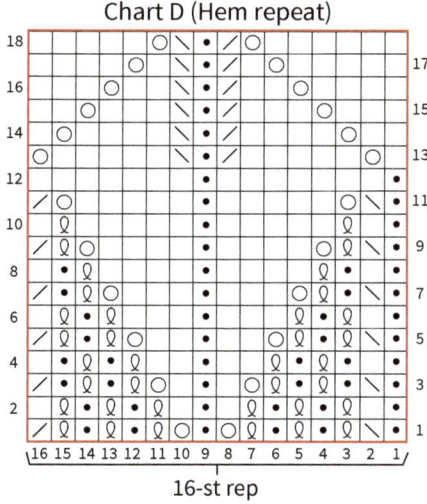

16-st rep

Chart F

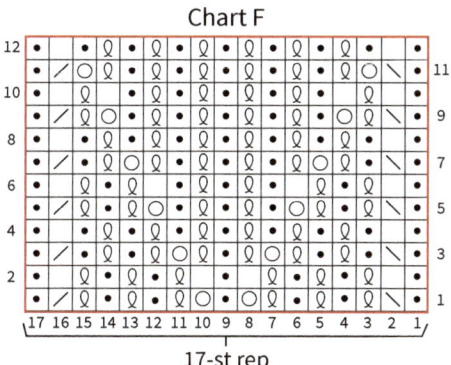

17-st rep

Chart E

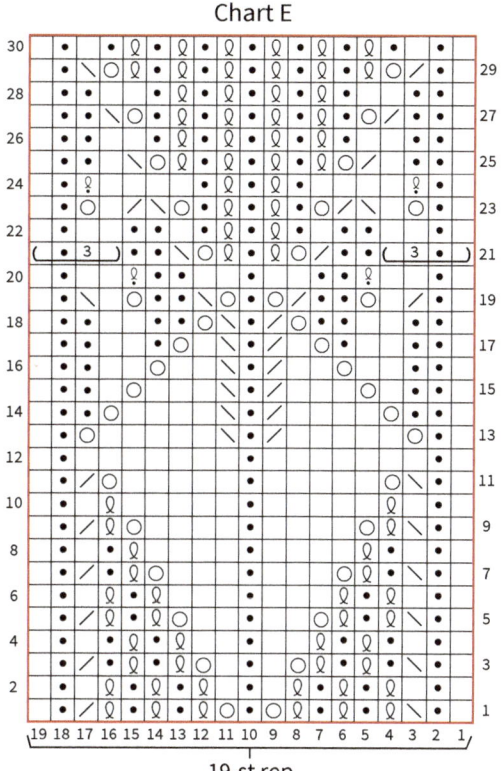

19-st rep

Chart G

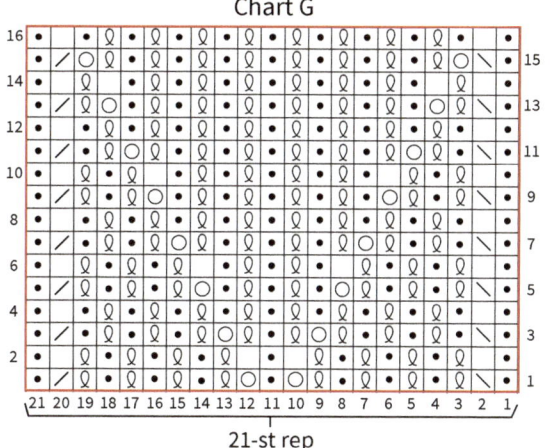

21-st rep

LINDEN HOODIE | 209

Linden Hoodie

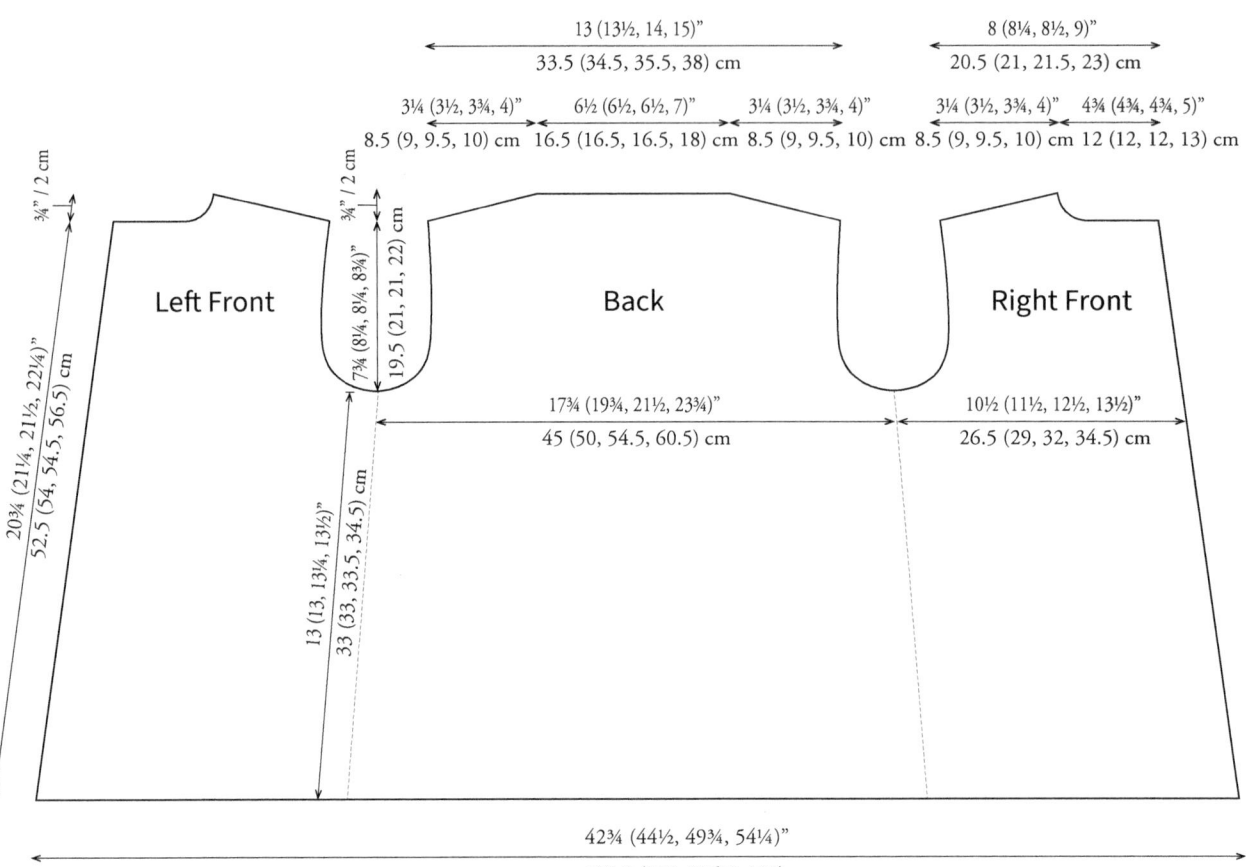

Linden Hoodie

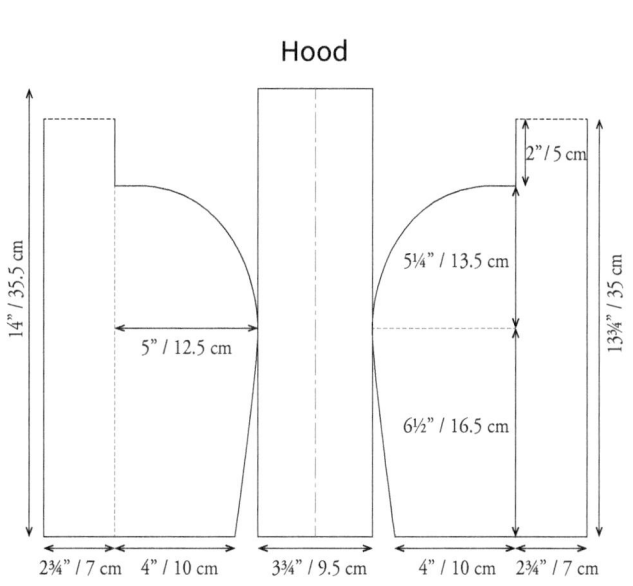
Hood

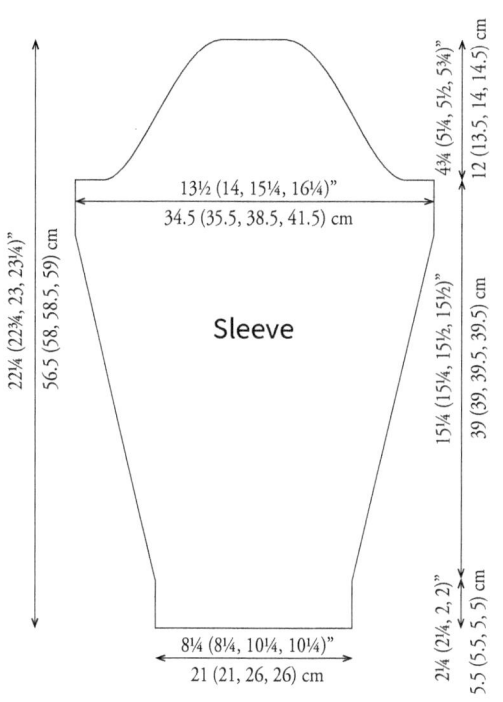
Sleeve

Mesa Poncho

FINISHED SIZES

Women's S (M)
Length from shoulder to bottom point: 26 (34)" / 66 (86) cm
Front/Back width after seaming: 32.75 (42.75)" / 83 (108.5) cm

Sample Size: S

YARN

Rowan Pure Wool Superwash Worsted (100% Wool; 219 yds [200 m] / 3.5 oz / 100 g): color Windsor 4 (7) balls

NEEDLES

Size US 6 (4 mm) circular needle
Adjust needle size if necessary to obtain the correct gauge.

NOTIONS

stitch marker; tapestry needle

GAUGES

Border pattern:
17.5 sts and 32 rows = 4" / 10 cm in Seed stitch

Lacy Butterfly pattern:
34 sts and 32 rows = 7" x 6.25" / 17.8 x 15.9 cm (1 patt rep)

STITCH GUIDE

Wrap 4 sts: K4 onto cn and hold to front. With working yarn, wrap these 4 sts front to back twice or 5 times, as indicated on chart. Yarn should be wrapped snugly in order to gather the stitches and form the pattern. Then slip the sts purlwise to the RHN.

Seed Stitch
(worked flat over an even number of sts)
RS rows: [K1, p1] to end.
WS rows: [P1, k1] to end.
Note: Always knit the purls and purl the knits.

2x2 Rib
(worked in the round over an even number of sts)
All rnds: [K2, p2] to end.

NOTES
- Poncho is worked flat in 2 pieces, then joined. Collar is picked up and worked in the round.
- Garter selvedge is worked throughout: Knit first and last sts of every row.

INSTRUCTIONS

Body Panels (make 2)

CO 124 (154) sts loosely with long-tail cast on or other stretchy method.

Seed Stitch Border

Row 1 (RS): K1 (selvedge st), [k1, p1] to last st, k1 (selvedge st).
Row 2 (WS): K1 (selvedge st), [p1, k1] to last st, k1 (selvedge st).
Work in patt for 15 (17) more rows, ending with a RS row.

Size S only:

Next row (WS), inc as follows: K1 (selvedge st), [p8, m1p] 13 times, [p9, m1p] 2 times, k1 (selvedge st) – 139 sts.

Size M only:

Next row (WS), inc as follows: K1 (selvedge st), [p8, m1p] 19 times, k1 (selvedge st) – 173 sts.

Lacy Butterfly Pattern

Estab patt from chart Row 1 as foll: K1 (selvedge st), work 34-st patt rep 4 (5) times, work 1 "plus" st (rev St st), k1 (selvedge st).

Cont in patt and work all chart rows 3 (4) times – 96 (128) rows total.

Bind off all sts loosely.

Assemble

Block pieces lightly to measurements.

Seam as follows, making sure stitches are not too tight:

With RS facing, join left edge of one panel to top edge of other panel as shown in diagram. Then join left edge of 2nd panel to top edge of 1st panel, matching A and B.

Collar

With RS facing and beginning at center back neck (C), pick up and knit 76 (84) sts evenly around neck edge. Join and pl mar for beg of rnd. Work in 2x2 Rib until collar measures 5.75 (6.5)" /14.5 (16.5) cm.

Bind off.

Assembly Diagram

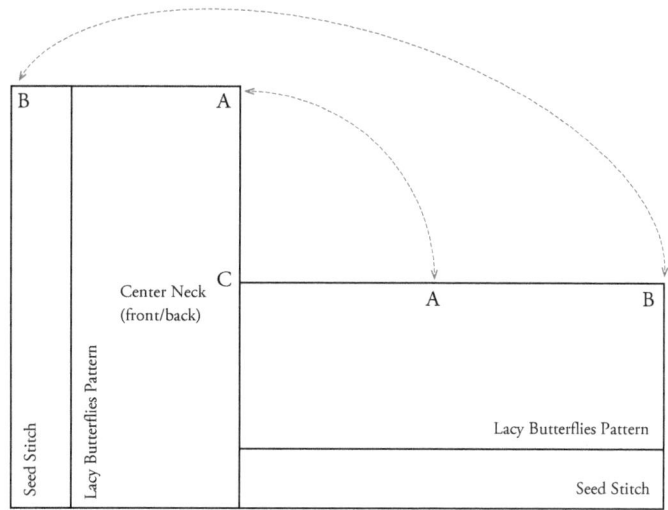

Assembled Poncho

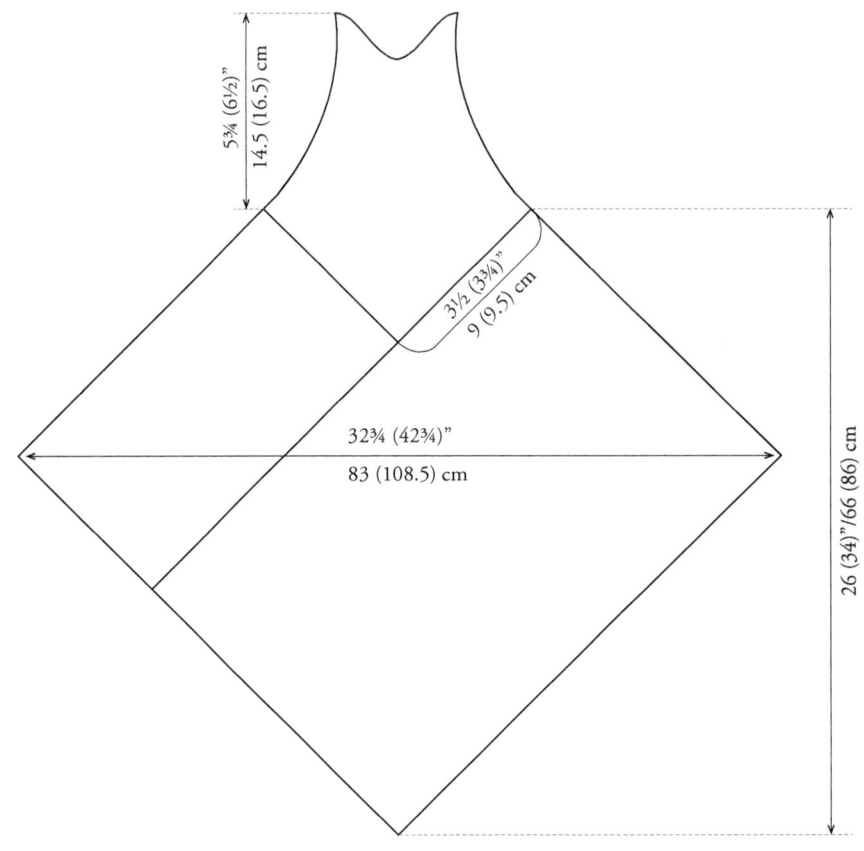

Body Panels

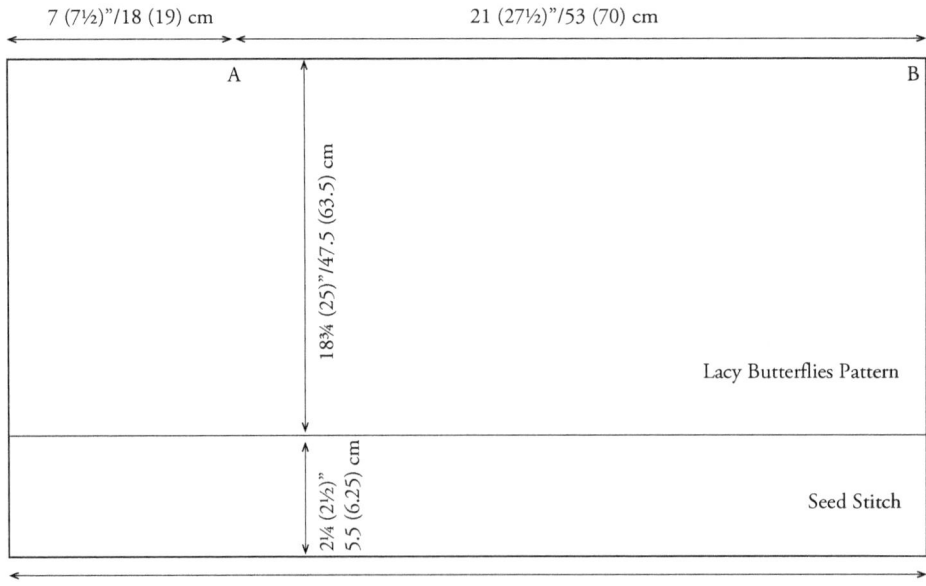

Mesa Poncho
(mult of 34 + 1 + 2 selvedge sts)

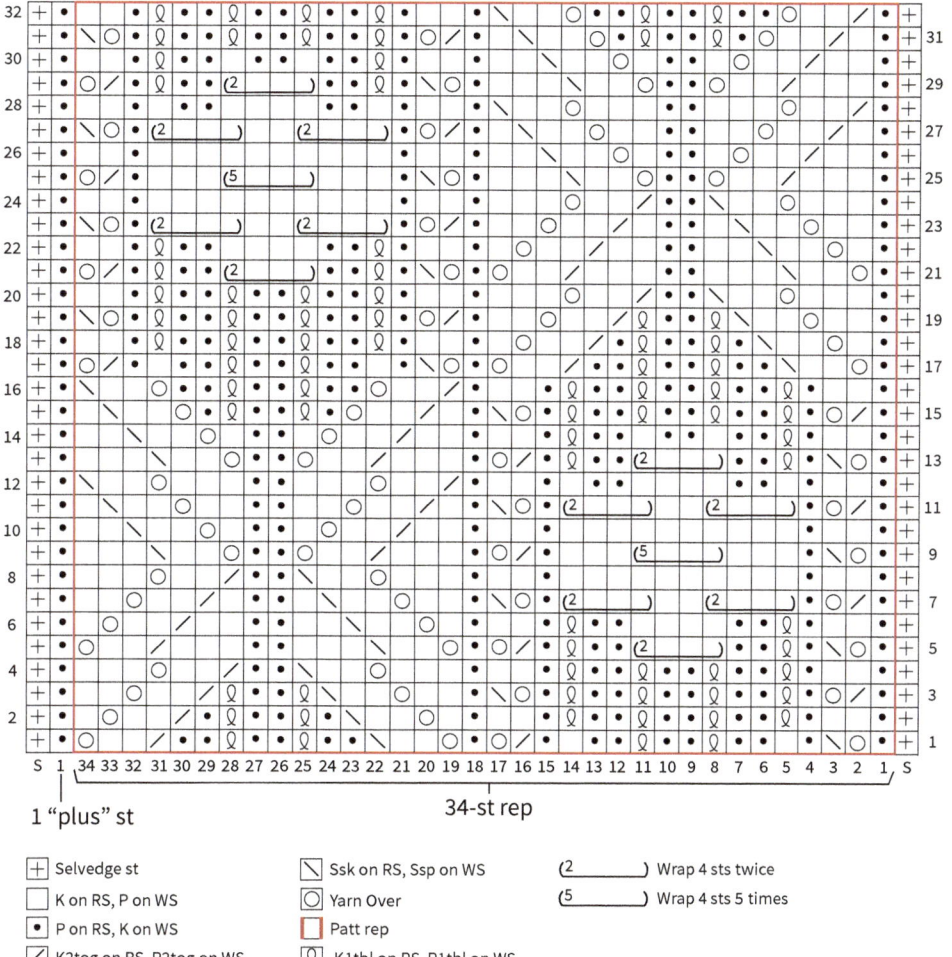

+	Selvedge st	
□	K on RS, P on WS	
•	P on RS, K on WS	
╱	K2tog on RS, P2tog on WS	
╲	Ssk on RS, Ssp on WS	
○	Yarn Over	
▭	Patt rep	
ℚ	K1tbl on RS, P1tbl on WS	
(2____)	Wrap 4 sts twice	
(5____)	Wrap 4 sts 5 times	

Nikki Reeves Pullover

FINISHED SIZES

Women's S (M, L, XL)
Finished bust: 35¼ (40½, 45¾, 51)" / 90 (103, 116, 130) cm
To fit bust sizes: 32-34 (35-38, 39-43, 44-48)" / 81-86 (89-96.5, 99-109, 111.5-122) cm

Sample Size: L

YARN

Plymouth Yarn Galway Worsted (100% wool; 210 yd [192 m] / 3.5 oz / 100 g): colorway 756 Sunflower Heather, 5 (7, 9, 9) skeins

NEEDLES

Size US 7 (4.5mm)

Adjust needle size if necessary to obtain the correct gauge.

NOTIONS

Stitch markers; tapestry needle

GAUGES

Interlocking Cables Pattern:
40 sts and 28 rows = 5¼" / 13.5 cm

Reverse Stockinette Stitch:
40 sts and 43 rows = 8" / 20.5 cm

Note: Both stitch and row gauge are important for intended sizing.

STITCH GUIDE

C4F – Sl2 to cn, hold front, K2, then K2 from cn.
C6B – Sl3 to cn, hold back, K3, then K3 from cn.
T5B – Sl2 to cn, hold back, K3, then P2 from cn.
T5F – Sl 3 to cn, hold front, P2, then K3 from cn.

NOTES

- A garter stitch selvedge is worked at both edges of all pieces: Knit the first and last sts of every row.
- Body length to armholes is the same for all sizes. If desired, work additional repeats of Chart 1 Rows 8-13 to extend the bottom ribbing pattern.
- The Double Diamonds pattern (Chart 3) is worked one time at the waist in place of Rows 21-26 of Chart 2.

- Decreases in cables - When a decrease affects the number of sts in a cable, work the remaining sts as follows: If an even number of sts remains, divide in half and cross in same direction as original cable. If an odd number of sts remains, divide as evenly as possible and cross the larger number over the smaller number in the same direction as the original cable.

INSTRUCTIONS

Back/Front (make 2)

CO 136 (156, 176, 196) sts.

Establish Cabled Ribbing patt from Row 0 of Chart 1 as foll (WS): K1 (selv), beg at left of chart work 2 "plus" sts, work 10-st patt rep 13 (15, 17, 19) times, work 2 "plus" sts, k1 (selv).

Cont in estab patt as foll: Work chart rows 1-13, repeat Rows 2-13 once, then work Row 14 – 27 total rows worked.

Establish Interlocking Cables patt from Row 1 of Chart 2 as foll (RS): K1 (selv), work 2 "plus" sts, work 20-st patt rep 6 (7, 8, 9) times, work 12 "plus" sts, k1 (selv).

Cont in estab patt as foll: Work Rows 2-20 once, work Chart 3 Double Diamonds Rows 1-14 once, then Chart 2 Rows 27-40, then rep Chart 2 Rows 1-26 – 74 rows from end of ribbing; 101 rows total.

Shape Armholes

Note: Use the Sloped Bind Off Technique beginning with the 2nd bind off row on each side.

Cont in estab patt, working Chart 2 Rows 27-40, then rep from Row 1, shaping armholes as foll: BO 5 sts at beg of next 2 (2, 2, 6) rows, then BO 3 (4, 4, 4) sts at beg of next 2 (2, 4, 6) rows, then BO 2 (3, 3, 3) sts at beg of next 2 rows, then BO 2 sts at beg of next 0 (2, 4, 2) rows, then BO 1 st at beg of next 4 (6, 4, 0) rows – 112 (122,132,132) sts rem.

Next row (RS), re-establish selv and cont in patt until armhole measures 7½ (7½, 8¼, 9)"/ 19 (19, 21, 23) cm.

Funnel Collar

BO 32 (35, 40, 42) sts at beg of next 2 rows – 48 (52, 52, 48) sts rem for neck.

Next row (RS), re-establish selv and cont in patt for 22 rows, ending with a WS row. (Note: Finished collar will be half this height.) Bind off in purl.

Sleeves (make 2)

Notes: 1) Read entire section before beginning. 2) Increases begin after the 27 ribbing rows are complete and are worked in the rev St st patt at edges, while the cable chart is worked at the center.

CO 70 (80, 90, 90) sts.

Establish Cabled Ribbing patt from Row 0 of Chart 1 as foll (WS): K1 (selv), k2 (rev St st), pl mar, beg at left of chart work 2 "plus" sts, work 10-st patt rep 6 (7, 8, 8) times, work 2 "plus" sts, pl mar, k2 (rev St st), k1 (selv).

Cont in estab patt as foll: Work Rows 1-13, repeat Rows 2-13 once, then work Row 14 – 27 total rows worked.

Next row, establish sleeve pattern from Row 1 of Chart 4 as foll (RS): K1 (selv), work to mar (rev St st), sl mar, work 2 "plus" sts, work 20-st patt rep 3 (3½, 4, 4) times, work 2 "plus" sts, sl mar, work to last st (rev St st), k1 (selv).

Cont in estab patt, working all rows of Chart 4, then rep from Row 1, working increases as instructed below.

At the same time, shape sleeves as foll

Size S (M) only: Inc 1 st at beg and end of every foll 4th row 8 times, then every foll 6th row 3 times – 22 sts increased over 50 rows; 92 (102) sts on needles.

Size L only: Inc 1 st at beg and end of the foll 4th row, then [inc 1 st at beg and end of the foll 6th row, then the foll 4th row] 5 times – 22 sts increased over 54 rows; 112 sts on needles.

Size XL only: Inc 1 st at beg and end of the foll 6th row, then [inc 1 st at beg and end the of foll 4th row, then the foll 6th row] 5 times – 22 sts increased over 56 rows; 112 sts on needles.

All Sizes: Work even until piece measures 17 (17, 17½, 18)"/ 43 (43, 44.5, 46) cm, ending with a WS row.

Sleeve Cap Shaping

BO 5 sts at beg of next 2 rows, then cont shaping cap as foll:

Size S only: [BO 3 sts at beg of next 2 rows, then 2 sts at beg of foll 4 rows] 3 times, then BO 4 sts at beg of next 4 rows – 24 sts rem. BO all rem sts.

Size M only: BO 4 sts at beg of next 2 rows, then 3 sts at beg of foll 2 rows, then 2 sts at beg of foll 4 rows, then 3 sts at beg of foll 10 rows, then 4 sts at beg of foll 4 rows – 24 sts rem. BO all rem sts.

Size L only: BO 4 sts at beg of next 2 rows, then [BO 3 sts at beg of next 2 rows, then 2 sts at the beg of the foll 2 rows] 5 times, then BO 4 sts at beg of the next 4 rows – 28 sts rem. BO all rem sts.

Size XL only: BO 4 sts at beg of next 2 rows, then 3 sts at beg of foll 2 rows, then 2 sts at beg of foll 2 rows, then 3 sts at beg of foll 2 rows, then 2 sts at beg of foll 6 rows, then 3 sts at beg of foll 2 rows, then 2 sts at beg of foll 8 rows, then 4 sts at beg of foll 4 rows – 28 sts rem. BO all rem sts.

Finishing

Block pieces to measurements. Sew shoulder seams and side neck seams. Fold collar in half to the inside and stitch in place. Sew side and sleeve seams. Set in sleeves. Weave in ends.

Chart 1 - Cabled Ribbing
multiple of 10 + 4

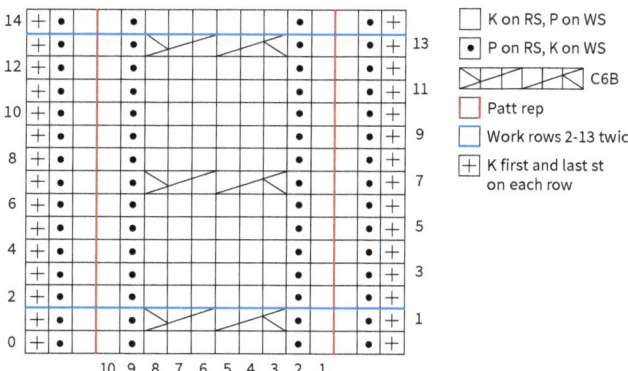

Chart 2 - Interlocking Cable Pattern
multiple of 20 + 14 / 40 rows

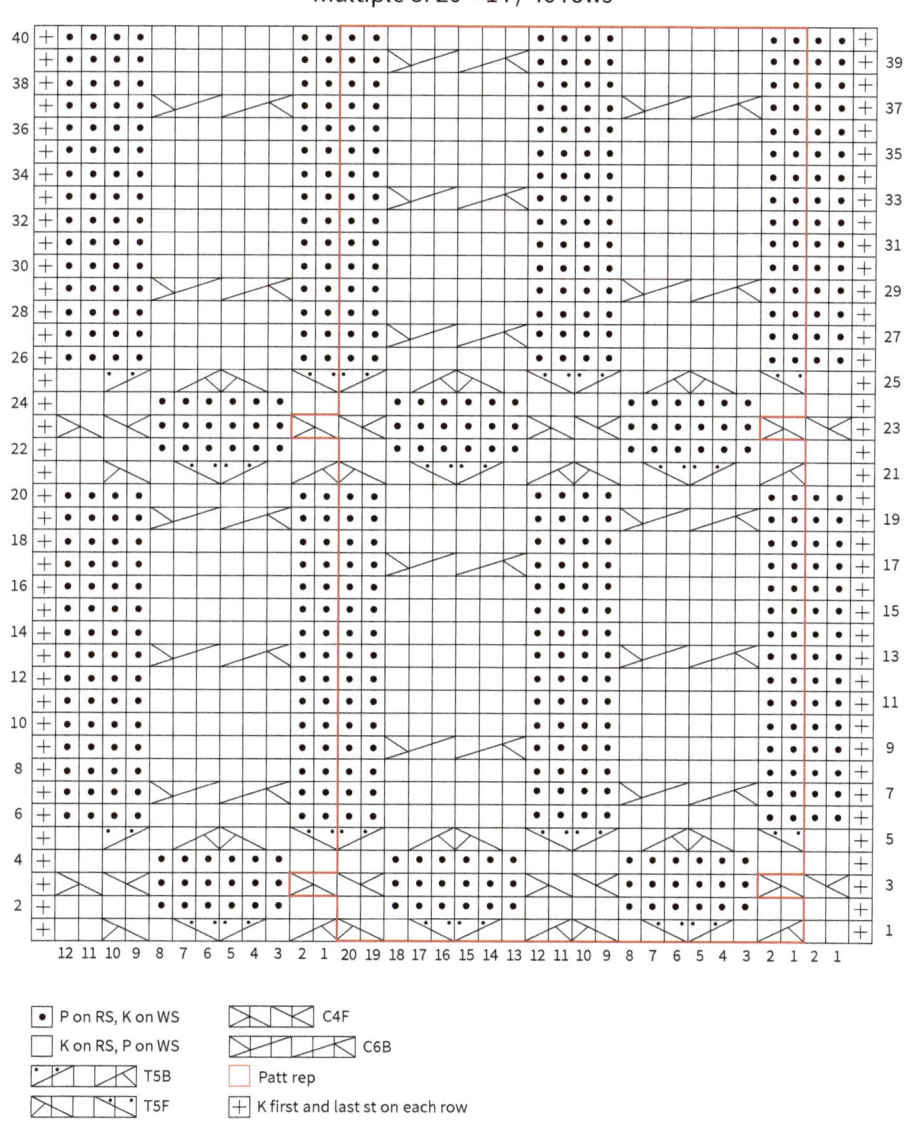

Chart 3 - Double Diamond Pattern
multiple of 20 + 14 / 14 rows

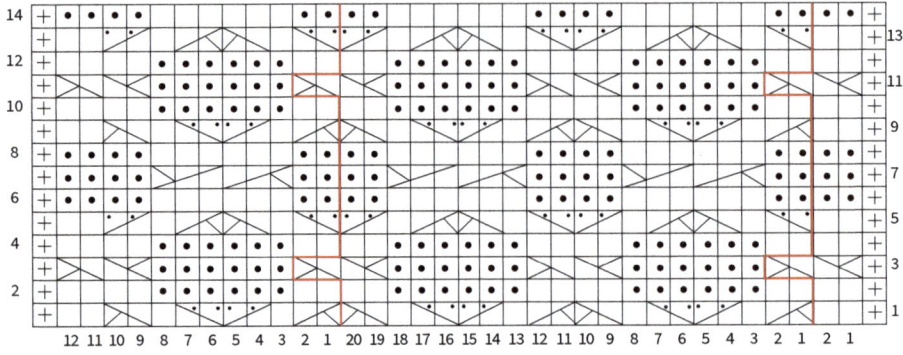

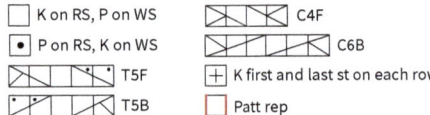

Chart 4 - Sleeve Pattern
multiple of 10 + 4 / 40 rows

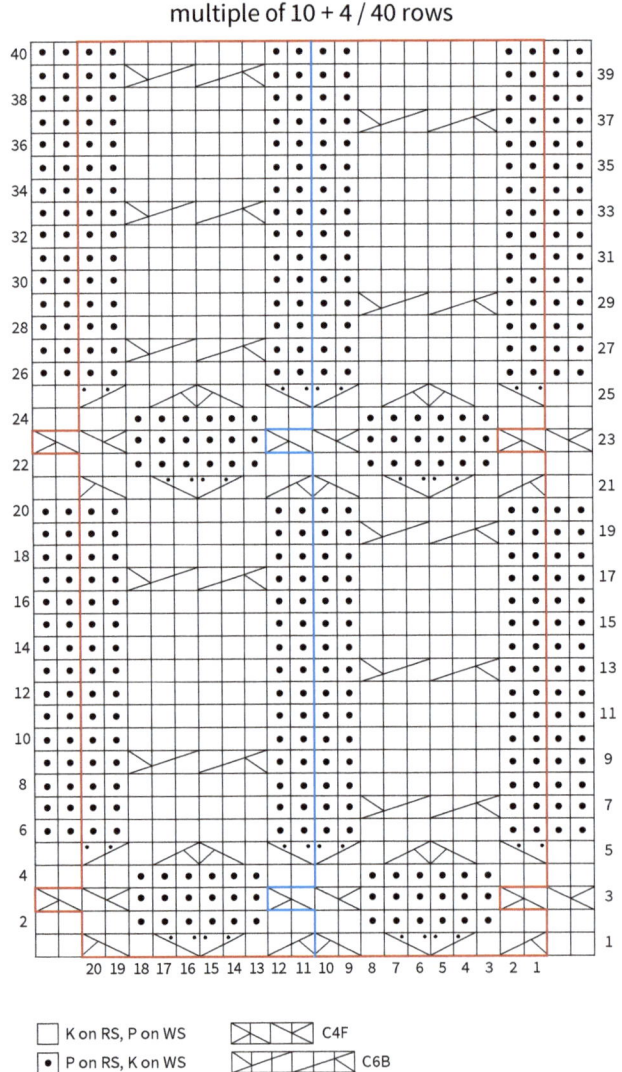

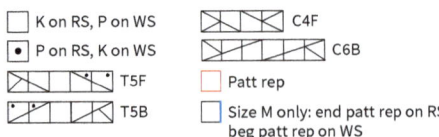

Nikki Reeves Body Schematic

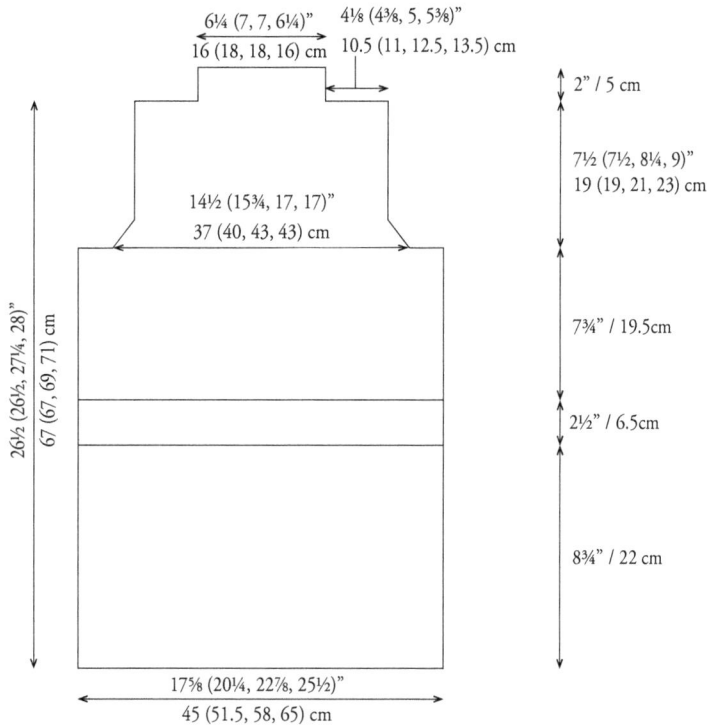

Nikki Reeves Sleeve Schematic

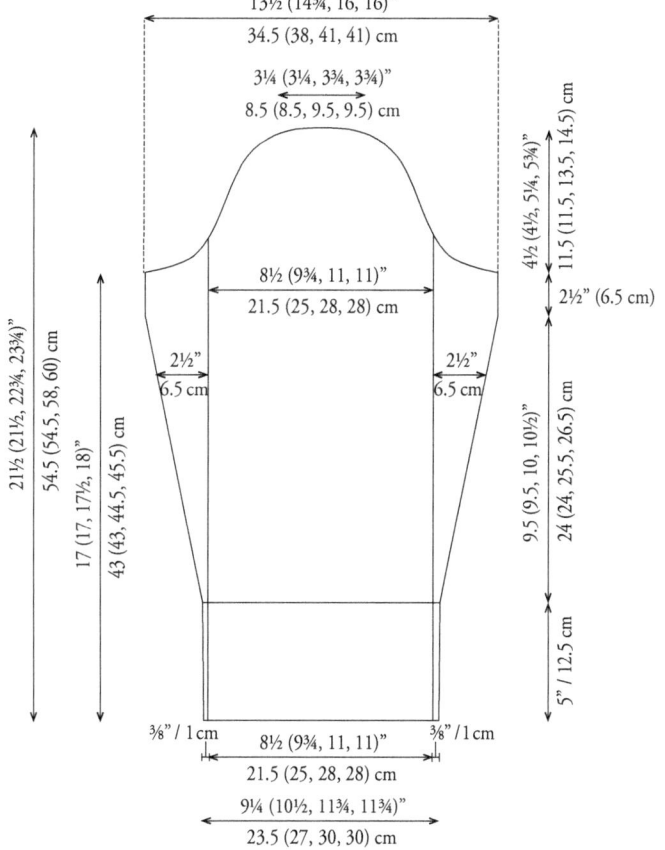

Open Bud Shawl

FINISHED MEASUREMENTS

Wingspan: 57¾" / 146.5 cm
Depth: 28" / 71 cm

YARN

Shibui Knits Cima (70% superbaby alpaca / 30% fine Merino; 328 yds [300 m] / 1.75 oz / 50 g): #2018 Bordeaux (A), 1 skein and #2022 Mineral (B), 2 skeins

Shibui Knits Silk Cloud (60% kid mohair / 40% silk; 328 yds [300 m] / 0.88 oz / 25 g): #2018 Bordeaux (C), 1 skein and #2022 Mineral (D), 2 skeins

NEEDLES

Size US 7 (4.5 mm)

NOTIONS

3 stitch markers, 2 dpns, blocking wires, blocking pins, tapestry needle

GAUGES

Lace Pattern:
17 sts and 37 rows = 4" / 10 cm in lace patt, blocked

Stockinette Stitch:
19 sts and 34 rows = 4" / 10 cm in St st, blocked

Gauge is not critical to this project's construction, however a change in gauge will affect the finished measurements and the yarn requirements.

NOTES

- The semi-circle shawl is worked from the lace border to neck.
- Two yarns are held together in different combinations throughout.
- The first and last 4 sts of every row are knit to create a garter edge along the wingspan of the shawl.
- Blocking this shawl is crucial to its shape.

INSTRUCTIONS

Lace Border

With yarns A and C held together, CO 4 sts, pl mar, CO 256 sts, pl mar, CO 4 sts - 264 sts total.

Establish the Lace Border chart as foll: K4 (garter edge), sm, work the 17-st patt rep a total of 15 times, work the 1 "plus" st, sm, k4 (garter edge). Cont in patt as estab, working Rows 2-28 once. Break C.

With A and D held together, work Rows 1-28 once. Break A.

With B and D held together, work Rows 1 – 28 once, then rep Rows 1 – 4 once more.

Stockinette Body

Cont with B and D, work 24 rows in St st with 4-st garter edge, placing marker at center on final row – 128 sts between markers on each side.

Next row - dec (RS): K4, sm, [ssk] until center m, sm, [k2tog] until last m, sm, k4 – 136 sts rem.
Maintaining garter edge, cont in St st for 57 rows then rep dec row – 72 sts rem.
Maintaining garter edge, cont in St st for 29 rows then rep dec row – 40 sts rem.
Maintaining garter edge, cont in St st for 15 rows then rep dec row – 24 sts rem.
Maintaining garter edge, cont in St st for 7 rows then rep dec row – 16 sts rem.
Maintaining garter edge, cont in St st for 5 rows then rep dec row – 12 sts rem.
Maintaining garter edge, cont in St st for 3 rows.

Next row (RS): K4, rem m, ssk, rem m, k2tog, rem m, k4 – 10 sts rem.

Next row (WS): K3, k2tog, ssk, k3 – 8 sts rem.

Divide rem sts evenly on 2 dpns and graft in garter st to join top edge of shawl.

Finishing

After soaking, use blocking wires along garter edge (wingspan) of shawl. Pin this edge in a straight line to form the diameter of the semi-circle. Then pin the lace border to form the outer edge of the semi-circle. Allow to dry. Weave in all ends.

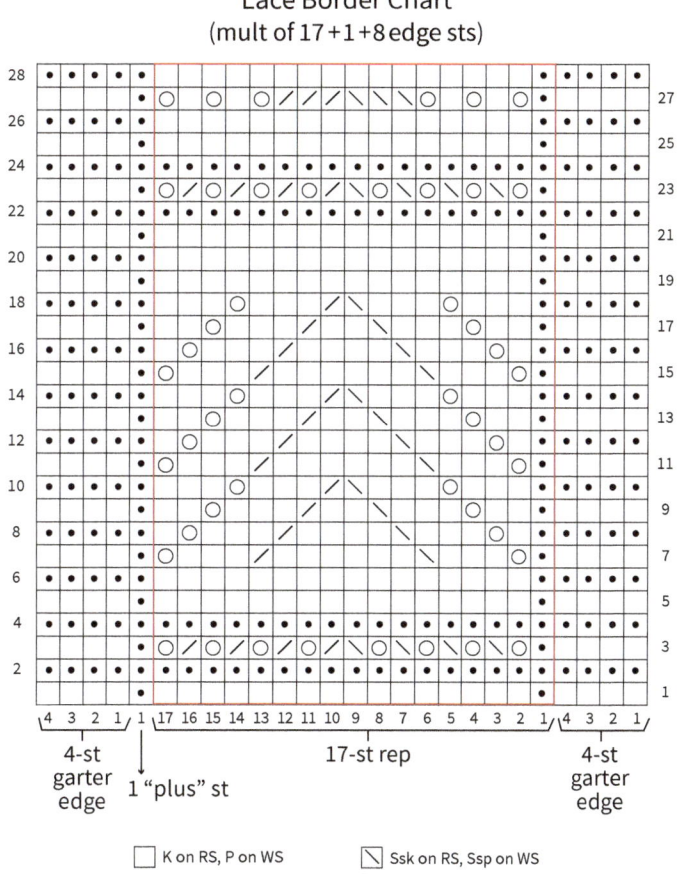

Open Bud Shawl
Lace Border Chart
(mult of 17 + 1 + 8 edge sts)

OLGA JANKELOVICH

Primavera Dress

FINISHED SIZES

Women's S (M, L)
Finished bust: 35 (42, 49)" / 89 (106.5, 124.5) cm
To fit bust: 28-30 (32-38, 40-44)" / 71-76 (81-96.5, 101.5-111.5) cm

Sample Size: S, length 34" / 86.5 cm

YARN

The Knitting Boutique Chesapeake Fingering (67% Superfine Merino / 33% Cashmere; 430 yds [393 m] / 3.5 oz / 100 g): in color "Lilac" 5 (6, 6) skeins

NEEDLES

Size US 5 (3.75 mm) and size US 3 (3.25 mm) straight and 32" (80 cm) circular needles
Adjust needle size if necessary to obtain the correct gauge.

NOTIONS

cable needle; tapestry needle; stitch markers

GAUGES

22 sts and 28 rows = 4" / 10 cm in Twisted Ribbing on larger needles
30 sts and 32 rows = 4" / 10 cm in Twisted Ribbing on smaller needles

Wraps patt (Rows 1 - 14 of Double Leaves and Twists chart):
24 sts and 14 rows = 3½" x 2⅛" / 9 x 5.5 cm on larger needles and 3⅛" x 1⅝" / 8 x 4 cm on smaller needles

Double Leaves patt (Rows 15 - 36 of Double Leaves and Twists chart):
24 sts and 22 rows = 3¾" x 2¾" / 9.5 x 7 cm on larger needles and 3½" x 2½" / 9 x 6.4 cm on smaller needles

Note: All measurements were taken on blocked swatches.

STITCH GUIDE

Twisted Ribbing pattern:
(worked flat over multiple of 3 sts + 2 edge sts)
Row 1 (RS): P1 (selvedge st), p1, [k1tbl, p2] to last 3 sts, k1tbl, p1, p1 (selvedge st).
Row 2 (WS): [k2, p1tbl] to last 2 sts, k2.

4-stitch double wrap (W4) - (see Double Leaves and Twists chart Rows 1 – 14)
Sl 4 sts to cn and hold to front. With working yarn, wrap these 4 sts by taking the yarn behind the cn and then to front and around twice. Yarn should be wrapped loosely enough so that when blocked, the 4 sts do not appear distorted. Then work 4 sts from cn: k1tbl, p2, k1tbl. See page 120.

INSTRUCTIONS

Back and Front

Ruffle Shaping

Note: The ruffle begins with 4 purl sts bet twisted knit sts and dec to 2 purl sts bet twisted knit sts over 40 rows.

With size 5 (3.75 mm) needles, CO 202 (242, 282) sts.

Row 1: (RS) P1 (selvedge st), p2, k1tbl, *p4, k1tbl; rep from * to last 3 sts, p2, p1 (selvedge st).

Row 2: (WS) K3, p1tbl, *k4, p1tbl; rep from * to last 3 sts, k3.

Rows 3 – 8: Work in estab patt.

Row 9 (RS): P3, k1tbl, *p1, p2tog, p1, k1tbl, p4, k1tbl; rep from * to last 8 sts, p1, p2tog, p1, k1tbl, p3. 182 (218, 254) sts rem.

Row 10: K3, p1tbl, *k3, p1tbl, k4, p1tbl; rep from * to last 7 sts, k3, p1tbl, k3.

Row 11: P3, k1tbl, *p3, k1tbl, p4, k1tbl; rep from * to last 7 sts, p3, k1tbl, p3.

Rows 12 – 16: Work in est patt.

Row 17 (RS): P3, k1tbl, *p3, k1tbl, p1, p2tog, p1, k1tbl; rep from * to last 7 sts, p3, k1tbl, p3. 163 (195, 227) sts rem.

Row 18: *K3, p1tbl; rep from *to last 3 sts, k3.

Row 19: *P3, k1tbl; rep from * to last 3 sts, p3.

Rows 20 – 24: Work in estab patt.

Row 25 (RS): P3, k1tbl, *p2tog, p1, k1tbl, p3, k1tbl; rep from *to last 7 sts, p2tog, p1, k1tbl, p3. 143 (171, 199) sts rem.

Row 26: K3, p1tbl, *k2, p1tbl, k3, p1tbl; rep from * to last 6 sts, k2, p1tbl, k3.

Row 27: P3, k1tbl, *p2, k1tbl, p3, k1tbl; rep from * to last 6 sts, p2, k1tbl, p3.

Rows 28 – 32: Work in est patt.

Row 33 (RS): *P1, p2tog, k1tbl, p2, k1tbl; rep from * to last 3 sts. 122 (146, 170) sts rem.

Row 34 – 40: Work 7 rows in Twisted Ribbing beg and end with a WS row.

Ruffle measures 5¾" / 14.5 cm.

Skirt

Beg Wraps patt (Rows 1 - 14 of chart) as foll: work 3 plus sts once, then 24-st rep 4 (5, 6) times and finish the row with 23 plus sts. Work through Row 14 as estab.

Change to size 3 (3.25 mm) needles and beg Double Leaves patt (Rows 15 - 36), estab patt as for Wraps patt (3 plus sts + 24-st rep 4 (5, 6) times + 23 plus sts).

For the next rep of Double Leaves patt, estab patt from chart Row 15 as foll:

RS: Work sts 10 - 24 once, then work entire patt rep 4 (5, 6) times, then work sts 1 - 11.

WS: Work sts 11 - 1 once, then work entire patt rep 4 (5, 6) times, then work sts 24 - 10.

Work as estab through row 36 of chart.

Then, rep Rows 15 - 36 of chart again, working as for first rep.

Waist

Work in Twisted Ribbing (p2, k1tbl) for 50 rows. Piece measures 21½" / 55 cm from CO edge.

Bodice

Change to size 5 (3.75 mm) needles.

Sizes S and L: Work Wraps patt (Rows 1 - 14) twice, placing mars on final row 14 as foll: work 25 (49) sts in patt, pl mar, cont in patt for 72 sts, pl mar, work in patt to end.

Size M: Work Wraps patt (Rows 1 - 14) twice, establishing patt as foll:

RS: Work sts 10 – 24 of patt rep once, then work entire patt rep 5 times, then work sts 1-11 once more (you may not work Wrap 4 at both ends at Row 9 and Row 13). WS: Work sts 11-1 of patt rep once, work entire patt rep 5 times, then work sts 24 -10 once more. Pl mars on final row 14 as foll: work in patt for 37 sts, pl mar, cont in patt for 72 sts, pl mar, work in patt to end.

Piece measures 25¾" / 66 cm from CO edge.

Armhole and Raglan Shaping

Note: Read the entire section before proceeding. Pattern stitch is worked simultaneously with armhole shaping followed by raglan decreases.

You will work over 72 center sts bet mars, Double Leaves patt first (Rows 15 - 36) with larger needles, then with smaller needles, Wraps patt (Rows 1-14) once, then finish with 12 (16, 24) rows in Twisted rib patt.

Double Leaves and Wraps patt are worked as foll: work sts 2-3 of plus 3 sts, then 24-st rep 2 times, then sts 1-22 once.

Next row (RS): BO 2 (3, 4) sts, work in twisted rib to mar, sl mar, work Double leaves patt, foll the layout described as above, sl mar, work in twisted rib to end. 120 (143, 166) sts rem.

BO 2 (3, 4) sts at beg of next 11 (15, 15) rows, maintaining patt and ending with chart row 26 (30, 30). 98 (98, 106) sts rem.

Beg raglan dec as foll, cont working patt (change to smaller needle when beg Wraps patt).

(RS) P2, p2tog, work to last 4 sts, p2tog tbl, p2. 2 sts dec'd.

(WS) K3, work to last 3 sts, k3.

Rep these two rows 17 (17, 21) more times, switching to Twisted rib patt after Row 14 of chart and cont 12 (16, 24) rows until 62 sts rem. BO all sts.

Sleeves

With size 5 (3.75 mm) needles, CO 131 (163, 195) sts.

Bell-cuff Ruffle Shaping

Work bell-cuff ruffle similar to body ruffle.
Row 1: *P3, k1tbl, to last 3 sts, p3.
Row 2: *K3, p1tbl, to last 3 sts, k3.
Rows 3 – 12: Work in estab patt.
Row 13: P3, k1tbl, *p1, p2tog, k1tbl, p3, k1tbl; repeat from * to last 7 sts, p1, p2tog, k1tbl, p3. 115 (143, 171) sts rem.

Row 14: K3, p1tbl, *k2, p1tbl, k3, p1tbl; rep from * to last 6 sts, k2, p1tbl, k3.
Row 15: P3, k1tbl, *p2, k1tbl, p3, k1tbl; rep from * to last 6 sts, p2, k1tbl, p3.
Rows 16 – 24: Work in est patt.
Row 25: P1, p2tog, k1tbl, *p2, k1tbl, p1, p2tog, k1tbl; rep from * to last 6 sts, p2, k1tbl, p2tog, p1. 98 (122, 146) sts rem.
Rows 26 – 36: Work 11 rows in Twisted Ribbing beginning and ending with a WS row.

Work Wraps patt (Rows 1 - 14) twice, estab patt as foll:

Sizes S & L: work sts 2-3 of 3 plus sts, then 24-rep 3 (-, 5) times, then sts 1-22.

Size M: work sts 11-24 once, then 24-st rep 4 times, then sts 1-10.

In the final row, pl mars as foll: work in patt for 25 (37, 49) sts, pl mar, cont in patt for 48 sts, pl mar, work in patt to end.

Armhole shaping

Note: the patts are worked in the foll order, as for front and back: Rows 15-36, then Rows 1-14, then 12 (16, 24) rows in twisted ribbing.

Change to size 3 (3.25 mm) needles.

Next row (RS): BO 2 (3, 4) sts, work in rib to mar, sl mar, work sts 2-3 of plus 3 sts, then 24-st rep once, then sts 1-21 once, sl mar, work in rib to end. 96 (119, 142) sts rem.

BO 2 (3, 4) sts at beg of next 11 (15, 15) rows, maintaining patt. 74 (74, 82) sts rem.

Beg raglan dec as foll, cont working patt (beg Wraps patt after Row 36).

(RS) P2, p2tog, work to last 4 sts, p2tog tbl, p2. 2 sts dec'd.

(WS) K3, work to last 3 sts, k3.

Rep these two rows 17 (17, 21) times, switching to Twisted rib patt after Row 14 of chart and cont 12 (16, 24) rows until 38 sts rem. BO all sts.

Finishing

Block all pieces according to the measurements on schematics stretching evenly the body ruffles on the bottom up to 36 (44, 50)" / 92 (110, 128) cm and sleeves ruffles up to 23 (29, 35)" / 60 (74, 88) cm. Sew the side and raglan seams. Weave in the ends.

If desired to prevent stretching sew a narrow ribbon around the neckline from WS.

Primavera Dress Front and Back

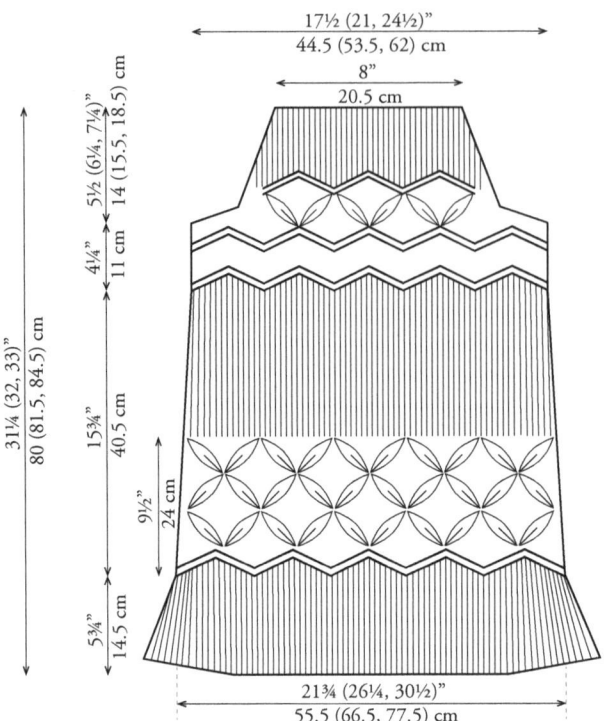

Primavera Dress Sleeves

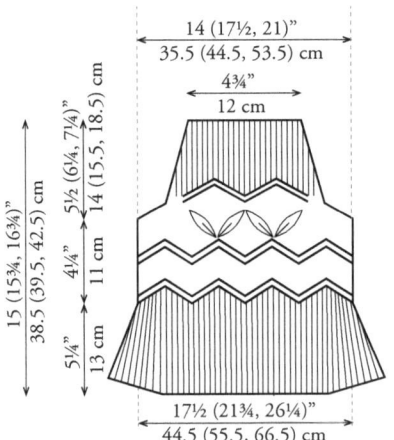

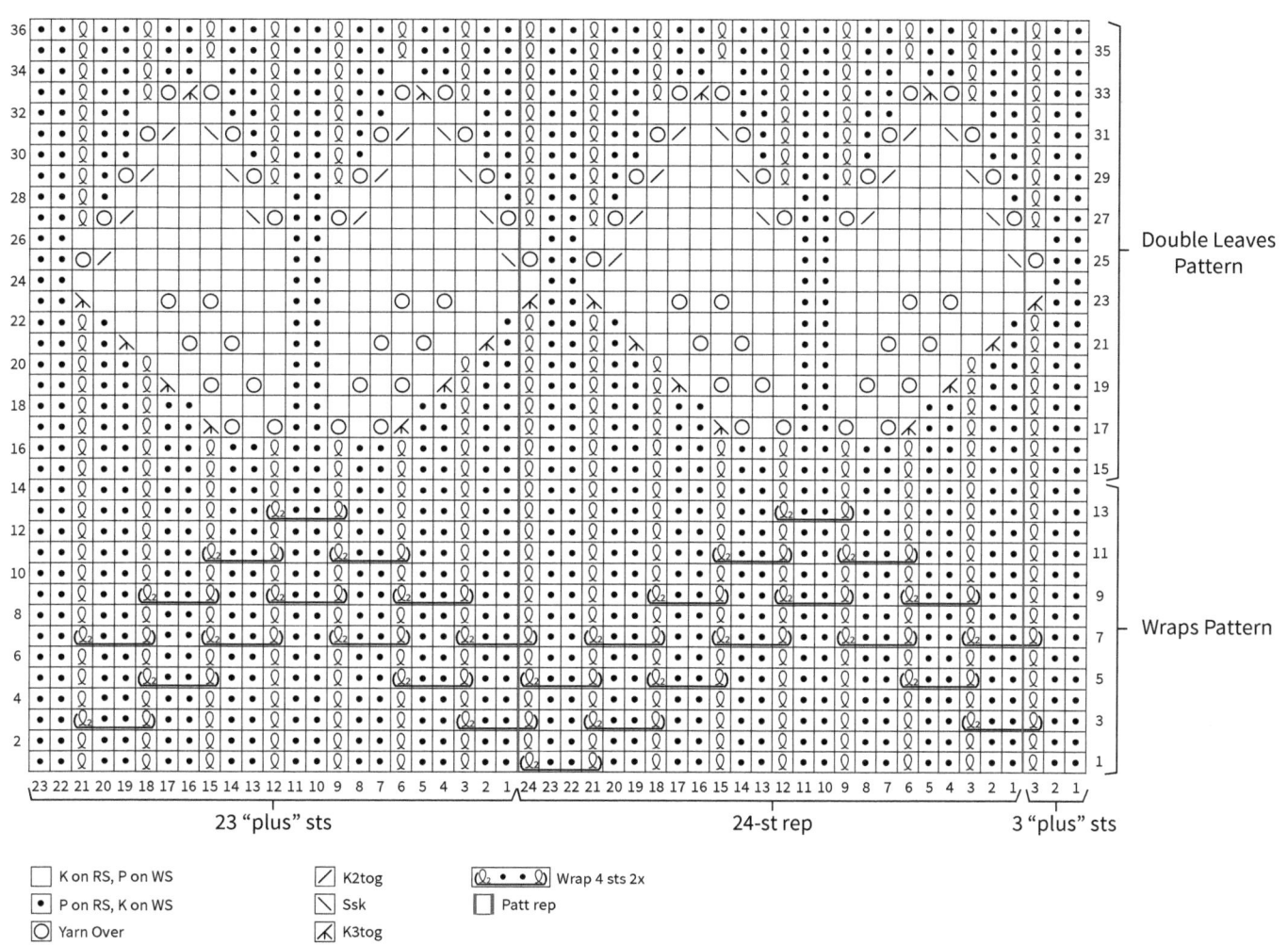

Sazanami Mini Dress

FINISHED SIZES

Women's XS (S, M, L)
Finished bust: 32¼ (36, 40¾, 43¾)" / 82 (91.5, 101.5, 111) cm
To fit bust sizes: 31 (35, 38½, 42)" / 78 (87.5, 97, 106.5) cm
Length: 29⅞ (33⅛, 36½, 39)" / 75.5 (84, 92.5, 99) cm

Sample Size: XS

YARN

Cascade Ultra Pima Fine (100% Cotton; 136 yds [124 m] / 1.75 oz / 50 g): colorway 3734 Teal, 9 (11, 13, 15) balls

NEEDLES

Size US 4 (3.5 mm)
Adjust needle size if necessary to obtain the correct gauge.

NOTIONS

Stitch markers; tapestry needle

GAUGES

Stockinette Stitch:
21 sts and 28 rows = 4" (10 cm)

Cable and Twist Pattern:
29 sts and 29 rows = 4" (10 cm)

STITCH GUIDE

Cr2L - K 2nd st tbl crossing behind the 1st st, then k the 1st st, sl both tog to RHN

Cr2R - K 2nd st crossing in front of 1st st, then k 1st st, sl both tog to RHN

C4F - Sl2 to cn, hold front, k2, then k2 from cn

C8B - Sl4 to cn, hold back, k4, then k4 from cn

C8F - Sl4 to cn, hold front, k4, then k4 from cn

NOTES

- Back and Front are identical and are worked flat from the bottom up.
- Horizontal cable panels are worked separately and seamed to the body as you go.
- Cable panels are worked with a Stockinette selvedge st at either side: knit first and last sts on RS rows; purl first and last sts on WS rows.

INSTRUCTIONS

Back / Front (make 2)

CO 126 (136, 151, 163) sts using long-tail method.

Purl 2 rows.

Pleats

Row 1 (RS): P3, *k20 (22, 20, 22), p5; rep from * 3 (3, 4, 4) more times, k20 (22, 20, 22), p3.

Row 2 and all WS rows: Work all sts as they appear (knit the knits and purl the purls).

Rep these 2 rows 5 (5, 7, 7) more times.

Next row (RS) – 1st dec: P1, p2tog, *k20 (22, 20, 22), p2tog, p1, p2tog; rep from* 3 (3, 4, 4) more times, k20 (22, 20, 22), p2tog, p1 - 116 (126, 139, 151) sts.

Next RS row, re-estab patt: P2, *k20 (22, 20, 22), p3; rep from * 3 (3, 4, 4) more times, k20 (22, 20, 22), p2.

Work as estab for 5 (7, 7, 9) more rows, ending with WS row.

Next row (RS) – 2nd dec: P2tog, *k20 (22, 20, 22), p3tog; rep from * 3 (3, 4, 4) more times, k20 (22, 20, 22), p2tog - 106 (116, 127, 139) sts.

Next RS row, re-estab patt: *P1, k20 (22, 20, 22); rep from * 4 (4, 5, 5) more times, p1.

Work as estab for 3 (5, 5, 7) more row(s), ending with WS row.

BO all sts on RS.

Horizontal Cable Insert (Chart #1)

All sizes, CO 12 sts using long-tail method.

Sizes XS (S, M) only:

Work Rows 1-16 of Cable & Twist Pattern #1 9 (10, 11) times – 144 (160, 176) rows total.

Size L only:

Work Rows 3-16 of Cable & Twist Pattern #1, then work Rows 1-16 ten times, then rep Rows 1-14 once more - 188 rows total.

BO all sts on RS.

With RS facing, sew top edge of Pleats to right edge of Horizontal Cable Insert using either backstitch or mattress stitch.

Body

With RS facing, pick up and knit 107 (117, 127, 139) sts evenly across the top edge of Horizontal Cable Insert.

Work back and forth in St st, decreasing as follows:

Dec 1 st at each edge of every 5th (6th, 7th, 6th) RS row 1 (5, 8, 1) time(s), then every 6th (7th, 8th, 7th) RS row 8 (4, 1, 9) time(s) - 89 (99, 109, 119) sts.

Work even for 21 (23, 25, 27) rows, or desired length to underarm, ending with WS row. Piece measures 23⅜ (25¾, 28¼, 30½)" / 59 (65, 71.5, 77.5) cm from CO edge.

Armhole shaping

Size M only: BO 3 sts at beg of next 2 rows – 103 sts.

Size L only: BO 5 sts at beg of next 2 rows – 109 sts.

All sizes: BO 2 sts at beg of next 2 (2, 2, 4) rows, then BO 1 st at beg of next 6 (8, 8, 8) rows - 79 (87, 91, 93) sts.

Work even for 6 (10, 14, 14) rows.

BO all sts on RS.

Top Cable (Chart #2)

Note: Use sloped bind off to shape neckline.

All sizes, CO 35 sts using long-tail method.

Beg with Row 13 (15, 13, 11) of Cable & Twist Pattern #2, work in patt for 21 (27, 29, 31) rows, ending with chart row 1 (9, 9, 9). BO 3 sts at the beg of next 2 WS rows, then work even in patt for 56 rows, ending with chart row 12 (4, 4, 4). CO 3 sts at end of next 2 RS rows. Work even in patt for 21 (27, 29, 31) more rows, ending with chart row 4 (2, 4, 6) - 104 (116, 120, 124) rows total.

BO all sts on RS.

With RS facing, sew right edge of TOP CABLE to top edge of Body using either backstitch or mattress stitch.

Finishing

Block to finished measurements. Sew side seams. Sew shoulders.

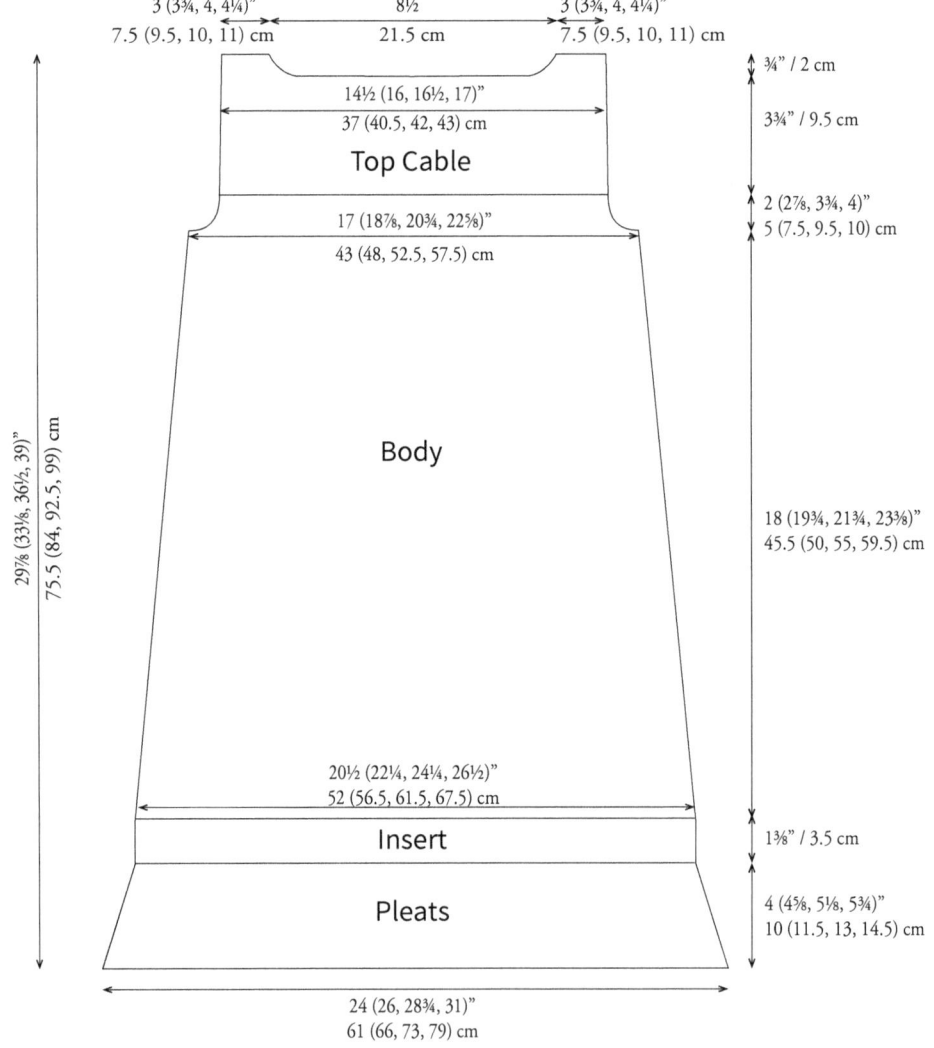

Sazanami Dress

Cable & Twist Pattern
Chart #1

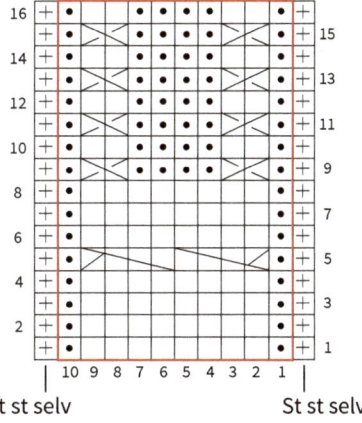

Cable & Twist Pattern
Chart #2

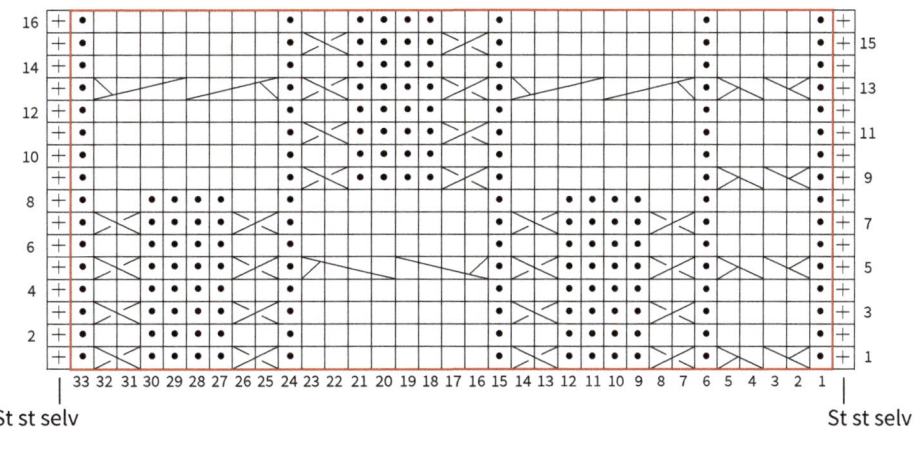

AYANO TANAKA

Seseragi Pullover

FINISHED SIZES

Women's S (M, L)
Finished bust: 37¼ (41½, 44)" / 95 (105.5, 112) cm
To fit bust sizes: 32-34 (36-38, 39-41)" / 81-86 (91.5-96.5, 99-104) cm

Sample Size: S

YARN

Blue Sky Fibers Alpaca Silk (50% alpaca / 50% silk; 145 yds [133m] / 1.75 oz / 50 g): colorway 110 "Ecu", 9 (10, 11) balls

NEEDLES

Size US 7 (4.5 mm) & US 5 (3.75 mm)
Adjust needle size if necessary to obtain the correct gauge.

NOTIONS

Locking markers or waste yarn; stitch holder; stitch markers; tapestry needle

GAUGES

Twisted Hearts Pattern:
29.5 sts and 30 rows = 4" / 10 cm in patt with larger needles
31 sts and 34 rows = 4" / 10 cm in patt with smaller needles

Side Panel Pattern:
23 sts and 32.5 rows = 4" / 10 cm in patt with larger needles
25 sts and 36 rows = 4" / 10 cm in patt with smaller needles

STITCH GUIDE

Twisted Rib Pattern
(worked flat over an even number of sts)
Row 1 (RS): [K1tbl, p1]
Row 2 (WS): [K1, p1tbl]

NOTES

- A Garter stitch selvedge is worked at both edges of all pieces: Knit the first and last sts of every row.
- Work all twisted sts as k1tbl on RS and p1tbl on WS.
- Shoulder shaping is worked with the sloped bind off method.
- When increasing and decreasing in pattern, omit yarn overs when there is no offsetting decrease, and vice versa.

INSTRUCTIONS

Back

With larger needles and Tubular cast on, CO 114 (128, 142) sts.

Set up Twisted Rib as foll (WS): K1 (selv), [k1, p1tbl] to last st (Twisted Rib), k1 (selv).

Work in patt as estab for 4 more rows. (½"/ 1.5 cm)

Next row (RS) estab patt from Row 1 (11, 11) of Twisted Hearts chart as foll: K1 (selv), k1tbl (twist st), work 14 (21, 0) "plus" sts, then work 3 (3, 4) full patt reps, then work 13 (20, 27) plus" sts, M1 (twist st), k1 (selv) – 115 (129, 143) sts.

Cont in patt as estab for 17 more rows. Piece measures 3"/ 7.5 cm from CO edge.

Waist-to-shoulder shaping

Change to smaller needles and work 6 rows in patt.

Next row (RS) - inc: K1 (selv), k1tbl (twist st), M1, work Twisted Hearts patt to last 2 sts, M1, k1tbl (twist st), k1 (selv) – 2 sts inc.

Rep inc row every 6th row 4 (4, 8) more times, then every 4th row 10 (11, 5) times – 145 (161, 171) sts. Work even 2 rows then place locking markers at beg and end of row to mark underarms. Resume incs every 4th row 13 (15, 15) more times – 171 (191, 201) sts.

Work even 3 rows.

Piece measures 17½ (18¾, 18¾)" / 44.5 (48, 48) cm.

Shoulder and neck shaping

Cont in patt and BO for shoulders as foll: BO 4 (6, 6) sts at beg of next 6 (8, 12) rows, then 5 (7, 0) sts at beg of next 8 (2, 0) rows – 107 (129, 129) sts rem.

Note: From this point, neck and shoulder shaping will be worked at the same time, first for the right shoulder, then for the left.

Back Right Shoulder

Next row (RS): BO 5 (7, 7) sts, leaving one st on the RH needle. Work 33 (41, 41) sts in patt - 34 (42, 42) sts on the RH needle. Place rem 68 (80, 80) sts from LH needle onto a stitch holder.

BO at neck edge (WS rows) then work to end as foll: BO 8 sts once, then BO 5 sts once, then BO 1 st once, then work 1 WS row even.

At the same time, work rem shoulder shaping at beg of RS rows as foll: BO 5 (7, 7) sts 3 times, then BO rem 5 (7, 7) sts.

Back Left Shoulder

Return all held sts to needle. With RS facing, join new yarn and BO 29 (31, 31) sts for back neck then work to end.

Work rem shoulder shaping at beg of WS rows as foll: BO 5 (7, 7) sts 4 times.

At the same BO for neck at beg of RS rows as foll: BO 8 sts once, then BO 5 sts once, then BO 1 st once.

Then BO rem 5 (7, 7) sts.

Front

Work as for Back to beg of waist-to-shoulder shaping, change to smaller needles, work 6 rows even in patt then work inc row as for Back. Rep inc row every 6th row 4 (4, 8) more times, then every 4th row 23 (25, 19) times, placing locking markers to mark underarms – 171 (189, 199) sts.

Work even 3 (1, 1) WS row(s).

Note: Waist-to-shoulder shaping is complete for size S. Other sizes must work rem incs while beginning the neck shaping. Next row for all sizes should be chart row 1. Shoulder BO will begin on chart row 3 (7, 7).

Neck and shoulder shaping

Next row (RS) work 76 (84, 90) sts in patt, then place rem 95 (105, 109) sts from LH needle onto a stitch holder.

Left Front

Note: Neck shaping, rem waist-to-shoulder incs, and shoulder shaping is worked at the same time. Read the instructions completely before continuing.

Work neck shaping at beg of next 9 (9, 10) WS rows as foll: BO 6 sts once, then BO 4 sts once, then BO 3 sts once, then BO 2 sts twice, then BO 0 (0, 1) st 0 (0, 1) time, then BO 1 st every other WS row twice. Work even at neck edge for rem rows.

Size S only: At the same time, work shoulder shaping at beg of RS rows as foll: BO 4 sts 3 times, then BO 5 sts 9 times - no sts rem.

Sizes M & L only: At the same time in next RS row work inc as estab – waist-to-shoulder shaping is complete. Work even at beg of next RS row, then beg with foll RS row work shoulder shaping as foll: BO 6 sts at beg of RS row - (4, 6) times; then BO 7 sts - (5, 4) time(s); then BO rem 7 sts.

Right Front

Return all held sts to needle. With RS facing, join new yarn and BO 19 (21, 19) sts for front neck then work chart row 1 in patt to end – 76 (84, 90) sts on the needle. Work 0 (1, 1) WS row.

Note: Neck shaping, rem waist-to-shoulder incs, and shoulder shaping is worked at the same time. Read the instructions completely before continuing. Shoulder BO will begin on chart row 2 (6, 6).

Work neck shaping at beg of next 9 (9, 10) RS rows as foll: BO 6 sts once, then BO 4 sts once, then BO 3 sts once, then BO 2 sts twice, then BO 0 (0, 1) st 0 (0, 1) time, then BO 1 st every other RS row twice. Work even at neck edge for rem rows.

Size S only: At the same time, work shoulder shaping at beg of WS rows as foll: BO 4 sts 3 times, then BO 5 sts 9 times - no sts rem.

Sizes M & L only: At the same time work inc as estab in first RS row – waist-to-shoulder shaping is complete. Work even at beg of next 2 WS rows, then beg with foll WS row work shoulder shaping as foll: BO 6 sts at beg of WS row - (4, 6) times; then BO 7 sts - (5, 4) time(s); then BO rem 7 sts.

Side Panels (make 2)

With larger needles and Tubular cast on, CO 28 (34, 32) sts.
Set up Twisted Rib as foll (WS): K1 (selv), [k1, p1tbl] to last st (Twisted Rib), k1 (selv).
Work in patt as estab for 4 more rows. (½"/1.5 cm)

Estab patt from Row 1 of Side Panel chart as foll: K1 (selv), k0 (1, 0) (extra St st), work 0 (2, 2) "plus" sts, work patt rep #1 twice, pl mar, k2, ssk, k2 (center), work patt rep #2 twice, work 0 (2, 2) "plus" sts, k0 (1, 0) (extra St st), k1 (selv) – 27 (33, 31) sts.

Work even in patt as estab for 19 rows. Piece measures 3"/ 7.5 cm.

Size S only: Rows 3 and 13: Omit the first and last decreases of Patt Reps 1 and 2 once, replace them with k1.

Change to smaller needles work even in patt for 6 rows, rep from chart row 11.

Next row (RS) - dec: K1 (selv), k2tog, work in patt to mar, work center, work in patt to last 3 sts, ssk, k1 (selv) – 2 sts dec.

Note: To maintain pattern while decreasing at edges, omit yo's, ssk's and k2tog's when no longer offset by charted dec/inc, replacing with k1 as necessary.

Cont in patt and rep dec row every 6 rows 8 (9, 3) more times, then every 4 rows 1 (3, 9) time(s), then every 10 (6, 0) rows 1 (1, 0) time – 5 sts rem.

Work even 7 (1, 19) row(s) then BO rem sts.

Sleeves (make 2)

Made with Twisted Hearts Lace patt.
With smaller needles and Tubular cast on, CO 88 sts.
Work Twisted Rib as for body and side panels.

Next row (RS), referring to the 28-st patt rep of the Twisted Hearts chart, estab patt from Row 1 as foll: K1 (selv), work 2 "plus" sts beg at st #27, work patt rep three times, M1 ("plus" st), k1 (selv) – 89 sts.
Work even in patt as estab for 29 more rows. Piece measures 4"/ 10 cm from CO edge.

Next row (RS) – inc: K1 (selv), M1, work in patt to last st, M1, k1 (selv) – 2 sts inc.
Cont in patt and rep inc row every 10 (6, 6) rows 4 (6, 2) times, then every 8 (4, 4) rows 1 (7, 11) time(s) – 101 (117, 117) sts.
Work even in patt for 9 (3, 3) rows, then BO all sts.

Finishing

Block pieces to measurements. Sew shoulder seams, side seams and sleeves.

Neck band

With smaller circular needles or dpns and with RS facing, beg at left shoulder seam. pick up and knit 77 (81, 87) sts from front neck edge and 59 (61, 67) sts from back neck edge – 136 (142, 154) sts.

Work 1x1 twisted rib 10 rows. (1¼"/ 3 cm). BO all sts.

Weave in ends.

Seseragi Pullover

Body

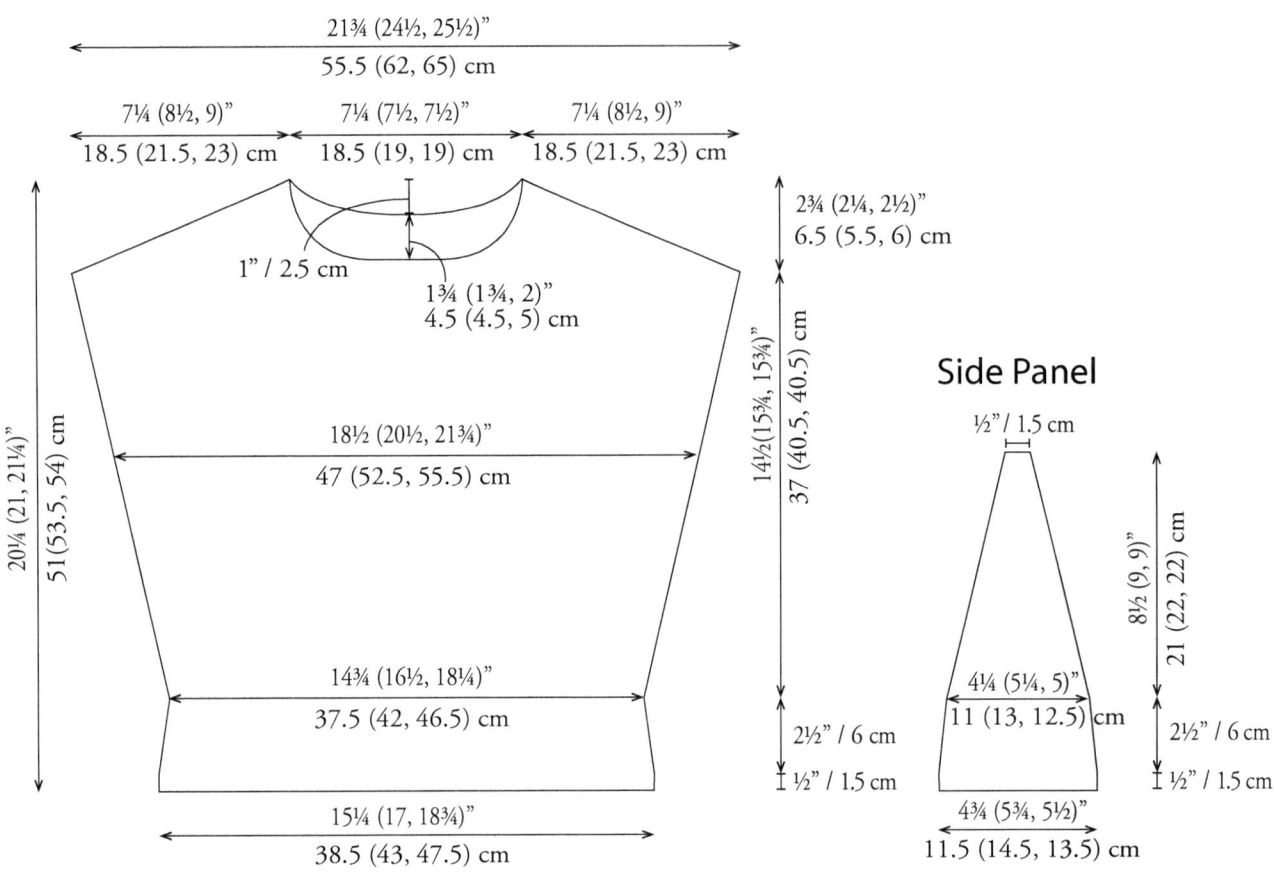

Side Panel

Sleeves

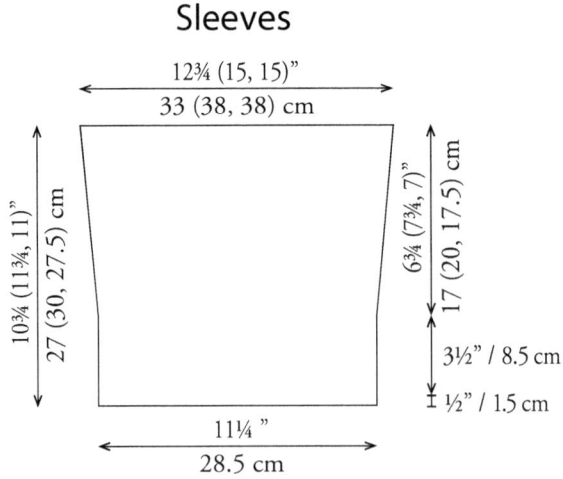

Side Panel Chart

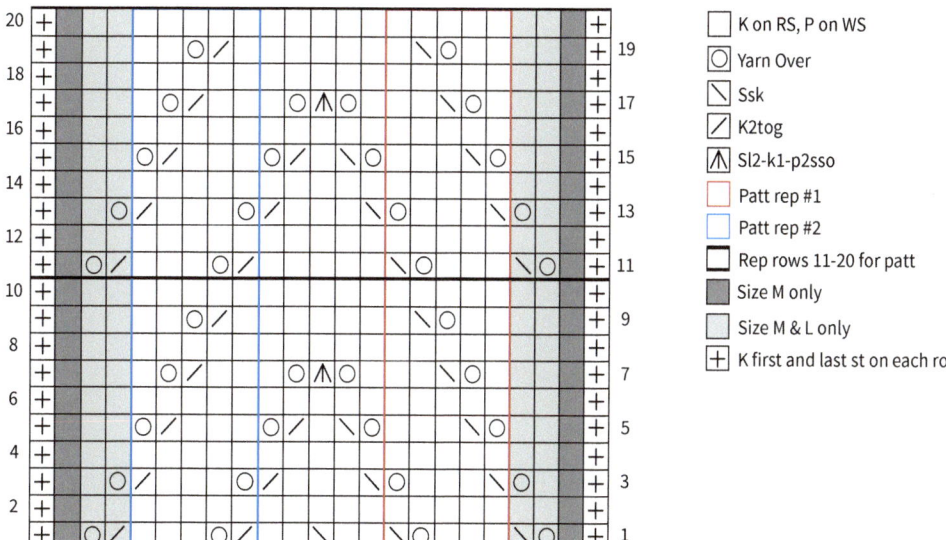

Twisted Hearts Size S

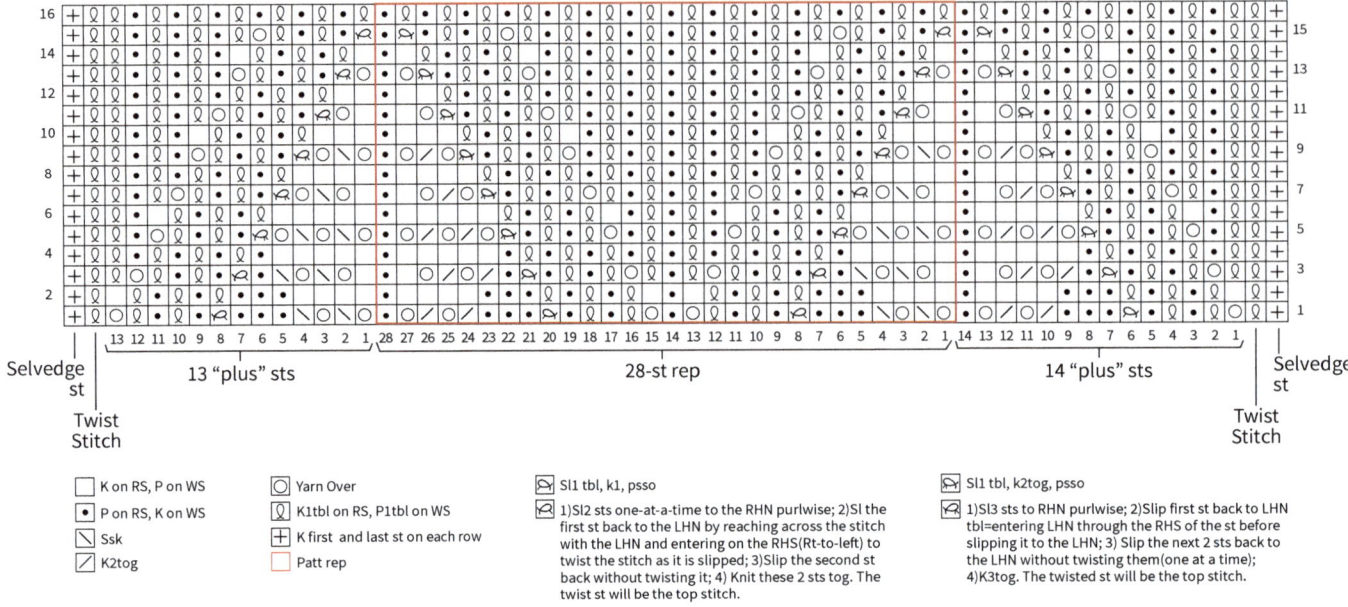

Twisted Hearts Size M

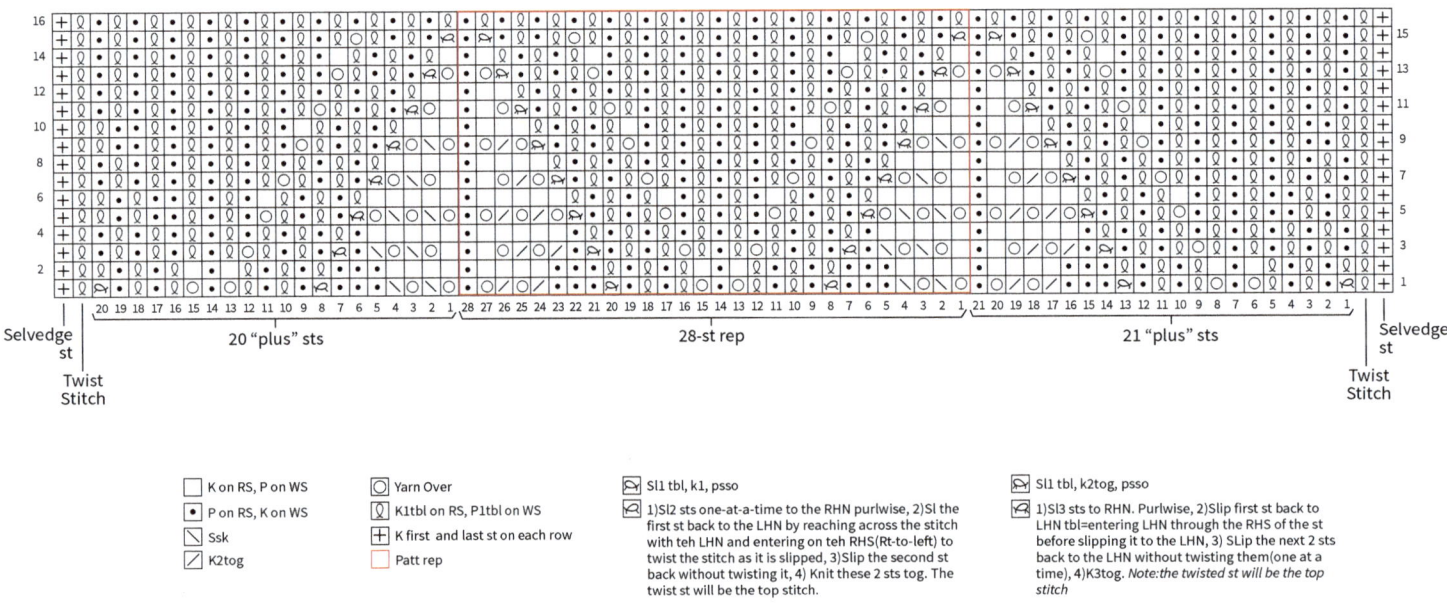

Twisted Hearts Size L

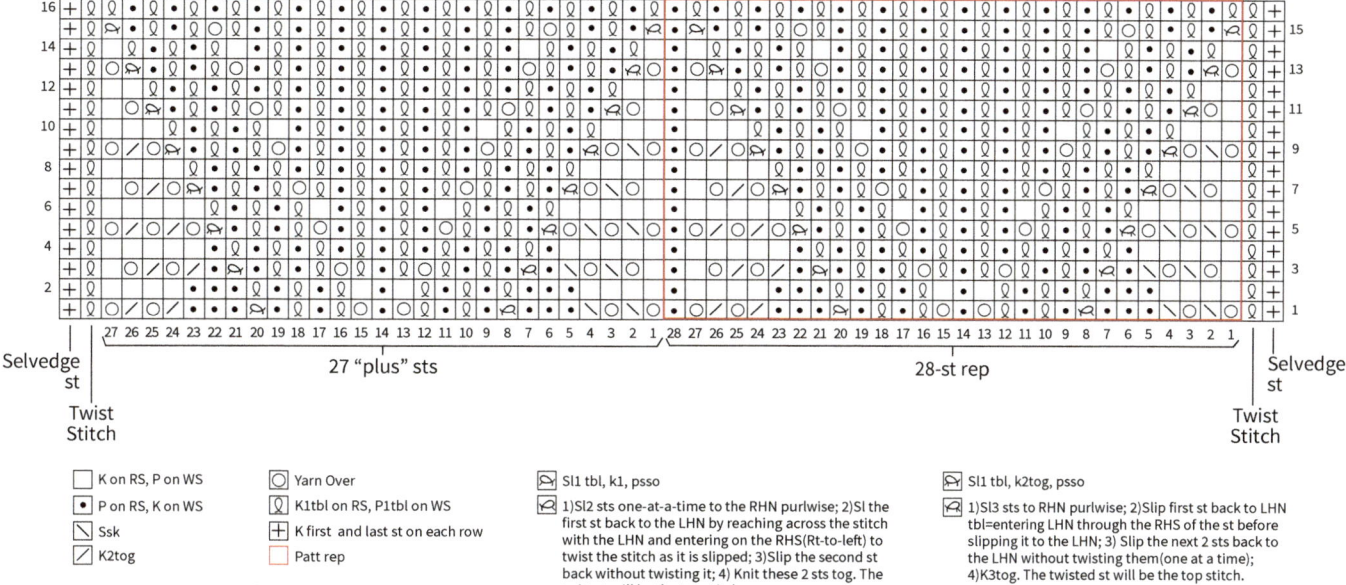

Legend:
- ☐ K on RS, P on WS
- • P on RS, K on WS
- \ Ssk
- / K2tog
- ○ Yarn Over
- Ⓠ K1tbl on RS, P1tbl on WS
- + K first and last st on each row
- ▭ Patt rep
- ⋈ Sl1 tbl, k1, psso: 1) Sl2 sts one-at-a-time to the RHN purlwise; 2) Sl the first st back to the LHN by reaching across the stitch with the LHN and entering on the RHS (Rt-to-left) to twist the stitch as it is slipped; 3) Slip the second st back without twisting it; 4) Knit these 2 sts tog. The twist st will be the top stitch.
- ⋈ Sl1 tbl, k2tog, psso: 1) Sl3 sts to RHN purlwise; 2) Slip first st back to LHN tbl = entering LHN through the RHS of the st before slipping it to the LHN; 3) Slip the next 2 sts back to the LHN without twisting them (one at a time); 4) K3tog. The twisted st will be the top stitch.

DIANE MARTINI

Skihytte Cardigan

FINISHED SIZES

XS (S, M, L, XL)
To Fit Bust Sizes: 30 (34, 38, 42)" and 76 (89, 96.5, 106.5) cm
Finished Sizes: 35¼ (38½, 41¾, 45)" / 89.5 (97.5, 106, 113.5) cm

Sample Size: S

NEEDLES

24-36" (60-80 cm) circular needles in size 5 (3.5 mm) for bands, size 6 (4.0 mm) for lower body/sleeves, and size 7 (4.5 mm) for upper body/sleeves, plus optional spare for working sleeves. Adjust needle sizes to obtain gauge.

YARN

MC (darker): 800 (880, 950, 1050) yds / 730 (805, 870, 960) m of Mystic Inca Alpaca 50% merino / 50% Alpaca in Navy

CC (lighter): 570 (630, 680, 750) yds / 520 (575, 625, 685) m of Ellens Half Pint Farm Yarn Alpaca Sportweight 100% Alpaca in colorway Forest Pansy.

Note: The yarns used are no longer available. Berroco Ultra Alpaca Light (50% Super Fine Alpaca/50% Peruvian Wool, 1.75 oz / 50 g / 144 yds) has been test knit to the same gauge and may be substituted. Other DK weight yarns may also be used.

NOTIONS

stitch markers
stitch holders
cable needle
tapestry needle
clasps - 5 each 1½-2" / 4-5 cm wide (or 7 buttons, 5/8" diam.)

GAUGES after blocking

Medallions Pattern: 24.5 sts and 23.5 rows = 4" / 10 cm on size 6 (4 mm) needles
Lattice Pattern: 24.5 sts and 23.5 rows = 4" / 10 cm on size 7 (4.5 mm) needles
Corrugated Rib Bands: 24.5 sts and 12 rows = 4" / 10 cm wide x 1¼" / 3 cm long on size 5 (3.75 mm) needles

STITCH GUIDE

Fair isle (stranded knitting) for Medallion and Lattice patterns
Corrugated ribbing for Checked Border pattern

DESCRIPTION

Skihytte means "ski lodge" in Norwegian – A product of Design-A-Long #4 with Shirley Paden (SPDAL4 on Ravelry), this Fair Isle Cardigan is perfect for the ski lodge or the office. The body is worked back and forth in one piece to the armholes, with set-in sleeves worked flat. Directions include charted colorwork. For intermediate knitters.

PATTERN NOTES

Get Gauge – Check all of the stitch patterns. Larger needles are used on the upper sleeves and body pattern to get gauge, and smaller needles on the band pattern.

Row Gauge: The measurements provided are rounded to the nearest ¼ inch, and nearest even row. Your results may be slightly different. If you cannot get both stitch and row gauge, choose the needle size that matches the stitch gauge and adjust the rows to match the measurements.

Make The Sleeves First – and block them. They will help to get familiar with the fair isle patterns, confirm your gauge and practice maintaining the patterns while shaping.

Selvedge stitches: All charts and instructions include garter selvedge sts for sleeves worked flat, and Stockinette selvedge sts for body. If working in the round (see below), the sleeve selvedges are not needed, and you will have 2 fewer sts.

Pattern repeats: Sizes XS and M use full pattern repeats, rather than the half repeat used in the other sizes. The patterns at the center front will not be exactly the same as the sample shown.

To break up pooling for hand dyed yarn: Use 2 skeins at once, alternating every 1 or 2 rows, carrying on WS. This also helps to blend any variation between skeins.

If working sleeves in the round: Try working with the WS OUT (floats on the outside of the tube), to help keep the float tension even.

Self-striping and hand painted yarns: Self-striping or hand painted yarns will pattern differently on the sleeves than on the body, and when sleeves are worked separately the striping may not match. One way to keep them even and closer to matching the body is to work both sleeves at once using steeks. Cast on 5 to 7 steek sts, first sleeve sts (per "flat" instructions), 5 to 7 more steek sts, then second sleeve sts. Join into rnd. Work the sleeves, maintaining steeks between. When done, secure and cut steeks, then block and sew sleeve seams. This method allows you to work both sleeves at the same time with only one set of yarn. The trade-off is that the sleeves must be sewn together instead of being seamless.

Binding off at neck edge: For cardigans, it is best to BO the back neck sts, then add the neck band. The BO edge helps to prevent the neck from stretching and keeps the fit at the armhole. If the sts of the back neck are left live the neck will stretch and the sleeve will hang low on the arm.

INSTRUCTIONS

Sleeves

CO 50 (50, 50, 54) sts on size 5 (3.75 mm) needles in DC (darker color) (OR If working in the rnd, CO 2 fewer sts.)

Begin Checked Border pattern. Work 4 rows in rev St st (p on RS, k on WS). Then work in two-color corrugated ribbing as follows:

RS row: K1 (selv) lighter color (LC), *k2 LC, p2 DC; rep from * to last st, k1 (selv) DC.
WS row: K1 (selv) DC, *k2 DC, p2 LC; rep from * to last st, k1 (selv) LC.

Maintain two-color corrugated ribbing for 5 total rows.

Next row (Row 10 WS): Change to DC, k1, p until 1 st rem, k1 (OR k all sts AROUND).
Next Row (RS) 1 more row in rev St st. 11 rows completed.
Next Row (WS) change to size 6 (4 mm) needles and k 1 row (OR p 1 rnd), inc evenly across row 12 (12, 12, 8) sts to total 62 sts (OR inc 2 less sts if working in the rnd to total 60 sts.). 12 rows completed.

Begin Sleeve Chart, Medallion pattern, maintaining garter selv sts. Work even for 36 rows.
At Row 37, inc 1 st at both ends, then every 8 (6, 4, 4) rows 4 (1, 4, 12) time(s), then every 10 (8, 6, -) rows 1 (5, 5, -) times to total 74 (76, 82, 88) sts. AT THE SAME TIME, at Row 74, change to size 7

(4.5 mm) needle and cont with Trellis patt for remainder of sleeve.

Work even for 1¾" / 4.5 cm, about 11 rows, until sleeve measures 16½ (17, 17, 17½)" / 42 (43, 43, 44.5) cm including the cuff band [about 90 (94, 94, 96) rows of Medallion and Trellis pattern].

Shape Cap: Bind off 4 (6, 6, 7) sts at beg of next 2 rows. 66 (64, 70, 74) sts rem. (If working in the rnd, from here forward the sleeve cap is knit flat.)

Keeping 1 st at each edge for seaming, dec 1 st at each end every row 11 (9, 9, 9) times, then every 4 rows 2 (5, 7, 8) times, then every 2 rows 11 (9, 9, 9) more times.

BO rem 18 (18, 20, 22) sts.

Block to measurements and set aside.

Check gauge before proceeding.

Body and Back

CO 202 (226, 250, 274) sts on size 5 (3.75 mm) circular needle in DC. Work Flat.

Begin Checked Border pattern. Work 4 rows in rev St st (p on RS, k on WS). Then, work in two-color corrugated ribbing as follows:

> **RS row:** K1 (selv) LC, *k2 LC, p2 DC; rep from * to last st, k1 (selv) DC.
>
> **WS row:** K1 (selv) DC, *k2 DC, p2 LC; rep from * to last st, k1 (selv) LC.

Maintain two-color corrugated ribbing for 5 total rows.

Next row (Row 10 WS): Using DC, k1, p to last st, k1.

Next row (RS): K1, p to last st, k1.

Next row (WS): Change to size 6 (4 mm) needles and k across, dec evenly 1 (5, 9, 13) sts. 201 (221, 241, 261) total sts. 12 rows completed.

Begin Body Chart, Medallion Pattern, with Stockinette selv sts from here on. Work even for 14 (14, 13½, 13¼)" / 35.5 (35.5, 34.5, 34) cm [about 82 (82, 80, 78) rows not counting hem]. AT THE SAME TIME, change to size 7 (4.5 mm) needles and Trellis Pattern at Row 74.

On LAST RS ROW, mark side seams as follows: Work 50 (55, 60, 65) sts, pl mar, work 101 (111, 121, 131) sts, pl mar, work 50 (55, 60, 65) sts.

Begin Armhole

Divide for armhole (RS) as foll: Work first 50 (55, 60, 65) sts (to side seam m). Place right front just worked on holder. BO 4 (6, 6, 7) sts for back underarm, work to next m. Place rem 50 (55, 60, 65) sts on holder for left front.

Turn work (beg WS row). BO 4 (6, 6, 7) sts, work to end of row: 93 (99, 109, 117) sts rem for back.

Then, dec 1 st at each edge every 2 rows a total of 2 (4, 4, 5) times as foll: K1, ssk work to last 3 sts, k2tog, k1.

Work even on rem 89 (91, 101, 107) sts until armhole measures 6¾ (7¼, 7½, 8¼)" / 17 (18.5, 19, 21) cm, ending after a WS row [about 40 (42, 44, 48) rows total]. BO 9 (9, 10, 11) sts at beg of next 4 rows, BO 8 (8, 9, 9) sts at beg of next 2 rows.

BO rem 37 (39, 43, 45) sts. Total about 128 (130, 130, 132) rows not counting hem and 23 (23¼, 23¼, 23¾)" / 53.5 (54, 53.5, 54) cm, including hem.

Fronts

Right side worked first.

Transfer right body front sts from holder to needle. Join yarn with WS facing.

Begin armhole shaping at armhole edge as for back as foll: BO 4 (6, 6, 7) sts, then on foll WS rows, dec 1 st 2 (4, 4, 5) times. 44 (45, 50, 53) sts rem.

When piece measures 21 (21¼, 21, 21¼)" / 53.5 (54.5, 53.5, 54) cm [about 116 (118, 116, 118) rows not counting hem], begin front neck shaping.

Pl mar at 26 (26, 29, 31) sts from armhole edge to mark shoulder BO sts for future.

Begin FRONT NECK shaping as foll: Sl 9 (10, 11, 11) sts at neck edge to holder. Then, dec 1 st at neck edge every row 9 (9, 10, 11) times, continue working even until shoulder BO is completed.

AT THE SAME TIME, when armhole measures 6¾ (7¼, 7½, 8¼)" / 17 (18.5, 19, 21) cm [about 40 (42, 44, 48) rows], beg shoulder BO as for back: BO 9 (9, 10, 11) sts at shoulder edge twice, 8 (8, 9, 9) sts at shoulder edge once.

Left front: Work as for right side, reversing shaping.

Blocking:

Block pieces to measurements as shown in the schematic before proceeding.

Shoulder Seams:

After blocking, sew shoulder seams.

Neck Band

With RS facing, pick up 1 st for each st and row along neck edge as follows: k 9 (10, 11, 11) sts from right front holder, pick up 19 (19, 22, 25) sts from right neck edge, 37 (39, 43, 45) sts from back neck, 19 (19, 22, 25) sts from left front neck edge and k 9 (10, 11, 11) sts from holder. Total 93 (97, 109, 117) sts picked up.

Turn work and p 1 row, decreasing 9 (5, 9, 13) sts evenly to total 84 (92, 100, 104) sts. Work Rows 1 – 12 of Checked Collar Pattern. BO on Row 13.

Front Bands:

With smallest needles (size 5 / 3.75 mm) and RS facing, pick up and knit about 4 sts for each 5 rows along cardigan front between bottom of collar band and top of hem, plus 8 sts from the hem. 110 (110, 110, 110) sts. Work as for collar EXCEPT AT BOTTOM EDGE – Match the bottom hem pattern by placing 2DC sts and 4LC sts at bottom edge in pattern.

Work both bands the same if using clasps.

Alternate: Right Front Buttonhole Band:

Note: Instructions are for 7 buttons, 5/8" diameter.

With RS facing, pick up sts and work buttonhole band the same as for left front through Row 4.

Row 5 (RS): Mark buttonhole locations as foll: 5 sts from neck edge, and 6 sts from bottom edge. Pl mar 5 more times evenly distributed between the first two markers (about 20-21 sts apart). Work to first m (at bottom edge of garment) *yo, p2tog LC, work to next m, yo, k2tog DC; rep from * to end of row using k2tog or p2tog as needed to maintain patt. Work rem rows of collar pattern.

Tip: Floats on WS of band may block the buttonholes. This can be fixed by basting the rolled edge of the button band to the WS of the band, catching the floats at the buttonholes and securing them to the edge as you go.

Band Finishing:

To complete the rev St border along the front edges of the neck band and top edge of the button band, pick up sts using DC as foll: Beg at outer edge, with RS facing, skip 2 sts, then pick up 8 sts along neck band, 1 st at "joint" between neck band and button band, and 8 sts from button band, leaving last 2 sts free to roll under. 17 total sts. Mark the center st.

Rows I & 3(WS): K to 1 st before m, s2kp, k to end of row.
Rows 2 & 4 (RS): P.
Row 5 (WS): BO all sts k'wise.

Finishing

Pin sleeves into armholes, with right sides facing. Sew armhole seams easing to fit.

Sew sleeve seams.

Weave in all ends.

Sew on clasps or buttons.

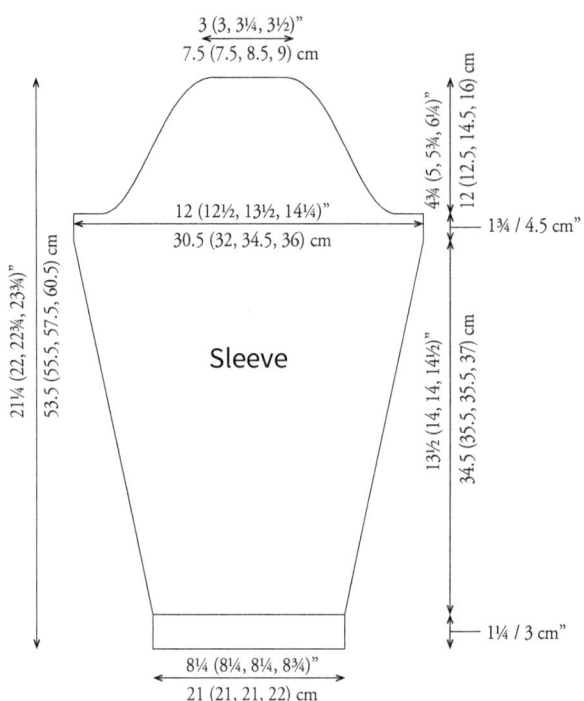

Skihytte Cardigan Sleeve

Skihytte Cardigan Body

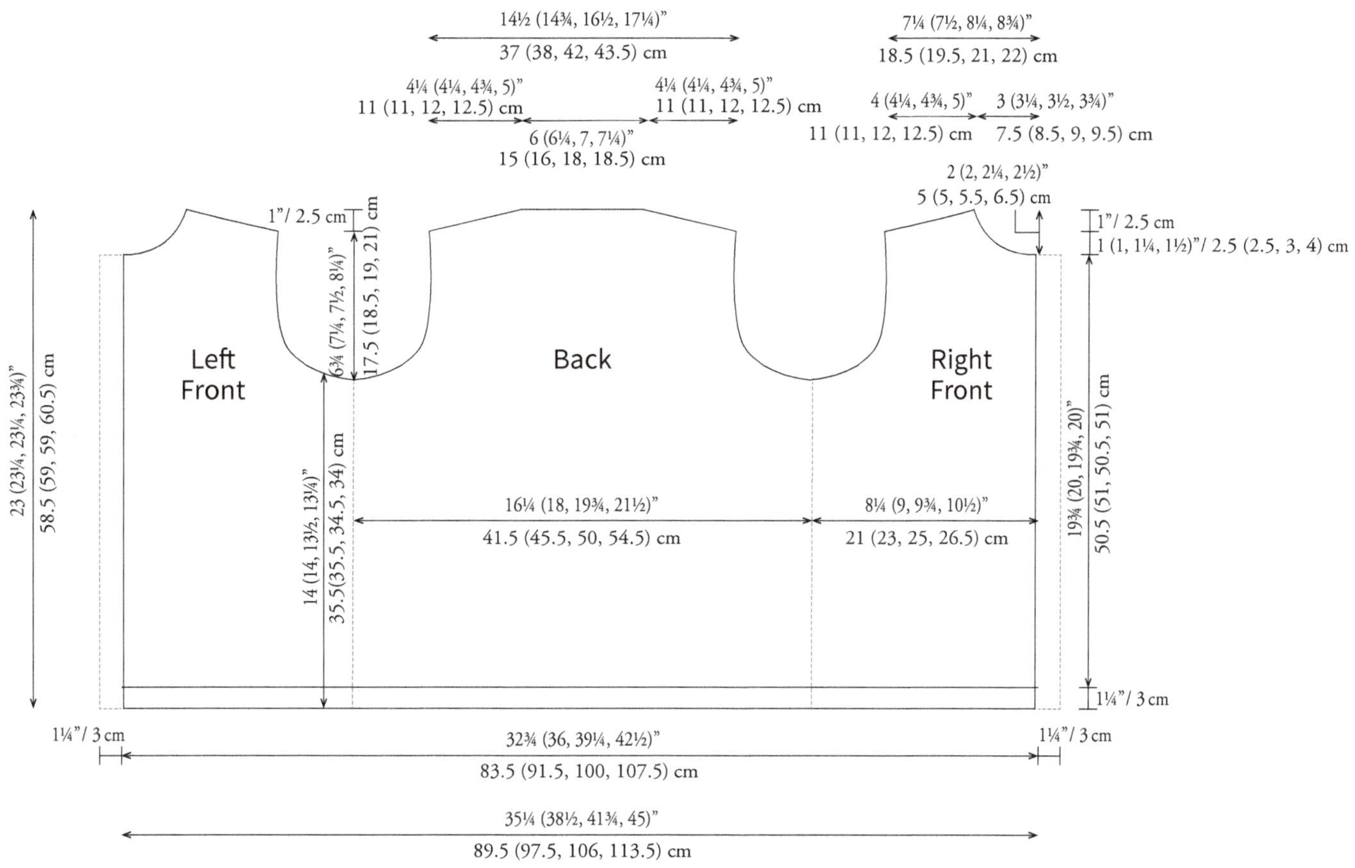

Schematic measurements:
- Top widths: 14½ (14¾, 16½, 17¼)" / 37 (38, 42, 43.5) cm; 7¼ (7½, 8¼, 8¾)" / 18.5 (19.5, 21, 22) cm
- 4¼ (4¼, 4¾, 5)" / 11 (11, 12, 12.5) cm
- 4¼ (4¼, 4¾, 5)" / 11 (11, 12, 12.5) cm
- 6 (6¼, 7, 7¼)" / 15 (16, 18, 18.5) cm
- 4 (4¼, 4¾, 5)" / 11 (11, 12, 12.5) cm
- 3 (3¼, 3½, 3¾)" / 7.5 (8.5, 9, 9.5) cm
- 2 (2, 2¼, 2½)" / 5 (5, 5.5, 6.5) cm
- 1" / 2.5 cm
- 1 (1, 1¼, 1½)" / 2.5 (2.5, 3, 4) cm
- 6¾ (7¼, 7½, 8¼)" / 17.5 (18.5, 19, 21) cm
- Left Front, Back, Right Front
- 23 (23¼, 23¼, 23¾)" / 58.5 (59, 59, 60.5) cm
- 14 (14, 13½, 13¼)" / 35.5 (35.5, 34.5, 34) cm
- 16¼ (18, 19¾, 21½)" / 41.5 (45.5, 50, 54.5) cm
- 8¼ (9, 9¾, 10½)" / 21 (23, 25, 26.5) cm
- 19¾ (20, 19¾, 20)" / 50.5 (51, 50.5, 51) cm
- 1¼" / 3 cm
- 1¼" / 3 cm
- 1¼" / 3 cm
- 32¾ (36, 39¼, 42½)" / 83.5 (91.5, 100, 107.5) cm
- 35¼ (38½, 41¾, 45)" / 89.5 (97.5, 106, 113.5) cm

Skihytte Checked Border

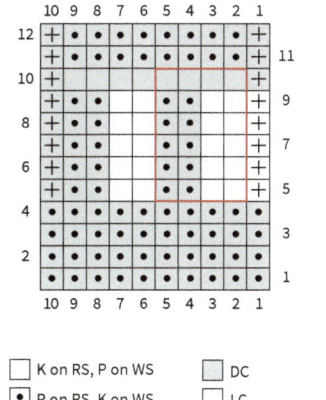

- ☐ K on RS, P on WS
- • P on RS, K on WS
- ▢ 4-st patt rep (red)
- ▨ DC
- ☐ LC
- + K first and last sts on each row

Skihytte Checked Collar and Front Bands

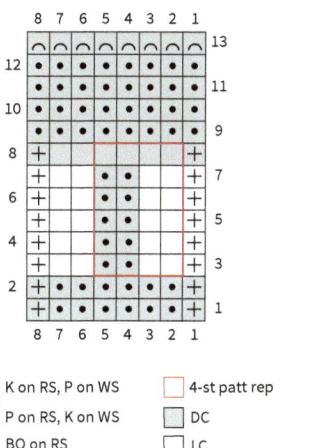

- ☐ K on RS, P on WS
- • P on RS, K on WS
- ⌒ BO on RS
- ▢ 4-st patt rep (red)
- ▨ DC
- ☐ LC
- + K first and last sts on each row

Skihytte Body

- ☐ K on RS, P on WS
- ☐ DC
- ☐ LC
- ☐ Medallions
- ☐ Trellis

Skihytte Sleeve

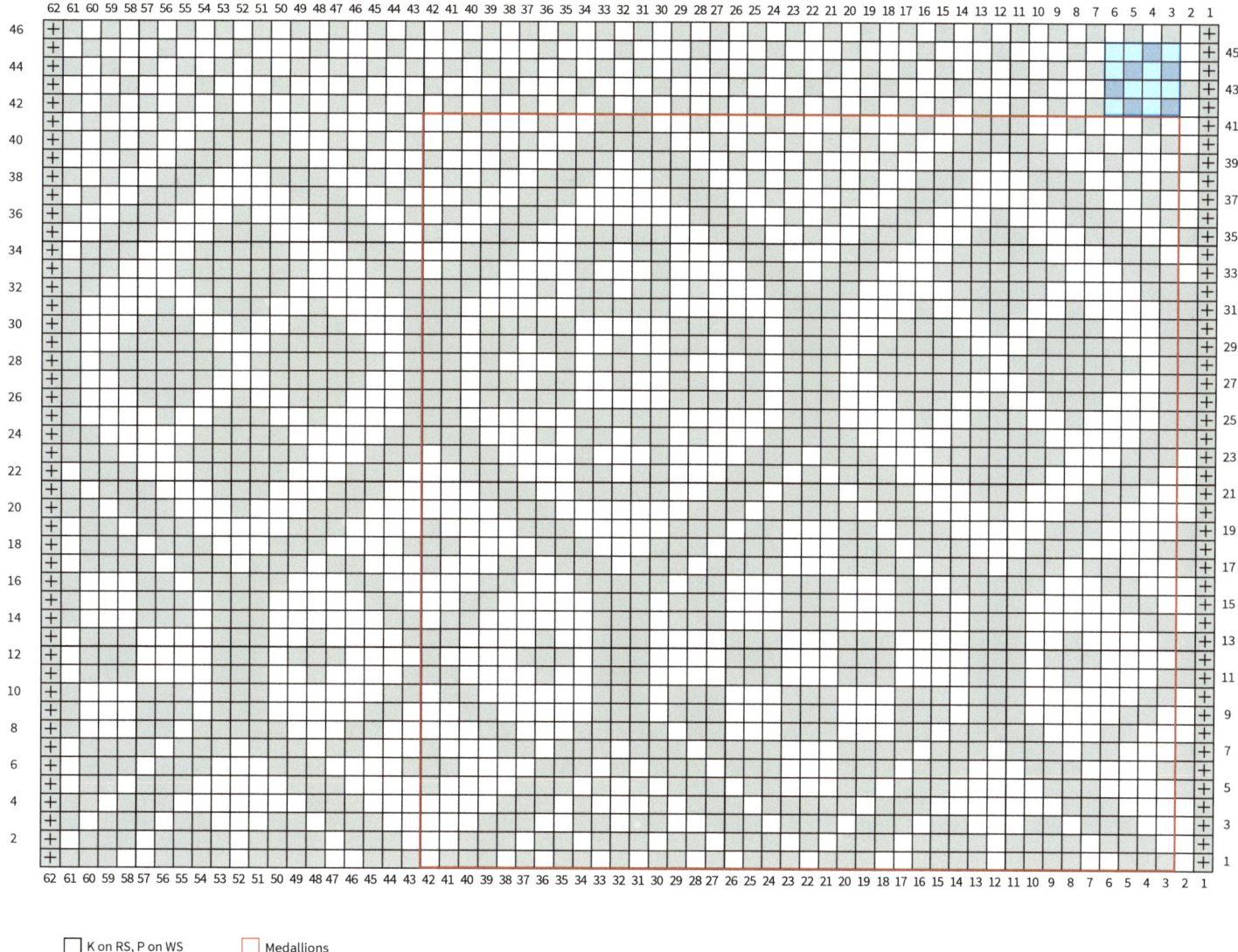

- ☐ K on RS, P on WS
- ☐ DC
- ☐ LC
- ☐ Medallions
- ☐ Trellis
- ± K first and last st on each row

AYANO TANAKA

Sunset Skirt

FINISHED SIZES

S (M, L, XL)
Waist: 30 (33, 36¼, 39¼)" / 76 (84, 92, 100) cm
Hip: 37¾ (41, 45, 49½)" / 96 (104, 114, 126) cm
Length: 22" / 56 cm
Choose size based on your waist measurement. Suggested ease: 1½-2"/ 4-5 cm.

Sample Size: S

NEEDLES

US 2½ (3 mm) straight and circular needles
*About circular needles, 32" (60cm) for size S. 40" (80 cm) for other sizes.
It is used when working the waist band in the round.*
Crochet Hook: Size C (2.75 mm)

YARN

MC: Kauni Wool "8/2 Effektyarn" (100% Wool; 656 yds [600 m] / 5.3 oz / 150 g): color EN 2 skeins
CC: Jameison's of Shetland Spindrift (100% Wool; 115 yds [105 m] / 0.88 oz / 25 g):
CC1: #125 Slate, 1 (1, 2, 2) ball(s)
CC2: #103 Sholmit, 1 (1,1,2) ball(s)
CC3: #290 Oyster, 1 (1, 2, 2) ball(s)
CC4: #104 Natural White, 2 (2, 2, 3) balls
CC5: #1390 Highland Mist, 1 ball
CC6: #274 Green Mist, 1 ball
CC7: #140 Rye, 1 ball
CC8: #1200 Nutmeg, 10 yds/ 10 m.

Jamieson & Smith 2ply Jumper weight (100% wool; 125 yds [114 m] / 0.88 oz / 25 g):
CC9: #1284, 1 ball
CC: #FC38, 1 ball

NOTIONS

tapestry needle
1"/ 2.5 cm wide elastic, 1"/ 2.5 cm longer than your waistband size.

GAUGES

Fair isle pattern:
31 sts and 35 rows = 4"/ 10 cm with US 2½ (3 mm) needle.

Stockinette stitch:
25 sts and 34 rows = 4"/ 10 cm with US 2½ (3 mm) needle.

STITCH GUIDE

Fair isle pattern:
See chart. Work back and forth in Stockinette stitch.

Reverse Single Crochet (Crab St) - worked from left to right:
*Insert hook into st, yarn round hook
(yrh), draw loop through, yrh, draw yarn through 2 loops on hook; rep from * to end.

PATTERN NOTES

Skirt body is worked flat in Fair isle patt from the bottom up and the stitches are set on hold at waist. Sides of two pieces are seamed, then waistband is knitted in the rnd. Edging is crocheted around the bottom.

The MC is a gradient yarn (gray-orange-cream). If you'd like to obtain the back ground color similar to the sample's color (S size), you will need more than 2 skeins to follow the color changes specified in the chart, in particular for larger sizes.

INSTRUCTIONS

Skirt (make 2)

With US 2½ (3 mm) size needles and MC, CO 211 (223, 239, 257) sts.
Starting with a RS row and St 16 (10, 2, 41) of Fair isle patt, work back and forth 8 rows.
Dec Row (RS): k1, ssk, work to last 3 sts, k2tog, k1. 209 (221, 237, 255) sts.
Rep Dec Row every 4th row 13 times, every other row once. 181 (193, 209, 227) sts.
Rep Dec Row every 4th row 14 times, every other row once. 151 (163, 179, 197) sts.
Rep Dec Row [every 4th row 15 (15, 7, 1) time(s), every other row 0 (0, 1, 1) time] 1 (1, 2, 10) time(s).
121 (133, 147, 157) sts.

L size only
Rep Dec Row 2 rows later once more. 145 sts.

All sizes
Work 2 (2, 0, 2) rows even, then dec on next row (WS) as foll: p2tog, p to last 2 sts, ssp.
119 (131, 143, 155) sts.

Place all sts on a holder or waste yarn.

Make another piece of skirt.
Sew side seams of two pieces with mattress stitch.

Waist band

Waist band is worked in the rnd with MC.
Move back all sts from stitch holder to circular needles. 238 (262, 286, 310) sts.
Join MC and dec as follows:

S size only
*K2, k2tog, (k3, k2tog) 23 times; rep from * once. 190 sts.

M & L sizes only
*[K4, k2tog] 1(3) time(s), [k3, k2tog] 25 times; rep from * once. 210 (230) sts.

XL size only
*K4, k2tog, [k3, k2tog] 5 times; rep from * 9 more times. 250 sts.

All sizes

K 8 rnds.

P 1 rnd (= turning ridge).

K 9 rnds.

Waistband measures 2¼"/ 5.5 cm.

Bind off all sts loosely.

Edging

With size C (2.75 mm) crochet hook and MC, crochet around the bottom edge.

Row 1: Sc.

Row 2: Rev sc.

Finishing

Sew elastic ends to desired length. Put elastic around waistband, fold band to WS along turning ridge. Sew band in place using whipstitch. Weave in ends.

Sunset Skirt

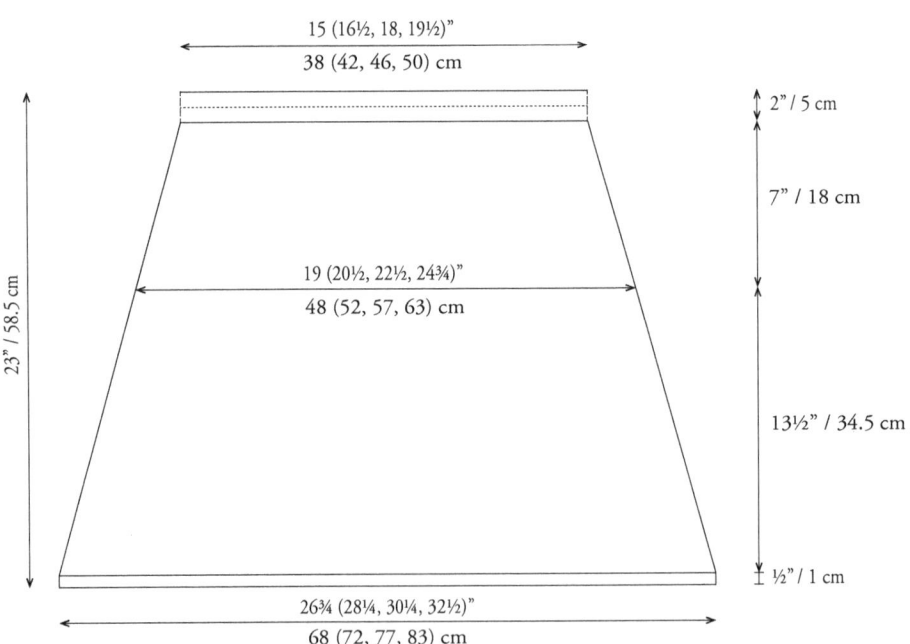

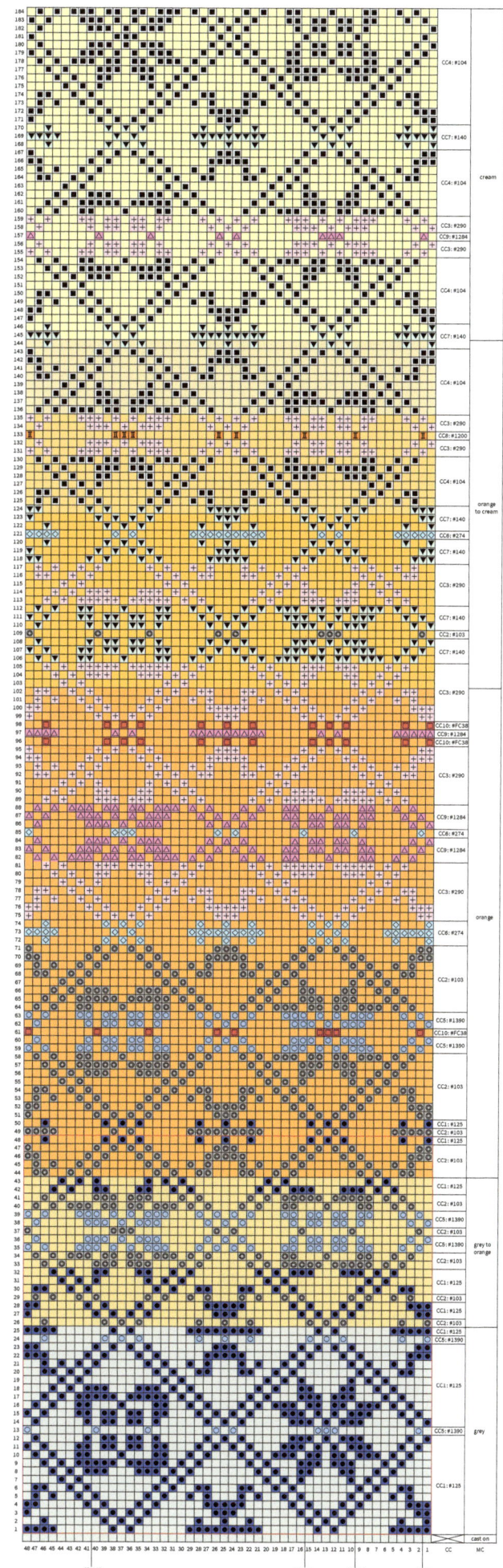

SUNSET SKIRT | 253

MIKI OHARA

Teardrop Cardigan

FINISHED SIZES

Sizes: S (M, L)
Finished bust: 37 (39½, 42½)" / 93.5 (100, 108) cm
To Fit Bust Sizes: 34-36 (37-39, 40-42)" / 86-91 (94-99, 101-106) cm
Ease: 0-2" / 0-5 cm

Sample Size: M – body, S – Sleeve length

YARN

MC: Madelinetosh Pashmina (75% Merino / 15% Silk / 10% Cashmere; 360 yds [329 m] / 3.5 oz / 100 g): color Lapis 4 (5, 5) skeins
CC: Fiberspates Scrumtious 4 Ply (55% Merino / 45% Silk; 399 yds [365 m] / 3.5 oz / 100 g): color Water 1 (1, 1) skein

NEEDLES

One pair each sizes 3 (3.25 mm) & 4 (3.5 mm) straight needles and one 40" / 100 cm size 3 circular needle - or size needed to obtain gauge

NOTIONS

stitch markers
buttons: 5 - ¾" / 19 mm buttons

GAUGES

1. **Twisted Cables Pattern:** 25.5 sts and 32 rows = 4" / 10 cm with US 4 (3.5 mm) needles
2. **Stockinette stitch**: 26 sts and 33 rows = 4" / 10 cm with US 4 (3.5 mm) needles
3. **Ribbing:** 24 sts and 36 rows = 4" / 10 cm with US 3 (3.25 mm) needles.

STITCH GUIDE

Twisted Cable - see chart
Stockinette stitch
3x2 Ribbing for collar

NOTES

- Selvedge: Garter selvedge (knit the first and last st on every row) is used throughout, excluding the collar.
- Partial cables: There will be instances on the edge increases/decreases where you will not have enough sts left to complete a cable st as per the chart. In these cases, just omit the cable and knit the knit sts and purl the purl sts.

INSTRUCTIONS

Back

With size 3 (3.25 mm) needles, CO 110 (118, 126) sts.

Beg with a WS row, establish rib patt as foll:

Row 1 (WS):

S: k1 (selv), k1, p1, pl mar, work ALL sizes to last 3 sts, p1, k1, k1 (selv).

M: k1 (selv), (k2, p1) 2 times, pl mar, work ALL sizes to last 7 sts, (p1, k2) 2 times, k1 (selv).

L: k1 (selv), k2, p2, (k2, p1) 2 times, pl mar, work ALL sizes to last 11 sts, (p1, k2) 2 times, p2, k2, k1 (selv).

ALL sizes (see Rib patt chart): [(p1, k2) 4 times, p1, pl mar] 8 times.

Next row: k1 (selv), k the knit sts and p the purl sts to last st, k1 (selv)

Keeping selv sts in garter st, work in rib patt for a total of 12 rows, ending with a RS row.

Inc row (WS):

S: k1 (selv), k1, p1, sl mar, work ALL sizes, p1, k1, k1 (selv).

M: k1 (selv), (k2, p1) 2 times, sl mar, work ALL sizes, (p1, k2) 2 times, k1 (selv).

L: k1 (selv), k2, p2, (k2, p1) 2 times, sl mar, work ALL sizes, (p1, k2) 2 times, p2, k2, k1 (selv).

ALL sizes (see Rib patt chart Inc row): [(p1, k2) 2 times, p1, M1P, (k2, p1) 2 times, sl mar] 8 times.

You have 118 (126, 134) sts.

Change to size 4 (3.5 mm) needles and start working Twisted Cable chart as foll:

Next row (RS): K1 (selv), work chart starting with st 13 (9, 5) through st 14, then sts 1-14 eight times, then work 2 (6, 10) sts from chart, k1 (selv).

There are 8 sections of 14 sts each (112 total) for the cable patt + 2 (6, 10) sts of a partial cable patt on each side + 2 selv sts and 9 total markers.

Work even in patt for 8 more rows, keeping selv sts in garter st and slipping markers as you go. End with a RS row.

Hip-to-waist shaping

Cont working Twisted Cable chart, dec 1 st at each side of next row. Then dec every 9th row 7 more times, ending with a RS row. 8 sts dec'd each side = 102 (110, 118) total sts.

At the same time, after working 44 rows of the chart, begin working the Intarsia Teardrop chart over the 4 middle patt rep (56 sts). Cont working the cable patt on sides and intarsia pattern in the middle for 108 rows. Upon completion of the intarsia chart, resume cable patt over the 4 middle patt rep.

Waist

After the last dec, work even for 11 rows, ending with a WS row.

Waist-to-bust shaping

On next row (RS), inc 1 st at each end of next row. Then inc every 4th row 7 more times. 8 sts inc'd each side = 118 (126, 134) total sts.

Work even for 19 rows, ending with a WS row. Piece should measure 18" / 45.5 cm from CO edge.

Shape Armholes

BO 5 (6, 7) sts at beg of next 2 rows, then BO 3 (3, 4) sts at beg of next 2 rows, then BO 2 (3, 3) sts at beg of next 2 rows, then BO 2 sts at beg of foll 4 rows, then 1 st at beg of foll 6 rows. 84 (88, 92) sts rem. Work even in patt for 42 (48, 52) more rows. Armholes should measure 7¼ (8, 8½)" / 18.5 (20.5, 21.5) cm.

Work 20 (22, 24) sts in patt, and place sts just worked on a holder or length of yarn. BO next 44 sts, then work next 20 (22, 24) sts in patt and place them on a holder or length of yarn.

Right Front

With size 3 (3.25 mm) needles, CO 52 (56, 60) sts.

Beg with a WS row, establish rib patt as foll:
Row 1(WS):

S: k1 (selv), kl, p1, pl mar, work All sizes.

M: k1 (selv), (k2, p1) 2 times, pl mar, work All sizes.

L: k1 (selv), k2, p2, (k2, p1) 2 times, pl mar, work All sizes.

ALL sizes (see Rib patt chart): [(p1, k2) 4 times, p1, pl mar] patt 3 times, (p1, k2) 3 times, k1 (selv).

Next row: k1 (selv), k the knit sts and p the purl sts to last st, k1 (selv)
Keeping selv sts in garter st, work in rib patt for a total of 12 rows, ending with a RS row.

Inc row (WS):

S: k1 (selv), kl, p1, sl mar, work All sizes.

M: k1 (selv), (k2, p1) 2 times, sl mar, work All sizes.

L: k1 (selv), k2, p2, (k2, p1) 2 times, sl mar, work All sizes.

ALL sizes (see Rib patt chart Inc row): [(p1, k2) 2 times, p1, M1P, (k2, p1) 2 times, sl mar] 3 times, p1, pl mar, k2, pl mar, p1, k2, p1, M1P, k2, k1 (selv).

You have 56 (60, 64) sts.

Change to size 4 (3.5 mm) needles.
Beg to work Twisted Cable chart and Intarsia chart for right front as foll:

Next row (RS): k1 (selv), work Intarsia chart over next 7 sts, sl mar, p2 (to be carried all the way through in rev St st), sl mar, work Twisted Cable chart starting at st 14, then sts 1-14 three times, sl mar, work 2 (6, 10) sts from chart, k1 (selv).

***Work even in patt for 8 more rows, keeping selvedge sts in garter st and 2 sts between Cable patt and Intarsia patt in rev St st. End with a RS row.

Hip-to-waist Shaping
Dec 1 st at beg of next row (WS). Then dec every 9th row at the side edge (beg of WS rows, end of RS rows) 7 more times. 8 sts dec'd = 48 (52, 56) total sts.

Waist
Work even for 11 rows, ending with a WS row.

Waist-to-bust Shaping
Inc 1 st at end of the next row (RS). Then, inc 1 st every 4th row 7 more times. 8 sts inc'd = 56 (60, 64) total sts.

Work even for 20 rows, ending with a RS row. Piece should measure 18" / 45.5 cm from CO edge.

Shape Armhole - (see next page for neckline shaping before proceeding)

BO 5 (6, 7) sts at beg of next WS row, then 3 (3, 4) sts at beg of next WS row, then 2 (3, 3) sts at beg of next WS row, then 2 sts at beg of foll 2 WS rows, then 1 st at beg of foll 3 WS rows. 39 (41, 43) sts rem.

Work even in patt for 42 (48, 52) rows.

At the same time – shape neckline
The beg of the V-Neck shaping is incorporated into the front intarsia chart.
After working the final row of the intarsia chart (RS row),

S: *Dec 1 st every other row twice, then every 3rd row once; rep from * 3 more times. 20 sts.

M: *Dec 1 st every other row once, then every 3rd row twice; rep from * 3 more times. 22 sts.

L: Work 1 row even, then dec 1 st, then dec 1 st every 3rd row 11 more times. 24 sts.

Work 3 (5, 6) rows even in patt, then place rem sts on a holder or length of yarn.

Left Front

With size 3 (3.25 mm) needles, CO 52 (56, 60) sts.

Beg with a WS row, establish rib patt as foll:

Row 1 (WS):

S: Work All sizes to last 3 sts, k2, k1 (selv).

M: Work All sizes to last 7 sts, (k2, p1) 2 times, k1 (selv).

L: Work All sizes to last 11 sts, (k2, p1) 2 times, k2, p2, k1 (selv).

All sizes: k1 (selv), (k2, p1) 3 times, pl mar, [p1, (k2, p1) 4 times, pl mar] 3 times.

Next row (WS): k1 (selv), k the knit sts and p the purl sts to last st, k1 (selv)

Keeping selv sts in garter st, work in rib patt for a total of 12 rows, ending with a WS row.

Inc row (WS):

S: Work All sizes to last 3 sts, k2, k1 (selv)

M: Work All sizes to last 7 sts, (k2, p1) 2 times, k1 (selv)

L: Work All sizes to last 11 sts, (k2, p1) 2 times, k2, p2, k1 (selv)

All sizes: k1 (selv), k2, M1P, p1, k2, p1, pl mar, k2, pl mar, p1, [sl mar, (p1, k2) 2 times, M1Lp, p1, (k2, p1) 2 times] 3 times.

You have 56 (60, 64) sts.

Change to size 4 (3.5 mm) needles.

Beg working Intarsia chart for left front and Twisted Cable chart as foll: k1 (selv), work Cable chart starting at st 13 (9, 5) through st 14, sl mar, then sts 1-14 three times, sl mar, work st 1, sl mar, p2 (to be carried all the way through in rev St st), then Row 1(RS) of Intarsia chart for left front over next 7 sts, k1 (selv).

For remainder of left front, work as for the right front from ***, reversing all shaping.

Sleeves (Make 2)

With size 3 (3.25 mm) needles, CO 47 (47, 53) sts.

Beg with a WS row, establish rib patt as foll:

Row 1 (WS): k1 (selv), [k2, p1] 1 (1, 2) times, pl mar, [(p1, k2) 4 times, p1, pl mar] 3 times, [p1, k2] 1(1, 2) times, k1 (selv)

Next row: K1 (selv), k the knit sts and p the purl sts to last st, k1 (selv)

Keeping selv sts in garter st, work in rib patt for a total of 12 rows, ending with a RS row.

Inc Row (WS): k1 (selv), [k2, p1] 1 (1, 2) times, sl mar, [(p1, k2) 2 times, p1, M1P, (k2, p1) 2 times, sl mar] 3 times, [p1, k2] 1 (1, 2) times, k1 (selv). 50 (50, 56) sts.

Change to size 4 (3.5 mm) needles.

Next Row (RS): k1 (selv), start Row 1 of Twisted Cable chart at st 12 (12, 9) through st 14, work 14-st rep 3 times, work 2 (2, 6) sts from chart, k1 (selv).

Work 5 rows even.

Sleeve Shaping Increases

On next row, inc 1 st each side, then inc every 7th (6th, 6th) row 3 (2, 6) more times, then every 6th (5th, 5th) row 12 (17, 13) time(s). 32 (40, 40) sts inc'd, 82 (90, 96) sts.

Work 24 rows even, ending on a WS row. Sleeve measures 17 (17½, 18½)" / 43 (44.5, 45.5) cm from CO edge.

Shape Sleeve cap

BO 5 (6, 7) sts at beg of next 2 rows.

S: *Dec 1 st at each end of next 2 rows, work 1 row even, then dec 1 st each end of next row; rep from * 6 more times. 30 total rows worked, 30 sts rem.

M: *Dec 1 st at each end of next 2 rows, work 1 row even; rep from * 10 more times. Then dec 1 st at each end of next row. 36 total rows worked, 32 sts rem.

L: Dec 1 st at each end of next row, then *(dec 1 st at each end of next row, work 1 row even) 2 times, dec 1 st at each end of next row; rep from * 6 more times, dec 1 st at each end of next 2 rows. 40 total rows worked, 34 sts rem.

All Sizes: BO 3 sts at beg of next 4 rows, then BO rem 18 (20, 22) sts.

Collar

Shawl Collar - Button Bands

The buttonholes in this section are 3-row vertical buttonholes.

Row 1 (RS): Double yo (wrap yarn around right needle twice), k2tog
Row 2 (WS): Knit first loop of double yo, drop second loop from needle
Row 3 (RS): Purl into center of hole, and drop stitch on needle above the hole

With size 3 (3.25 mm) circular needle, CO 343 (353, 358) sts.
Row 1 (WS): *p3, k2; rep from * until last 3 sts, p3 (the first time you work this row, pl mar after 99 sts - this will tell you where to start the first buttonhole).
Row 2 (RS): *k3, p2; rep from * until last 3 sts, k3.
Rep Rows 1-2 twice more, then Row 1, for a total of 7 rows.

Buttonhole row 1 (RS): work in patt to mar, sl mar, *yo2, k2tog, cont in patt for 21 sts, rep from * 3 more times, yo2, k2tog, cont in patt to end.

Buttonhole row 2 (WS): Cont in patt, knitting first loop and dropping second loop from needle at each double yo.

Buttonhole row 3 (RS): Cont in patt, purling into center of hole and dropping st on needle above the hole at each buttonhole.

Then continue in patt for a total of 13 rows, ending with a WS row.

Bind off sides

BO 114 sts, cont in patt for 116 (126, 130) sts, BO rem 113 (113, 114) sts. Cut yarn.

Shape collar at back of neck

Re-attach yarn to middle sts on RS.

Size S: *Dec 1 st at each end of next 2 rows, (dec 1 st at each end of next row, work 1 row even) 3 times; rep from * 5 more times. Then dec 1 st at each end of next row, work 1 row even.

Size M: *Dec 1 st at each end of next 3 rows, work 1 row even, then dec at each end of next 2 rows, work 1 row even; rep from * 6 more times. Then dec 1 st each end on next row.

Size L: *Dec 1 st at each end of next 3 rows, work 1 row even; rep from * 11 more times, then dec 1 st at each end of next 2 rows.

62 (72, 76) sts dec'd. BO rem 54 sts.

Finishing

Block pieces to measurements. Sew shoulder seams using the 3-needle BO technique. Sew side seams. Set in sleeves. Sew BO edge of shawl collar to body, pinning the center of the collar to the center of back neck, and the end of the diagonal lines to the beg of the V.

Sew buttons to left side opposite of button holes.

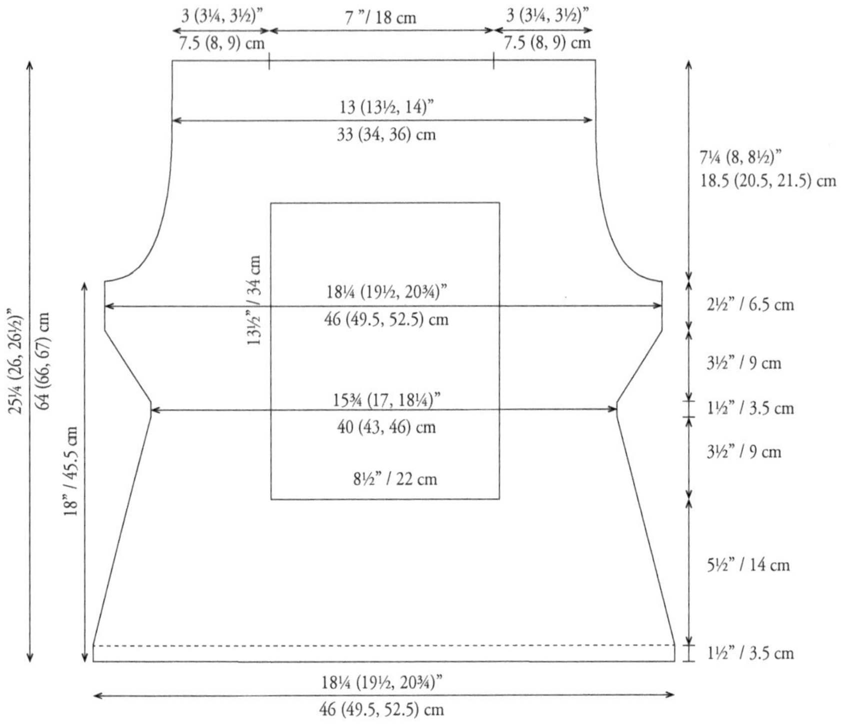

Miki Ohara Teadrops Cardigan

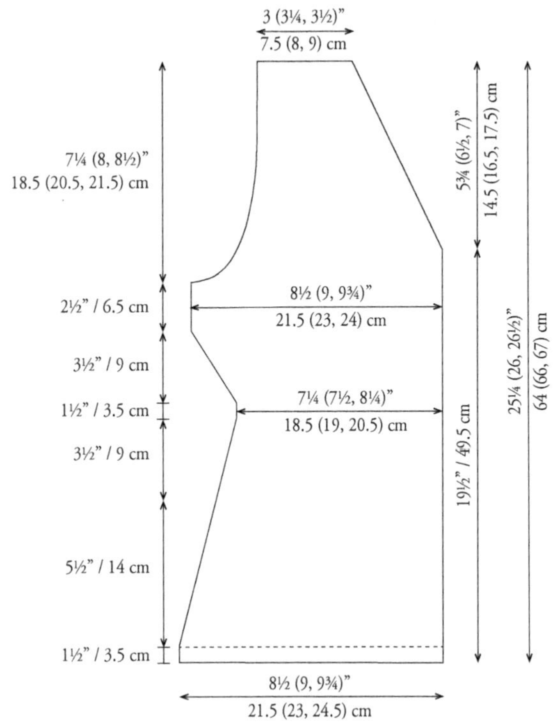

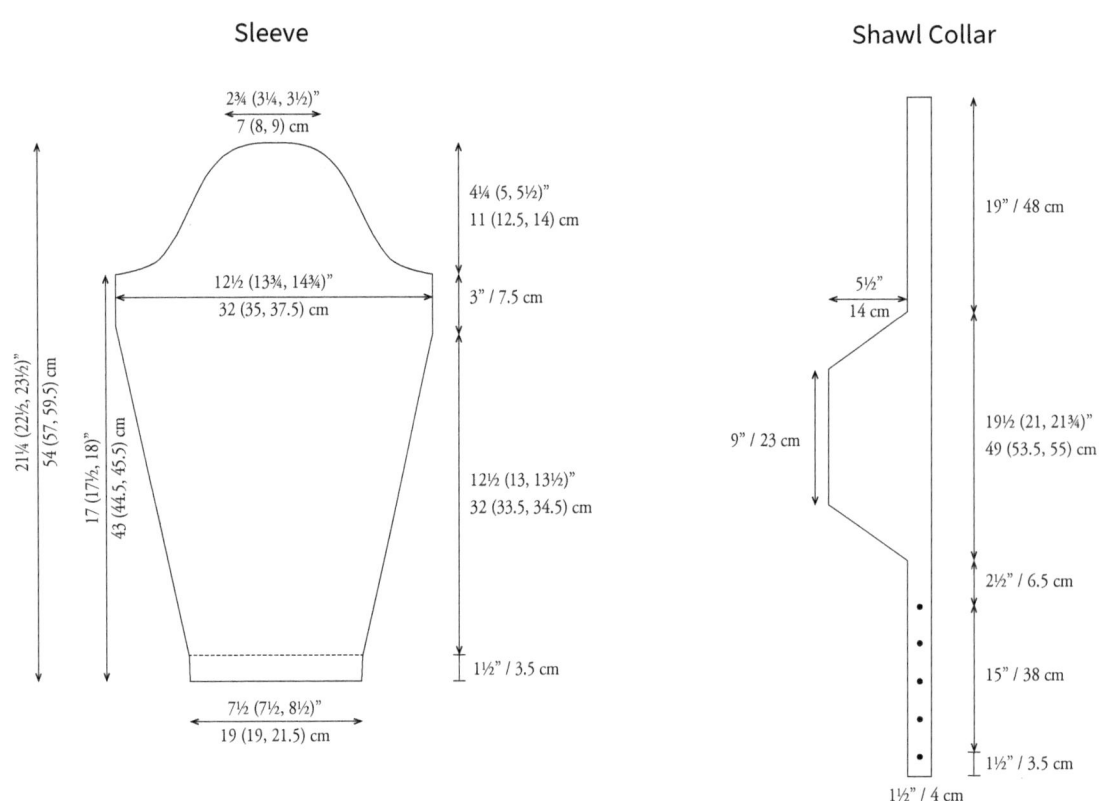

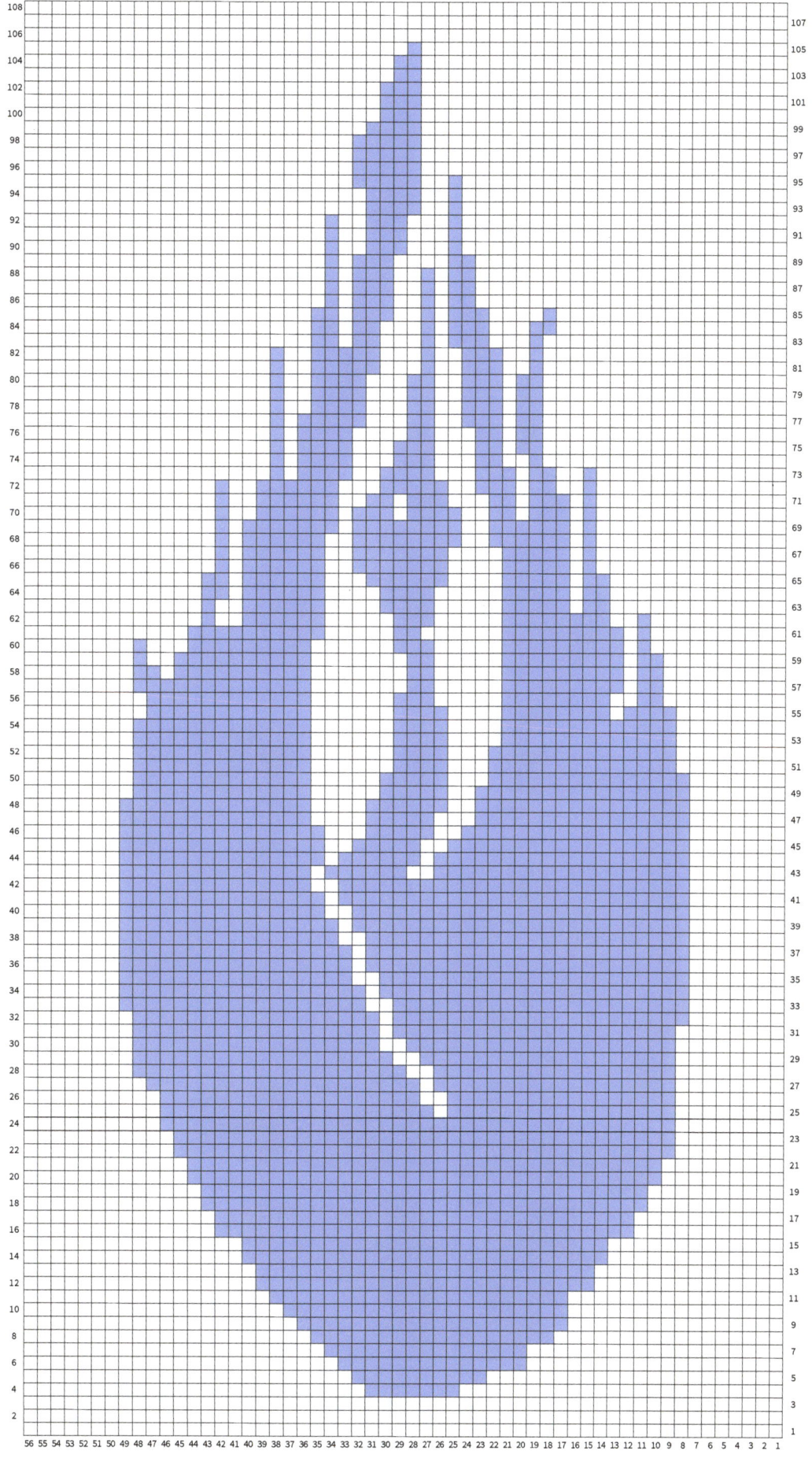

TEARDROP CARDIGAN | 261

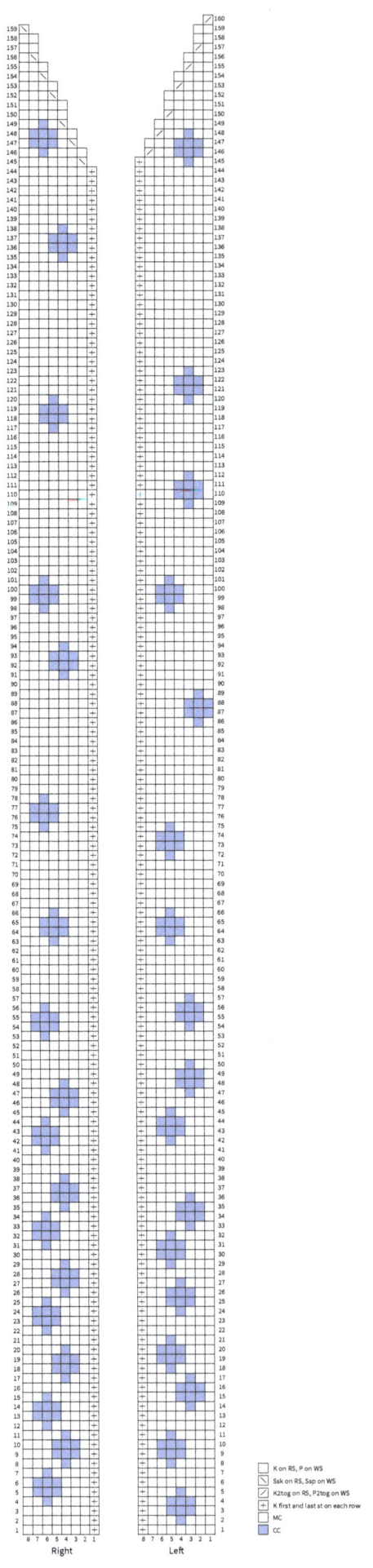

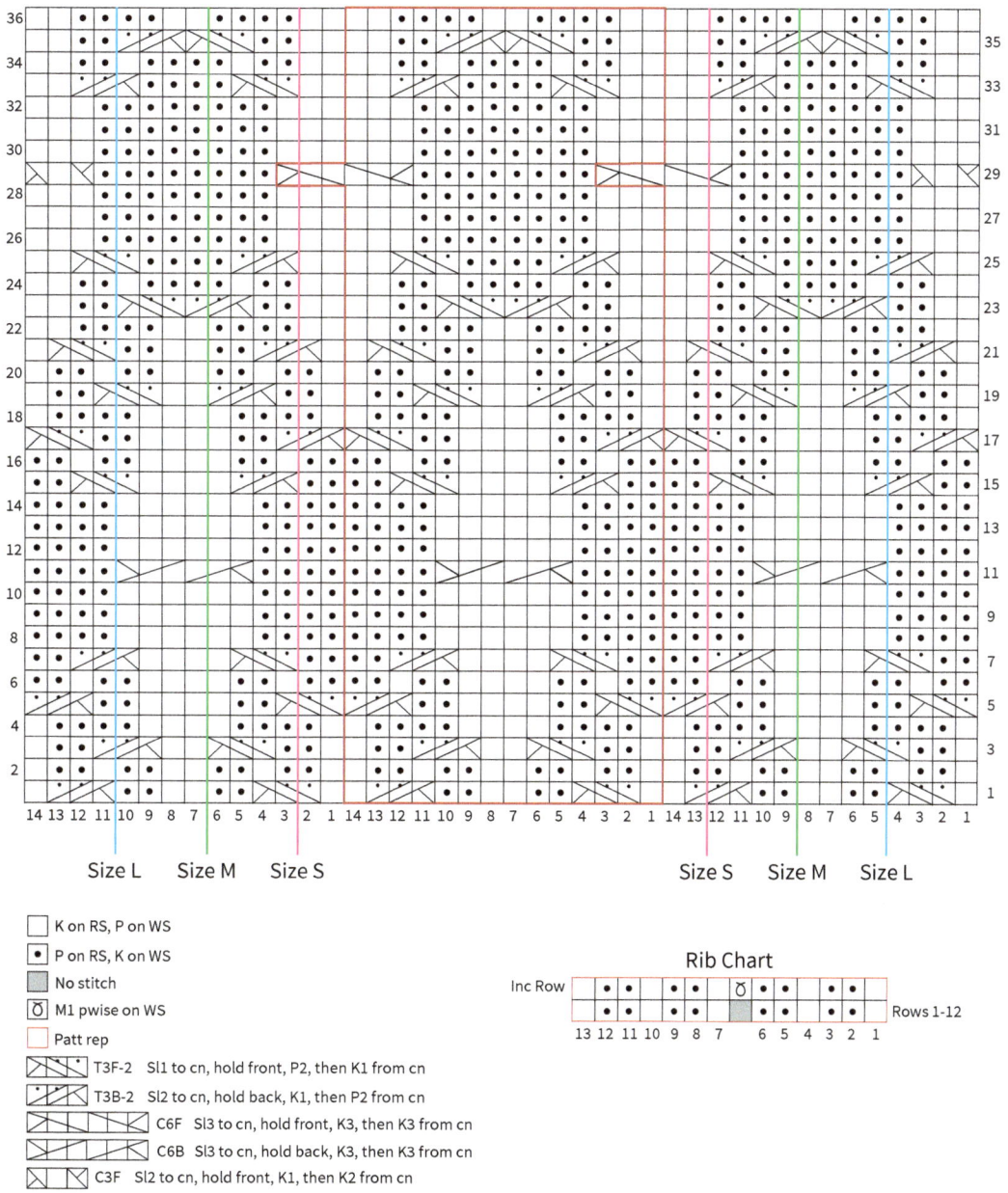

Twisted Cable Chart

Size L, Size M, Size S

- ☐ K on RS, P on WS
- • P on RS, K on WS
- ▨ No stitch
- ⊽ M1 pwise on WS
- ▭ Patt rep
- T3F-2 Sl1 to cn, hold front, P2, then K1 from cn
- T3B-2 Sl2 to cn, hold back, K1, then P2 from cn
- C6F Sl3 to cn, hold front, K3, then K3 from cn
- C6B Sl3 to cn, hold back, K3, then K3 from cn
- C3F Sl2 to cn, hold front, K1, then K2 from cn

Rib Chart

Inc Row, Rows 1-12

TEARDROP CARDIGAN | 263

Tige Cardigan

FINISHED SIZES

Sizes: S (M, L)
To Fit Bust Sizes: 33-35 (36-38, 39-43)" / 84-90 (92-97, 100-110) cm

Sample Size: S

YARN

Trendsetter Yarns Merino VI (100% Extrafine Merino Wool Superwash; 136 yds [124 m] / 1.75 oz / 50 g): color 621 Red 20 (22, 24) balls

NEEDLES & HOOKS

Knitting Needles: One pair size 6 (4 mm)
Crochet Hook: Size 3 (3.5 mm)

NOTIONS

Stitch Markers
Tapestry Needle
Buttons: Three 1" (25 mm) buttons

GAUGES

Mixed Panels
Width – 55 sts = 7$\frac{1}{8}$" (18 cm), 7.72 sts = 1" / 2.5 cm
Length – 48 Rows = 6$\frac{3}{8}$" (16 cm), 7.53 rows = 1" / 2.5 cm

Chart Components
Zigzag Lace Patt = "Z3" 3 sts = $\frac{5}{8}$" / 1.5 cm
Cornstalk Patt = "CS" 11 sts = 1$\frac{1}{2}$" / 4 cm
Cables, Lace & Twists Patt = "CLT" (Center) 17 sts = 2$\frac{1}{8}$" / 5.5 cm
"P2" = 2 sts = $\frac{1}{8}$" / 0.3 cm

Swatch
Selv + P1, CS 11, P2, Z3, P2, CLT 17, P2, Z3, P2, CS 11, P1+ Selv = 55 sts + 2 Selv = 57 sts
Twisted Rib: 31.5 sts and 30 rows = 4" / 10 cm
Reverse St st: 32 sts and 30 rows = 4" / 10 cm
Single Crochet: 28 sts = 6" / 15 cm wide – Button Backs

STITCH GUIDE

Lacy Cables & Vines Pattern (9 Panels): See Chart

Selvedge Stitch: See "Pattern Notes"

Single Crochet: Working from right to left *insert hook into a st, yarn round hook (yrh), draw loop through, yrh, draw yarn through 2 loops on hook*; Rep from * to *.

Reverse St. st: Purl on RSRs, Knit on WSRs.

Twisted Rib Patt: Multiple of 2 +1 / 2 Rows
Row 1- P1, *K1tbl, P1 *; Rep * to *
Row 2 - *K1, P1tbl*; Rep * to *, end K1

PATTERN NOTES / TECHNIQUES USED

Garter Stitch Selvedge – Edge technique used throughout = Knit the first and last sts on every row. All shaping worked inside the selvedge stitches.

Sloped Bind Off (Used to smoothly shape the armholes, neckline and sleeve caps)

Work the first bind off row as usual. Beg the technique with the 2nd bind off row. On the row before the bind off row do not work the last stitch. When you turn the work, this will be the first stitch on the RHN. On the bind off row, slip the first stitch on the Left Hand Needle purlwise to the RHN, then bind off the leftover stitch from the previous row over the slipped stitch. If there are additional bind off sts on this row work them as usual.

Crocheted Button Backs: See sc instructions above. Using the size E (3.5mm) crochet hook, make 2 Button Backs as foll: Begin by Making a slip knot, then ch2. **Rnd1:** work 8 sc in the 2nd ch from the hook (in the slip knot). **Rnd2:** *Work 2 sc in the first sc, then 1 sc in the foll sc *; repeat from * to * = 12 sc. **Rnd3:** Work 1 sc in each of the 12 sc. Slip the last st to the first sc. Return to the center and slip the starting tail onto a tapestry needle. Pull the starting yarn through the first row of sts to close the center hole.

INSTRUCTIONS

Center Back

With size 6 (4 mm) needles, cast on 105 (119, 131) sts including 2 side selvedge sts. Set up rows for each size as foll:

S: Selv + P2, Z3, P2, CS 11, P2, Z3, P1 [P1, CS 11, P2, Z3, P2 + CLT 17 + P2, Z3, P2, CS 11, P1] P1, Z3, P2, CS 11, P2, Z3, P2 + Selv = 103 + 2 Selv = **105 sts**

M: Selv + P2, Last Half CS =5, P2, Z3, P2, CS 11, P2, Z3, P1 [P1, CS 11, P2, Z3, P2 + CLT 17 + P2, Z3, P2, CS 11, P1] P1, Z3, P2, CS 11, P2, Z3, P2, First Half CS = 5, P2 + Selv = 117 + 2 Selv = **119 sts**

L: Selv + P2, CS 11, P2, Z3, P2, CS 11, P2, Z3, P1 [P1, CS 11, P2, Z3, P2 + CLT 17 + P2, Z3, P2, CS 11, P1] P1, Z3, P2, CS 11, P2, Z3, P2, CS 11, P2 + Selv = 129 + Selv = **131 sts**

Work even on these stitches as foll:
S: Rows 1-32 twice, then Rows 33-48 once, then Rows 1-32 twice more = 144 rows.
M & L: Rows 1-48 three times, then Rows 1-8 = 152 rows.
Piece should measure 19¼ (20¼, 20¼)" / 49 (51.5, 51.5) cm.

Work across the selv + 24 (31, 37) shoulder sts, BO the center 55 back neck sts, work across the rem 24 (31, 37) shoulder sts + 1 selv = 25 (32, 38) total sts in shoulders on each side. Place shoulder sts on holders in prep for the 3-needle bind off seaming technique.

Twisted Rib Side Panels

For all sizes the total width of the back and fronts will include panels that will be made separately in the Twisted Rib Patt and seamed to each side edge = 4 total panels, 2 RHS panels and 2 LHS panels. All side and armhole shaping will be worked on these side panels.

With size 6 (4 mm) needles, cast on 25 sts (23 + 2 selv).
Establish patt as foll: Selv, P1, [K1tbl, P1] 11 times, selv.
Work the Garter st. selv technique throughout. Panel widths should be 3" (7.5 cm) when measured inside the selv sts. Work all inc's and dec's inside the selv sts.

Hip-to-Waist Shaping

The way of working the dec's and inc's will depend on the position of the K1tbl and P1 sts in the Twisted Rib Patt at the beg and end of the dec or inc rows. All dec's and inc's will be worked on RSRs.

RHS Panels: Foll the dec instructions below on RSRs on RHS edges. Begin on row 3, work as foll: Dec 1 st on row 3, then 1 st on the foll 4th row, then [dec 1 st on the foll 2nd row, then 1 st on the foll 4th row 2 times] twice, then dec 1 st on the foll 2nd row, then 1 st on the 4th row = 33 rows worked, 10 sts dec'd, 15 sts (13 + 2 selv sts) rem.

LHS Panels: Foll the dec instructions below on RSRs on the LHS edges.

Panel Decreases (All worked on RSRs)
1) Decreases #1 RHS Edge
Row Beg - When the row begins with Selv, P1, K1tbl, exchange places with the P1 and K1 to place the K1 first on the LHN, then work a K2tog tbl dec on the 2 sts. The P1 tucks neatly beneath the K1tbl.

2) Decrease #2 RHS Edge
Row Beg - When the row begins with Selv, K1tbl, P1, work a P2tog dec on the 2 sts after the Selv.

3) Decrease #1 LHS Edge
Row End - When the row ends with K1tbl, P1, Selv, work a K2tog tbl dec on the last 2 sts before the Selv. The P1 tucks nearly under the K1tbl

4) Decrease #2 LHS Edge
Row End - When the row ends with P1, K1tbl, Selv, slip the 2 sts Knitwise, to the RHN one at a time, then slip them back to the LHN in the twisted position. Next, work a P2tog through the front loops.

Waist

Both RHS and LHS Panels: Work 13 rows even on the rem 15 sts. Piece should measure 6" (15 cm).

Waist-to-Bust Shaping

RHS Panels: Foll the inc instructions below and beg on the next RSR row, inc 1 st on the RHS, then inc 1 st on the foll 4th row, then [inc 1 st on the foll 2nd row, then on the foll 4th row] 4 times. 10 sts added = 25 sts (23 sts + 2 selv) on the needles. Then work even until piece measures 12" (30.5 cm).
LHS Panels: inc's are worked foll the instructions below on RSRs on LHS edges.

Panel Increases (All worked on RSRs)
Increase #1 RHS Edge
1) Row Beg - After the Selv, when the row begins with a K1tbl, work a P1, then a K1tbl in the same stitch.
Increase #2 RHS Edge
2) Row Beg - After the Selv when the row begins with a P1, work K1tbl, then P1 in the same stitch.

Increase #1 LHS Edge
3) Row End - When the row ends with K1tbl, Selv, work K1tbl then P1 in the same stitch, then the selv.

Increase #2 LHS Edge
4) Row End - When the row ends with P1, Selv, work P1, then K1tbl in the same stitch, then Selv.

Shape Armholes

RHS Edge and LHS Edge: Bind off 4 sts twice, 3 sts 1 (3, 3) times, 2 sts 2 (3, 3) times, 1 st 3 (2, 2) times = 7 (0, 0) sts rem = S: 5 Twisted Rib sts and 2 selv. Work even on these 7 sts until piece measures 19¼" (49 cm).

Fronts

With size 6 (4 mm) needles, cast on 81 (88, 94) sts including 2 side selvedge sts. Set up Right Front following the layout:

S: Selv + [P1, CS 11, P2, Z3, P2 + CLT 17 + P2, Z3, P2, CS 11, P1] P1, Z3, P2, CS 11, P2, Z3, P2 + Selv = 79 + 2 Selv = **81 sts**

M: Selv + [P1, CS 11, P2, Z3, P2 + CLT 17 + P2, Z3, P2, CS 11, P1] P1, Z3, P2, CS 11, P2, Z3, P2, First half CS = 5 sts, P2 + Selv = 86 + 2 Selv = **88 sts**

L: Selv + [P1, CS 11, P2, Z3, P2 + CLT 17 + P2, Z3, P2, CS 11, P1] P1, Z3, P2, CS, P2, Z3, P2, CS 11, P2 + Selv = 92 + 2 Selv = **94 sts**

Left front: Work the layout in reverse, as well as the buttonhole.

Note: On the Right Front the layout is worked from closing edge to the LHS that will be seamed to the Twisted Rib Panel. On the Left Front, the layout is worked from the RHS edge that will be seamed to the Twisted Rib Panel to the underlap closing edge. The legnthwise flow of the patterns is the same as for the Center Back.

Work even on these 81 (88, 94) sts for 45 (53, 53) rows foll center Back row flow (end with a RS row). Piece should measure 6¼ (7¼, 7¼)" / 16 (18.5, 18.5) cm.

Work Buttonhole

Note: I recommend practicing this buttonhole on a swatch before working it on the main garment.

You will be working a vertical ½" (1.2 cm) buttonhole on the center purl st of the first 11-st Cornstalk (CS) Patt on the Right Front and on the center purl st of the last 11-st Cornstalk (CS) Patt on the Left Front. The buttonholes should end approx ½" (1.2 cm) below the beg of the V neck shaping.

On the next WS row = row 12 (6, 6) of the Cornstalk Patt, begin the separation for the Vertical Buttonhole (hiding the separation yarns will be neater if the separation is made on a WSR). **S:** P1tbl, P1, P1tbl, K1, then P2tog tbl. **M & L:** [P1tbl] twice, P2, P2tog tbl.

Note: The P2tog tbl will include both the next P1tbl and the center K1 st. For the buttonhole the center K1 stitch has been eliminated.

Next, tie on a second ball of yarn leaving a length at the bottom and complete the 2nd side of the Cornstalk pattern as follows: **S:** P1tbl, K1, P1tbl, P1, P1tbl; **M & L:** P1tbl, P2, [P1tbl] twice.

There are now 5 sts on each side being worked separately with a separate ball of yarn. Work the separate halves of the pattern over the 4 buttonhole rows as foll: work to the center, drop 1 yarn and continue across the sts on the opposite side of the center opening with the 2nd ball of yarn. There are Twist sts bordering the buttonhole at the center on each side.

On the next WS row (= Row 50 (58, 58)), as you work the stitch before the gap at the center, work the final P1tbl then pull the yarn to the back and work a K1 on the same stitch. The K1 is the restoration of the center stitch. Using the main ball of yarn continue working across all stitches. Then, continue working with only the main ball of yarn. Leave a length of yarn as you snip the second ball for weaving the ends in. Use the ends left at the bottom and top to add a strengthening border all around the buttonhole.

After completing the buttonholes work even through Row 54 (62, 62) on the Right Front and on Row 55 (63, 63) on the Left Front. Piece should measure 7¼ (8¼, 8¼)" / 18.5 (21, 21) cm.

Shape V

(Use Sloped Bind Off Technique)

Begin V neck shaping on row 55 (63, 63) on the Right Front and row 56 (64, 64) on the Left Front. On both fronts you will be binding off the 56 neck sts over 84 rows, then working even through row 90 on the 25 (32, 38) remaining shoulder stitches (including one selv stitch).

For the Right Front you will be working all bind offs on RSRs. On the Left Front, because all bind offs are done at the neck edge, you will be working on WSRs. Work as foll: Begin by [BO 1 stitch at the neck edge twice, then, 2 sts at neck edge once] 14 times = 25 (32, 38) sts rem for shoulders. Work even on these sts until piece measures 19¼ (20¼, 20¼)" / 49 (51.5, 51.5) cm. Place the rem shoulder sts on holders in prep for the 3-needle bind off seaming technique.

Sleeves

With size 6 (4 mm) needles, cast on 67 sts, including 2 side selvedge sts. Set up Sleeve following the layout:

Selv + P1, Z3, P2, CS 11, P2, Z3, P2 + CLT 17 + P2, Z3, P2, CS 11, P2, Z3, P1, Selv = 65 + 2 Selv sts = 67 sts. Width should measure 8½" (21.5 cm).

Work even on the center sleeves on the mixed cables layout above foll the Lacy Cables and Vines Patt to a length of 19¼ (19½, 19¾)" / 49 (49.5, 50.5) cm, 146 (148, 150) rows = 9 reps of 16-row Cornstalk Patt + 0 (2, 4) rows.

Shape Cap (Use Sloped BO Technique)

[3 sts at the beg of the next 2 rows, 2 sts at the beg of the foll 2 rows] twice, 3 (2, 1) st(s) at the beg of the next 2 rows, 4 sts at the beg of the foll 4 rows = 25 (27, 29) sts rem. BO all rem sts.

Twisted Rib Panels

The side edges of the sleeves will be worked in Twist Stitch Panels following the inc's as explained above. As with the side panels for the body, the width of each side panel will be based on the garment size.

RHS Panel: Cast on 11 (11, 15) sts = 9 (9, 13) sts + 2 selv. Patt layout at cast on is as foll: Row 1: Selv, P1, [K1tbl, P1] 4 (4, 6) times, Selv. Working in the Twisted Rib Patt and foll the RHS and LHS increase technique explained above, at the RHS edges work inc's after working selv sts on RSRs as foll: **S:** Inc [1 st on the 10th row, then on the foll 8th row twice] 4 times = 12 sts inc'd. **M & L:** Inc [1 st on the foll 8th row, then 1 st on the foll 6th row 3 times] 4 times = 16 sts inc'd. Piece should measure 14" (35.5 cm). Work even on these sts for 3" (7.5 cm) = approximately 22 rows. Piece should measure 17" (43 cm). End with a WSR.

LHS Panel: Work as for RHS. Also work increases on the RSRs, only work the increases at the LHS edge.

Shape Cap (Use Sloped BO Technique)

Twisted Rib dec's RHS: Bind off 5 sts at the beg of the next RSR, then [3 (2, 2) sts at the beg of the foll RSR, 2 (3, 3) sts at the beg of the foll 3 (1, 2) RSRs] 2 (4, 3) times, then Sizes M & L only, 2 sts at the beg ot the next RSR = 23 (27, 31) Twisted Rib sts BO.

LHS: Work as for RHS only working BOs at beg of WSRs.

Collar

Notes: You will be working six 16-row repeats of the 11-st Cornstalk Motif = 96 rows. The repeat across the row as you set up the pattern layout will be as foll: P2 + 11-stitch Cornstalk Motif = 13 sts in each of the 26 repeats. For symmetry each side will end with a P2.

Patt Flow Layout: *P2 + 11-st Cornstalk Motif*; Rep from * to * 25 times, end with P2.

Collar Width = 42½" (108 cm) at Base.
Collar Depth = 12¾" (32.5 cm)

Use Sloped Bind Off Technique for binding off sts to shape the collar side edges.

With size 6 (4 mm) needles CO 340 sts and work across rows 1 and 2 in Patt following the chart.

Beg dec'ing by working as follows:

Rows 3 through 10
BO 1 stitch at the beg of the next 8 rows = 332 sts.

Rows 11 through 22
BO [2 sts at the beg of the next 2 rows, then 1 st at the beg of the foll 4 rows] 2 times = 316 sts

Rows 23 through 40
BO [2 sts at the beg of the next 4 rows, then 1 st at the beg of the foll 2 rows] 3 times = 286 sts.

Rows 41 through 52
BO [3 sts at the beg of the next 2 rows, then 2 sts at the beg of the foll 4 rows] 2 times = 258 sts.

Rows 53 and 54
BO 3 sts at the beg of the next 2 rows = 252 sts.

Rows 55 through 66
BO [4 sts at the beg of the next 2 rows, then 3 sts at the beg of the foll 4 rows] 2 times = 212 sts.

Rows 67 through 88
BO 4 sts at the beg of the next 2 rows, 3 sts at the beg of the foll 2 rows, 4 sts at the beg of the foll 2 rows, 5 sts at the beg of the foll 4 rows, 4 sts at the beg of the foll 4 rows, 5 sts at the beg of the foll 4 rows, 6 sts at the beg of the foll 4 rows = 110 sts.

Rows 89 through 96
BO 7 sts at the beg of the final 8 rows = 54 sts

Row 97: BO all rem sts.

Bias Band

With size 6 (4 mm) needles, cast on 3 sts and work as foll: Row #1 - Inc in first and last sts.

Row #2 - Purl. Repeat rows 1 & 2 until there are 9 sts on the needles. Work on these 9 sts as foll: RSRs - Inc in first st by KFB, work across row and K2tog on last 2 sts. WSR - Purl 9. Continue to work in this way. Measure the needed length of the band as foll: Baste the collar onto the jacket, then turn the tape measure on its side and measure along one side of the front, around the collar, then down the other side of the front. See finishing instructions below for ending the knitting.

Finishing

Block pieces to measurements. Slip Back and Front Shoulder sts back onto needles from holders, then using a 3rd needle, seam shoulders using the 3-needle bind off technique, making certain that the patterns are aligned.

Sides: Sew side panels to the backs and fronts making certain that the armhole shaping is in the correct (outer) position. Sew side seams. Collar: This piece has been basted to the neckline for planning the length of the Bias Band. For an invisible join, sew collar to neck edge using the Whipstitch technique with very close stitches. The RS of the collar should be facing inward (collar will turn outward when worn).

Bias Bands: Seam Bias Band to jacket before attaching the sleeves working as follows: Steam Bias Band to the correct measurement. Pin band around the fronts and collar, beginning at the lower Right Front. Fold the band in half over the edges. Add more length or rip back until the band fits to within 1" (2.5 cm) of completion. Bind off as foll: RSRs: K2tog, work to last 2 sts, K2tog. WSRs: Purl. Rep these 2 Rows 3 times. There will be 3 sts rem. Bind off all rem sts. Baste the band to the jacket. Next, seam the band using mattress stitch to attach the band on the RS. Then, use the Whipstitch technique to attach the band on the WS.

Button Backs: The 2 Button Backs are sewn on the WS of work beneath the button placement areas of the Cornstalk Patt motifs on each side. Sew one on the Left Front and one on the Right Front as foll: Place the first on the section of the Left Front that will lie beneath the buttonhole on Right Front closing edge. Place the second beneath the location on the center of the Right Front that will sit above the underlapping edge buttonhole on the Left Front. Sew the button for the Right Front closing onto the button back on the center Left Front. Sew the under button onto the button back on the inside of the Right Front. This button will close the left front. Sew a second button to top of this button back for the dbl breasted appearance when the jacket is closed.

Sleeves: Sew side panels to sleeves, then sew center sleeve seams. Set sleeves into the armholes. Baste the sleeves in, then backstitch the sleeves in place.

Tige Jacket Back

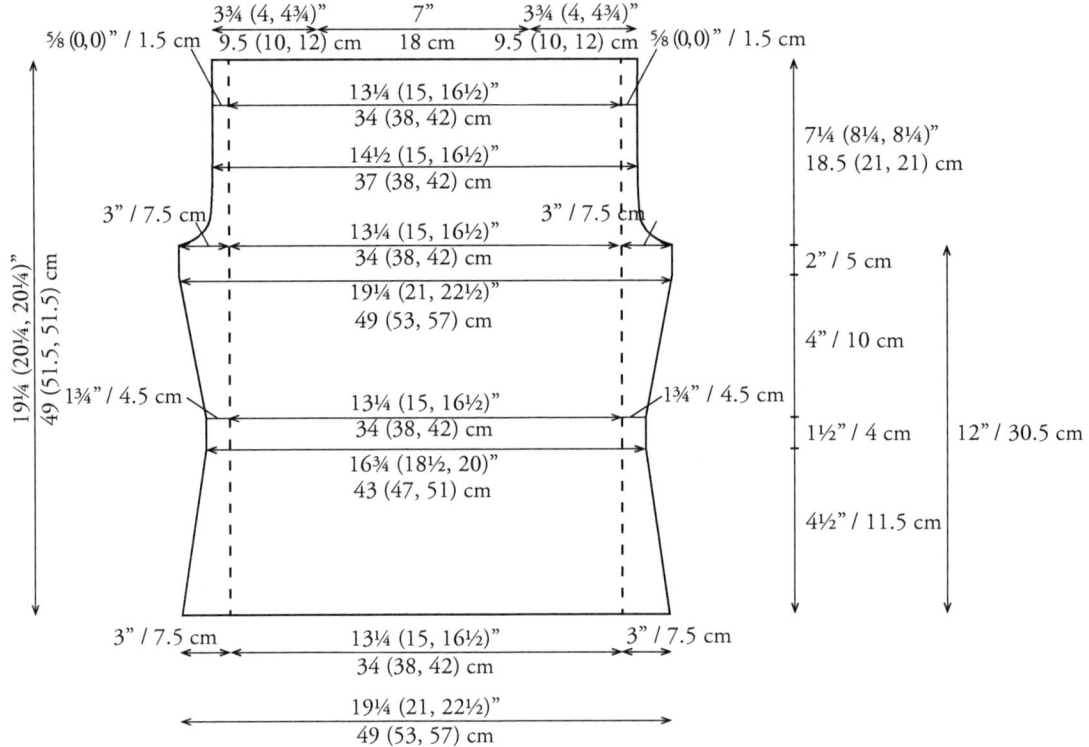

Tige Jacket Fronts

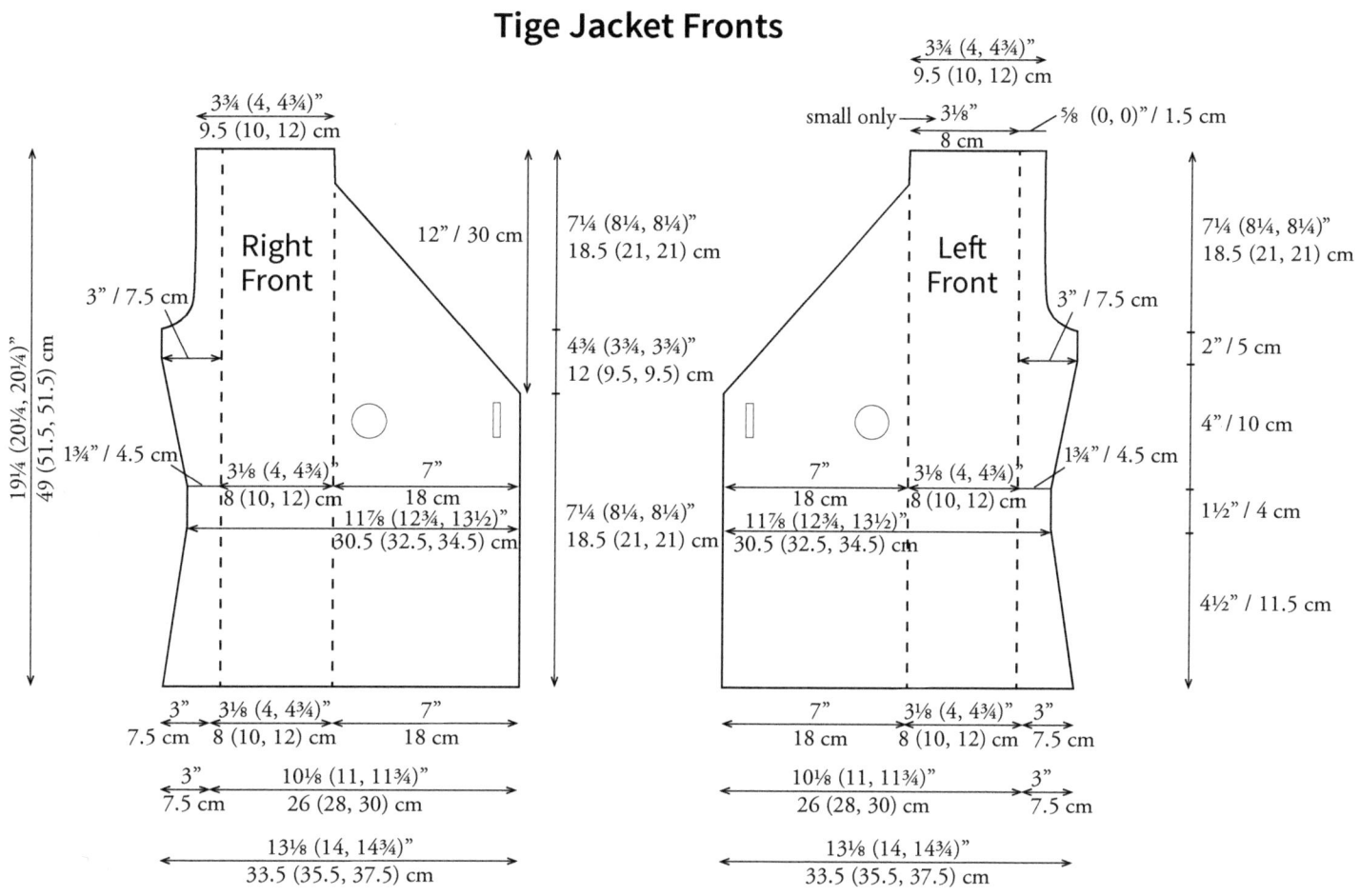

Tige Jacket Sleeve

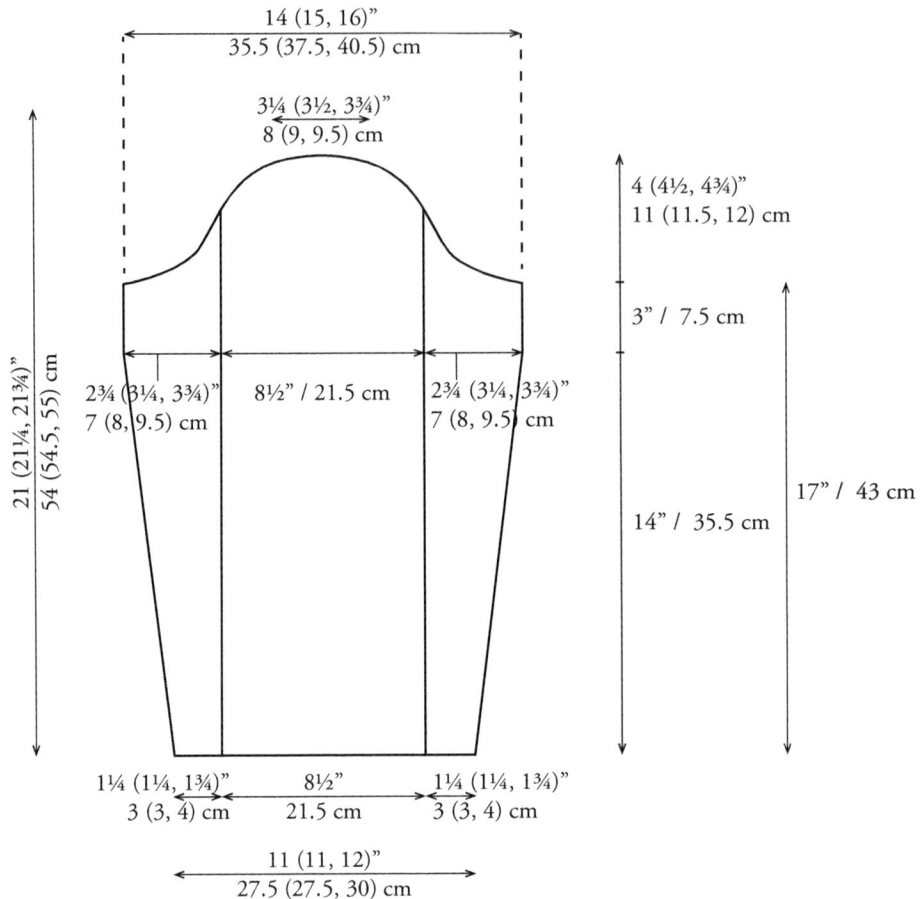

Collar

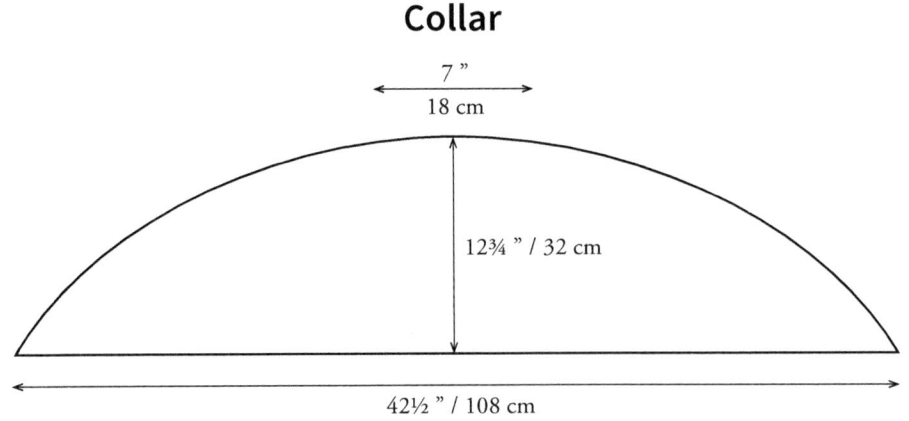

Lacy Cables & Vines

On the chart there are 69 sts shown. They include a selvedge and 6 stitches on each side that fall outside the center layout of 55 sts that have been placed inside the [brackets] in the written instructions. That bracketed layout is the same for all sizes. The number of sts on each side changes for each size.

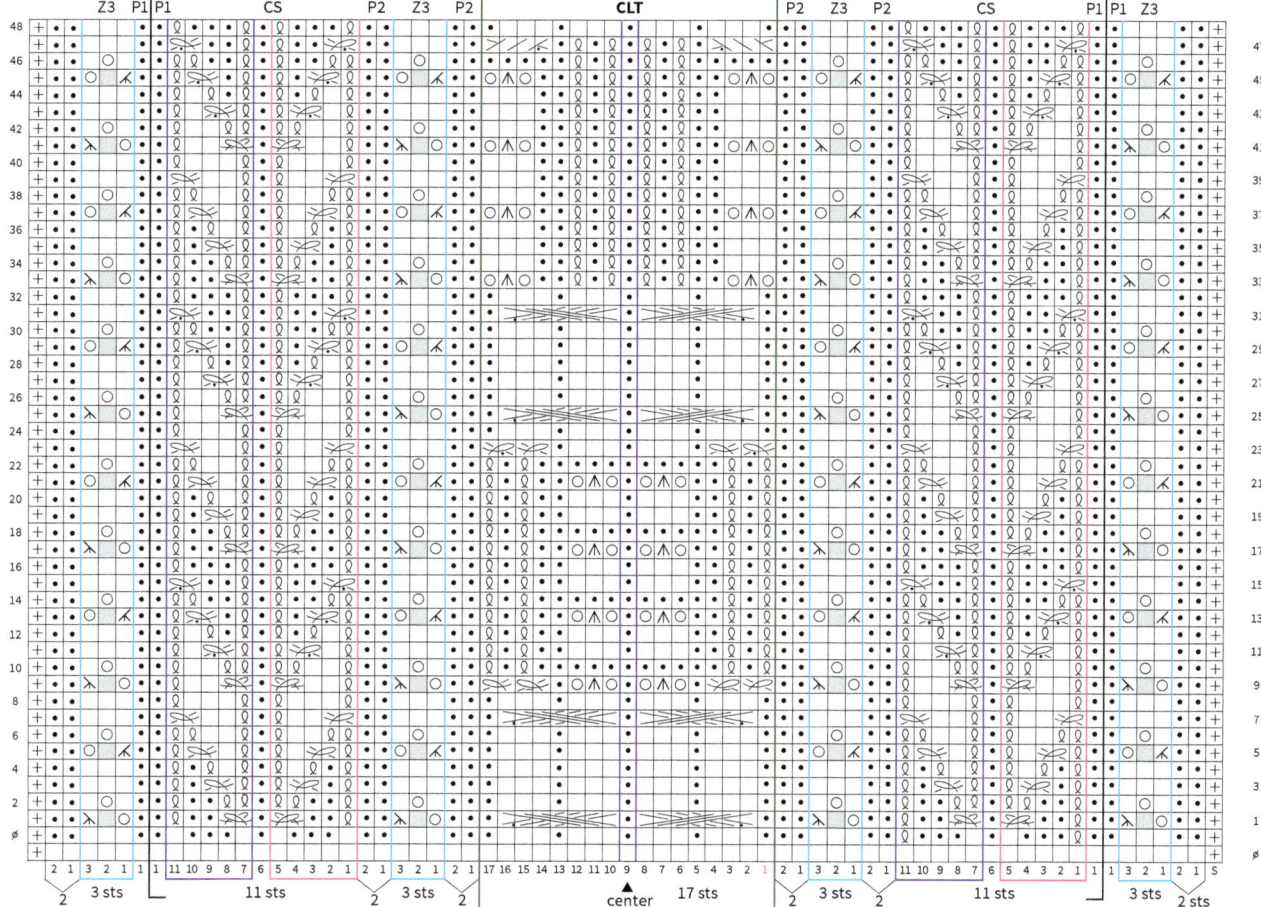

- K on RS, P on WS
- P on RS, K on WS
- Yarn Over
- Sl1-k2tog-psso 1)Sl1 st to RHN, 2)K next 2 sts tog, 3)Pass sl st over the st made by k2tog
- K3tog
- Sl2-k1-p2sso 1)Sl2 sts to RHN, 2)K next st, 3)Pass 2 sts over the k st
- Selvedge st = k first and last st each row
- No stitch
- K1tbl on RS, P1tbl on WS

Z3   Zigzag lace patt
CS   Cornstalk patt
CLT   Center Lace and Twists Patt

Tw2-B 1)Reach in front across the first st, 2)K the 2nd st tbl, 3)K the first st. Drop both sts tog from the LHN.

Tw2-F 1)Reach behind the first st, 2)K1 on 2nd st, 3)K the first st tbl, 4)Drop both sts tog from the LHN

Tw2-B-P 1)Reach in front across the first stitch, 2)K the 2nd st tbl, 3)P1 on the skipped st, 4)Drop both sts from the LHN

Tw2-F-P 1)Reach behind the first st, 2)Pull the 2nd st forward then purl it, 3)Ktbl on the first st, 4)Drop both sts tog from the LHN

Tw2 CrB 1)Reach in front across the first stitch, 2)K the 2nd st tbl, 3)K1tbl on the skipped st, 4)Drop both sts from the LHN

Tw2 CrF 1)Reach behind the first st, 2)K1tbl, 3) K1tbl on the first st, 4)Drop both sts tog from the LHN.

C7B-P Sl4 to cn, hold back, k3, then p1, k3 from cn
C7F-P Sl3 to cn, hold front, k3, p1 then k3 from cn
Cr4 B-P 1)Sl1 to CN, hold at back, 2)K3, p1 from CN
Cr4 F-P 1)Sl3 sts to CN, hold at front, 2)P1, then k3 from CN

Notes: The center purl stitch is at the bottom of the fabric. You will see when you knit #18 that you will have to cross CN1 and CN2.

JOAN FORGIONE

Trellised Arbor Shawl

FINISHED MEASUREMENTS

Width along top edge: 73½" / 187 cm
Vertical length at deepest point: 24½" / 62 cm

YARN

Quince & Co. Tern (75% American wool / 25% silk; 221 yds [202 m] / 1.75 oz / 50 g): #423 Iron, 3 skeins

NEEDLES

Size US 6 (4mm)

NOTIONS

cable needle (cn); blocking wires (optional); blocking pins; tapestry needle

GAUGES

33 sts and 33 rows = 4" / 10 cm in twisted rib pattern before blocking
30 sts and 40 rows = 4" / 10 cm in twisted rib pattern after blocking

Gauge is not critical to this project's construction, however a change in gauge will affect the finished measurements and the yarn requirements.

STITCH GUIDE

Kfbf: Knit into the front, then the back, then the front of the same st– 2 sts inc

4-st double wrap (W4): Sl4 to cn and hold to front. With working yarn, wrap these 4 sts by taking the yarn behind the cable needle and then to the front and around twice. Yarn should be wrapped loosely enough so that when blocked, the 4 sts do not appear distorted. Then work 4 sts from cn: k1tbl, p2, k1tbl. See page 120.

NOTES

- The asymmetrical triangle shawl is worked from one tip to the opposite edge.
- Beginning with Row 3, 12 sts are increased every 18 rows throughout the body and edging.

INSTRUCTIONS

Twisted Rib Body

CO 9 sts.

Work chart 1, Rows 1-20, then rep Rows 3-20 thirteen (13) times more - 177 sts.

Lace Edging

Work chart 2, all rows - 213 sts.

Bind off all sts loosely on the WS.

Finishing

Use wet blocking method; after soaking the shawl, pin it to finished measurements and allow to dry. Weave in all ends.

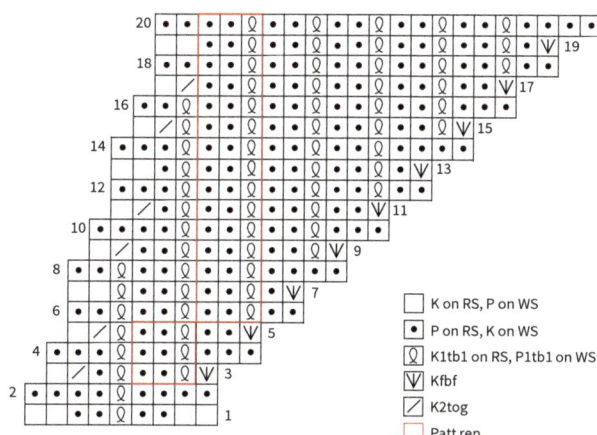

Trellised Arbor Shawl
Lace Edging (chart 2)

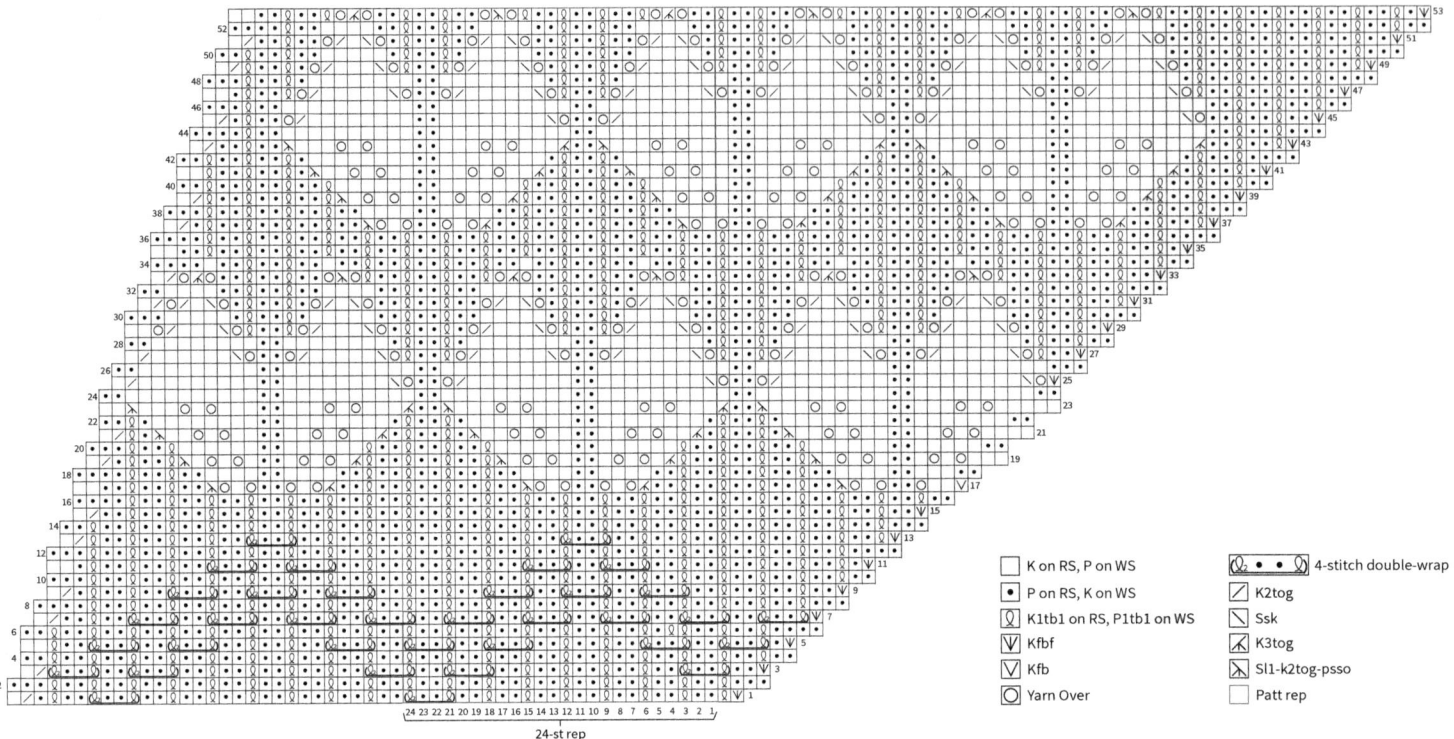

IRIS SCHREIER

Twist & Shout Shawl

FINISHED SIZE

Length tip to tip: 120" / 305 cm
Width: 23" / 57 cm

YARN

Artyarns Merino Cloud Gradients Kits (80% Extra Fine Merino / 20% Cashmere; 540 yds [496 m] / 4.2 oz / 120 g): Fuschias, one 4-skein set (Colors A1-A4); Olives, one 4-skein set (Colors B1-B4)

NEEDLES

Size US 6 (4 mm). Adjust needle size if necessary to obtain the correct gauge.

NOTIONS

tapestry needle

GAUGES

20 sts and 26 rows = 4" / 10 cm in pattern stitch after blocking

STITCH GUIDE

Transition Band
Row 1: With first specified color, kfb, k to last 2 sts, k2tog.
Row 2: K to end.
Row 3: With second specified color, kfb, k to last 2 sts, k2tog.
Row 4: K1, p to last st, k1.
Row 5: With third specified color, kfb, k to last 2 sts, k2tog.

NOTES

- Each skein in the gradient kit is numbered in order of shade, with 1 being the lightest and 4 being the darkest.
- The middle color in each Transition Band should be cut after working Rows 3 & 4. Otherwise, carry the resting yarn until it is replaced by the next shade.
- There is no RS/WS; the chart begins on alternating sides throughout.
- Each time you work the chart, work Rows 1-20 once, working the outlined pattern repeat 4 times per row.

INSTRUCTIONS

With A4 (darkest color A), CO 113 sts.

Work Transition Band in A4, B4, A4.

With A4, work chart.

Work Transition Band in A4, B3, A4.

With A4, work chart.

Work Transition Band in A4, B2, A3.

With A3, work chart.

Work Transition Band in A3, B1, A3.

With A3, work chart.

Work Transition Band in A3, B4, A2.

With A2, work chart.

Work Transition Band in A2, B3, A2.

With A2, work chart.

Work Transition Band in A2, B2, A1.

With A1, work chart.

Work Transition Band in A1, B1, A1.

With A1, work chart.

Work Transition Band in A1, B4, B1.

With B1, work chart.

Work Transition Band in B1, A4, B1.

With B1, work chart.

Work Transition Band in B1, A3, B2.

With B2, work chart.

Work Transition Band in B2, A2, B2.

With B2, work chart.

Work Transition Band in B2, A1, B3.

With B3, work chart.

Work Transition Band in B3, A4, B3.

With B4, work chart.

Work Transition Band in B4, B3, B4.

BO loosely with B4. Cut yarn, weave in ends. Block as desired.

Twist & Shout Shawl

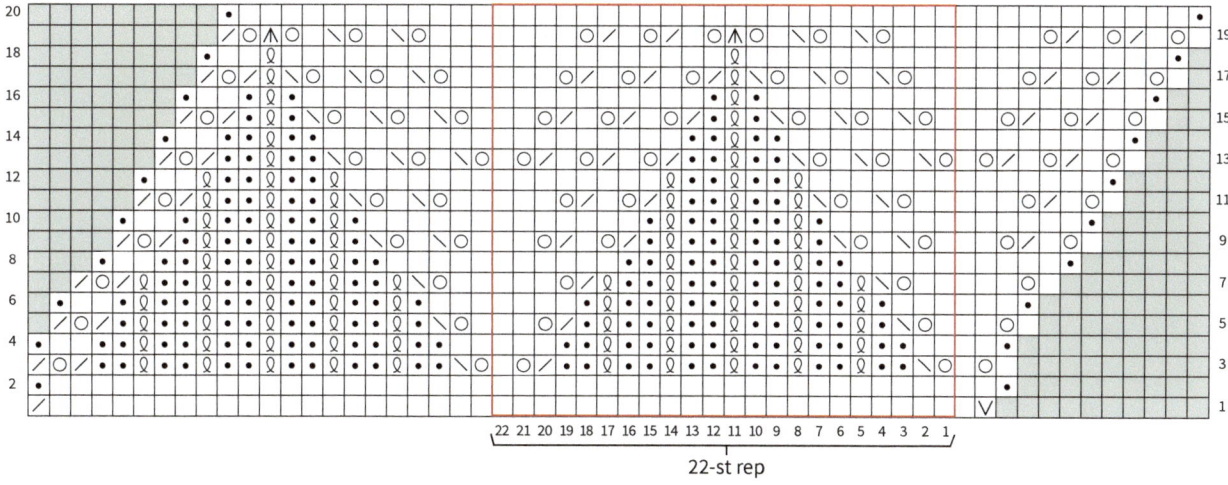

TRUDIE JOSEPH

Twisted Rhythms

FINISHED SIZES

Women's S (M, L)
Finished bust: 38½ (44¼, 49¼)" / 97.5 (112.5, 125) cm
To fit bust sizes: 36 (42, 47)" / 91.5 (106.5, 114.5) cm

Sample Size: L

YARN

MC: Cleckheaton Superfine Merino 8 Ply (100% Merino; 142 yds [130 m] / 2.29 oz / 65 g): color 47 Denim 11 (14, 15) balls
CC: color 02 Dark Grey 1 (2, 2) balls
Note: If making single-color version, replace CC skeins with additional MC skeins.

NEEDLES

Size US 7 (4 mm)
Size US 8 (5 mm)
Adjust needle size if necessary to obtain the correct gauge.

NOTIONS

stitch markers, stitch holders or waste yarn, five 1" (25.5 mm) buttons

GAUGES

Diamond Moss Pattern:
24 sts and 25 rows = 4" / 10 cm in patt with smaller needles

Cables & Twists Pattern:
24 sts and 28 rows = 4" / 10 cm in patt with smaller needles
21 sts and 28 rows = 4" / 10 cm in patt with larger needles

Sleeve Pattern:
20 sts and 24 rows = 4" / 10 cm in patt with smaller needles

STITCH GUIDE

Twisted Rib Pattern
(worked flat over an even number of sts)
Row 1 (RS): [K1tbl, p1]
Row 2 (WS): [K1, p1tbl]

Diamond Moss Pattern
See Chart 1.

Cables & Twists Pattern
See Charts 2, 3 & 4.

Moss Stitch
(worked flat over an odd number of sts)
Rows 1 & 2: K1 (selv), k1, [p1, k1] to last stitch, k1 (selv).
Rows 3 & 4: K1 (selv), p1, [k1, p1] to last stitch, k1 (selv).

NOTES

- A Garter stitch selvedge is worked at all seamed edges until the armhole shaping: Knit the first and last sts of every row. These sts are not shown on the charts but are included in the pattern instructions.
- The sloped bind off method.
- The Diamond Moss pattern may be worked in a single color. If knitting the two color option, consider working the cuffs and colors in CC as well.
- Pay close attention to the chart instructions, as the "plus" sts are worked differently for the Back, Right Front, and Left Front in order to position the pattern properly and symmetrically.

INSTRUCTIONS

Back

With US 7 (4.5mm) needles, CO 123 (139,155) sts.

Establish Diamond Moss patt from Chart 1, Row 1 as foll: K1 (selv), work blue patt rep 0 (1, 2) times (= 0 (8, 16) "plus" sts), work red patt rep 3 times, work to end of chart row working green patt rep 0 (1, 2) times (= 22 (30, 38) "plus" sts), k1 (selv).

Work in patt as estab for Rows 2-64 of Chart 1, decreasing as indicated in final row – 119 (135, 151) sts rem.

Establish Cables & Twists patt from Chart 2, Row 1 as foll: K1 (selv), work 27 (19, 27) "plus" sts, work 32-st patt rep 2 (3, 3) times, work 26 (18, 26) "plus" sts, k1 (selv).

Cont in patt as estab for 49 more rows or 7" (18 cm), ending with a WS row.

Change to US 8 (5.0mm) needles.
Cont in patt as estab and shape armholes as foll:
BO 5 sts at beg of next 2 rows.
BO 2 (4, 5) sts at beg of next 2 rows.
BO 1 (3, 4) st(s) at beg of next 2 rows.
BO 1 (2, 3) st(s) at beg of next 2 rows.
BO 0 (2, 3) sts at beg of next 2 rows.
BO 0 (1, 2) st(s) at beg of next 2 rows.
BO 0 (0, 1) st(s) at beg of next 4 rows – 101 (101, 103) sts rem.

Cont in Cables & Twists pattern until Back measures 8 (8½, 9)" / 20.5 (21.5, 23) cm from beg of armhole shaping, ending with a WS row.

Left shoulder

Next row (RS): Work 40 sts in patt then place these sts on holder or waste yarn for right shoulder, BO **21 (21, 23) sts for back neck, work to end – 40 left shoulder sts rem.**

Cont in patt, shaping neck as foll: BO 7 sts at beg of next RS row, then BO 3 sts at beg of next RS row, then BO 2 sts at beg of next 2 RS rows – 26 sts rem.

Place left shoulder sts on holder.

Right shoulder

With RS facing, place 40 right shoulder sts back on needle.
Join working yarn and work 1 RS row in patt then shape neck as foll: BO 7 sts at beg of next WS row, then BO 3 sts at beg of next WS row, then BO 2 sts at beg of next 2 WS rows – 26 sts rem.

Place right shoulder sts on holder.

Right Front

With US 7 (4.5mm) needles, CO 57 (65, 73) sts.

Note: All RS rows beg with a sl st (center front edge).

Establish Diamond Moss patt from Chart 1 as foll:

Row 1 (RS): Sl1, skip blue patt rep and work red patt rep once, work 22 sts in patt, then work green patt rep 0 (1, 2) times (= 22 (30, 38) "plus" sts), k1 (selv).

Row 2 (WS): K1 (selv), work green patt rep 0 (1, 2) times, work 22 sts in patt then work red patt rep once, k1 (selv).

Work in patt as estab for Rows 3-64 of Chart 1, decreasing as indicated in final row - 55 (63, 71) sts rem.

Establish Cables & Twists patt from Chart 3, Row 1 as foll:

Row 1 (RS): Sl1, work Chart 3 for your size, k1 (selv).

Row 2 (WS): K1 (selv), work chart, k1 (selv).

Cont in patt as estab for 48 more rows or same length as Back to armhole.

Change to US 8 (5.0mm) needles.

Cont in patt as estab and shape armhole as foll:

BO 5 sts at beg of first WS row.
BO 2 (4, 5) sts at beg of next WS row.
BO 1 (3, 4) st(s) at beg of next WS row.
BO 1 (2, 3) st(s) at beg of next WS row.
BO 0 (2, 3) sts at beg of next WS row.
BO 0 (1, 2) st(s) at beg of next WS row.
BO 0 (0, 1) st(s) at beg of next 2 WS rows – 46 (46, 47) sts rem.

Work even in patt for 22 (26, 30) rows or until armhole measures 5½ (6, 6½)"/14 (15, 16.5) cm, ending with a WS row.

Cont in patt and shape neckline as foll:

BO 6 sts at beg of next RS row.
BO 4 sts at beg of next RS row.
BO 3 sts at beg of next RS row.
BO 2 sts at beg of next 2 RS rows.
BO 1 st at beg of next 3 (3, 4) RS rows – 26 sts rem.

Work even in patt until armhole measures same as for back, then place right shoulder sts on holder.

Left Front

With US 7 (4.5 mm) needles, CO 57 (65, 73) sts.

Note: All WS rows beg with a sl st (center front edge).

Establish Diamond Moss patt from Chart 1 as foll:

Row 1 (RS): K1 (selv), work blue patt rep 0 (1, 2) times, work red patt rep once, work 22 sts in patt, skip green patt rep, k1 (selv).

Row 2 (WS): Sl1, skip green patt rep, work 22 sts in patt, work red patt rep once, work blue patt rep 0 (1, 2) times, k1 (selv).

Work in patt as estab for Rows 3-64 of Chart 1, decreasing as indicated in final row - 55 (63,71) sts rem.

Establish Cables & Twists patt from Chart 4, Row 1 as foll:

Row 1 (RS): K1 (selv), work Chart 4 for your size, k1 (selv).

Row 2 (WS): Sl1, work chart, k1 (selv).

Cont in patt as estab for 48 more rows or same length as Back to armhole.
Change to US 8 (5.0mm) needles.

Cont in patt as estab and shape armhole as foll:
BO 5 sts at beg of first RS row.
BO 2 (4, 5) sts at beg of next RS row.
BO 1 (3, 4) st(s) at beg of next RS row.
BO 1 (2, 3) st(s) at beg of next RS row.
BO 0 (2, 3) sts at beg of next RS row.
BO 0 (1, 2) st(s) at beg of next RS row.
BO 0 (0, 1) st(s) at beg of next 2 RS rows – 46 (46, 47) sts rem.

Work even in patt for 22 (26, 30) rows or until armhole measures 5½ (6, 6½)"/14 (15, 16.5) cm, ending with a RS row.

Cont in patt and shape neckline as foll:
BO 6 sts at beg of next WS row.
BO 4 sts at beg of next WS row.
BO 3 sts at beg of next WS row.
BO 2 sts at beg of next 2 WS rows.
BO 1 st at beg of next 3 (3, 4) WS rows – 26 sts rem.

Work even in patt until armhole measures same as for back, then place right shoulder sts on holder.

Sleeves

Note: If making the two-color version, work cuffs in CC, then change to MC after moss stitch.
With US 7 (4.5 mm) needles, CO 69 sts.
Work Moss Stitch for 2½"/6.5 cm, ending with a WS row.

Next row estab ribbing patt as foll:
Row 1 (RS): K1 (selv), p3 (Rev St st), pl mar, *[k1tbl, p1] x2, k1tbl, p3; rep from * to last 9 sts, [k1tbl, p1] x2, k1tbl, pl mar, p3 (Rev St st), k1 (selv).
Row 2 (WS): K1 (selv), k to mar (Rev St st), sl mar, [p1tbl, k1] x2, p1tbl, *k3, [p1tbl, k1] x2, p1tbl; rep from * to mar, sl mar, k to last st (Rev St st), k1 (selv).
Size S only: Work even in patt until sleeve measures 17½"/44.5 cm.
Sizes M & L only: Cont in patt and inc 1 st at beg and end of every - (11th, 5th) RS row - (4, 8) time(s) - (8, 16) sts inc; - (77, 85) sts total.
Work even in patt for – (5, 13) rows or until sleeve measures – (18, 18)"/– (45.5, 45.5) cm.

All sizes: Shape sleeve cap
BO 5 sts at beg of next 4 rows – 49 (57, 65) sts rem.
Dec 1 st at beg and end of every 3rd row 2 (7, 16) times, then every 4th row 9 (6, 0) times – 22 (26, 32) sts dec; 27 (31, 33) sts rem.
BO 5 sts at beg of next 2 rows, then BO rem 17 (21, 23) sts.

Finishing

Block all pieces to measurements. Join fronts to back at shoulders using 3-needle bind off. Sew body side seams. Sew sleeve seams. Set in sleeves. Add front bands and collar, using CC if desired.

Front Bands

With US 7 (4.5 mm) needles and RS facing, pick up sts evenly along Right Front edge from beg of Cables & Twists patt to neckline, making sure the total number is odd.

Beg with WS row, work 3 rows in Moss Stitch, slipping the first st of every row (no selvedge).

Place 5 markers, evenly spaced, to mark desired location of buttonholes. Each buttonhole will be 3 sts long.

Next row (RS): *Work in patt to mar, re mar, BO 3 sts; rep from * 4 times more, work in patt to end.

Next row (WS): *Work in patt to bound off sts, CO 3 sts using backwards loop method; rep from * 4 times more, work in patt to end.

Work 4 more rows in patt then BO all sts on RS.

Rep for Left Front band, working 9 rows in Moss Stitch with no buttonholes.

Collar

With US 7 (4.5mm) needles and WS facing, pick up sts evenly along neck edge (do not pick up sts on front bands) placing markers 12 sts from beg and end and making sure the total number is odd.

Work back and forth in Moss Stitch and shape collar as foll:

Row 1: Sl1, work to 2 sts before 2nd mar, W&T.
Row 2: Work to 2 sts before mar, W&T.
Rows 3-4: Work to 8 sts before mar, W&T.
Rows 5-6: Work to 14 sts before mar, W&T.
Rows 7-8: Work to 20 sts before mar, W&T.
Next row: Work to end, picking up wraps and working them together with wrapped sts.

Cont in Moss Stitch, slipping the first st of every row and picking up and working remaining wraps on first row. Work back and forth until collar measures 6"/15 cm at center or see option below.
BO all sts.

Optional collar edging:

When collar measures 4½" (11.5 cm), cont as foll:
Work 2 rows in MC.
Work 2 rows in CC.
Work 2 rows in MC.
Work 4 rows in CC.
BO all sts.

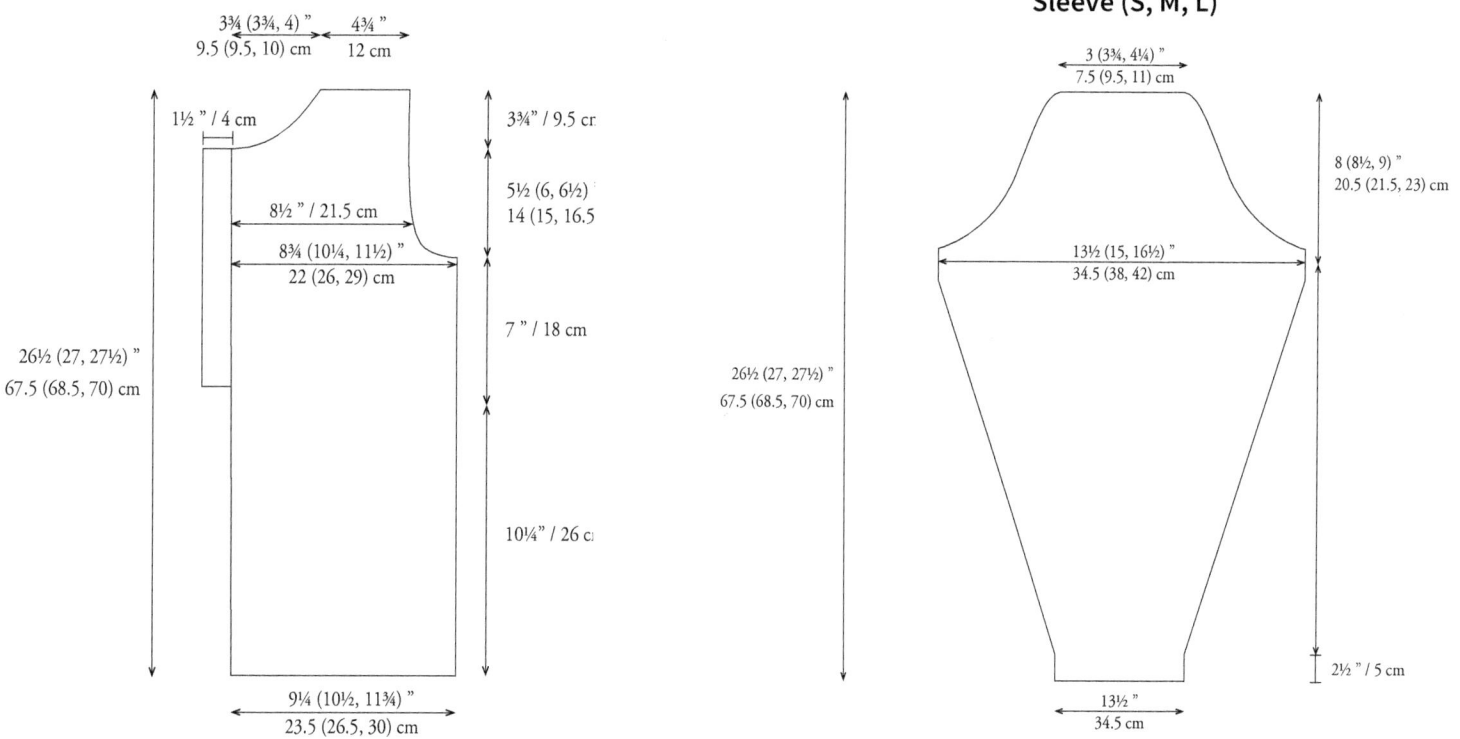
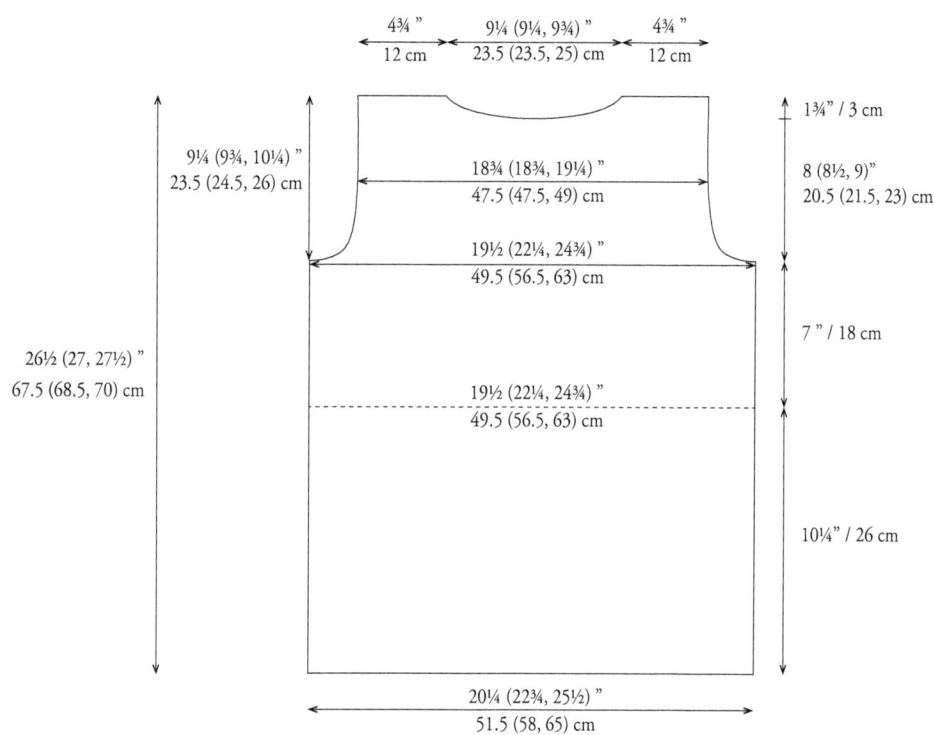

TWISTED RHYTHMS | 287

Chart 1 - Diamond Moss Pattern

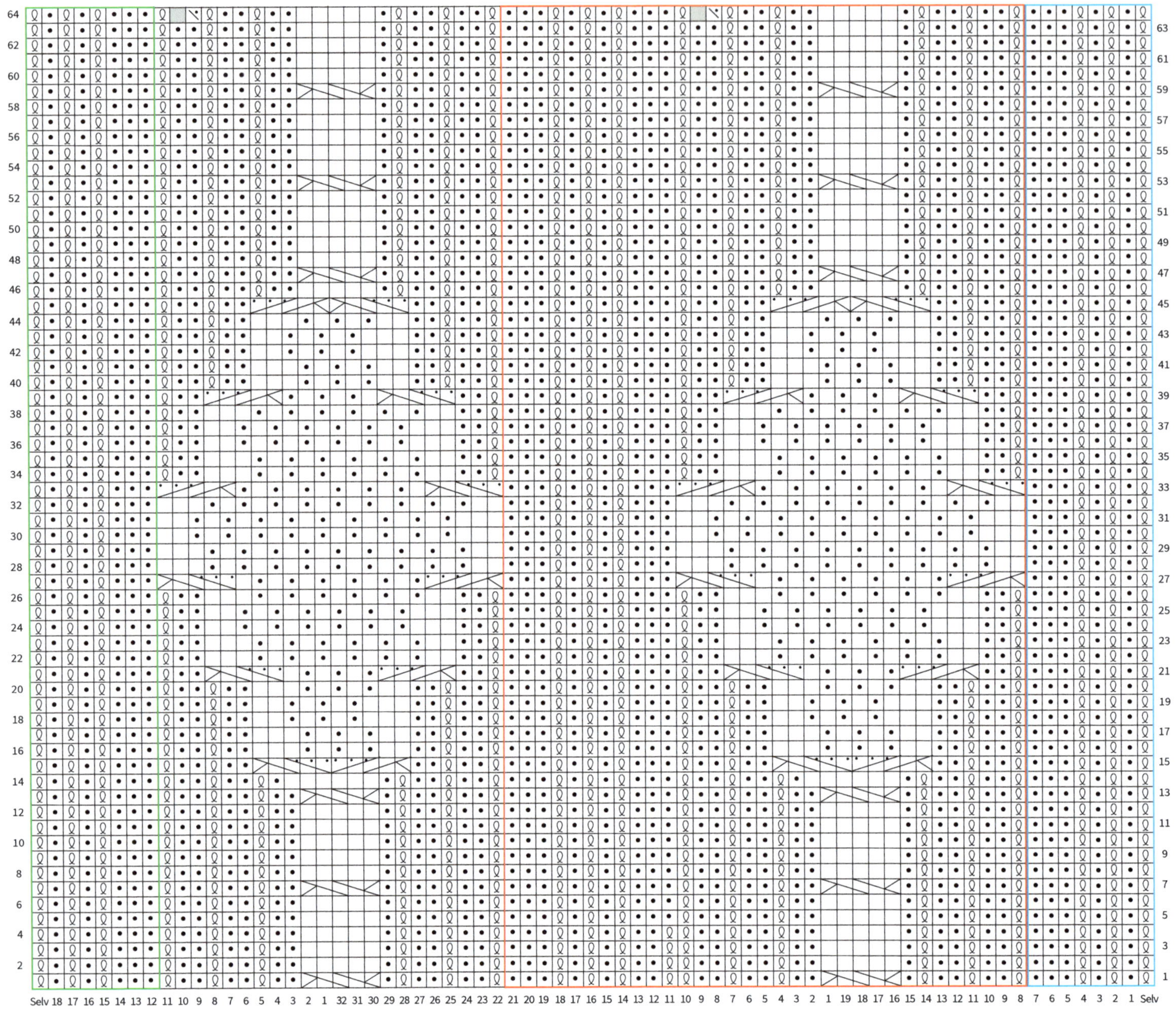

Chart 2 - Cables & Twists Patterns - Size M - Back

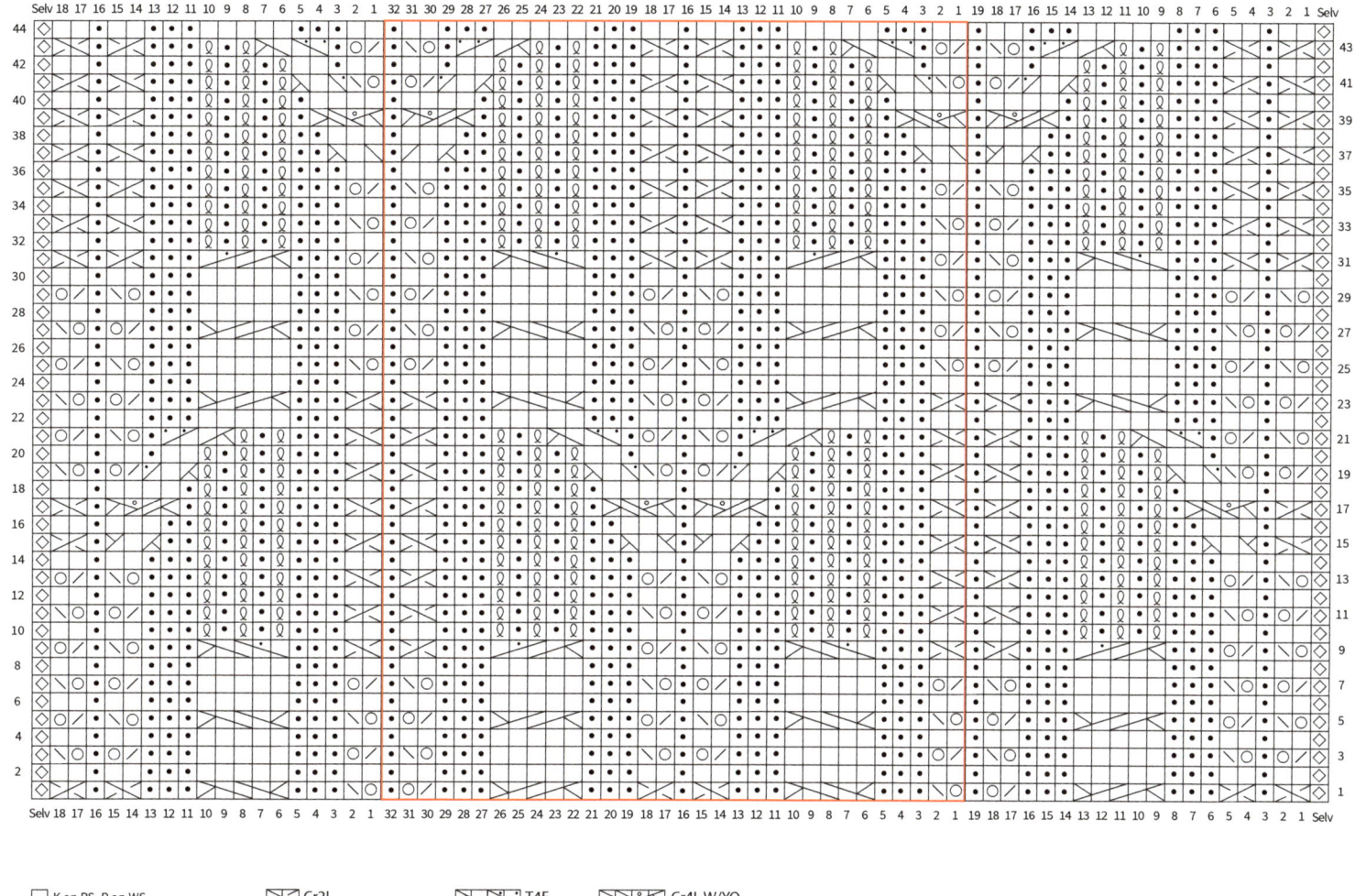

Chart 2 - Cables & Twists Pattern - Size S & L - Back

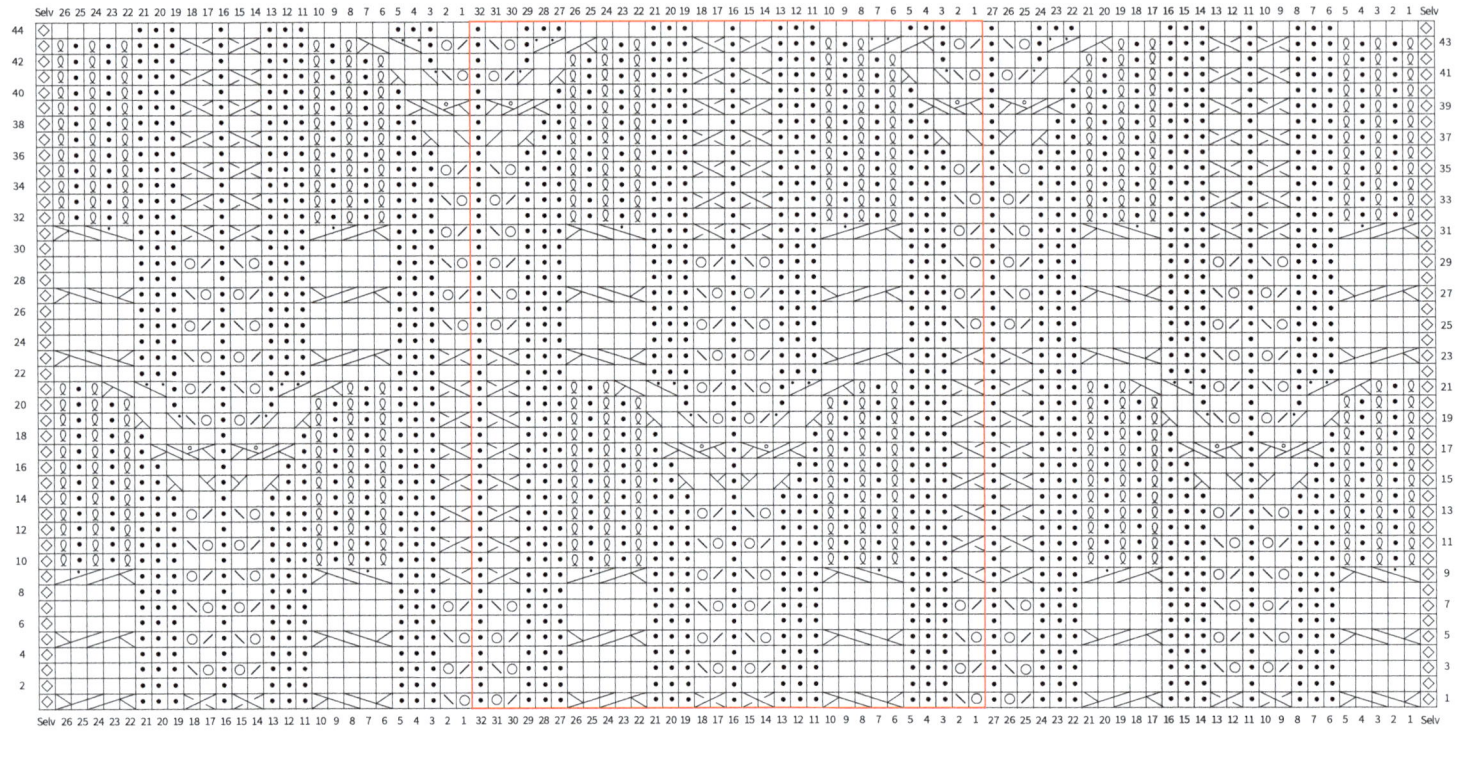

Chart 3 - Size M - Right Front

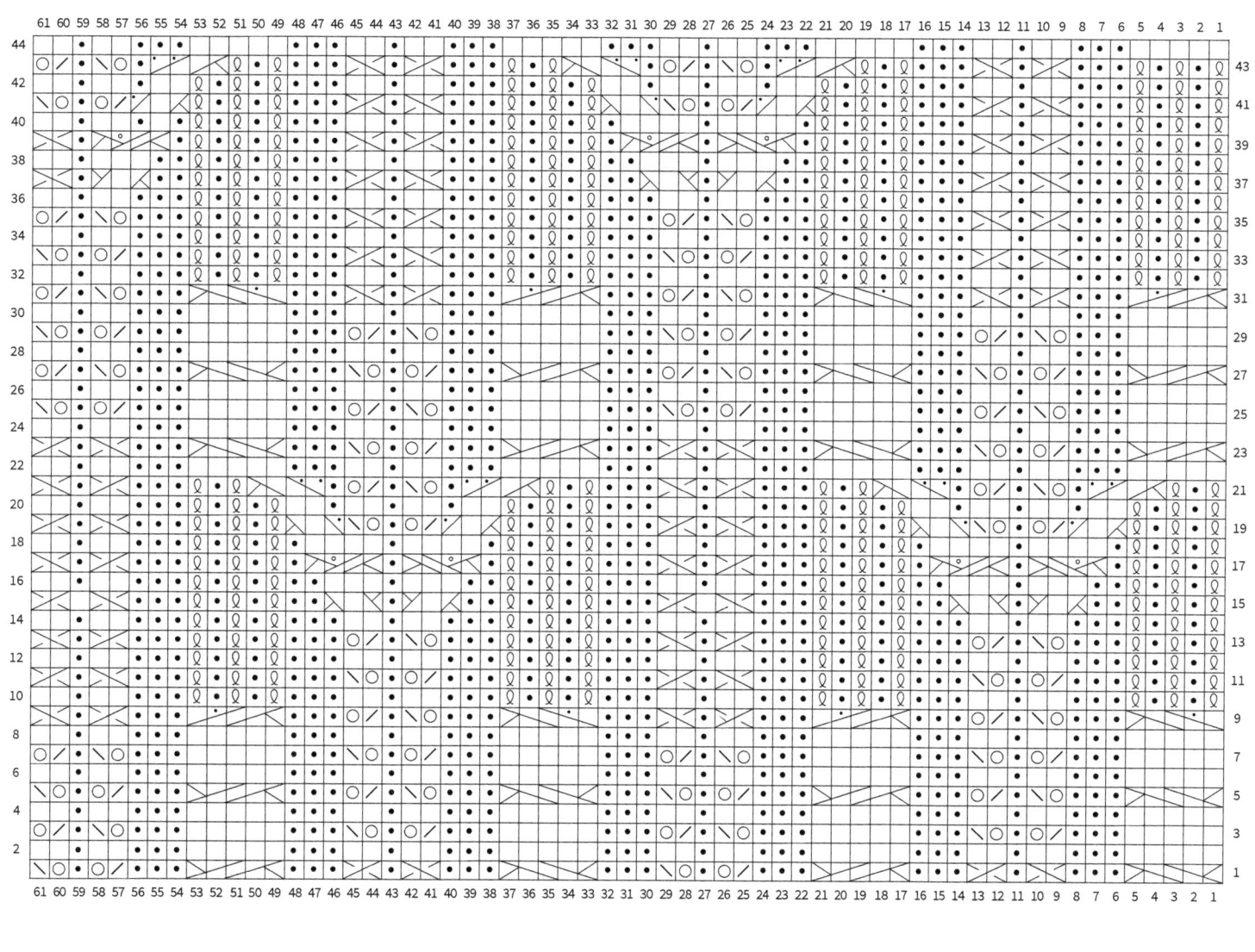

- ☐ K on RS, P on WS
- • P on RS, K on WS
- ○ Yarn Over
- ℚ K1tbl on RS, P1tbl on WS
- ╲ Ssk
- ╱ K2tog
- Cr2L
- Cr2R
- C3F
- C3B
- T3F
- T3B
- T4F
- T4B
- T5L
- T5R
- C5F
- C5B
- Cr4L W/YO
- Cr4R W/YO

TWISTED RHYTHMS | 291

Chart 3 - Cables & Twists Pattern - Size L - Right Front

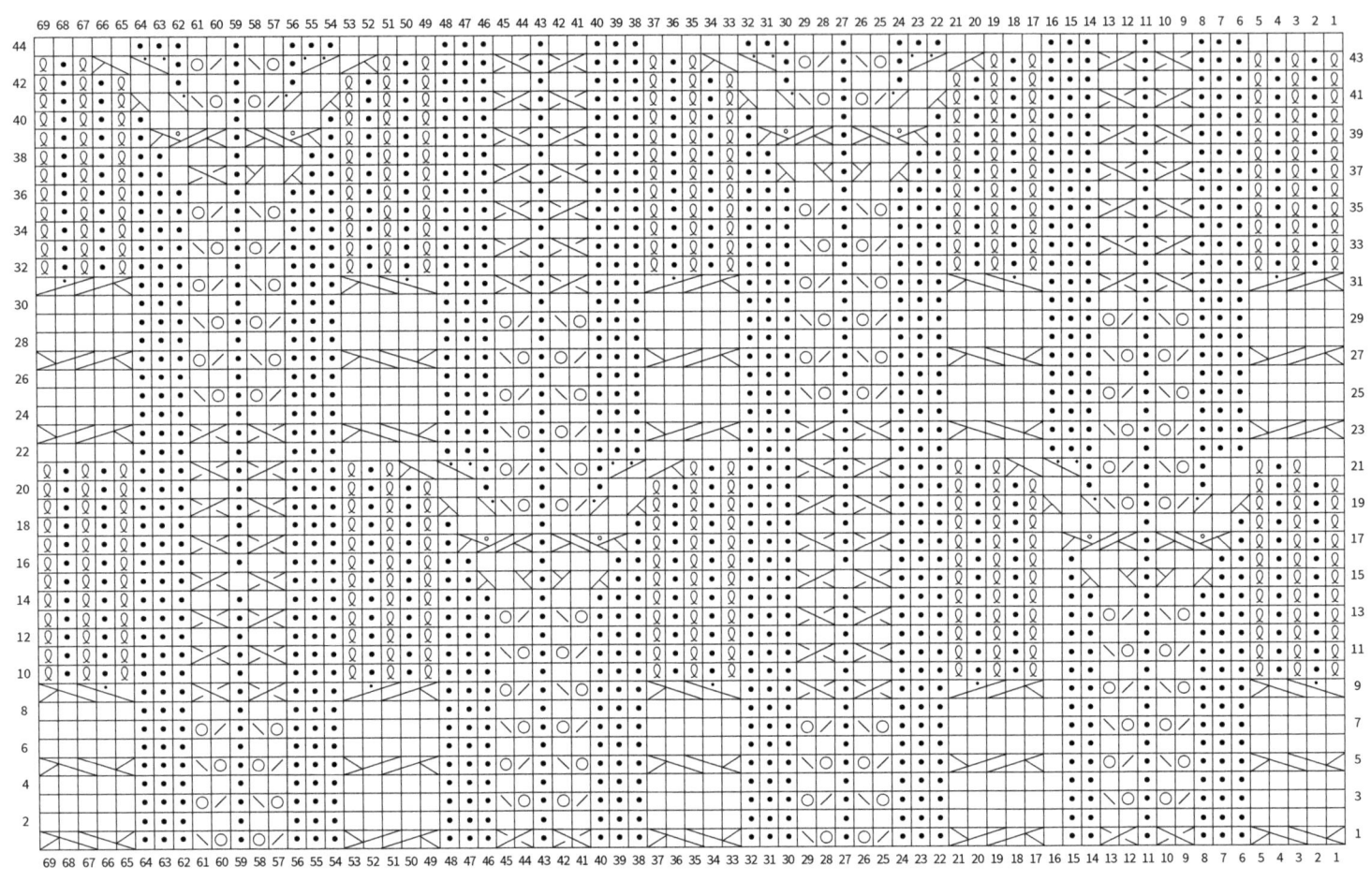

Chart 4 - Cables & Twists Pattern - Size M - Left Front

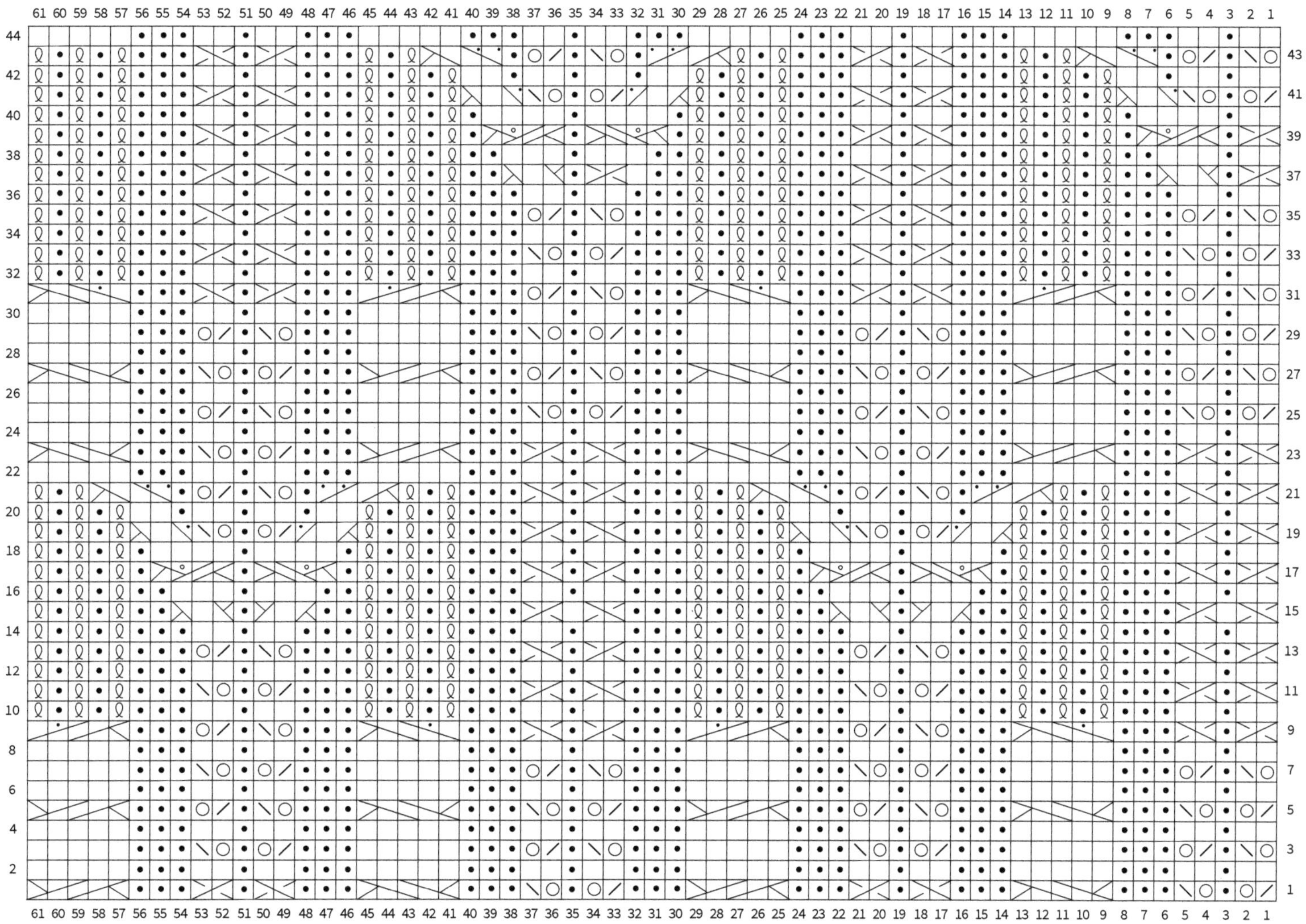

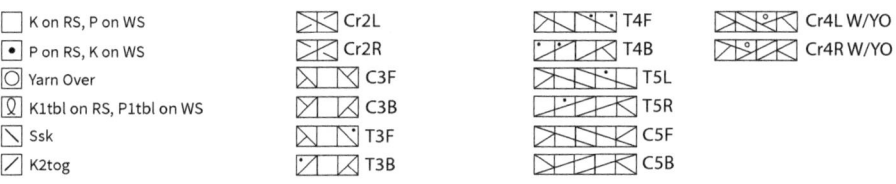

- ☐ K on RS, P on WS
- • P on RS, K on WS
- ◯ Yarn Over
- ℚ K1tbl on RS, P1tbl on WS
- ╲ Ssk
- ╱ K2tog
- Cr2L
- Cr2R
- C3F
- C3B
- T3F
- T3B
- T4F
- T4B
- T5L
- T5R
- C5F
- C5B
- Cr4L W/YO
- Cr4R W/YO

Chart 4 - Cables & Twists Pattern - Size L - Left Front

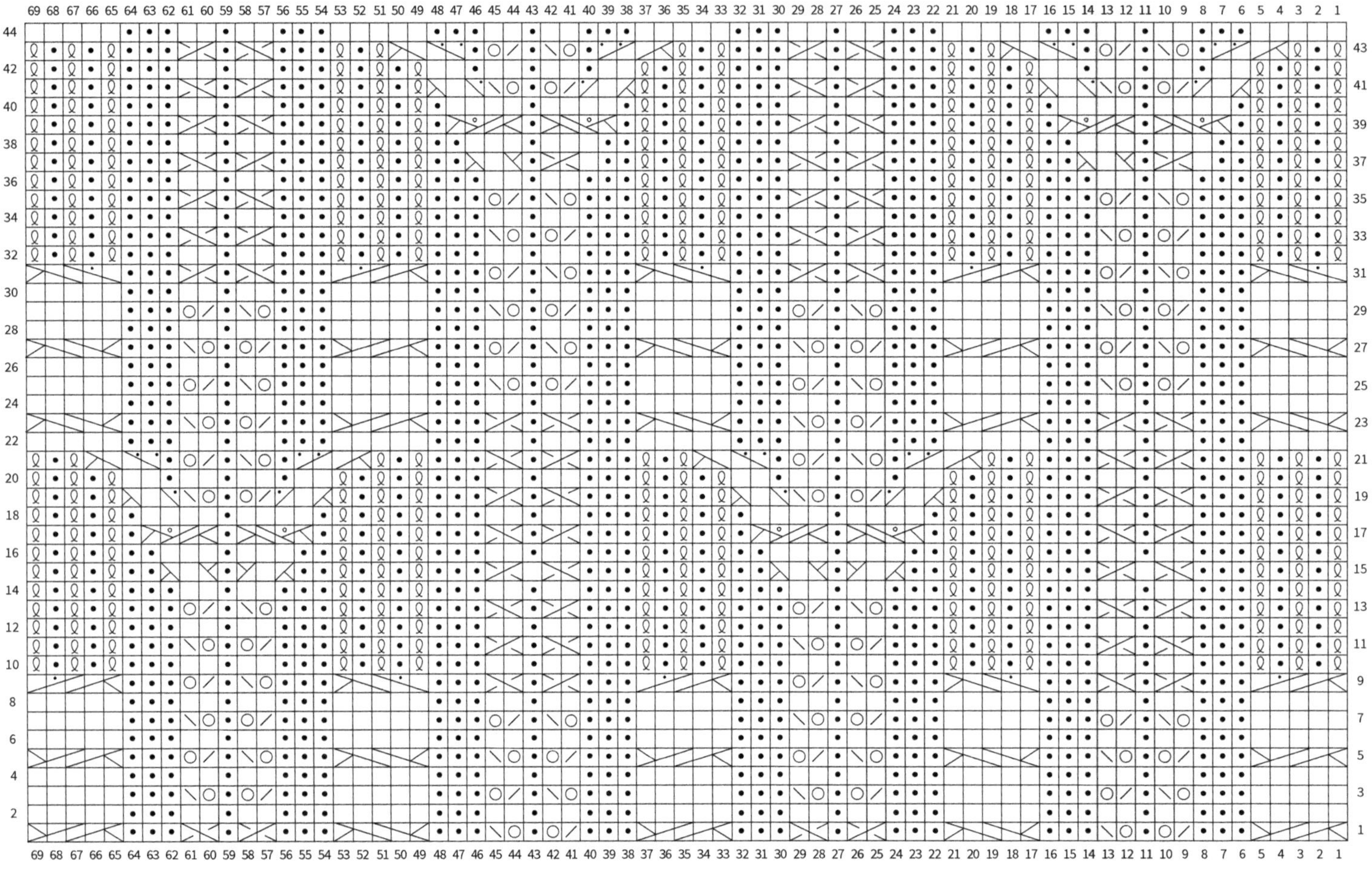

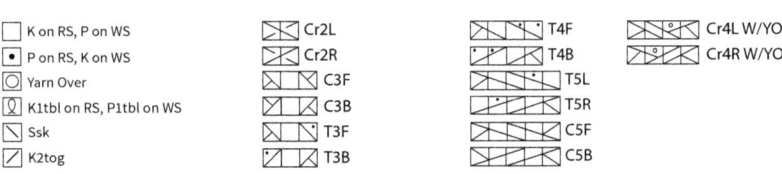

- ☐ K on RS, P on WS
- • P on RS, K on WS
- ○ Yarn Over
- ℚ K1tbl on RS, P1tbl on WS
- \ Ssk
- / K2tog

- Cr2L
- Cr2R
- C3F
- C3B
- T3F
- T3B
- T4F
- T4B
- T5L
- T5R
- C5F
- C5B
- Cr4L W/YO
- Cr4R W/YO

Chart 3 & 4 - Cables & Twists Pattern - Size S - Right & Left Front

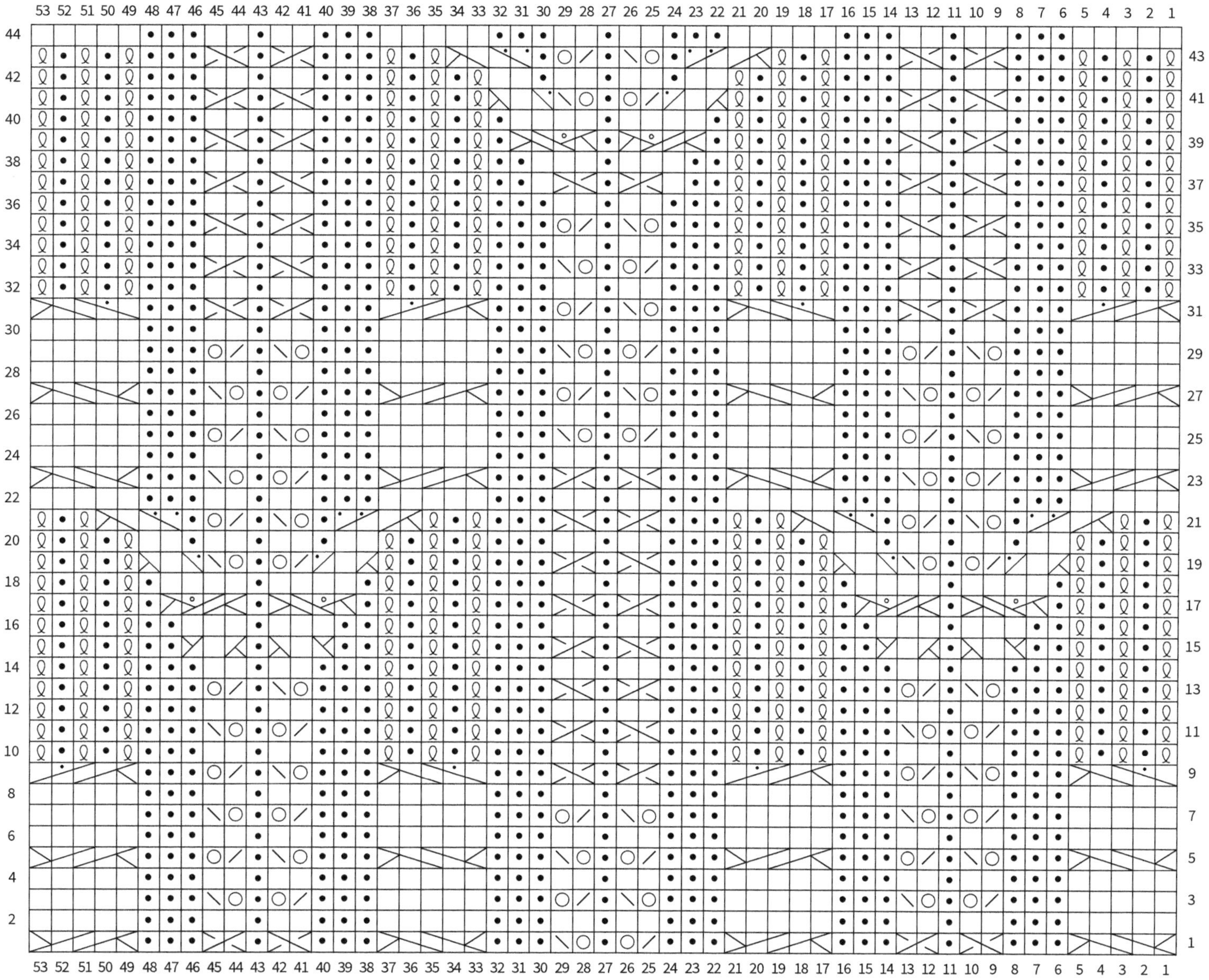

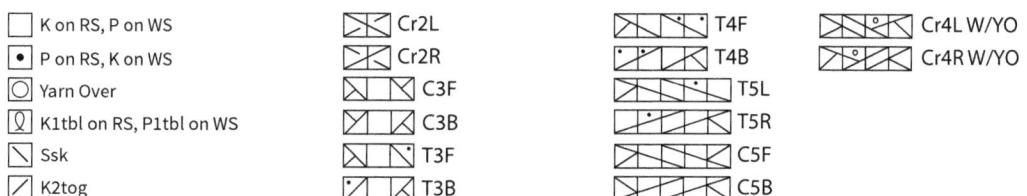

- ☐ K on RS, P on WS
- • P on RS, K on WS
- ○ Yarn Over
- ℚ K1tbl on RS, P1tbl on WS
- \ Ssk
- / K2tog
- Cr2L
- Cr2R
- C3F
- C3B
- T3F
- T3B
- T4F
- T4B
- T5L
- T5R
- C5F
- C5B
- Cr4L W/YO
- Cr4R W/YO

SHIRLEY PADEN

Volare Capelet

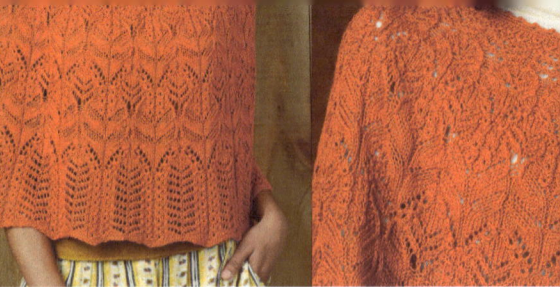

FINISHED SIZES

Women's S/M (L/XL)

Circumference at lower edge: 54 (60)" / 137 (152) cm
Circumference at neck edge: 21 (22½)" / 53 (57) cm
Length at deepest scallop point: 18¼" / 46.5 cm

Sample Size: S/M

YARN

Mariposa Yarn Atelier Viceroy (100% Silk; 410 yds [375 m] / 3.5 oz / 100 g): #2011, 3 (4) skeins

NEEDLES AND HOOKS

Size US 3 (3.25 mm) – 32" / 80 cm circular needle
Size US 2 (2.75 mm) – 32" / 80 cm and 24" / 60 cm circular needles
US Size E/4 (3.5 mm) crochet hook

GAUGES

Note: Each pattern rep has 21 sts. Swatch widths were based on 3 reps = 63 sts.

1. Lacy Chevron Wings Patt:
63 sts = 9" / 23 cm with Size 3 (3.25 mm) needles
28 rnds = 3½" / 9 cm

2. Wings & Circles Patt:
63 sts = 8" / 20.5 cm with Size 3 (3.25 mm) needles
36 rnds = 4½" / 11.5 cm

63 sts = 7½" / 19 cm with Size 2 (2.75 mm) needles
36 rnds = 4" / 10 cm

3. Garter St. Patt:
63 sts = 9" / 23 cm with Size 3 (3.25 mm) needles
30 rnds = 3" / 7.5 cm

4. Alternating Wraps Patt:
60 sts = 7" / 18 cm with Size 2 (2.75 cm) needles
36 rnds = 6" / 15 cm

STITCH GUIDE

Lacy Chevron Wings (multiple of 21 sts/ 4 rnds)
See chart.

Wings & Circles (multiple of 21 sts/ 36 rnds)
See chart.

Alternating Wraps (multiple of 6 sts/ 4 rnds)
Wrap 3: Lift the 3rd st backwards over the first 2 sts and off the LHN; then work k1, yo, k1.

Rnd 1: *Wrap 3, k3; rep from * to end.
Rnd 2: Knit.
Rnd 3: *K3, wrap 3; rep from * to end.
Rnd 4: Knit.
Rep Rnds 1-4 for patt.

Note: When working flat, odd rows are RS and even rows are WS; purl WSR's.

Crochet Picot Edging (2 rnds)
Rnd 1 – Work 1sc in each bind-off st around.
Rnd 2 – Work 1sc in each of the first 3sc of the previous rnd, *ch3, sk 1sc, work 1sc in each of the foll 3sc; rep from * to end.

TECHNIQUES GUIDE

Sloped Bind Off (Used to smoothly shape the neckline)

Work the first BO row as usual. Beg the technique with the 2nd BO row. On the row before the BO row do not work the last stitch. When you turn the work, this will be the first stitch on the RHN. On the BO row, slip the first stitch on the LHN purlwise to the RHN, then BO the leftover stitch from the previous row over the slipped stitch. If there are additional BO sts on this row work them, then BO (as usual).

NOTES

- Capelet is worked from lower edge to neck.
- Sloped Bind Off Technique is used for neck shaping.
- Change to the shorter circular needle when there are too few stitches for the work to slide comfortably around the longer needle.
- If necessary, adjust the needle size to successfully attain the correct gauge.

INSTRUCTIONS

With larger needles CO 378 (420) sts. Join to work in the rnd being careful not to twist the sts, and pl mar to indicate the beg of rnd.

Work 5 rnds in Garter st, beg and ending with a knit rnd.

Work 4-rnd Lacy Chevron Wings patt a total of 7 times, 18 (20) times per rnd (28 rnds total). If desired, place markers between each patt rep. Piece should measure 4" (10 cm).

Next, work Rnds 1-36 of Wings & Circles patt.

Change to smaller needles and rep Rnds 1-36 of Wings & Circles patt. Piece should measure 12" (30.5 cm).

Shape Yoke

On the next rnd = first rnd of the 3rd 36-rnd rep of the Wings & Circles Patt, continuing on the Size 2 (2.75 mm) 32" (81 cm) needle, beg dec'ng 198 (220) sts over the next 31 rnds. There are 6 dec rnds. 18 (20) sts will be dec'd on the first dec rnd, then 180 (200) sts will be dec'd over the foll 5 dec rnds = 36 (40) sts per dec rnd. **Decrease Method:** Dec at each edge of the 18 (20) patt reps using a P2tog on the beg and ending purl sts of the first dec rnd, and on rnds that beg and end with purl sts. On dec rnds that beg and end with knit sts, work a ssk dec at the rep beg and a K2tog at the rep end.

Important Note: **Both Sizes:** On the first dec rnd, work as foll: Sl the last P1 st of the last rep worked before the dec rnd to the opposite side of the beg rnd mar and work a p2tog on that last P1 st and the first P1 st of the first rep of the dec rnd. At the end of that first rep, sl the last P1 st to the foll rep. The first rep will have 20 sts. Continue to work each rep as the first by sl the final P1 st to the other side of the rep separation mar and working a P2tog on that last st and the first st of the next rep. After this first dec rnd has been worked, 18 (20) sts will have been dec'd. There will be 20 sts in each of the 18 (20) reps = 360 (400) sts on the needle. There will be a single line of P1 sts between each patt rep. The 5 rem dec(s) will be made at each end of every rep inside these P1 separation lines.

Each of the 18 (20) reps will beg with 21 sts, 21 x 18 (20) = 378 (420) sts) on the needles. After all dec's have been worked the st count will be 10 sts in each rep = 180 (200) sts on the needle at the neckline. Foll the dec chart, work dec's at the beg and end of each rep on every foll 6th rnd after foll the instruction above for Rnd 1. **Rnd 7:** Dec 2 sts to 18 sts each rep x 18 (20) reps = 324 (360) sts. **Rnd 13:** Dec 2 sts to 16 sts each rep x 18 (20) reps = 288 (320) sts. **Rnd 19:** Dec 2 sts to 14 sts each rep x 18 (20) reps = 252 (280) sts. **Rnd 25:** Dec 2 sts to 12 sts each rep x 18 (20) reps = 216 (240) sts). **Rnd 31:** Dec 2 sts to 10 sts each rep x 18 (20) reps = 180 (200) sts. There are 90 (100) sts rem in front and back. Work even on these rem sts for 9 rnds = 40 rnds worked in yoke. Piece should measure 16½" (42 cm). On the next rnd, begin working 6 rnds of the Alternating Wraps Patt (6-st multiple) - See Stitch Guide. **L/XL Only:** Dec 8 sts on the first rnd as foll: Work *[Wrap 3, K3] 3x, then Wrap 3, K1, K2tog, K1 on the 4th rep*; Rep * to * 8x = 192 sts rem, 96 sts Front & Back.

Shape Neck:

Important Notes: 1) After working the first center neck shaping BO, you will be working flat which means back and forth on RS and WS rows. 2) Because the Wrap 3 technique should be worked on RSRs, the first row of the front neck BOs should be worked on a RSR. 3) Use the Sloped Bind Off Technique (See Techniques Guide).

Row 1: Work the 90 (96) front sts continuing in the Alternating Wraps Patt binding off as foll: Work across 24 RHS front neck sts, then BO 42 (48) sts for the center front neck sts, then work across the 24 LHS front neck sts = 15 (16) 6-st reps worked. Continue working in patt across the 90 (96) back neck sts. Next, reattach yarn at neck edge on the RHS. **Row 2 (WSR):** To beg the Sloped BO, slip the first 2 sts to the RHN and BO one over the other, then BO the rem RHS front neck edge sts., then, work across the 90 (96) sts of the back neck and across the 24 LHS neck edge sts. **Row 3:** Turn and BO the 24 LHS front neck edge sts, then work across the 90 (96) back neck sts. **Row 4:** Turn and BO the back neck sts

Finishing

Block piece to measurements. With the Size E/4 (3.5 mm) crochet hook, work the two rnd Crochet Picot Edging around the neckline.

Volare Capelet

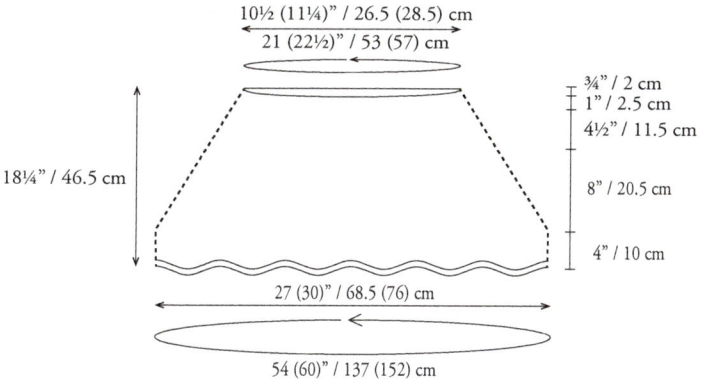

Lacy Chevron Wings
(Multiple of 21/ 4 rnds)

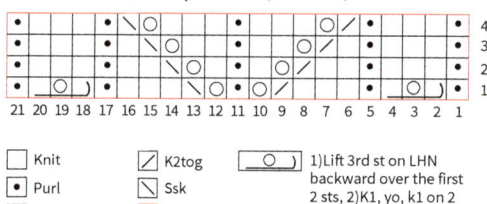

Wings & Circles
(Multiple of 21/ 36 rnds)

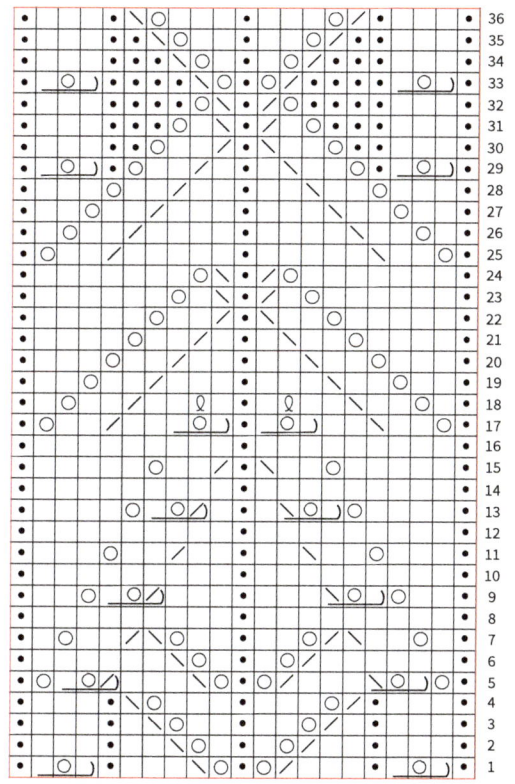

Wings & Circles Yoke Shaping Chart

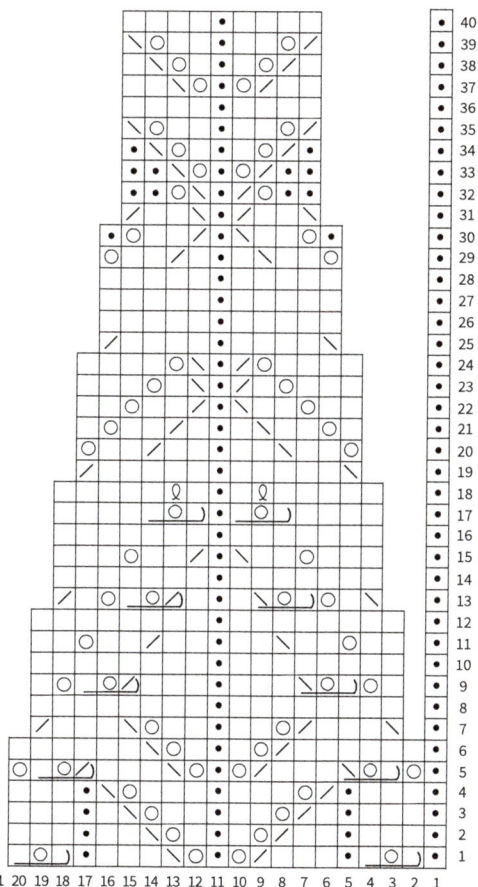

ELLEN M. SILVA

Winged Surplice

FINISHED SIZES

Women's S (M, L, XL)
Finished bust (back width x2): 34 (38, 42, 46)" / 86 (96.5, 106.5, 117) cm
To fit bust sizes: 28-32 (32-36, 36-40, 40-44)" / 71-81 (81.5-91.5, 91.5-101.5, 102-112) cm

Sample Size: L

YARN

Skacel HiKoo Sueño Worsted (80% wool / 20% bamboo; 182 yds [166 m] / 3.5 oz / 100 g): colorway 1364 Slated, 7 (8, 9, 10) skeins

NEEDLES

Size US 6 (4.0 mm) circular needle, 24" (60 cm) or longer
Adjust needle size if necessary to obtain the correct gauge.

NOTIONS

stitch markers, size US 2 (2.75) circular needle (used only for picking up sts for I-cord edging), 2 buttons approximately 5/8" (16 mm) – one decorative for use on outside of sweater and one plain for use on inside of sweater; tapestry needle

GAUGES

Winged Surplice Lace:
38 sts and 32 rows = 7 x 4¼" / 17.5 x 11 cm in patt

Stockinette Stitch:
20 sts and 30 rows = 4" / 10 cm

Note: The construction of this sweater is dependent on accurate stitch and row gauge; however, it is possible to make some allowance for differences in row gauge. Work the front panels first and base the length of the back panel on them – the side edge of the back should just fit the long edge of the front panel. This will have some effect on the finished size, but given the positive ease and surplice styling of the sweater, the garment will still fit adequately.

NOTES

- A Stockinette stitch selvedge is worked at both edges of all pieces: Knit the first and last sts of RS rows; purl the first and last sts of WS rows. These sts are included in the pattern instructions.
- Decreasing in Lace Patterns: whenever there are not enough sts to work BOTH a yarn over and its paired decrease (k2tog or ssk), do not work either; simply knit the st that would otherwise have been a yarn over or decrease. Do work shaping decreases at the edge if it is a decrease row; this note refers only to the decreases and yarn overs shown in the lace charts.
- Sleeve cap shaping is worked with the sloped bind off method.

INSTRUCTIONS

Right Front (as worn)

CO 107 (107, 116, 116) sts using a standard long-tail cast on. The first and last st are selvedge sts and are always knit on the RS and purled on the WS.
Knit two rows, working selvedge sts as directed above.

Establish the lace patt from Row 1 of the Front chart as foll: K1 (selv), work 19-st patt rep 5 (5, 6, 6) times, work 10 (10, 0, 0) "plus" sts, k1 (selv). Cont in patt for Rows 2-6. On Row 7, begin working decreases as described below.

Shaping will be worked by decreasing at outer edge every 2 out of 3 rows as foll: For RS rows, work to last 4 sts, k2tog, p1, k1 (selv) – 1 st dec. For WS rows, p1 (selv), k1, p2tog, work to end – 1 st dec. Refer to pattern note above for how to maintain lace pattern while working decreases.

Beg with chart row 7, work 2 dec rows (RS, WS), then work 1 row even, then 2 dec rows (WS, RS), then work 1 row even – 2 sts dec every 3 rows.

Cont working decreases as estab until 41 sts rem (including selvedges) then work even for 0 (0, 2, 2) rows for a total of 13 (13, 15, 15) complete pattern repeats, ending with a chart row 8. Next row (RS), K across dec 4 sts evenly – 37 sts rem. BO all sts on WS.

Left Front (as worn)

Cast on and knit 2 rows with St st selvedge as for Right Front, then establish lace patt from Row 1 of the Front chart as foll: K1 (selv), work 10 (10, 0, 0) "plus" sts, work 19-st patt rep 5 (5, 6, 6) times, k1 (selv). Cont in patt for Rows 2-6. On Row 7, begin working decreases as described below.

Shaping will be worked by decreasing at outer edge every 2 out of 3 rows as foll: For RS rows, k1 (selv), p1, ssk, work to end – 1 st dec. For WS rows, work to last 4 sts, p2tog tbl, k1, p1 (selv) – 1 st dec. Refer to pattern note above for how to maintain lace pattern while working decreases.

Beg with chart row 7, work 2 dec rows (RS, WS), then work 1 row even, then 2 dec rows (WS, RS), then work 1 row even – 2 sts dec every 3 rows.

Cont working decreases as estab until 41 sts rem (including selvedges) then work even for 0 (0, 2, 2) rows for a total of 13 (13, 15, 15) complete pattern repeats, ending with a chart row 8. Next row (RS), K across dec 4 sts evenly – 37 sts rem. BO all sts on WS.

Back

Using a standard long-tail cast-on, CO 107 (127, 137, 157) sts. Knit 2 rows with St st selvedge.

Next row (RS), establish patt from Row 1 of Back Panel chart as foll: K1 (selv), k23 (33, 38, 48) (St st), pl m, work across chart row once (lace panel), pl m, k to last st (St st), k1 (selv). Cont in patt as estab, working chart rows 2-16, then rep rows 9-16 until piece measures 18 (17½, 19, 18½)"/45.5 (44.5, 48.5, 47) cm from cast-on edge, ending with a WS row. The edge of the piece should be 1 (1½, 2, 2½)" /2.5 (4, 5, 6.5) cm shorter than the long edges of the Fronts.

Shape Armholes

Next row (RS): K6 (9, 11, 14), BO 10 (14, 10, 14) sts for right underarm, work as estab to last 16 (23, 21, 28) sts, BO 10 (14, 10, 14) sts for left underarm, knit to end – 6 (9, 11, 14) sts each side; 75 (81, 95, 101) sts rem for back.

Next row (WS): P6 (9, 11, 14) then CO 1 st with backward loop to RH needle (new selv) – 7 (10, 12, 15) sts.

Working left armhole only, dec at armhole edge every 2 out of 3 rows as foll: For RS rows, k1 (selv), ssk, k to end – 1 st dec. For WS rows, p to last 3 sts, p2tog tbl, p1 (selv) – 1 st dec. Work 2 dec rows then 1 row even and rep until 3 sts rem total (including selvedges) then sl1, k2tog, psso and pull end through final st to secure.

Place live Back stitches between the underarms on holder or waste yarn, and arrange the rem 6 (9, 11, 14) right underarm sts on the needles so you are ready to work a RS row. With new working yarn, k6 (9, 11, 14) then CO 1 st with backward loop to RH needle (new selv) – 7 (10, 12, 15) sts. Dec at armhole edge every 2 out of 3 rows as foll: For WS rows, p1 (selv), p2tog, p to end – 1 st dec. For RS rows, k to last 3 sts, k2tog, k1 (selv) – 1 st dec. Work 2 dec rows then 1 row even and rep until 3 sts rem total (including selvedges) then sl1, k2tog, psso and pull end through final st to secure.

Back Raglan Shaping

Place held sts back onto needles, ready to work a WS row. CO 1 st to RH needle for new selv, work as estab to end of row, then CO 1 st for second selv – 77 (83, 97, 103) sts total.

Work decs at both ends every 2 out of 3 rows as foll: For RS rows, k1 (selv), ssk, work to last 3 sts, k2tog, k1 (selv) – 2 sts dec. For WS rows, p1 (selv), p2tog, work to last 3 sts, p2tog tbl, p1 (selv) – 2 sts dec.

Work 2 dec rows then 1 row even and rep until 17 (19, 21, 23) sts rem (including selvedges), ending with a WS row. Knit one row even, then BO all sts on WS.

Sleeves (Make 2 with mirrored shaping)

Cuff

Using a standard long-tail cast-on, cast on 59 sts. Knit two rows with St st selvedges, then establish lace sleeve motif from Row 1 of Sleeve chart as foll: K1 (selv), work 19-st patt rep 3 times, k1 (selv). Cont in patt as estab for chart rows 2-24.

Note: From this point rep chart rows 17-24 only.

Next row – inc (RS): K1 (selv), m1, pl m, work in patt to last st, pl m, m1, k1 (selv) – 2 sts inc. Cont in patt and rep inc row every 16 (10, 8, 8) rows 6 (9, 12, 14) more times, working new sts in St st and working lace patt betw markers – 73 (79, 85, 89) sts . Work even in patt until sleeve measures 17½ (18, 18½, 19)"/ 44.5 (45.5, 47, 48.5) cm from cast-on edge.

BO 5 (7, 5, 7) sts at beg of next 2 rows – 63 (65, 75, 75) sts rem.

Sleeve Cap Shaping

Note: The first and last rem sts will be new selvedge sts. In order to create the proper drape for the garment, the sleeve cap decreases are worked at a different rate than the front and back raglan edges.

Work decs as instructed below as foll: For RS rows, k1 (selv), ssk, work to last 3 sts, k2tog, k1 (selv) – 2 sts dec. For WS rows, p1 (selv), p2tog, work to last 3 sts, p2tog tbl, p1 (selv) – 2 sts dec.

Alternate working decs every 3rd row then every 2nd row until you have worked 12 (16, 20, 24) dec rows and 30 (40, 50, 60) rows total – 39 (33, 35, 27) sts rem.

Cont decs every 2nd (2nd, 2nd, 3rd) row 11 (8, 6, 2) times more – 17 (17, 23, 23) sts rem.

Using Sloped Bind-Off method, shape the back raglan edge of the sleeve cap as follows:

Right Sleeve:

Row 1 (RS): BO 6 (6, 8, 8) sts, work even in pattern to end of row. 11 (11, 15, 15) sts rem including selvedge sts.

Row 2 (WS): Work even in patt to end of row.

Row 3: BO 5 (5, 7, 7) sts, work to end of row. 6 (6, 8, 8) sts rem.

Row 4: BO rem sts.

Left Sleeve:

Row 1 (RS): Work even in patt to end of row.

Row 2 (WS): BO 6 (6, 8, 8) sts, work in patt to end of row. 11 (11, 15, 15) sts rem.

Row 3: Work even.

Row 4: BO 5 (5, 7, 7) sts. 6 (6, 8, 8) sts rem.

Row 5: BO rem sts.

Finishing

Block pieces to measurements. Sew front panels to back along long edges using mattress stitch. Sew raglan seams, noting the number of sleeve cap rows differs from the number of front or back raglan rows. You will need to seam at a ratio of approximately 11 sleeve raglan sts to 10 front/back raglan sts.

Applied I-cord with button loops

With RS facing and using the US 2 (2.75mm) needle, starting at the bottom right front, pick up and knit 1 st for every row along right front lace panel, inserting the needle between the selvedge st and the first pattern stitch in each row. Then pick up and knit 1 st in every right sleeve cap st, inserting needle in the row below the bind off. Continue in the same manner across the back neck and left sleeve cap, then pick up sts along left front lace panel ending at bottom corner at center left front. Set aside.

With the US 6 (4.0 mm) needle, CO 3 sts. Work I-cord for button loop as follows: *K3, sl 3 sts back to LHN; repeat from * until I-cord is 1½"/4 cm long, ending with sts on LHN. Work applied I-cord beginning with right front panel as follows: *K2, ssk (joining last st of I-cord to first picked up st on spare needle); repeat from * until all picked up sts have been used. With main needle only, work I-cord for another 1½"/4 cm for second button loop. K3tog, cut yarn and pull end through. Using the yarn tails, tack the I-cord ends to the tips of the front lace panels to form button loops. Adjust the size of the loop as needed to fit your buttons. Sew buttons in place on the seam between front panels and back, with the decorative button on the outside of the left side of the sweater and the plain button on the inside on the right side. Place them so they will be even with the tips of the front panels when the sweater is lying flat. Weave in all ends.

Winged Surplice Lace Back Panel Chart

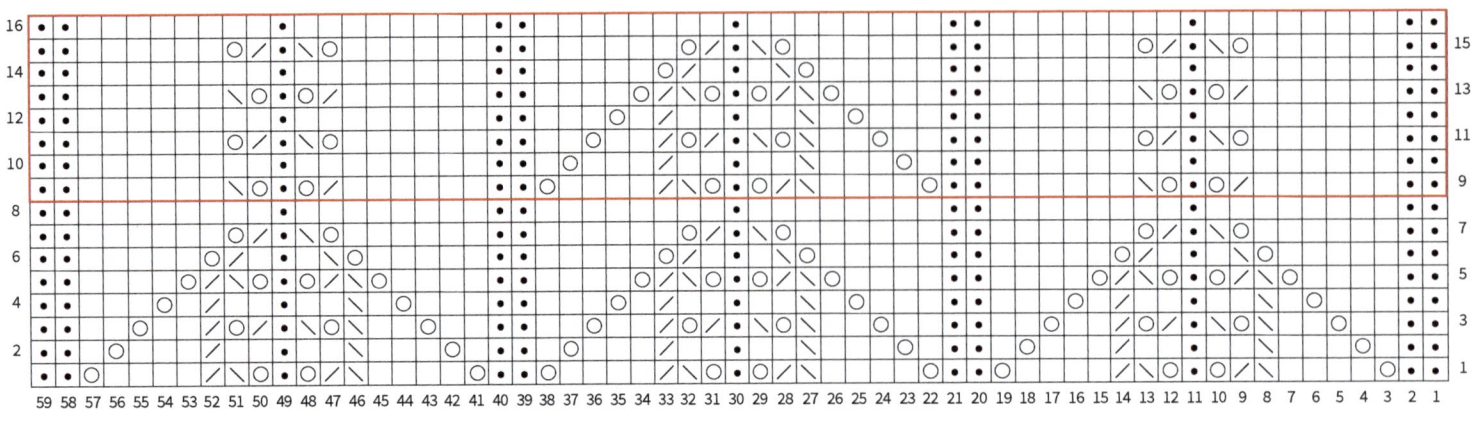

Winged Surplice Lace Front Chart

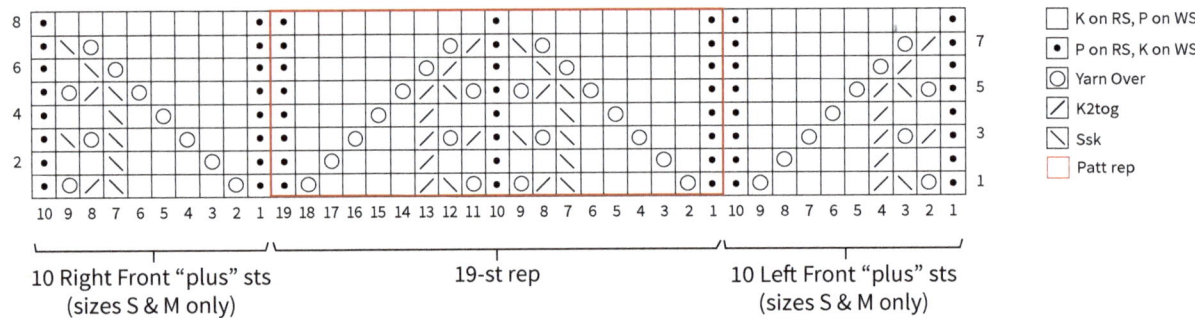

Winged Surplice Lace Sleeve Motif Chart

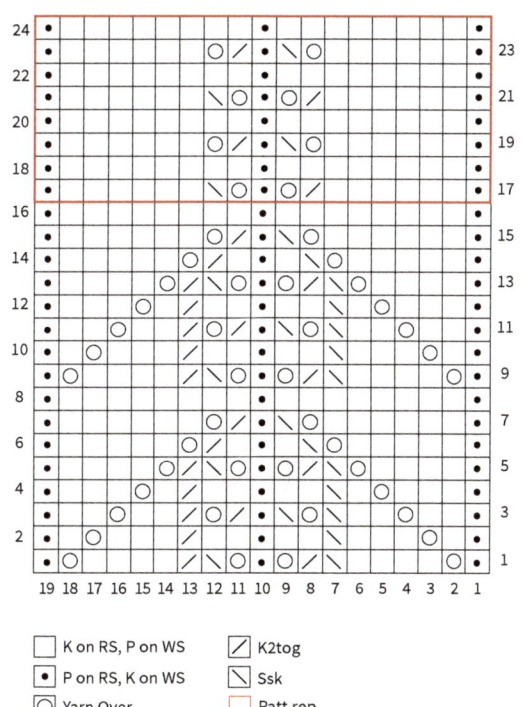

Winged Surplice

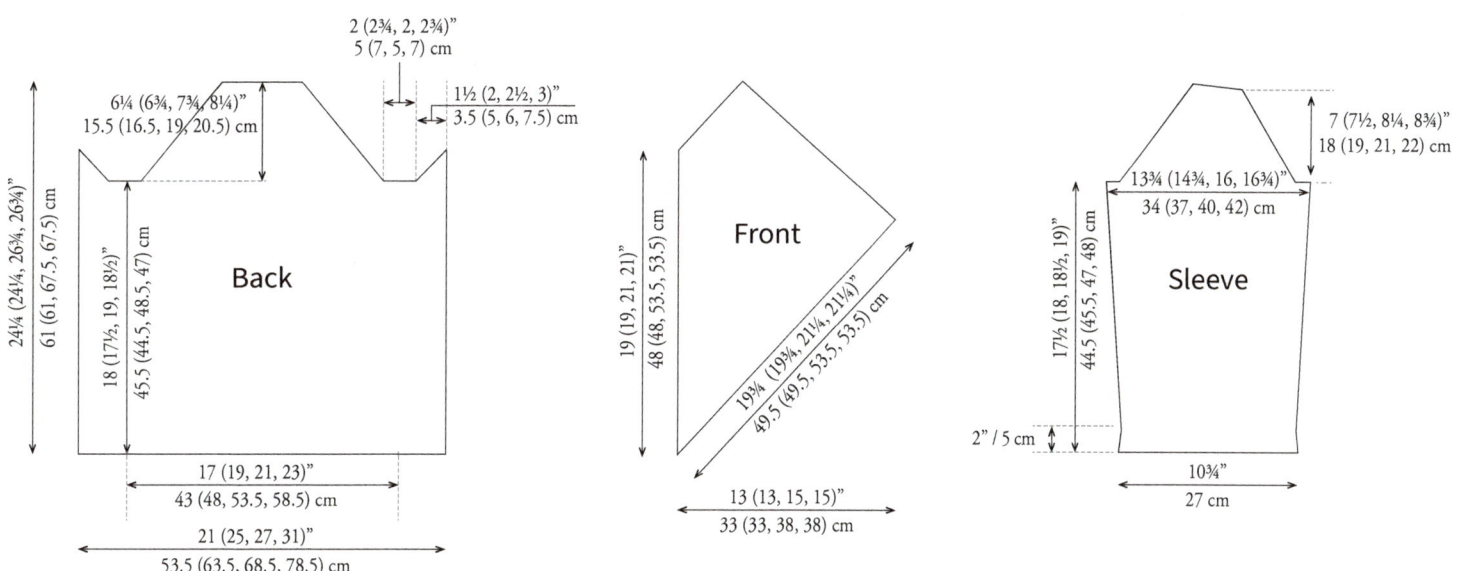

LISA HOFFMAN

Zigzag Gauntlets

FINISHED SIZE

Circumference: 7" / 18 cm, relaxed after blocking
Length: 13" / 32.5 cm

To fit woman's hand size Small to Medium.

Note: This ribbed fabric is very stretchy and accommodating of a generous range of sizes. Sample shown stretches to a circumference of approx. 10" / 25.5 cm. However, don't forget to take into account not only your hand size, but also your lower arm circumference, as these mitts extend almost to the elbow.

YARN

Artyarns Merino Cloud (80% Extrafine Merino / 20% Cashmere; 436 yds [400 m] / 3.5 oz / 100 g): color 2309 Natural, 1 skein

NEEDLES

Size US 4 (3.5 mm) dpn's
Adjust needle size if necessary to obtain the correct gauge.

NOTIONS

stitch markers (2); cable needle; locking markers and small stitch holder or scrap yarn to hold I-cord sts and thumb sts

GAUGES

40 sts and 33 rounds = 4" / 10 cm in Twisted Rib Pattern before blocking

STITCH GUIDE

I-Cord - Knit all sts. *Do not turn. Slide sts to right end of needle, pull yarn from behind, knit all sts. Rep from * to desired length.

I-Cord Bind Off - CO 3 sts using knitted cast-on method. *K2, k2togtbl, slip 3 sts back to left needle; rep from * to last 3 sts. Place these 3 sts on holder for finishing.

DBLT3B - Sl 1 st onto cn and hold in back, [k1tbl] 2 times, k1tbl from cn.

DBLT3F - Sl 2 sts onto cn and hold in front, k1tbl, [k1tbl] 2 times from cn.

T2B - Sl 1 st onto cn and hold in back, k1tbl, p1 from cn.

T2F - Sl 1 st onto cn and hold in front, p1, k1tbl from cn.

T3B - Sl 1 st onto cn and hold in back, [k1tbl] 2 times, p1 from cn.

T3F - Sl 2 sts onto cn and hold in front, p1, [k1tbl] 2 times from cn.

Right-leaning Double Decrease (RDD): K2tog, slip st back to LHN, pass 2nd st over the slipped st, slip st to RHN.

Left-leaning Double Decrease: Sl1-k2tog-psso.

Make one - twisted (M1t): With LHN lift bar between sts from back to front; knit into the back loop for a twisted st.

Make one purlwise – twisted (M1tp): With LHN lift bar between sts from back to front; purl into the back loop for a twisted st.

Twisted Rib Pattern
Rnd 1: [P1, k1tbl] to end.
Rep Rnd 1 for pattern.

INSTRUCTIONS

Left/Right Glove

CO 4 sts on 1 dpn. Work I-Cord for about 60 rnds then place 4 live sts on locking marker and cut yarn. Beg at last rnd of I-Cord, pick up 54 sts along length of I-Cord, 1 st per rnd. (Leave rem I-Cord hanging for finishing.) Join to work in the rnd.

Work Rnds 1-68 of Left or Right Glove chart, repeating last 2 sts to end of rnd.

Rep Rnds 37 to 54, placing markers on either side of blue border and working Thumb Gusset chart in place of 9 sts within blue border – 25 sts between markers; 70 sts total.

Next rnd, separate thumb as follows: Work Rnd 55 to mar, rm, p2, M1tp, k1tbl, sl1, place next 17 sts on holder or scrap yarn, slip st back to left needle and k2togtbl, k1tbl, M1tp, p2, rm, work chart to end – 54 sts rem.

Work rem chart rnds 56-69 (note: sts decrease on rnd 69) - 46 sts rem.

Work 3 rnds even in Twisted Rib Pattern. Bind off using I-Cord Bind-Off method.

Thumb

Place 17 sts from holder onto 3 dpns.

Rnd 1: [K1tbl, p1] 8 times, k1tbl, M1tp - 18 sts. Join to work in the rnd. Work as estab in Twisted Rib for 8 rnds. Bind off using I-Cord Bind-Off method.

Finishing

Carefully unravel I-Cord from cast-on edge up to the round of the last picked-up stitch; place sts on dpn. Graft I-Cord ends together using Kitchener Stitch, or bind off and seam. Seam I-Cord ends together at top and thumb. Darn ends. Steam lightly.

Thumb Gusset

Zig Zag Fingerless Gloves
Left Glove

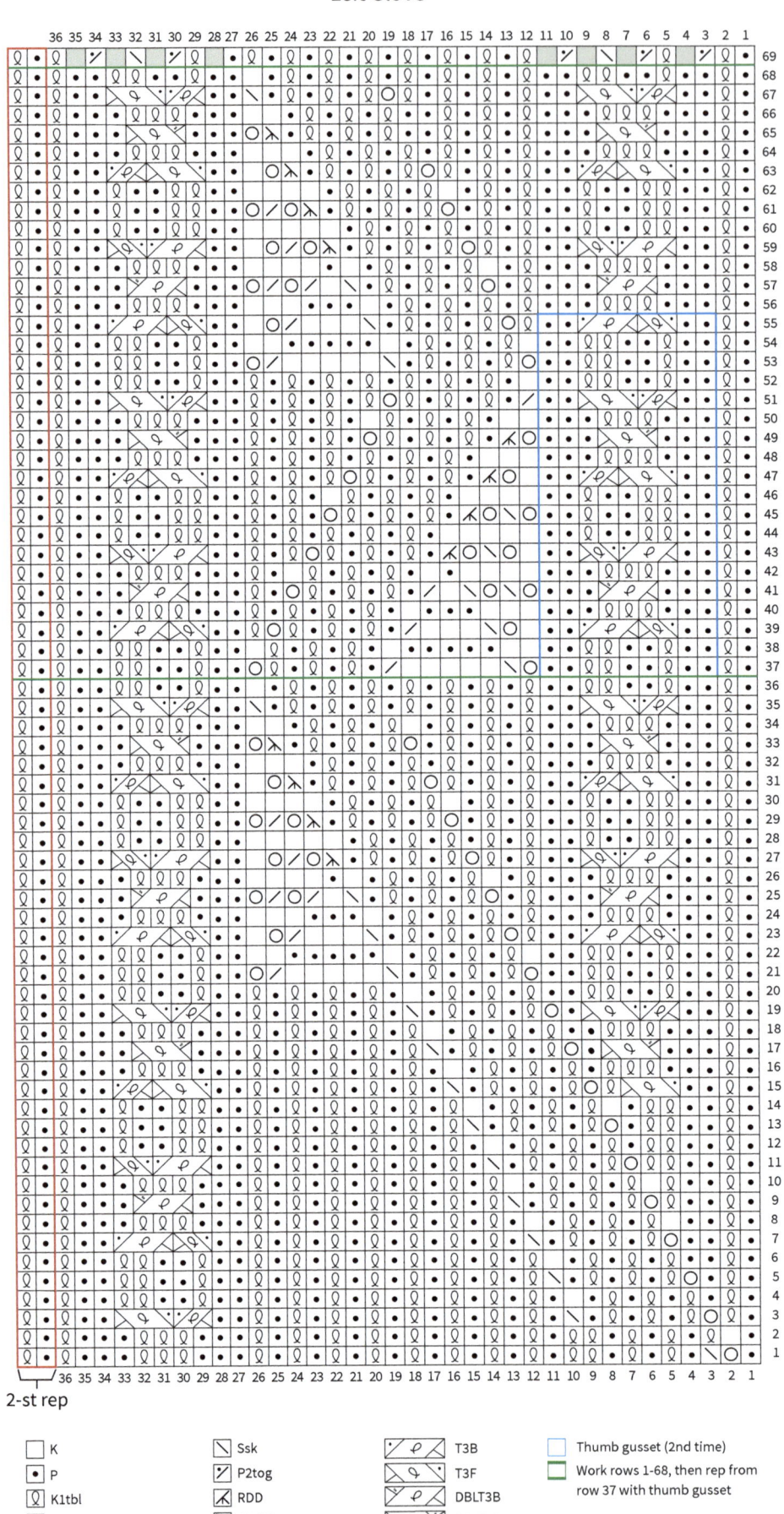

Zig Zag Fingerless Gloves
Right Glove

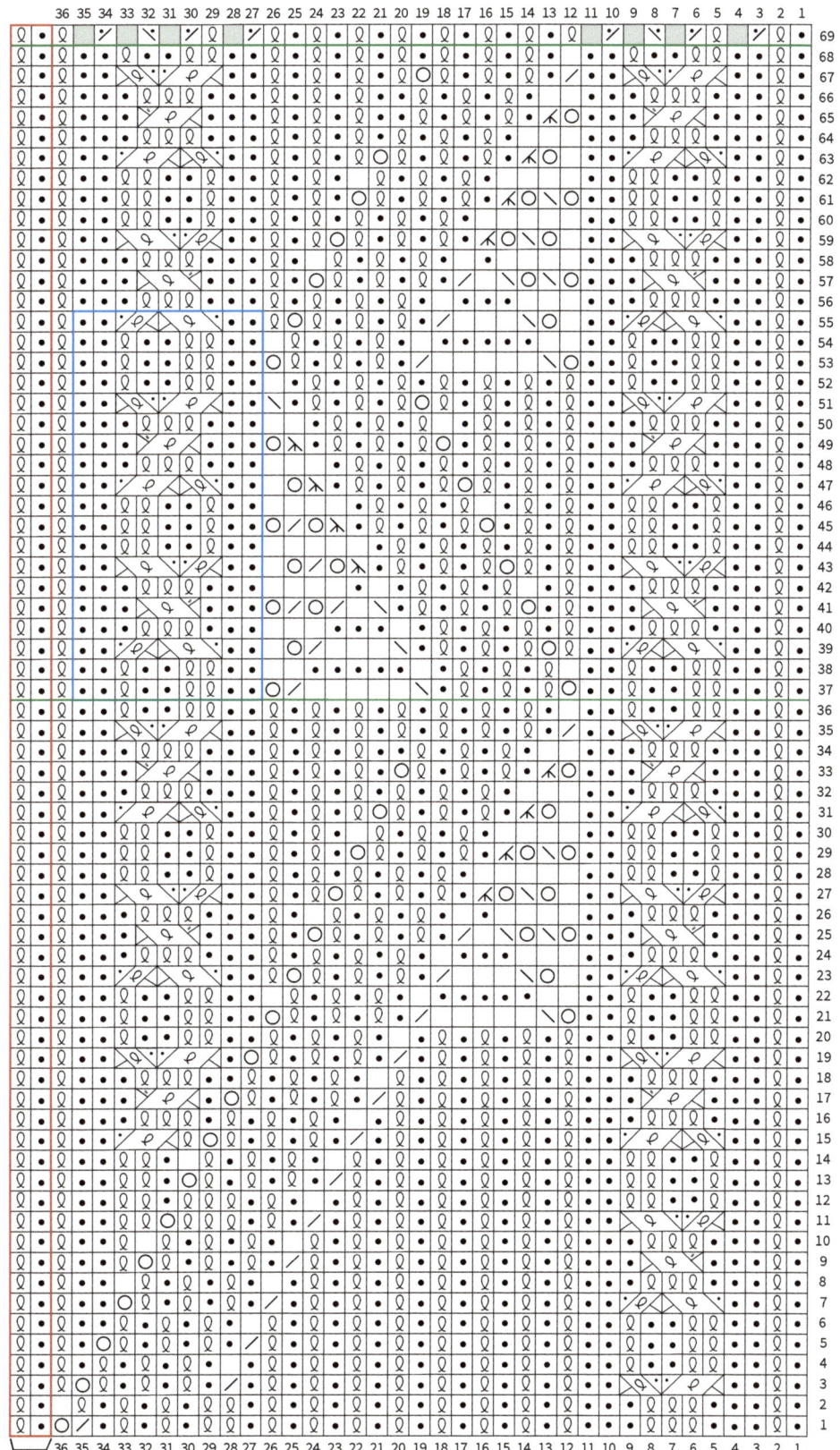

ZIG ZAG GAUNTLETS | 309

TECHNICAL CONTRIBUTORS

Eleanor Dixon

Eleanor Dixon first became a technical editor after hearing the term on a knitting podcast and intuitively knowing that this was her destined niche in the crafting industry. With over eight years of editing experience, and certification by The Knitting Guild of America, Eleanor enjoys working with independent designers from all over the world, as well as publishers and yarn companies. A native of Philadelphia, PA, and a graduate of Cornell University, Eleanor now lives in a little corner of paradise on the Florida coast, where she and her husband have raised three children.

Naoko Ogawa

Naoko Ogawa is a Japanese translator who has fallen in love with knitting. She is the founder/owner/translator of Atelier Knits, an online store selling Japanese translations of indie designers' knitting patterns. She has also become a technical editor for the love of working with designers to place better patterns in the marketplace. She occasionally also "patternizes" the things she makes for her family. She lives in France. Learn more at strandsoflife.com

Chie Ushio

Chie was born and raised in Tokyo, Japan. She graduated from the School of Visual Arts in New York City in 2004 and worked as a book designer at Penguin Random House for over 10 years. Now she works as a graphic design consultant for UN Women. She loves dogs, sewing, and good sushi.

TECHNICAL CONTRIBUTORS

Rafael De Peña

Born in the Dominican Republic and raised in New York City, Rafael De Peña is a fashion illustrator and designer, with a concentration in figurative work. Having studied fashion design in both Los Angeles and New York, Rafael has worked with major fashion brands including Halston and Club Monaco. His work can be found in projects around the world, including Shirley Paden's first book, *Knitwear Design Workshop: A Comprehensive Guide to Handknits*. Learn more at rafaeldepena.com

Anne Shannon

Originally from Cleveland, Ohio, Anne Shannon is a graduate of the University of Cincinnati, College of Design, Architecture, Art, and Planning. Some of her earliest graphic design work was in publishing, as a co-op student for Chronicle Books in San Francisco. In the years since, she has design numerous books and publications, including work for Interweave Press, F+W Media, and Menasha Ridge. Learn more at AnneShannonDesign.com

YARN SOURCES

Artyarns
70 Westmoreland Avenue
White Plains, NY 10606
artyarns.com

Australian Yarn Company
4 Lansell Street
Bendigo, Victoria 3550
ausyarnco.com.au

Berroco, Inc.
1 Tupperware Dr., Suite 4
N. Smithfield, RI 02896
berroco.com

Blue Sky Fibers
P.O. Box 88
Minneapolis, MN 55011
blueskyfibers.com

Brooklyn Tweed
128 NE 7th Avenue
Portland, OR 97232
brooklyntweed.com

Cascade Yarns
813 Thomas Avenue SW
Renton, WA 98057
cascadeyarns.com

Elsebeth Lavold
Distributed by Knitting Fever, Inc.
315 Bayview Avenue
Amityville, NY 11701
knittingfever.com

Jade Sapphire Exotic Fibres
146 Germonds Road
West Nyack, NY 10994
jadesapphire.com

Jamieson and Smith Shetland Wool
90 North Road
Lerwick, Shetland
ZE1 OPQ United Kingdom
shetlandwoolbrokers.com

Knitting Boutique Yarns
knittingboutique.com

Kuani Wool
Odderboekvj 13 7323 Give, Denmark
Distributed by: Beet Street Yarns
308 Pine Street
Plymouth, WI 53073
beetstreetyarn.com

Madeleine Tosh Co.
343 Alemeda Street, Suite 112
Fort Worth, TX 76126
madeleinetosh.com

Mariposa Yarn Atelier
3220 Cobb Pkwy SE, Suite 102
Atlanta, GA 30339
mariposayarnatelier.com

Neighborhood Fiber Company
700 N. Eutaw Street
Baltimore, MD 21201
neighborhoodfiberco.com

Plymouth Yarn Company, Inc.
500 Lafayette Street
Bristol, PA 19007
pyc@plymouthyarn.com

Quince & Co.
102 Main Street
Saco, ME 04072
quinceandco.com

Rowan Yarns
17F Brooke's Mill,
Armitage Bridge,
Huddersfield, West Yorkshire,
England, HD4 7NR
knitrowan.com

Shibui Knits
840 SE Washington Street
Portland, OR 97214
shibuiknits.com

Skacel Collection, Inc.
8041 S. 180th Street
Kent, WA 98032
skacel.com

Trendsetter Yarn Group
16745 Saticoy Street, Suite 101
Van Nuys, CA 91406
trendsetteryarns.com

Valley Yarns
WEBS
75 Service Center Road
Northampton, MA 01060
yarn.com

YARN WEIGHT GUIDE

Yarns are classified according to their diameter (thickness)—commonly referred to as the yarn weight. In general, yarn weights are categorized according to the number of stitches that comprise 4" (10 cm) of stockinette stitch. The categories indicate how fine or bulky a fabric produced by a particular yarn will be. This knowledge is critical if you want to substitute yarns for a project.

Specific yarn weight categories have changed over the past few decades, but the basic categories have remained essentially the same. For years, the groups were based on the size of needles used to knit them, with "fingering" or "fine weight" indicating the thinnest type of yarn to "extra bulky," indicating the thickest type of yarn. In the 1980s, the groups were renamed based on gauge—the number of stitches that comprise 4" (10 cm) of stockinette stitch.

The Craft Yarn Council of America has drawn up guidelines for a standard yarn weight system to bring uniformity to yarn labels and published patterns. Yarns are classified by number, according to the weight of the yarn and the manufacturer's recommendations for gauge and needle size.

STANDARD YARN WEIGHT SYSTEM

Yarn Weight Symbol & Category Name	0 LACE	1 SUPER FINE	2 FINE	3 LIGHT	4 MEDIUM	5 BULKY	6 SUPER BULKY
Type of Yarns in Category	Fingering, 10-count, Crochet Thread	Sock, Fingering, Baby	Sport, Baby, Aran	DK, Light Worsted, Rug	Worsted, Afghan,	Chunky, Craft,	Bulky, Roving
Knitted Gauge* Range in Stockinette Stitch to 4" (10 cm)	33–40 sts	27–32 sts	23–26 sts	21–24 sts	16–20 sts	12–15 sts	6–11 sts
Recommended Needle in Metric Size Range	1.25–2.25 mm	2.25–3.25 mm	3.25–3.75 mm	3.75–4.5 mm	4.5–5.5 mm	5.5–8 mm	8 mm and larger
Recommended Needle in U.S. Size Range	000–1	1–3	3–5	5–7	7–9	9–11	11 and larger

*Guidelines Only: The above reflect the most commonly used gauges and needles for specific yarn categories.

INDEX

A

Abbreviations 116-117
Ada Dress 38-39, 126-135
Aleria Pullover 52-53, 136-143
Alternating Longtail Cast On 121

B

Balineen Hat 68-69, 144-145
Bel Fiore Cape 36-37, 144-147, 148-151
Brason, Sima 110, 69, 156

C

Cabled Yoke Pullover 60-61, 152-155
Cascading Cables Cowl 68-69, 156-159
Coleus Coat 46-47, 84-85, 160-169
Coquilles Capelet 42-43, 170-171
Coquilles Pullover 40-41, 172-177
Cosmopolitan Consciousness 48

D

De Peña, Rafael 311
Designer's Notebook 106
Dixon, Eleanor 310
Duets & Inspirations 26-105
Design-A-Longs (DALs) 6

E

En Pointe Pullover 34-35, 178-181
Evening Elegance 28

F

Floating Triangles Hat & Cowl 58-59, 182-183
Forgione, Joan 57, 59, 69, 103, 110, 144, 182, 222, 276
Four-Stitch Double Wrap 120
Frost Flowers Pullover 96-97, 184-189

G

Gothic Tracery Cardigan 98-99, 190-197

H

Hoffman, Lisa 31, 110, 306

I

Inspirations 12-25
Instructions 116-309

J

Jankelovich, Olga 35, 37, 67, 105, 111, 148, 178, 224
Joseph, Trudie 73, 111, 282

K

Knit-A-Longs (KALs) 7

L

Laiken, Eloe Woolf 106
Linden Hoodie Blue 76-77
Linden Hoodie Burgundy 62-63, 78-79
Linden Hoodie Instructions 198-211

M

Martini, Diane 53, 55, 112, 136, 242
Mesa Poncho 82-83, 212-215

N

Nikki Reeves Pullover 64-65, 216-221

O

Ogawa, Naoko 310
Ohara, Miki 81, 112, 254
Open Bud Shawl 56-57, 222-223
Oshige, Noriko 83, 112, 212

P

Paden, Shirley 47, 71, 85, 87, 89, 91, 113
Page, Gale 99, 190, 113
Primavera Dress 66-67, 104-105, 224-229
Pullover Circles Motif 125

R

Reeves, Nicole 65, 113, 216
Restful Reflections 92
Rustic Reveries 74

S

Sazanami Mini Dress 32-33, 230-233
Schreier, Iris 101, 114, 280
Seseragi Pullover 94-95, 234-241
Shannon, Anne 311
Silva, Ellen M. 45, 114, 300
Skihytte Cardigan 54-55, 242-249
Special Techniques 120
Sunset Skirt 50-51, 250-253
Swatch Inspirations 25
Symbol Keys 118-119

T

Tanaka, Ayano 51, 95, 114, 234, 250
Teardrop Cardigan 80-81, 254-263
Technical Contributors 310-311
Three Needle Bind Off 0
Tige Cardigan 88-89, 264-275
Tobita, Mari 63, 79, 77, 115, 198
Trellised Arbor Shawl 102-103, 276-279
Tubular Cast On 122
Twisted Rhythms 72-73, 282-295
Twist & Shout Shawl 100-101, 280-281

U

Ushio, Chie - 310

V

Volare Capelet 70-71, 90-91, 296-299

W

Whipstitch Seam 124
Winged Surplice Cardigan 44-45, 300-305
Wolfstein, Ada 39, 106-109

Y

Yaple, Midori 33, 115, 230
Yarn Sources 312
Yarn Weight Guide 313

Z

Zig Zag Gauntlets 30-31, 306-309
Zukaite, Laura 61, 97, 115, 152, 184

www.ingramcontent.com/pod-product-compliance
Lightning Source LLC
Chambersburg PA
CBHW041829300426
44111CB00002B/26